DARK BRILLIANCE

DARK
BRILLIANCE

THE AGE OF REASON:
FROM DESCARTES TO PETER THE GREAT

PAUL STRATHERN

PEGASUS BOOKS
NEW YORK LONDON

DARK BRILLIANCE

Pegasus Books, Ltd.
148 West 37th Street, 13th Floor
New York, NY 10018

ISBN: 978-1-63936-797-9

10 9 8 7 6 5 4 3 2 1

Printed in the United States of America
Distributed by Simon & Schuster
www.pegasusbooks.com

To my sister Anne

CONTENTS

Significant Dates During the Age of Reason   viii
Dramatis Personae   x

Prologue   1

1   Reason and Rationale   5
2   Two Italian Artists   23
3   Spread of the Scientific Revolution   39
4   The English Civil War and Thomas Hobbes   61
5   The New World and the Golden Age of Spain   77
6   Two Transcendent Artists   95
7   The Money Men and the Markets   113
8   Two Artists of the Dutch Golden Age   133
9   The Sun King and Versailles   151
10   England Comes of Age   169
11   A Quiet City in South Holland   191
12   Exploration   209
13   A Courtly Interlude   225
14   Spinoza and Locke   251
15   The Survival and Spread of the Continent of Reason   271
16   New Realities   283
17   Logic Personified   303
18   On the Shoulders of Giants   317
Epilogue   337

Notes   343
Acknowledgements   361
Illustrations   363
Index   367

SIGNIFICANT DATES DURING THE AGE OF REASON

1600   English East India Company founded

1601   Death of Tycho Brahe in Prague; his observations are used by Johannes Kepler to establish the elliptical orbits of the planets

1602   Dutch East India Company (VOC) founded

1603   Death of Elizabeth I after ruling for forty-four years

1606   Willem Janszoon becomes the first European to set foot in Australia

1618–48   Thirty Years' War

1620   Pilgrim Fathers arrive in North America

1628   William Harvey publishes work on the circulation of the blood

1642   Blaise Pascal invents the adding machine

1642   Outbreak of the English Civil War

1643   Evangelista Torricelli invents the barometer

1650   René Descartes dies in Stockholm

1651   Thomas Hobbes publishes his *Leviathan*

1654   Queen Christina abdicates from the throne of Sweden

1665   Great Plague of London

1665   Death of Philip IV of Spain

1666   Great Fire of London

1669   Death of Rembrandt

1671   Gottfried Leibniz invents the calculating machine

1672   Lynching of the De Witt brothers

1673   Louis Jolliet and Jacques Marquette sail the upper reaches of the Mississippi

1674   Antonie van Leeuwenhoek discovers the microverse

1687   Isaac Newton publishes his *Principia*

1703   Peter the Great founds St Petersburg

1715   Death of Louis XIV after a reign of seventy-two years

DRAMATIS PERSONAE

Aristotle: Ancient Greek philosopher, lived during the fourth century BC. Much of his (often erroneous) philosophy persisted through the medieval era and beyond, because it was sanctioned by the Roman Catholic Church.

Ashley Cooper, Anthony (Lord Shaftesbury): Powerful political figure in seventeenth-century England, who acted as a benefactor for John Locke.

Aubrey, John: His gossipy but revealing *Brief Lives* carries much informal information about his seventeenth-century English contemporaries.

Bacon, Francis: A great mind, far ahead of his time, who championed an experimental approach to science.

Becher, Johann: German-born intellectual. His mind was a curious blend of genius and conman.

Boyle, Robert: Anglo-Irish scientist, whose experimental approach meant he is recognized by many as the founder of modern chemistry.

Brahe, Tycho: Danish astronomer, renowned for his vast practical knowledge of the stars, all obtained with the naked eye.

Bruno, Giordano: Visionary scientist and philosopher who was burned at the stake by the Church for promulgating 'heretical ideas'.

Caravaggio, Michelangelo Merisi da: Brilliant Italian artist in the chiaroscuro style, whose turbulent lifestyle led him to murder and eventually be murdered.

Cardinal Mazarin: Powerful political figure and diplomat during the reign of Louis XIV.

Castiglione, Baldassare: Wrote *The Courtier*, a book outlining the etiquette and manners recommended for courtiers.

Cervantes, Miguel de: Spanish author of *Don Quixote*.

Charles I, King of England: Deposed by parliament, lost the ensuing Civil War and was then beheaded.

Christina, Queen: Powerful, intellectual and wilful queen of Sweden, who renounced her throne.

Colbert, Jean-Baptiste: First minister of France during the reign of Louis XIV. Encouraged the arts and sciences – especially Huygens.

Copernicus, Nicolaus: Polish priest and astronomer who posited the solar system, i.e. claiming that the earth was not the centre of the universe as decreed by the Church.

Cromwell, Oliver: A leader of the Parliamentary army during the English Civil War, who eventually became ruler of England.

Cruz, Juana Inés de la: Extraordinarily talented woman whose talents and intellect were largely overlooked, as she lived in Mexico.

Descartes, René: Regarded by many as the first modern philosopher. Also a supremely talented scientist and mathematician.

Dryden, John: Gifted poet who was forced to compromise as England switched between Catholic and Protestant rule.

El Greco: Greek-born artist who came to prominence in Spain. His 'distorted' figures are now seen as wonders of spiritual expression.

Elizabeth I, daughter of Henry VIII: Became queen of England during its great but turbulent emergence as a European power.

Euclid: Ancient Greek mathematician from Alexandria, whose work *Elements*, written around 300 BC, influenced mathematicians throughout Europe.

Ferdinand II & III: Holy Roman Emperors, amongst the most powerful rulers in Europe.

Fermat, Pierre de: French mathematician and friend of Pascal.

Flamsteed, John: Scientist who became England's first Astronomer Royal.

Galen: Greek physician who flourished in Rome during the second century. His often-erroneous medicine was regarded as sacrosanct by the Church.

Galileo Galilei: Born in Florence during the sixteenth century, regarded as the father of modern science.

Gentileschi, Artemisia: Supremely talented baroque painter, who was raped by the artist Agostino Tassi.

Graunt, John: The father of modern statistics.

Guzmán, Gaspar de (Count-Duke of Olivares): Notoriously incompetent chief minister to Philip IV of Spain.

Halley, Edmund: Scientist in London during the time of Newton. Halley's Comet is named after him.

Harvey, William: Highly skilled English physician who was the first to correctly demonstrate the circulation of the blood.

Henry VIII: Ruler of England during the sixteenth century; father of Elizabeth I.

Hobbes, Thomas: English writer whose *Leviathan* revolutionized political thinking.

Hooke, Robert: Multi-talented English scientist.

Huygens, Christiaan: Supreme Dutch scientist who invented the first modern clock.

Janszoon, Willem: Dutch sailor for VOC who became the first European to set foot in Australia.

Jolliet, Louis: French explorer, who along with Jacques Marquette was the first to travel through the North American interior.

Kepler, Johannes: German astronomer who used Brahe's observations to plot the elliptical orbits of the planets.

La Varenne, François Pierre: French chef who is widely regarded as the founding father of modern French cuisine.

Leibniz, Gottfried: German scientist and rational philosopher who invented calculus independently of Newton.

Leopold I: Holy Roman Emperor.

Locke, John: English philosopher who launched empiricism.

Louis XIV: The Sun King, who ruled France from Versailles.

Lully, Jean-Baptiste: Italian-born French composer.

Mandeville, Bernard: Dutch-born physician whose pioneering work on political economy, *The Fable of the Bees*, caused a scandal.

Marquette, Father Jacques: French Jesuit explorer, who along with Jolliet was the first to travel through the North American interior.

Medici, Marie de': Descendant of the famous Florentine banking family who became queen of France.

Melani, Atto: Italian-born castrato singer who flourished in France.

Mersenne, Father Marin: French mathematician who circulated works by great scientists and philosophers from his monastic cell in Paris.

Milton, John: Finest English poet of his time, best known for his *Paradise Lost*.

Molière: Stage name of the great French dramatist best known for his satire *Le Bourgeois Gentilhomme*.

Montaigne, Michel de: French philosopher best known for his far-reaching *Essays*.

Monteverdi, Claudio: Italian musician and composer, who excelled in sacred and secular music, especially opera.

Mustafa Pasha, Kara: Grand Vizier of the Ottoman Empire who led the Siege of Vienna.

Newton, Isaac: Supreme mathematician and scientist of his age, best known for his work on gravity.

Oldenburg, Henry: German-born scientist who became secretary to the Royal Society in London. Corresponded with scientists throughout Europe.

Pascal, Blaise: Outstanding French mathematician and scientist, who abandoned science for religion.

Pepys, Samuel: English author of the most comprehensive diary of the period, which covers his time as a rising naval administrator.

Peter the Great: Tsar of Russia who attempted to modernize his country; founder of St Petersburg.

Petty, William: Maverick English surveyor of Ireland who produced pioneering ideas of political economy.

Philip IV: Ruler of Spain during its Golden Era.

Poussin, Nicolas: French painter.

Purcell, Henry: English composer.

Racine, Jean: Preeminent French dramatist, famed for his use of language.

Rembrandt van Rijn: Dutch artist now famed for his supreme self-portraits.

Rubens, Peter Paul: Flamboyant Flemish artist and diplomat, the best-known painter of his time.

Spinoza, Baruch: Dutch rationalist philosopher of Portuguese Jewish descent.

Tasman, Abel: Dutch explorer after whom Tasmania is named.

Torricelli, Evangelista: Italian student of Galileo whose inventions include the barometer.

van Dyck, Anthony: Dutch-born artist who flourished as a portrait painter in London during the reign of Charles I.

van Leeuwenhoek, Antonie: Pioneer Dutch observer of the microscopic world.

Velázquez, Diego: Supreme artist at the court of King Philip IV of Spain.

Vermeer, Johannes: Dutch artist who lived in Delft. His supreme gift was never properly recognized during his lifetime.

Witt, Johan de: Dutch politician and friend of Spinoza, who was lynched after he took power.

Wren, Christopher: English polymath who is now best remembered as the architect of St Paul's Cathedral.

DARK
BRILLIANCE

PROLOGUE

DURING THE 1600s, BETWEEN the end of the Renaissance and the start of the Enlightenment, Europe lived through an era known as the Age of Reason. This was a period that saw widespread advances in the arts and sciences. Artists such as Caravaggio, Rembrandt and Van Dyck flourished across the continent. Likewise, scientists such as Newton, Huygens and Pascal continued the Scientific Revolution instigated during the Renaissance by Galileo. Philosophy advanced through rationalists such as Descartes and Spinoza, as well as empiricists such as John Locke, whose ideas would later play a formative role in the American Constitution. At the same time, society began to investigate its own workings. Political theory took on a more profound aspect with *Leviathan* by Thomas Hobbes. Ideas on economics emerged from such disparate figures as the maverick Englishman Sir William Petty and the French mercantilists who advised Louis XIV, the Sun King, on how to run France.

Yet this was an age of unreason almost as much as it was an age of reason. The above accomplishments took place against a background of extreme political turbulence and irrational behaviour on a continental scale. These took the form of internal conflicts and international wars, as well as more localized manifestations – such as outbreaks of 'witchcraft' and the sadistic measures taken against the women deemed responsible. In just the length of a biblical lifetime – 'threescore years and ten' – the puritan Pilgrim Fathers who had emigrated to the New World in order to practise their religion in freedom underwent an outbreak of mass hysteria.

The result was the notorious Salem witch trials. And by now, the 'land of liberty' was also beginning to participate in another form of unreason: the transatlantic slave trade.

These are far from being the only major anomalies of the era, which might justifiably be called the Age of Reason and Unreason. Indeed, the Age of Reason itself was born in Europe at the same time as the greatest outbreak of mass violence yet witnessed on that continent. This was the Thirty Years' War, a brutal conflict which would devastate central Europe to an extent that would not be seen until the outbreak of the two world wars some three centuries later. Yet, out of this very same war came the Peace of Westphalia, a treaty which formulated the idea of the independent nation-state, a concept that remains a cornerstone of international politics to this day. The Thirty Years' War was followed by the English Civil War, which was the beginning of the end for the divine right of kings, at least in Britain. It was such turbulence that prompted Hobbes to write his *Leviathan*. Indeed, many of the greatest works and advances of the Age of Reason were to be inspired (or provoked) by the unreason that gripped Europe.

In some cases, leading figures themselves incorporated both aspects of this divided era. Perhaps none more so than the Italian artist Caravaggio, whose often-violent scenes dramatically capture effects of light and darkness, both literal and metaphorical – a conflict that frequently flared in his own brawling life, during which he committed murder and may even have been murdered himself.

This age also saw the development of European empires across the globe. The English and the Dutch East India Companies were pioneers of intercontinental trade with Asia, ousting the earlier Portuguese trader-explorers. In the process, these companies would develop financial instruments – shares and stock markets – which many regard as the beginnings of modern capitalism. But the subtlety and ingenuity of these rational structures contrast strongly with the grotesque barbarism exhibited by these same companies towards the indigenous populations of India and Indonesia. At the same time, a lucrative new transatlantic commerce opened with the New World. The silver mines of South

America, the sugar plantations of the Caribbean, and the cotton trade with the southern colonies of North America all brought transformative riches to western European society. Yet there was a dark underside to this brilliant new wealth: it was dependent upon mass slavery.

This book is intended to illustrate such paradoxes, which were present right from the beginnings of our progressive era. Previous narratives of the Age of Reason have usually concentrated on the rational aspect and the advances of this period. But what precisely is meant by the term 'reason'? It was viewed then, much as it still is today, as a method of thought which progresses by logical steps towards a proven conclusion. Reason's use of logic to establish a hitherto-unknown certainty is perhaps best illustrated by its offshoot, mathematics. Here, the entire system is based upon a series of self-evident axioms, upon which all are agreed. Like Euclidean geometry this builds up, step by step, to create an edifice of such certainty and abstract beauty that it is viewed as one of humanity's finest achievements. The rapture inspired by such a system is well expressed by the twentieth-century mathematician and philosopher Bertrand Russell:

At the age of eleven, I began Euclid, with my brother as tutor. This was one of the great events of my life, as dazzling as first love. I had not imagined there was anything so delicious in the world. From that moment until I was thirty-eight, mathematics was my chief interest and my chief source of happiness.

Not until the turn of the twentieth century was this sublime aspect of reason replaced, at least to a certain extent. Only then did another offshoot of philosophy, namely psychology, begin to discover that human reason is in reality based upon a far murkier world of instinctive impulses and dark irrational drives. Freud's unconscious mind is but one manifestation of this not wholly scientific discovery of a world beyond reason.

It now becomes clear that this darker aspect too was part of the Age of Reason, from which our western progressive, liberal, democratic world derives. And now this 'free' world is faced with the prospect of placing limits upon itself, in order for the world itself to survive our activities

– which have led to climate change, pollution, and the general degradation of our planet. Given such circumstances, it is worth examining
precisely how such 'rational' progress began. Can we learn from our
rational origins – in both their sublime and their darker aspects? Can we
discover from this founding myth how our rational world will be able to
limit itself in order to preserve the very world we inhabit? Can the world
that untrammelled progress has done so much to create, and at the same
time destroy, survive itself?

   In order to survive, rational progress will inevitably be forced to ration
itself. A telling pun. As some commentators have observed, not wholly
with irony: if ever there were a time for communism to be invented, it is
now! Does this mean that we must inevitably accept a command economy
– socialism, no less? It is worth remembering that socialism – especially
in its egalitarian aspect – was during the past centuries the great hope
of so many enlightened thinkers. Eventually the dream soured and the
command economy degenerated into the command of dictatorship. But
this would be a later development – a deviation from the original progressive idea that came into being during the Age of Reason, the era which
would give birth to western civilization. If this is to endure, what lessons
are to be learned from the Age of Reason and Unreason upon which our
modern world is founded?

CHAPTER 1

REASON AND RATIONALE

B Y THE EARLY 1600s, Europe was approaching the height of
the Little Ice Age. This had begun around two centuries previously, when a mysterious decrease in sunspots reduced solar radiation,
causing average temperatures across northern Europe to begin to fall
by as much as two degrees Celsius. Owing to the vagaries of meteo-
rological currents, this reduced the temperature in some locations by
more than ten degrees. Arctic glaciers and pack ice began to expand; the
Norse colonies in Greenland vanished, and contact between Europe and
Greenland itself was severed for three centuries. Regular fierce storms
in the North Sea flooded the German and Danish coasts, resulting in
offshore islands vanishing beneath the waves. In the Netherlands, the
dykes were breached, causing the inland Zuider Zee (Southern Sea) to
expand through the heart of the country. All over northern Europe there
were protracted icebound winters, followed by regular 'years without
summer'. This was the time when Flemish painters produced scenes filled
with padded figures breathing smoky breath as they skated along frozen
Dutch canals and ice-sheeted fields. Meanwhile, glaciers ground down
the mountainsides of the Alps, slowly but inexorably pulverizing entire

villages. Year upon year crops failed, and famine swept the lands of central Europe.

As if all this was not enough, in 1618 Europe plunged into the first pan-continental war in its history – the most vicious and widespread conflict it would endure until the world wars of the twentieth century. This was the Thirty Years' War, by the end of which the population of Europe would be slashed by more than 10 per cent, with some regions in Germany losing as many as 60 per cent of their inhabitants. Here was devastation almost on the scale of the Black Death some three centuries previously, when the bubonic plague is thought to have accounted for the loss of more than a third of the continent's population.

The Thirty Years' War began as a conflict between the major Catholic powers of northern Europe (essentially France and the Holy Roman Empire) and the Protestants (mainly newly converted German states allied to powerful Sweden). However, this simple generalization masks a host of particular anomalies.

Take, for instance, the case of the twenty-two-year-old French Catholic thinker René Descartes, who would later become known as one of the leading intellectuals of his era. In these early years, Descartes was unsure of precisely what he wanted to do with his life. He had a small amount of inherited money, and was possessed of the vague idea that he would follow a life of intellect. So that he could pursue his thoughts and experiments freely, without censure from the Catholic authorities in his native land, he had taken up residence in the newly independent Netherlands. Here a more liberal atmosphere prevailed, tolerant of Catholics, Protestants, and the numerous Jewish refugees fleeing persecution in countries ranging from Portugal to Poland.

Descartes's very name would become synonymous with rational thought; thus it comes as something of a surprise to witness his reaction to the outbreak of the Thirty Years' War. Despite being a Catholic, and devoid of military experience, he volunteered to join the army of Prince Maurice of Orange, a Dutch Protestant force. Indeed, he would later claim that he had taken a commission in the army because he felt sure that this would provide him with sufficient time and peace, devoid of social distractions, in order to think. Descartes was in the habit of rising late, and he had found that lying in bed in the morning best suited his mental processes.

It was during this period that he learned the rudiments of military engineering, which came easily to his superb mathematical mind. However, his life as a late-rising officer in Prince Maurice's army evidently proved too onerous, and around a year later he switched his allegiance and joined the Catholic army of Duke Maximilian of Bavaria. Here he was able to embark upon his philosophical pursuits in earnest, especially when the Bavarian army made its customary withdrawal from hostilities and took up winter quarters at Neuberg an der Donau, a small walled Bavarian town on the upper reaches of the Danube.

In common with previous years, the harsh winter set in early – and as a result the town and the surrounding countryside were soon smothered in a permanent blanket of solid snow. To escape from the cold, Descartes shut himself away in a small stove-warmed room where he was able to pursue his studies in peace. However, we know that something must have been bothering him, for he recorded that on the night of 10–11 November 1619 his sleep was disturbed by a series of unsettling dreams. At one point he imagined himself struggling against an overpowering wind as he tried to make his way down the street towards the church at his old school back in France. A friend called out to him from a nearby courtyard. Later, he heard 'a noise like a crack of lightning', after which the darkness of his room was filled with swirling sparks. Then he saw a dictionary and a book of poetry on his desk...

When Descartes awoke he was convinced that his dreams had revealed to him the purpose of his life. Through the irrational turmoil of unconscious images rising before his mind's eye, he had glimpsed his calling: he would devote himself to the rational pursuit of truth. By use of reason alone he would discover the answer to the ultimate philosophical questions: *Who am I? What do I know? How can I learn the truth? How do I know that this is the truth...?*

We must imagine Descartes lying in bed, in his cosy windowless room, its ceiling supported by solid wooden beams, in the corner a tiled Bavarian

stove radiating heat. Outside, at the lower end of the sloping cobbled
street, the ice-edged river would have been visible, tendrils of mist rising
from its dark gliding surface. The attics of the shabbier houses bordering
the river provided makeshift dormitories for the common soldiery of
Duke Maximilian's army, by now stirring from their chilly sleep beneath
heaped skins. In the rooms below, the families with whom they had been
billeted listened warily as they heard the curses and thumps from above.
Meanwhile, the mercenary units camped outside the town walls were also
coming to life. Burly figures breaking through the frozen entry flaps to
their coarse canvas tents; others huddled in blankets, coaxing life into the
smoking fires amidst the camp. The sergeants-at-arms shouting at the
bowed youngsters ferrying logs from the stacks beneath the town walls to
the glowing ashen circles of the fires.

As Descartes would later put it: 'Since I desired to devote myself
wholly to the search for truth, I thought it necessary… to reject as utterly
false anything in which I could discover the least grounds for doubt.' This
would cause him to embark upon a process of radical thought, an introspective intellectual exercise in which he sought to eliminate all possibility of delusion. To do so, he imagined that:

> some malicious demon of the utmost power and cunning has
> employed all his energies in order to deceive me. I shall think that
> the sky, the air, the earth, colours, shapes, sounds and all external
> things are merely the delusions of dreams which he has devised
> to ensnare my judgement. I shall consider myself as not having
> hands or eyes, or flesh, or blood or senses, but as falsely believing
> that I have all these things.

There remained but one thing that it was impossible for him to doubt.
No demon, however cunning and devious, could make him doubt that he
existed:

> While I wanted to think everything false, it must necessarily be
> that I who thought was something; and remarking that this truth,

I think, therefore I am, was so solid and so certain that all the most extravagant suppositions of the sceptics were incapable of upsetting it, I judged that I could receive it without scruple as the first principle of the philosophy that I sought.

Descartes would prove to be more than just a perceptive thinker. He would also become a scientist, not afraid to be as steadfast in the pursuit of truth in his experiments as he was in his rational thinking. His philosophy of reason would lead him to undertake vivisectional investigations of animals, such as cats and rabbits. As he recorded after one such experiment: 'If you cut off the end of the heart of a living dog, and insert your finger through the incision into one of the concavities, you will clearly feel that every time the heart shortens, it presses your finger, and stops pressing it every time it lengthens.'

Unflinching reason led him to conclude that all creatures were automata, governed entirely by the laws of physics, devoid of feelings or consciousness. Only humans were possessed of these qualities, because they alone had immortal souls. But the interaction of incorporeal spirit (the soul or mind) and mechanical matter puzzled him at first. How could the mind interact with the body? After further experiments he concluded that this interaction took place in the pineal gland, a small organ located deep within the human brain: 'There the soul comes in contact with the "vital spirits", and through this contact there is interaction between soul and body.'

However, as he continued with his cool-headed vivisection of splayed and pinned un-sedated animals, undeterred by their squirming bodies and shrill cries, he made a disquieting discovery. Some other vertebrates also possessed a pineal gland. This, he decided, could not be the same as the human variety. When questioned on how he accounted for this, he replied irritably: 'the most ignorant people could, in a quarter of an hour, raise more questions of this kind than the wisest men could deal with in a lifetime; and this is why I have not bothered to answer any of them'.

On returning to his rational pursuits, Descartes would philosophize:

Those long chains of perfectly simple and easy reasonings by means of which geometers are accustomed to carry out their most difficult demonstrations had led me to fancy that everything that can fall under human knowledge forms a similar sequence; and that so long as we avoid accepting as true what is not so, and always preserve the right order for deduction of one thing from another, there can be nothing too remote to be reached in the end, or too well hidden to be discovered.

In contrast to Descartes's petulant display of unreason concerning the pineal gland, this last passage is as lucid a manifesto for the Age of Reason as one is likely to find.

After wintering in Neuberg an der Donau, Descartes returned to the fray with Duke Maximilian's army. The precise details of his military role are few. He is known to have been present at one of the first major conflicts of the Thirty Years' War, the Battle of White Mountain outside Prague. Here, in November 1620, some 25,000 soldiers of the Holy Roman Emperor Ferdinand II's Catholic League defeated a Protestant army of 15,000 men. Though curiously, on this occasion, Descartes is said to have 'served with the Catholic League as an official observer'.

In 1627, Descartes is known to have been present at the Siege of La Rochelle, the Huguenot (Protestant) stronghold on the west coast of France. Once again, he appears to have been an 'observer' at this notorious event, during which 20,000 out of the port city's population of 25,000 were starved to death. Sometime after this he left the army, whereupon he spent several years travelling around Europe, visiting various shrines in Italy and other sights. It was a somewhat hazardous time to become a tourist – though there have been suggestions that he was in fact a spy.

Eventually, such was the devastation during the continuing Thirty Years' War that the entire ecology of central Europe was unbalanced. By the end of the war, the population of the German lands had been reduced from 12 million to 4 million. Rat colonies in the cities had multiplied; they devoured all hidden stores of grain, beets and other root vegetables, and gnawed the rotting flesh from cadavers with their tiny teeth, before fanning out into the countryside, ravaging crops, even stripping the bark from the trees.

In cities where a remnant of civic order prevailed, citizens frequently succumbed to 'frenzies of despair', causing widespread outbreaks of mass hysteria. In south-central Germany, Bishop von Ehrenberg mounted a sweeping campaign to rid Würzburg of Protestantism. As a result, nearly a thousand Lutherans were dragged from their homes and burned at the stake. In nearby Bamberg, the local bishop launched a campaign against witches: old women, especially widows, were rounded up, subjected to summary trials, and burned before mocking crowds of onlookers. Witch hunts soon began to spread throughout southern Germany.

First-hand descriptions of such calamitous events can be found in the few documents which have survived, a prime example being the recently discovered handwritten diary kept by the *Landsknecht* (a German common mercenary soldier) Peter Hagendorf, whose language indicates that he probably originated from the Rhineland.* Other harrowing tales of such scenes were passed by word of mouth down to ensuing generations, becoming a folk-memory amongst surviving families throughout much of central Europe. Some years later, these would inspire Hans Jakob Christoffel von Grimmelshausen to write Germany's earliest picaresque masterwork, *Simplicius Simplicissimus*, whose narrative is explained in its subtitle: 'The adventures of a simpleton named Melchior Sternfels von Fuchshaim: namely where and in what manner he came into this world, what he saw, learned, experienced, and endured therein; also why he again left it of his own free will'. (The last remark refers to the hero's eventual entry into a monastery.)

---

* This incomplete manuscript was discovered purely by chance in 1988 amongst bundles of old papers in the Berlin State Library. The 192 pages of notes describe Hagendorf's travels across almost 1,500 miles of war-ravaged Europe, from Italy and France to the Netherlands and the German states. His most memorable description is of the 1631 sack of the city of Magdeburg in Saxony. During the course of this event, the rape, pillage and murderous destructive mayhem were such that as many as 20,000 are thought to have been killed. Consequently, the word *Magdeburgisieren* (magdeburgization) entered the German language to describe total annihilation.

By 1648, the armies of Europe had for the most part fought themselves to a standstill, and it was agreed that a peace conference would be held in the north-west German state of Westphalia. Such was the remnant bitterness between Catholics and Protestants that they could not even agree upon a location for the conference. Instead, two cities were chosen, thirty miles apart. Osnabrück was under Protestant control, though many of its citizens remained Catholic; while the city of Münster remained firmly Catholic. By now, it has been estimated, between 4.5 and 8 million people throughout Europe had lost their lives during the course of this war. (The disparity between these figures speaks volumes; such was the near-universal breakdown of civil order that casualties could not be calculated with any real accuracy, and even estimates fluctuated wildly.)

The Peace of Westphalia, as this conference came to be known, faced further problems of divided loyalty. By now, Catholic France had switched to the Protestant cause in order to thwart the Catholic Holy Roman Empire in its bid to become the dominant power in Europe. Meanwhile the Protestants, for their part, had splintered into two major groups. The Lutherans adhered to the original theology of Martin Luther; while the teachings of the Calvinists, led by the extremist French theologian John Calvin, had been adopted in Sweden and by the Huguenots in France.

Although fighting still continued in some regions of Europe, the peace conference in Westphalia received delegations representing the full range of European interests. There were sixteen official delegations from European nations, some sixty-six delegates from the 140 states of the Holy Roman Empire, and no less than thirty-eight factional causes. These delegations were never present all at the same time. Some arrived early and left early; others remained; while others arrived late, to find the conference was over. The main delegations represented the Holy Roman Empire, France, Spain, Sweden, the Pope and the United Provinces of the Netherlands (the Dutch Republic, often informally known as Holland). They were led by a disparate collection of generals, aristocrats of varying degree, diplomats (professional and self-appointed) and other politicians, all intent upon cutting a dashing figure on the European stage.

The French delegation was led by Henri II, Duc de Longueville, who refused to speak to any candidate who did not address him as *Altesse* (Your Highness) on account of his royal descent. The powerful Swedish delegation was led by Count Johan Oxenstierna, who had received specific instructions from his father, the Lord High Chancellor of Sweden, with orders that he was not to deviate one iota from these demands. Meanwhile, his fellow Swedish delegate Baron Johan Adler Salvius received his orders from Queen Christina, which were delivered by royal messengers, constantly changed, and seldom agreed with his colleague Oxenstierna's instructions. The delegation of the Holy Roman Empire, which represented a large population of Catholics throughout Europe, was led by John Louis of Hadamar-Nassau, who was of German, Austrian and Dutch descent; he had been raised as a Calvinist and only converted to Catholicism while in Rome during the war. His main ally, the papal nuncio in Cologne, was the Italian Fabio Chigi, who decided from the outset that he would take no part in the negotiations as he 'refused to deal with heretics'. (Chigi would later be elected Pope Alexander VII – largely, it is said, because of the diplomatic qualities he had exhibited while serving as papal nuncio.) The Swiss Confederacy, which was determined to negotiate its freedom from the Holy Roman Empire, was represented by the ambitious Johann Rudolf Wettstein, who made an unexpected early arrival at Münster on a canal ship. Not only had he not been invited but he also had no official Swiss accreditation.

Neither of the small cities of Münster and Osnabrück was equipped to play host to a conference of any size, let alone the large delegations which continued to pour in from all over Europe – some unaccompanied by interpreters, others considering it beneath their dignity to pay for accommodation at such an event. Consequently, the Swiss envoy was 'lodged above a wool weaver's shop in a room that stank of sausage and fish oil', and the twenty-nine-strong delegation from Bavaria was only able to obtain eighteen beds.

The conference itself had no official agenda or even a mediator, and thus proceeded on an improvised basis, with several delegations arranging private meetings on neutral ground in small towns and villages in the countryside between Osnabrück and Münster. Many of the delegates had no authority to make decisions on their own and had to send messages by courier back to their rulers. Weeks, even months, would go by as messages and answers passed back and forth.

When official meetings did actually take place between senior delegations in the larger municipal buildings in Osnabrück and Münster, a strict protocol soon had to be devised. Delegates refused to mingle or leave themselves open to any slights which might be seen as diminishing their status, such as the late (or early) arrival of their opposite negotiators, the occupancy of the highest chairs at the conference table, and so forth. Thus, prior to an arranged meeting, each delegation would enter the hall through a different doorway, and proceed at the same slow pace so as to take their allotted seats at the conference table at precisely the same time.

Many meetings were arranged by delegations unaware that the opposing delegation with which they wished to negotiate had not yet arrived, or had unaccountably departed. Throughout the entire gathering, messages continued to arrive from various locations of continued fighting or unexpected cessations of hostilities. Indeed, although history has allotted the date 1648 to the Peace of Westphalia, its negotiations both preceded and continued after this date, sometimes in entirely different locations.* Indeed, the overall attendance of delegates in Osnabrück and Münster is reckoned to have peaked between January 1646 and July 1647. And even after 1648, when many of the separate peace treaties had been signed, publicised and widely acknowledged, some important players refused to accept the treaties to which they had agreed. Amongst these was the main loser in these negotiations, the pope (the treaties officially confirmed, once and for all, the end of papal hegemony throughout western Europe). An outraged Pope Innocent X declared the Peace to be:

---

* These include the premature peace negotiated in Hamburg as early as 1641 between all the major protagonists – including France, the Holy Roman Empire and Sweden – where documents were signed but promptly ignored by all concerned. To say nothing of the substantive but unresolved negotiations which took place between France and the Holy Roman Emperor in Cologne in 1646.

'null, void, invalid, iniquitous, unjust, damnable, reprobate, inane, empty of meaning and effect for all time'.

Astonishingly, despite the chaotic negotiations, uncoordinated behaviour, and downright irrationality of much that took place under the name of the Peace of Westphalia, this event would in many ways usher Europe into the Age of Reason. Its provisions were responsible for major, and often lasting, political transformation. And in practical terms, it literally changed the map. Most notably, the Swiss Confederacy gained its independence from the Holy Roman Empire, an autonomy that remains to this day. Similarly, the Dutch Republic was officially recognized. On the other hand, the awarding to Sweden of tracts of northern Germany – including Pomerania, parts of Brandenburg, and the strategic port of Bremen – would prove misguided and quickly become inoperable. Sweden was also granted an indemnity of 5 million thalers so that it could pay its long-suffering troops, who had resorted to scavenging, looting and pillage in order to provide for themselves. The Peace had its incontestable failures too: most notably, it failed to affect the conflict between Spain and France, which continued locally until the Treaty of the Pyrenees was signed in 1659.

More even than the creation of new countries, the main achievement of the Peace of Westphalia was its definitive effect upon the conduct of international politics. It has even come to be acknowledged as a formative event of European history by many; one whose influence would, over the centuries, spread across the entire globe. It is rightly seen as being responsible for the establishment of international law and the inviolability of the independent nation-state. And this, despite it producing no single definitive, universally recognized document.

This collection of treaties, self-contradictory documents, and multi-signed pieces of paper with secret added codicils would found – as if by a miracle – the principles that still govern modern Europe. And indeed, much of the world. It established the axiom that no nation was permitted to interfere with the cultural, religious or political developments of any neighbouring nation. State sovereignty was regarded as sacrosanct. And in order to reinforce and aid this development, nations could exchange diplomatic missions which themselves remained sacrosanct within the nations where they were established, with the ambassadors of these missions accorded the title 'excellency'.* Thus differences could be resolved before they resulted in outright conflict.

Diplomacy would also play a major role in the other highly significant development resulting from the Peace of Westphalia: notably, the balance of power between nations throughout Europe. This would ensure a more or less stable state of affairs for almost 150 years, until the outbreak of the French Revolution in 1789. In the words of Henry Kissinger, arguably the most skilful diplomatic operator during the last part of the twentieth century: 'The Westphalian concept took multiplicity as its starting point and drew a variety of multiple societies, each accepted as a reality, into a common search for order. By the mid-twentieth century this international system was in place on every continent; it remains the scaffolding of international order such as it now exists.'

After the Thirty Years' War, Descartes is known to have returned to Holland and arranged for his inherited property in France to be sold up and invested in bonds, sufficient to provide him with a private income so that he could pursue his intellectual interests for the rest of his life. But, despite his penchant for solitude and uninterrupted scientific activity, he would not be totally isolated through these years.

During the course of his European travels Descartes had been reunited with an old school friend called Marin Mersenne, who had entered the church and received intellectual visitors in his cell at the convent of L'Annonciade in Paris. It is difficult to overstate the influence of Father Mersenne on the scientific and philosophical life of Europe during the early 1600s. Mersenne was himself a talented polymath

---

* Such diplomacy had become well established in Italy during the previous century by Venice and a few other city-states, such as Mantua, who maintained ambassadors in other city-states – and particularly in Rome – in order to glean and sometimes influence papal policy. Now, this would increasingly become an international modus operandi.

and mathematician.* He had also met or corresponded with many of the leading intellectuals of the age – most notably Galileo, 'the father of modern science', the Dutch scientist Christiaan Huygens, and the English political theorist Thomas Hobbes – communicating with them as an equal. More importantly, he maintained links with these figures, and built up a network in order to exchange the latest findings in many fields, passing on original works to be read and criticized by his peers. In this way, Mersenne's cell overcame a serious flaw in the coordination of northern European scientific and intellectual knowledge, becoming a forerunner for the likes of the Royal Society in London, the Academy of Sciences in Berlin, and similar academies in places ranging from St Petersburg to Stockholm to Edinburgh. (In Italy, the Accademia dei Lincei already existed, disseminating the works of Galileo, but would barely outlive his condemnation by the Inquisition.)

The method by which Descartes had arrived at his ultimate axiom 'I think therefore I am', upon which he would base the entire structure of his thought, was a comprehensive scepticism previously unknown in European reasoning. Prior to this, medieval logic had for the most part been based upon Aristotle's reasoning, which used syllogisms to generate new knowledge. There are many forms of syllogism, but the basic structure can be seen in the classic example:

Socrates is a man.
All men are mortal.
Therefore Socrates is mortal.

Descartes defended his own thinking as follows, in his reply to one of the objections to his philosophy gathered by Mersenne:

---

* Mersenne's lasting claim to fame is his formula for generating 'Mersenne primes': $M_p = 2^p - 1$. Here M_p is a Mersenne prime, and p is some prime number (i.e. one that is divisible only by itself). This formula may only generate a small fraction of the known primes, but has so far proved infallible. As of 2020, computers had confirmed the existence of fifty-one Mersenne primes below 100 million.

When someone says 'I am thinking, therefore I am, or I exist', he does not deduce his existence from thought by means of a syllogism, but recognizes it as something self-evident by a simple intuition of the mind. This is clear from the fact that if he were deducing it by means of a syllogism, he would have to have had previous knowledge of the major premise 'Everything which thinks is, or exists'; yet in fact he learns it from experiencing in his own case that it is impossible that he should think without existing. It is in the nature of our mind to construct general propositions on the basis of our knowledge of particular ones.

Despite such insistence, Descartes's basic premise remains open to criticism. Some have asked: if you stop thinking, does this mean that you cease to exist? Though is it possible to cease thinking entirely, even in sleep or any other unconscious state? More serious is the objection that the introduction of 'I' into 'I think therefore I am' is illegitimate, and is only included because of syntax. As Bertrand Russell pointed out: 'The word "I" is grammatically convenient, but does not describe a datum... He nowhere proves that thoughts need a thinker, nor is there reason to believe this except in a grammatical sense.' This objection is reinforced by modern physiological research using brain scans, which indicate that decisive mental activity can often be observed in the brain *before* 'I' am aware of making a decision. Who then is doing the thinking, when the conscious 'I' is not aware of the decision made in my brain? This question remains unanswered – posing serious problems about human agency with regard to the law, as well as in other fields.

Descartes's thinking led naturally to his celebrated distinction between mind and body, which would remain one of the basic conundrums of philosophy and science for centuries to come. According to Descartes, the body is composed of matter, and is thus subject to the laws of physics. It is the incorporeal mind or soul which animates the body, making us human. Without the mind, the body is a mere automaton.

Descartes reached this distinction by introspective reasoning, which led him to his controversial conclusion that 'soulless' animals are mere automata. Some have suggested that he may in part have been influenced in this conclusion by some ingenious and very lifelike puppet-machines he had seen in Paris, where they had become the latest sensation.

Descartes never satisfactorily solved this 'mind-body' problem that he had raised. Indeed philosophers and scientists were unable to provide a convincing answer until the twentieth century, when the problem was declared to be illusory and the mind described as an 'emergent quality' that spontaneously arises from the complexities of the brain. As the Canadian psychiatrist Ralph Lewis put it: 'Clearly, the brain is a phenomenon in which the whole is greater than the sum of its parts, and its product, the mind or subjective sense of self, is radically different qualitatively from its parts – an emergent property.'

Indeed, Francis Crick, the co-discoverer of DNA, famously dismissed the idea of a separate mind or consciousness, declaring: 'You're nothing but a pack of neurons.' However, investigators of artificial intelligence have found the problem of 'mind' far more elusive: their ever-more-complex machines obstinately refuse to produce anything remotely resembling an emergent consciousness. And although the twentieth-century British philosopher Gilbert Ryle dismissed Descartes's idea of mind as 'the ghost in the machine', ironically his evocative phrase continues to haunt discussions of this problem. Descartes's fundamental distinction remains, for many, an unanswered problem. Though it is fair to say that nowadays the majority of scientists and philosophers insist that the mind-body problem is a pseudo-problem – an illusory category distinction. Despite this, they have yet to provide a fully convincing answer to the nature of consciousness.

Descartes also made a major contribution by applying rational thought to scientific method. Here, he advised scientists:

> to divide up each of the difficulties… into as many parts as possible… *Solve the simplest problems first*… commencing with objects that [are] the most simple and easy to understand, in order to rise little by little, or by degrees, to knowledge of the most complex, assuming an order, even if a fictitious one, among those which do not follow a natural sequence relatively to one another.

This is a literal prescription for the original Ancient Greek word αναλυση (analysis), which can be translated as 'to unravel or pick apart'.

In the field of mathematics, Descartes would point the way to a transformative step forward. Previously, algebra had been a matter of formulas such as $2x + 3y = 12$, where x and y are unknown quantities. On the other hand, geometry was a matter of lines and points drawn on a plane surface. (*Geo* derives from the Ancient Greek for 'earth' and *metron* means 'measurement'.) Descartes found an ingenious but simple way to combine these two apparently disparate branches of mathematics, by using what are still known as Cartesian coordinates. In this way, an algebraic formula could be plotted on a graph, with the unknown x being given values on the horizontal x-axis, and the unknown y plotted on the vertical y-axis, producing a line – or in other cases a curve – along values of x and y which provide a solution to the formula. For example, the equation $x^2 + y^2 = 1$ describes a circle of radius 1 centred on the origin point where the x-axis and y-axis intersect. Likewise, the equation $x^2 + 2y^2 = 5$ produces an ellipse. Similarly, geometric figures could be reproduced as algebraic formulas. One big advantage of this latter method was the introduction of greater precision to geometry. No matter how precisely one tries to draw a line of length two inches, or a triangle with sides two inches, three inches and four inches, absolute precision is impossible – even with the aid of a ruler. However, as soon as these lengths become numerical parts of an algebraic formula, they inevitably become exact, and can be manipulated to produce precise answers. With some justification, Descartes would claim: 'My geometry is to ordinary geometry as Cicero's Rhetoric to a child's A, B, Cs.'

Descartes's scientific and philosophical ideas mark the beginning of a new age in western thought as it began to emerge from the straitjacket of Aristotelian orthodoxy. Nonetheless, the latter remained the official teaching of the Church, and Descartes's method of comprehensive doubt, in particular, left him open to censure. (If everything can be doubted – so can the existence of God.) Even so, Descartes continued sending his works to the sympathetic Father Mersenne in Paris, asking that they be distributed amongst his intellectual contacts for criticism. As already noted, Descartes did not always take kindly to criticism of his work. However, when in 1633 he learned that Galileo had been hauled before the Inquisition in Rome, charged with heresy on account of his Copernican views, Descartes immediately panicked. He wrote to Mersenne, asking him not to send out any copies of his latest scientific work, which contained many ideas in accord with those of Galileo, including the Copernican 'heresy'.

Even in Holland, Descartes's new ideas had begun to attract criticism from certain Protestant leaders and academics. Some have seen this as an explanation for why Descartes was forever moving from place to place within the country – a wish to elude direct confrontation with those who disputed his findings and indeed his entire philosophy. Descartes is known to have lived in 'at least twenty addresses' during the twenty years he spent in Holland. However, this personal quirk appears to have been more a matter of his restless temperament and his longing for solitude.*

After these constant changes of address, the move he would make in 1649 was far more drastic, and undertaken with deep misgivings. Descartes's fame as a thinker had by this time spread through Europe, and the intellectually ambitious Queen Christina of Sweden invited him to become her tutor. Coerced by letters from the French ambassador in Stockholm, Descartes eventually gave in and travelled north on a ship despatched by the queen herself. On his arrival in Stockholm, Descartes was horrified to learn that Christina expected to receive her philosophy lessons at 5 a.m. For a man accustomed to a lifetime of rising after noon, this would prove the last straw. Riding by coach through the dark frigid winter streets of Stockholm to the Royal Palace soon caused his fragile health to fail. Within months of arriving in Sweden he had caught a

---

* However, this solitude was by no means absolute. As was customary for a gentleman of his time, he invariably employed a servant to cater for his domestic needs. On one occasion he had an affair with a maidservant called Helena Jans, who consequently gave birth to a daughter fathered by Descartes. The child was named Francine, and Descartes was in the habit of passing her off as his niece. But when Francine died at the age of five, Descartes was overcome with grief. He never married Helena, but is known to have provided her with a handsome dowry of 'one thousand guilders, a considerable sum', which enabled her to marry well.

serious chill. Despite the concerned ministrations of the French ambassador, Descartes's condition quickly worsened, and in February 1650, at the age of fifty-three, he died.

However, such was the pervasive and lasting influence of Descartes's thought throughout Europe that, thirteen years later, the Catholic Church felt obliged to place all of Descartes's works on the Index (the list of books Catholics were forbidden to read). The religious authorities argued that his philosophy relied upon reason and mind, rather than belief in God. This is undeniable, though ironically Descartes himself remained a devout Catholic throughout his life, and even used his philosophy to develop a rational proof of the existence of God. Indeed, he would eventually produce two such proofs of God's existence, which would seem to indicate an element of Cartesian doubt concerning this problem.

Descartes's main proof of the existence of God uses a variant of what is known as the ontological argument. This was first proposed by the eleventh-century theologian St Anselm, who despite being Italian was appointed Archbishop of Canterbury, the senior religious post in England. The ontological argument reasons that, as God is the most perfect being, he must be possessed of all possible perfections. A being who possesses all other perfections is even more perfect if he exists than if he does not. Therefore God exists.

The entire tenor of this argument is medieval, though its power of reasoning evidently appealed to Descartes more than the questionable assumptions upon which it rests. This aspect of the ontological argument would continue to appeal to logicians, especially those of a mathematical inclination. The finest logician of the twentieth century, the Austrian Kurt Gödel, would achieve the remarkable feat of disproving mathematics (showing it to be incomplete, and thus open to inconsistency). Having exposed this drastic flaw in humanity's most rigid form of reasoning, Gödel then set down a logical proof of the existence of God, using a variant of the ontological argument. Here, it would seem, the Age of Reason continued to venture into the realms of unreason.

CHAPTER 2

TWO ITALIAN ARTISTS

ITALY REMAINED COMPARATIVELY UNSCATHED during the religious wars which devastated so much of Europe during the early decades of the 1600s. According to the contemporary British historian Diarmaid MacCulloch, 'Italy was less inclined to the ideals of the Reformation to begin with, and lacked the anti-clerical sentiment that was present in other parts of Europe'. He ascribes this to the widespread participation of the laity in Italian religious life, especially in such organizations as religious guilds, confraternities and oratories.

On the other hand, individuals who publicly proclaimed heretical ideas were liable to fall foul of the Roman Inquisition. Amongst these was the Neapolitan-born Franciscan friar Giordano Bruno, a scientist whose ideas were both far ahead of his time and way behind. In particular, he extended the Copernican view of the solar system to the entire universe, insisting that the stars were also like the sun and had their own orbiting planets. Yet interwoven with such advanced scientific ideas was a curious hermeticism involving Thoth, the Ancient Egyptian god of wisdom, and the moon. Such heresies led to him being burned at the stake in Rome in 1600. Thirty-three years later, it was Galileo's terror of suffering the same

fate which led to him renouncing the Copernican views that he knew to
be correct.

Meanwhile, although armies were raised in Italy during this period,
their soldiers had little taste for actual combat. The experience of Odoardo
Farnese, Duke of Parma, appears to have been typical: 'Desertion, it
seems, was a reality of life more than battle was. Large engagements of
entire armies were rare in Italy; a skirmish that killed a few dozen men
was on the bloody side. By contrast, Odoardo lost half his army to desertion before he reached his allies' camp, some 1,500 men in total. Deserters
would often be recruited by the other side, and some crossed the lines
repeatedly in search of signing bonuses.'

Italy itself may have enjoyed comparative calm during these years, but
the same cannot be said for the lives of two leading Italian artists of this
period. Namely, the baroque painter and fugitive murderer Michelangelo
Merisi da Caravaggio, and the pioneering woman painter Artemisia
Gentileschi, who suffered rape, the theft of her works, and even judicial
torture by thumbscrew in order to determine the truth of her evidence.

The painter we know as Caravaggio was born in Milan in March 1571.
His father was named Fermo Merixio, whose surname has led some
to suggest that he may have been of Catalan or Greek origin. Merixio
was employed as an architect-designer by the marquis of Caravaggio, a
small town some thirty miles east of Milan. When Caravaggio was five,
his family left Milan to avoid an outbreak of the plague, and settled in
Caravaggio. Here his father, his grandfather and later his mother all died
of the plague. In the words of the British art critic Andrew Graham-
Dixon: 'By the age of six, Caravaggio had lost almost every male member
of his family, and the art of his maturity would be saturated in the
ineradicable memory of night terrors, filled with images of turmoil in
dark places.' These early events would colour Caravaggio's entire life: he
would forever resent the traumatic blow that fate had inflicted upon him.

Taking on the name of the town where he had grown up, at thirteen
Caravaggio returned to Milan, where he was apprenticed to the painter

Simone Peterzano, who had been a pupil of Titian and painted in the popular mannerist style that was emerging in Italy in the wake of the Renaissance. (Early mannerism can be seen in the works of Michelangelo, who exaggerated various features and mannerisms in his figures to achieve a heightened effect.) During his apprenticeship, Caravaggio became acquainted with the many art treasures in Milan, especially Leonardo da Vinci's famous fresco of the Last Supper on the wall of the refectory of the monastery of Santa Maria delle Grazie. Here Caravaggio appears to have been intrigued by the variety of precisely rendered expressions on the faces of the disciples.

At the age of twenty-one, Caravaggio's time in Milan came to an abrupt end when he fled the city after becoming involved in a number of brawls, during one of which he wounded a police officer. According to a contemporary witness, Caravaggio arrived in Rome 'naked and extremely needy... without fixed address and without provision... short of money'. Caravaggio's talent was already evident, and he soon found employment with the successful artist Giuseppe Cesari, whose mannerist works had proved popular with Pope Clement VIII. Cesari's studio was little more than an art factory, churning out paintings to adorn the walls of all the new palazzi and churches that were being built in Rome. Caravaggio's first works for Cesari were mainly paintings of fruit and flowers. Although this was mere hack-work, the paintings were distinguished by their penetrating precision and realism. This is unmistakably the case in his first full-fledged paintings, *Boy Peeling a Fruit* and *Boy with a Basket of Fruit*. (Indeed, the fruit in the latter painting has recently been scrutinized by a professor of horticulture, who identified a fig leaf disfigured by an unusual form of fungal infection – an effect so precisely rendered that it was even possible for the expert to distinguish the particular rare disease.)

During this period, Caravaggio himself succumbed to a spell of disease, which was evidently quite prolonged, for it put an end to his employment by Cesari. While Caravaggio was convalescing he painted a self-portrait entitled *Young Sick Bacchus*, which was probably produced a couple of years after his arrival in Rome. In this painting, the young Bacchus (the god of wine and revelry) is clutching a bunch of pallid grapes as he turns towards the spectator, revealing the sallow, fleshy face of a man in his early twenties.

This picture also confirms the direction in which Caravaggio's painting was developing. Where the mannerists exaggerated elements of their portraits for effect, Caravaggio turned this style on its head. Instead of distorting his images, he sought to achieve a very precise realism of expression, heightened by the use of chiaroscuro – the sharp contrast between light and shadow – to imbue the scene with an element of drama. This was not new; it had been used in the previous century by Renaissance painters from the German Holbein to the Italian Raphael. Chiaroscuro enabled the artist to build up a form, such as an arm or a female breast, giving it substance and a three-dimensional appearance on the flat smooth surface of the painted two-dimensional canvas.

Caravaggio, in line with his personal psychology, chose to give his chiaroscuro a particularly dramatic flourish – now known as tenebrism, involving a more exaggerated form of *tenebroso* (gloom, or shadow). Such contrasted darkness must in its own way have been a very precise form of realism at the time, when the only form of illumination at night or in darkened rooms was candlelight. It brings out the whiteness of human flesh, dramatically shining through the dusky gloom.

This effect was heightened by Caravaggio's choice of subject matter, which had veered closer to the way of life he was leading in Rome. *The Fortune Teller* depicts a young Romani fortune teller deftly running her fingers over the outstretched palm of a fashionably dressed young beau, complete with a large feather in his cap, the proportions of his torso flattered by the fine tan doublet he is wearing. Her fingertips are tracing the lines in his palm, but from the way her eyes are holding his, it seems that a more emotional mutual reading is taking place. Yet on closer inspection, this initial reading of the scene is subtly undermined by the duplicity that later becomes apparent: her fingers are surreptitiously slipping the ring from his finger.

Another novelty of this scene is shown in Caravaggio's choice of models. He chose a girl he had seen in the street for his fortune teller. And the naive beau with his sword on his left hip was modelled on

Caravaggio's friend, the sixteen-year-old Sicilian painter Mario Minniti.

The Fortune Teller is a consciously contemporary scene, and the faces of his models echo this contemporaneity. Caravaggio was intentionally breaking with the Renaissance tradition of painting classical scenes complete with recognizable classical figures. An elaborate new style was beginning to replace the Renaissance and mannerist styles of the previous century. Here we see the emergence of the baroque, exhibiting a richness of colour and dress and gesture – all intended to contrast with the austerity of the emergent Protestant art, which eschewed the adornments and flamboyant effects of Catholic art.

Other pictures from this period hint further at Caravaggio's character and the life he was leading in Rome. *The Cardsharps* is a similarly ambiguous scene, showing two well-dressed young men playing cards. The one facing away from us is reaching behind his back, craftily removing a card tucked into his belt. Meanwhile, an older figure standing behind the other player is holding out his frayed-gloved fingers to indicate which cards the player has in his hand. The sardonic look on his bearded face contrasts with the fresh-faced youth of the players, although only one of them is in fact possessed of the youthful innocence that his face would seem to indicate.

By now Caravaggio was beginning to make a name for himself, with his work attracting wealthy buyers. Amongst these was Cardinal Francesco del Monte, a connoisseur of the arts who became Caravaggio's patron and introduced him to his circle of fellow art-lovers.

Encouraged by del Monte, Caravaggio began to paint religious subjects. Unsurprisingly, he introduced a dramatic realism into the biblical scenes he portrayed. His *Penitent Magdalene* depicts the biblical prostitute slumped in a low chair, the finery of her dress rumpled about her knees, her hands folded despairingly in her lap beneath her bowed face. Beside her on the floor are a broken string of pearls, various trinkets and a three-quarters-empty flask of liquid (white wine? perfume? oil?), emblematic of the misguided life she now wishes to put behind her. A tear courses down her cheek, and her downcast face is reminiscent of Christ's head on the cross.

Critics have been divided over the spirituality of this painting. Is it just a surface element, a mere suggestion – is *Penitent Magdalene* no more than the painting of a weeping young woman? Or is Caravaggio successful in catching the genuine profundity of Magdalene's remorse? One thing is certain: he manages to render this portrait devoid of any hint of the sentimentality which could so easily have crept into such a scene. This alone gives it a gravitas that provokes thought in the onlooker.

A similar complaint relating to a lack of spirituality was made of Caravaggio's most sensational painting of this time: *Judith Beheading Holofernes.** In this painting Caravaggio takes the biblical story of how the Jewish widow Judith encouraged the Assyrian general Holofernes to get drunk, then lured him to his tent and seduced him. While Holofernes slumbered, she slipped from his bed, seized his sword and cut off his head. Characteristically, Caravaggio portrays this scene at the actual moment of Holofernes's grisly murder: his neck half severed from his body, his upturned face crying out in mortal agony. Judith's white-bloused figure stands out against the shadowy background of the tent's red canvas, the wizened features of her maid urging her on as she grasps Holofernes's hair and slices the razor-sharp blade through his neck as it gushes blood.

Some critics have noted a certain lack of power in the cutting gesture with which Judith wields the large sword. Others have argued, more convincingly, that the initial blow has already been struck, and that the seeming lack of determination in her gesture is merely an echo of the subtly rendered expression on Judith's face. This masterfully captures her feeling of ambiguity at what she is doing. She is determined to murder Holofernes, to avenge his cruelty to the Israelites, yet she cannot disguise her distaste at the horrific violence and bloodshed of her actions. Caravaggio manages to convey all this by means of the slight frown which distorts her delicate yet determined face.

There is no denying the sheer mastery with which Caravaggio manages

---

* Caravaggio painted two different versions of this scene. I have chosen to describe the earlier version, probably painted in the first years of the seventeenth century.

to suggest the complex psychology of this moment. This is certainly a religious painting in that it portrays a biblical scene, but the question of its spirituality is another matter. Like tragedy, it purges the emotions. It even touches the soul – this, after all, is death, the passing of a human life – yet it is hardly uplifting in any ethereal sense.

A contemporary described Caravaggio's behaviour around this time: 'After a fortnight's work he will swagger about for a month or two with a sword at his side and a servant following him, from one ball-court to the next, ever ready to engage in a fight or an argument, so that it is most awkward to get along with him.' As Caravaggio gained in repute, artistically and at street level, so his behaviour began to deteriorate. He became notorious for his violent temper. While a guest at Cardinal del Monte's palazzo, he is said to have attacked an aristocratic fellow guest with a club. Several times he was arrested for brawling and even duelling. Little wonder that Caravaggio's painting of Holofernes's murder was infused with such telling realism.

Then, in 1606, during the course of a duel, Caravaggio killed his opponent, the notorious scion of a noble Roman family. As with so much of Caravaggio's wild life, the details of this sensational incident remain blurred. It has been suggested that the duel concerned gambling debts; other sources suggest that Caravaggio killed his opponent while trying to castrate him, and that they were fighting over a courtesan named Fillide Melandroni. Interestingly, this was the very woman Caravaggio had used as the model for Judith.

After this incident, not even his powerful patron could protect him. Caravaggio immediately fled Rome, wanted for murder. In his absence a court sentenced him to death by beheading. Caravaggio ended up in Naples, beyond the jurisdiction of the Roman courts, where he found protection with a relative of the Sforza family, who had once employed Caravaggio's father in Milan. Here, once more, Caravaggio's sheer talent enabled him to secure a steady stream of work – especially from church patrons, who commissioned him to paint religious subjects. And once more, Caravaggio often found his art in conflict with the spirituality expected by those patrons.

Most typical of this conflict in all of Caravaggio's works is his painting *Conversion on the Way to Damascus*, which was in fact completed in Rome. This refers to St Paul's dramatic conversion to Christianity while pursuing his campaign to persecute Christians. The Bible tells of St Paul being blinded by a vision. Caravaggio goes one further, showing Paul flat on his back, having fallen from his horse, his arms outstretched towards the blinding vision. This is suggested by a light which appears to emanate from beyond the frame of the canvas, illuminating Paul and the large flank of his horse, whose hoofs are trampling his legs.

The composition prompted the exasperated patron to complain: 'Why have you put a horse in the middle, and St Paul on the ground?'

'Because!'

'Is the horse God?'

'No, but he stands in God's light.'

Conversion on the Way to Damascus was initially commissioned by Tiberio Cerasi, Pope Clement VIII's treasurer-general, who died before Caravaggio could complete the work. Cerasi's heirs initially rejected it, but were eventually persuaded to hang it in the Cerasi Chapel, though they deducted 100 scudi from Caravaggio's payment.*

The controversy over Caravaggio's perceived lack of spirituality remains. There is no doubting the dramatic flair and realism of his paintings. But is this all simply surface sensationalism, superbly rendered yet somehow devoid of any deeper content? There is certainly psychological penetration, as in the expression on Judith's face... After the religious paintings of the medieval era, and the classical subjects of Renaissance art – culminating in works such as the sculptures of Michelangelo – Caravaggio's work inevitably seems to lack a truly spiritual dimension. Drama, of itself, can be profound – as his contemporary Shakespeare

---

* The initial commission was for 400 scudi. Relative values are all but impossible to calculate with any great accuracy, but suffice to say that at this time a Roman artisan could expect to earn around 100 scudi in a year, while a wealthy cardinal could build a palazzo for 2,000 scudi. Caravaggio was a prolific painter, and is reputed to have completed some works in two weeks, though larger works, such as *Conversion on the Way to Damascus*, would have taken him some months.

makes plain. But Shakespeare has the metaphorical resonance of litera-ture. Caravaggio seems to have but the surface brilliance of evocation – in a supreme, if secular, sense. This is superbly characterized by the twenti-eth-century British art critic John Berger, who suggests of Caravaggio's art that: 'His darkness smells of candles, over-ripe melons, damp washing waiting to be hung out the next day: it is the darkness of stairwells, gambling corners, cheap lodgings, sudden encounters.'

Caravaggio's chiaroscuro may suggest the contrast between spiritual light and mortal darkness, yet it barely succeeds in capturing any transcen-dent element. Not surprisingly, Caravaggio was never fully appreciated in the centuries following his death, which took place in 1610 at the age of just thirty-eight, possibly through murder.

The last years of his life would be spent largely on the run from 'enemies'. From Naples he went to Malta, then Sicily, then back to Naples. His was at heart a secular life, and his art reflects this. As Graham-Dixon writes: 'A lot has been made of Caravaggio's presumed homosexuality, which has in more than one previous account of his life been presented as the single key that explains everything, both the power of his art and the misfortunes of his life. There is no absolute proof of it, only strong circumstantial evidence and much rumour.'

Graham-Dixon concurs with the notion of Caravaggio's homosex-uality, but points out that the artist also had female lovers. The truth of Caravaggio's character seems to lie in an inner conflict that permeated his entire personality, giving it that volatility alluded to by his contemporary in Rome. Caravaggio was always ready to take offence, to pick a fight. He seems seldom to have been at ease with himself – in his life outside his studio, away from his easel, that is.

Curiously, for all his work's violence, its drama of light and darkness, there is an unmistakable aspect of peace in its realized brilliance. Beyond the 'sudden encounters' mentioned by Berger, beyond the uneasiness of character suggested by Graham-Dixon, there is an air of fulfilment in Caravaggio's paintings. These are works of art. Their violence is aesthetic – not intended to provoke, but to be viewed as an object of silent contem-plation on the wall of a public gallery. Little wonder that they seemed out of place adorning some rich church dignitary's palazzo. These are scenes – religious or otherwise – seen through a secular eye, and painted with the clarity of reason, even though they often hark back to events of unreason.

Caravaggio's art would not be fully appreciated until it was 'rediscovered' in the twentieth century – a secular age imbued with violence, where religious scenes became no more than reminders of supremely human acts.

Caravaggio took out his resentment on the world around him. His contemporary, the pioneer woman painter Artemisia Gentileschi, suffered the opposite fate. As a talented woman in a machismo Italian society, she was resented, attacked and despised.

Gentileschi was born in Rome, probably in 1593, the oldest child of the Tuscan artist Orazio Gentileschi. Orazio had arrived in Rome from his native Pisa around 1600, already an accomplished mannerist painter. However, despite being almost ten years older than Caravaggio, he immediately fell under his spell and developed a chiaroscuro baroque style, though without the sheer flair and bravado of his young master.

When Artemisia was just twelve, her mother died, and in order to look after her Orazio took her into his studio, where she learned to mix paints and stretch canvases. It soon became apparent that she had a precocious talent for drawing, and then painting. Unsurprisingly, her first works were influenced by Caravaggio, by way of her father. But instead of copying her father's somewhat idealized figures, she drew from life, and these realistic figures began to exhibit an extraordinary accomplishment.

Artemisia's first known work is *Susanna and the Elders*, painted in 1610 when she was just seventeen. Its biblical subject is Susanna, whose naked figure is depicted at the baths, turning away awkwardly from the lewd proposals the two elders leaning over her shoulder are attempting to whisper into her ear. The work skilfully combines chiaroscuro effects (the darkness of one elder's face whispering into the ear of his bearded colleague) with classical influences (such as the wholly intentional and fully realized awkwardness of Susanna turning away from the pestering male figures). However, above and beyond such influences, the painting resoundingly expresses the travails of oppressed woman-hood: Gentileschi herself had undoubtedly suffered, and resisted, such unsolicited attentions.

The following year, her father, along with the artist Agostino Tassi, was commissioned to decorate the vaults of a palazzo owned by Cardinal Scipione Borghese, a wealthy connoisseur who had previously commissioned Caravaggio before his flight from Rome some years earlier.* Consequently, the thirty-two-year-old Tassi became a regular visitor to the Gentileschi household. One day, when Artemisia was alone, Tassi persuaded her to show him a painting beside the bedroom. He then bundled her inside, pushed her on to the bed and attempted to rape her, smothering her mouth with his hand so that she could not cry out for help. Artemisia frantically scratched at his face and managed to grasp a knife and slash at his chest, but was unable to prevent him from dishonouring her.

Tassi was surprised to discover that Gentileschi was a virgin, and afterwards promised that he would marry her. Later, on the strength of that promise, he browbeat Artemisia into a sexual relationship. It seems likely that Artemisia was inclined to go along with this in order to recoup her honour by means of marriage – though some have claimed that she eventually fell in love with Tassi.

Orazio soon became aware of rumours concerning his daughter and Tassi. When he questioned Tassi, he denied everything, but Orazio was unconvinced. He went to the authorities and pressed charges against Tassi. At the trial, Artemisia recounted the details of her rape, and in line with contemporary judicial practice she was subjected to torture, in order to 'prove' that her evidence was the truth. In particular, she was subjected to thumbscrews and having her hands bound ever tighter by cords. She refused to retract her evidence, risking her painter's hands in the process – always replying, when questioned, 'It is true, it is true.'

---

* Cardinal Borghese would build the magnificent white Villa Borghese, now an art gallery, which stands amidst the Borghese gardens on a hill overlooking central Rome.

Tassi's evidence, on the other hand, was so blatantly false and self-contradictory that the judge intervened on several occasions, insisting that he cease lying. At one point, Tassi even claimed that Gentileschi had written him erotic poems. This could not be true because, despite her painterly skills, Gentileschi remained unable to write. The only school she had ever attended was her father's studio.

Tassi called up half a dozen of his friends as witnesses. In their testimonies they claimed that Gentileschi was a whore, that her house was a bordello, and that she had committed incest with her father. Once again the judge made clear how preposterous he found this evidence. In all, the trial lasted seven months, with news of its proceedings spreading throughout Italy, leaving Gentileschi's reputation in tatters. However, in a rare verdict Gentileschi was declared innocent and Tassi was sentenced to two years in prison (which was, however, annulled the following year). During the trial it had emerged that Tassi already had a prison record, had been convicted of rape, and was known to have raped his sister-in-law and his first wife. And it was further revealed that his present wife had gone missing under suspicious circumstances. Not until this point did Gentileschi even know that Tassi was married.

Following the trial, Orazio did what he thought best to salvage his daughter's reputation. A marriage was arranged for her – to a Florentine artist named Pierantonio Stiattesi – and the couple left Rome for Florence. Here Gentileschi's talent soon achieved recognition from the ruling Medici family, who had previously patronized Renaissance artists such as Botticelli and Michelangelo.

During her years in Florence, Gentileschi would paint a number of works alluding to the trauma of her rape. But this should not be seen as overshadowing her work as a whole. Far from it. If anything, her work is dominated by her supreme talent as a colourist, evolving far beyond the chiaroscuro and drama she learned from Caravaggio by way of her father. Many of these later works include self-portraits, and she is unsparing of her features as they evolved beyond the first blush of youthful beauty to a plumper maturity. She captures her changing face with such telling character that you seem to know her, almost as if you are recognizing this woman of growing years – who looks directly at you as she is playing the lute, or gazes upward as St Catherine, her serious features seemingly prepared for the suggested martyrdom to come.*

However, there is no escaping the direct violence to which she returns again and again. And the most gruesome example of this is the very same scene chosen by Caravaggio: *Judith Slaying Holofernes*. In contrast to Caravaggio's rendering, Gentileschi's painting focuses on Judith's intent as she hacks off the head of Holofernes, her servant beside her, holding him down. Judith's face is a recognizable self-portrait, and although it is marked by a slight frown (echoing Caravaggio), this is a frown of determination. Even so (again like Caravaggio), Judith remains at arm's length from her victim – it is her servant who is closer. Judith's frown does not register distaste for the hideous act she is committing; instead her distaste seems to be for her victim. Gentileschi also uses chiaroscuro to add drama to the scene. Indeed, her painting is certainly more dramatic, more realistic, more convincing in its violence. It is filled with emotion. Unexpectedly, it is only in Caravaggio's depiction of Judith – the complexity of emotions in her face – that his work excels.

In Florence, Gentileschi became part of the cultured court of the Medici ruler Grand Duke Cosimo II, who is best remembered for his patronage and protection of Galileo from the papal authorities. At court, Gentileschi learned to read and write, and soon developed a fully rounded cultural persona. Her art was quickly appreciated, and recognized as superior to that of the local artists. In 1615, she – along with some of these artists – was commissioned by Michelangelo Buonarroti the Younger (a descendant of Michelangelo himself), who was building the Casa Buonarroti to commemorate his illustrious forebear. Gentileschi was given the leading commission to decorate the ceiling of the main gallery with a figure portraying the *Allegory of Inclination*, representing inborn talent.

---

* St Catherine was a Christian who suffered martyrdom in fourth-century Alexandria under the brutal emperor Maxentius, who sentenced her to death on the spiked breaking wheel that became known as the Catherine Wheel.

For this, Gentileschi produced a superb nude, whose face is a youthful self-portrait in keeping with the innocence of untutored natural aptitude. (This figure would later have parts of her nudity overpainted with covering scarves as the moral climate of Florence took on a more prudish aspect.*) Fittingly, the nude figure of Inclination holds a compass directed at a star. Legend has it that Gentileschi consulted Galileo himself regarding the shape of this compass, though this is unlikely as the compass is rendered as a simple object, with no attempt at realistic detail. However, it is known that Gentileschi corresponded with Galileo during these years; and the possible shape of the compass was unlikely to have been her only topic.

Recently discovered letters reveal that, during her time in Florence, Gentileschi fell in love with one of her noble patrons, Francesco Maria Maringhi. Gentileschi's husband appears to have been more than complaisant, even going so far as to add messages to his friend Maringhi on the back of Gentileschi's love letters. However, after four years this happy arrangement became the subject of gossip-mongers, which meant that Gentileschi and her husband were obliged to leave Florence in 1620.

During the last three decades of her life, Gentileschi lived largely in Rome and Naples, and even spent a year in England at the court of Charles I. Here Gentileschi painted *Self-Portrait as the Allegory of Painting*. This followed the prescription by the contemporary art iconographer Cesare Ripa that the figure of Painting should be portrayed as:

> A beautiful woman, with full black hair, dishevelled, and twisted in various ways, with arched eyebrows that show imaginative thought… with a chain of gold at her throat from which hangs a mask, and has written in front 'imitation'. She holds in her hand a brush, and in the other the palette, with clothes of evanescently covered drapery.

In Gentileschi's painting we look down over the shoulder of a

---

* By now the nude statue of Michelangelo's *David* had been defaced with a gilded fig leaf, which would remain in place well into the Victorian era.

younger version of herself, though with the dark dishevelled hair of Ripa's description.

Gentileschi would live well into her sixties, fulfilling commissions for patrons as diverse and discerning as Charles I of England and Philip IV of Spain. She probably died sometime in 1656, when a virulent outbreak of plague swept through Naples.

Like Caravaggio, her work suffered an eclipse after her death. During the ensuing centuries, she was regarded as an oddity: a 'woman painter' dogged by the scandal of her rape and the consequent trial. Few seem to have looked beyond this caricature and studied the actual works, until in 1916 she was 'rediscovered' by the Italian art expert Roberto Longhi, who somewhat misguidedly described her as 'the only woman in Italy who ever knew about painting, colouring, drawing, and other fundamentals'.

In the later decades of the twentieth century, her full worth and unique pioneering role would be recognized by many feminist writers, who noted her skill as well as her preoccupation with innocent wronged women and revenge on men. Her art is, of course, much more than this, her range far wider – though the fully realized violence of many of her works is undeniable. This would also be the case in a work not redis-covered until 2020 – namely, *David with the Head of Goliath* (a subject also chosen by her father Orazio, as well as Caravaggio). Gentileschi's chiaroscuro version has Goliath's head lying at David's bare feet, a bloody gash in the centre of the giant's forehead where he was slain by David's slingshot. The youthful, almost androgynous victor rests his arm on the hilt of the great sword he has just used to cut off Goliath's head. It is not one of Gentileschi's best works – subdued in both treatment and reali-zation, especially when seen in the light of her many masterpieces. This very fact alone should give the lie to contemporary art professor Camille Paglia's short-sighted judgement that 'Artemisia Gentileschi was simply a polished, competent painter in a Baroque style created by men'.

Such pioneers as Gentileschi seldom occur in a vacuum. Other women artists would emerge during this period – most notably the Italian Giovanna Garzoni, and the Dutch Judith Leyster (several of whose works were initially thought to have been the work of Frans Hals). But none of these was a maestra of the calibre of Gentileschi. It would be two centuries before women began to emerge as major artists, and then it would be in the field of literature. Only later would leading painters of the calibre of Gentileschi begin to emerge, such as the French multi-styled Suzanne Valadon (who taught her son Maurice Utrillo to paint) and the utterly original Mexican Frida Kahlo. It would take major changes in (male) society for such figures to thrive.

CHAPTER 3

SPREAD OF THE
SCIENTIFIC REVOLUTION

I N ORDER TO UNDERSTAND the spread of the Scientific Revolution
during the Age of Reason, we must first take note of its founding
figures, who emerged during the preceding Renaissance period.

The Florentine Galileo Galilei is widely recognized as the father
of modern science. There are two main reasons for this. The first is that
he believed in subjecting scientific 'truth' to experiment. (The contemporary Italian word for this was *cimento*, which means 'test' or 'trial'.)
His second fundamental contribution is summed up in his declaration
'mathematics is the language in which God has written the universe'.
From now on, measurement would become central to scientific truth.

Advances are seldom the work of a single individual. Discoverers –
both in science and in other fields – are often accompanied by contemporaries of similar intent. Several such figures would appear during Galileo's
lifetime.

In England, the flamboyant maverick polymath Francis Bacon
managed to combine his multiple pursuits of knowledge with a

ruthless ambition for high office. Indeed, he is one of the few people in history of whom it can be said that he was wasting his time ruling his country. Sheer ambition (and the need to pay off his extravagant debts) impelled Bacon to climb the greasy pole of politics to its highest point, in the process dislodging his main competitors by the most underhand methods at his disposal. In 1617, when King James I travelled to Scotland, Bacon was appointed regent of England and briefly became de facto ruler of the country. Fortunately for science, his enemies made sure that he later fell from grace and was dismissed from his post as Lord Chancellor for accepting bribes. (In his defence, he pointed out that he could not possibly have been biased, as he accepted bribes from both sides.)

Bacon's firm belief in experimental science, and his understanding of how it proceeded, led to him extending Galileo's insights. He asserted that science was more than simply mathematical: for instance, its truths could not be discovered by deductive reason, like mathematical theorems. Scientific laws were discovered by *inductive* reason: generalizations that could only be drawn from a large quantity of repeated experimental observations.

Ironically, despite his great insight into scientific method, Bacon himself undertook few practical experiments. And on one occasion when he did, the consequences would prove fatal. In March 1626, while travelling by coach through snow, he had a sudden inspiration that the coldness of snow might preserve living flesh from putrefaction. He ordered the coach to stop, leapt out and bought a plucked chicken from a woman by the wayside. He at once began stuffing it with snow with his bare hands, intent upon testing his idea. Unfortunately, this impulsive experiment led to him catching a chill, of which he eventually died – before he could demonstrate his far-sighted hypothesis concerning the power of refrigeration.

Bacon's English contemporary William Harvey studied medicine at the University of Padua, at the time the finest university in Europe (Galileo was professor of mathematics there, and Harvey received lectures from

Fabricius, 'the father of embryology').* After years of painstaking research – 'the very exemplar of Baconian methodology' – Harvey was the first to describe correctly the circulation of the blood throughout the human body. This was widely considered 'the greatest contribution to anatomy and medicine of any century'. Consequently, he was appointed royal physician, but was curiously unimpressed by Francis Bacon, remarking: 'He writes philosophy like a Lord Chancellor.'

Harvey was also active in the realms of unreason. A superstitious fear of alleged witchcraft was prevalent in England at the time, and many so-called witches were persecuted. Harvey was opposed to such persecution, and became involved in a celebrated incident. When travelling with the king to Newmarket, he was sent to investigate a woman suspected of being a witch. On entering her house he introduced himself as a travelling wizard who had come to discuss witchcraft with her. At the time, it was believed that all witches had their 'familiar' – a supernatural agent in the form of an animal – and Harvey asked the woman if she had a familiar. The woman beckoned to a toad, which hopped across the floor and then drank from a saucer of milk at her feet. Claiming to feel thirsty, Harvey despatched the woman to a nearby tavern to fetch him a pitcher of ale. In her absence, he caught the toad and dissected it – finding it to be in 'no wayes different from other toades... ergo it was a plain natural toad'. Unfortunately, he had become so immersed in his dissecting that

---

* Later in the century, the infant prodigy Elena Cornaro would study there. The illegitimate daughter of a Venetian aristocrat and a peasant woman, Elena had mastered four foreign languages by the time she was seven. During her youth she became fluent in Hebrew and Arabic, learned to play four musical instruments, and studied philosophy, geometry, physics and astronomy. Initially, she was forbidden to study theology by the Bishop of Padua, though her father used his influence to overcome this objection. He also ensured that she was able to study at the University of Padua, despite a statute forbidding women from entering the university. There she studied philosophy, theology, physics and astronomy, gaining a doctorate in philosophy in 1678 – the first woman recorded as achieving this feat. Consequently, Padua dropped its statute forbidding women, and a number of other female students soon followed. On leaving university, Cornaro devoted her life to study and charitable works, dying just seven years later at the age of thirty-eight.

he did not notice when the woman returned and saw what he was doing. Whereupon 'she flew like a Tigris at his face', scratching and screeching at him. Harvey eventually managed to calm her down, informing her that he was the king's physician, and that if he had discovered she was a witch and her familiar proved supernatural, she would have been tried and burned at the stake. It seems unlikely that this convoluted, if incontrovertible, reasoning consoled her for the loss of her pet toad.

In Italy, the revolution of science started by Galileo was continued by his pupil Evangelista Torricelli, who like his master was a physicist and mathematician. Descartes had speculated that the earth was subject to pressure from the weight of its atmosphere, but it was Torricelli who proved this to be the case. He filled a long glass tube with mercury, placed his thumb over the open end to temporarily seal it, and upended the tube so that the open end was plunged into a bowl of mercury. The mercury in the glass tube sank, but always remained higher than the surface of the mercury in the bowl.

In doing this, Torricelli had shown that the pressure of the earth's atmosphere on the mercury in the bowl was able to support the column of mercury in the tube, which was not subject to the earth's atmosphere. Following in Galileo's footsteps, Torricelli understood how mathematics could be used to describe this phenomenon: the length of the column of mercury in the tube could be measured, thus indicating the precise weight of the atmosphere pressing down on the mercury in the bowl. Here was a prime example of Galileo's belief that the language of the universe was written in mathematics.

Torricelli found that the column of mercury in the tube was always about thirty inches higher than the surface of the bowl, though he noticed that this varied from time to time. By carrying out this experiment Torricelli had invented the barometer, which was capable not only of measuring the pressure of the earth's atmosphere but also of indicating variations in this pressure. Such measurements would become a central feature of the science of meteorology, which began to develop during the following century. (Torricelli had also created a vacuum in the upper section of the glass tube. This was the first experiment to create a sustainable vacuum.)

Meanwhile, in Prague, the German Johannes Kepler was mapping the orbits of the planets, using tables containing a multitude of precise astronomical observations made by his mentor, the Danish astronomer Tycho Brahe. By following the evidence provided by these tables, Kepler realized that the orbits of the planets around the sun were not circular, as Copernicus had posited. Instead, each planet's orbit followed the course of an ellipse (the curve which is revealed when a cone is sliced diagonally). Unfortunately, Kepler's experimental method – another case of exemplary Baconian inductive reasoning – was somewhat marred by his inclination towards irrational mysticism. This led him to subscribe to the Ancient Greek belief in the 'music of the spheres'– the ethereal sound the planets reportedly made as they passed through the heavens. Fortunately, this 'music' could not be heard by mere mortals, and was only audible to the soul, and thus it had no deleterious effect on Kepler's supremely painstaking and rational mapping of orbits.

Such were the Renaissance scientists who laid the groundwork for the ever-expanding Scientific Revolution. It was no accident that the first great scientist of the Age of Reason would appear in the Dutch Republic, which had officially been recognized by the Peace of Westphalia. Though technically Protestant, the Dutch Republic had fostered a more liberal attitude towards religion and indeed freedom of thought in general. It was this which drew Descartes to pursue his new rational philosophy there. The liberal atmosphere would also attract Huguenots from France and Jews from all over Europe – Sephardic Jews from Spain and Portugal,* and Yiddish-speaking Ashkenazi Jews from the German lands and the Habsburg Empire.† Similarly it would attract a number of freethinkers, especially from England. This wide diversity and tolerance would play a large part in turning the comparatively small Dutch Republic into a

---

* *Sepharad* was the Hebrew word for Spain.

† Yiddish retained elements of Hebrew, but was largely derived from German and Slavonic languages, though it was written in Hebrew characters.

leading European centre of commercial and cultural innovation during the Age of Reason.

The first great scientist of this era would be Christiaan Huygens (pronounced HY-genz), who was born in 1629 in The Hague, the capital of the Dutch Republic. He was the second son of Constantijn Huygens, a wealthy diplomat and influential adviser to the ruling House of Orange.* Outside his government duties, Constantijn pursued a range of polymathic interests, becoming a fine poet and an amateur scientist of sufficient expertise that he corresponded with the likes of Galileo, Mersenne and Descartes.

Young Christiaan was educated at home with his elder brother, Constantijn, by a series of tutors who instructed them in subjects ranging from music to mathematics, history to literature – to say nothing of fencing and horse riding. In other words, all the requirements befitting two young gentlemen destined for prestigious careers in public service. Their father also insisted that they follow him in his polymathic pursuits. As a result, Christiaan became a skilled painter as well as a meticulous draughtsman (as is evidenced in the detailed scientific notebooks he kept in later life). The boys' father was frequently away on diplomatic missions, but he expected regular reports on his sons' progress. One of these would note of Christiaan that 'he might almost be called a prodigy', but complained that he wasted too much of his time on 'devices of his own invention, on constructions and machines, which, though they might be ingenious, are but distractions that will always break down'.

Christiaan's father also disapproved of such unscholarly activity. Fortunately, he would later hire as his son's tutor Jan Stampioen, previously a professor of mathematics and then tutor of the stadtholder's son William (who would succeed his grandfather William the Silent

---

* As the Dutch Republic achieved freedom from Habsburg rule, a leading role in this struggle was played by the Protestant William the Silent, head of the House of Orange. Consequently, the House of Orange would provide stadtholders (governors) for the new republic. These were elected by the States General (parliament). The House of Orange originated from the Principality of Orange in French Provence.

to become William II, Prince of Orange). It was Stampioen who fired Christiaan's imagination, and by his early teens his pupil had already attained a prodigious expertise in mathematics.*

At the age of sixteen, Christiaan left home with his older brother Constantijn to study law at the University of Leiden. However, on the recommendation of Descartes, Christiaan was also tutored in mathematics by Frans van Schooten, a follower of Descartes who was also abreast of the latest developments in science and mathematics.

Four years later, Christiaan's father obtained a post for him on a Dutch diplomatic mission travelling through various German states and north into Denmark. Here Christiaan planned to cross into Sweden and go to Stockholm to meet Descartes, but this trip came to nothing when he learned that Descartes had died that winter. So Christiaan continued with the diplomatic mission, travelling though Germany into Italy, where he visited Rome, before returning home in late 1650.

There now followed a series of events which changed young Huygens's life. In November 1650 the new stadtholder, the twenty-four-year-old Prince William II of Orange, died of smallpox after reigning for just three years, whereupon the Estates General decided against appointing his infant son William as stadtholder.† Thus began a truly republican era in Dutch history, known as the First Stadtholderless Period.

These unprecedented events were accompanied by a number of ominous developments that gripped the Dutch populace. First the country suffered such a prolonged and heavy snowfall that everything ground to a halt. Mourners were unable to travel to The Hague and the funeral of William II had to be postponed. When the spring thaw finally arrived, it was accompanied by violent storms, with tidal surges causing the worst flooding the country had seen in eighty years.

---

* Stampioen was of sufficient prowess to have bested Descartes in a mathematical argument, which had so enraged the 'rational' philosopher that he challenged Stampioen to a duel – before Christiaan's father stepped in to smooth the ruffled feathers on both sides.

† Thirty-nine years later, in 1689, this William of Orange would become King of England, Scotland and Ireland.

The death of William II meant that Christiaan Huygens's father no longer held a position of political influence. At the same time, he also realized that Christiaan was not cut out for a diplomatic career, and allowed him to retire to Hofwijck, the family's 'moated chateau... modelled on the hunting lodges of the Princes of Orange, but surrounded by formal gardens of mathematical precision'. Here Huygens was able to pursue his scientific interests at will.

However, although he was now able to live a life of some luxury, and was able to devote himself entirely to his favourite scientific pursuits, Huygens was hardly happy. His health was frail, and he was prone to bouts of severe depression. A putative portrait from this time depicts a rather plump young man wrapped in a loose, richly patterned gown, wearing the fashionable wig of the period, all tumbling curls and ringlets. Huygens would never marry, and his brother Constantijn was his closest companion, aiding him in setting up his experiments.

By now, Huygens was already corresponding with Father Mersenne in his cell in Paris. Indeed, Mersenne was so enthused by Huygens's mathematical knowledge that he referred to him as 'the new Archimedes', and put him in touch with several of the mathematicians and scientists with whom he corresponded. In this way, Huygens received an unpublished paper by Torricelli (who had died in 1647), and indirectly made contact with the leading French mathematician Pierre de Fermat. Unfortunately, nothing came of the latter contact, as Fermat's interests remained confined to pure mathematics, while Huygens was becoming more involved in applied mathematics, such as that pursued by Torricelli.

Huygens now had the temerity to point out mistakes in Descartes's laws of collision, replacing these with his own theory of collisions. This is of some note, as the latter contained the first suggestion of an idea that Newton would later develop into the fundamental concept of 'force' (which would transform the entire scope of physics – from small colliding bodies to the movements of the planets). In doing so, Huygens was proposing an early version of Newton's first law of motion, which states that in the absence of any external force, such as gravity, a body will continue moving in a straight line. And Huygens further developed

Descartes's ingenious idea that gravity was caused by a universal vortex. Huygens proposed that gravity was the result of 'a system of multiple vortices acting through "subtle matter" in space'. Here it is possible to detect, though only through hindsight, how the ideas of contemporary scientists were beginning to evolve towards Newton's comprehensive explanation of gravity.*

In 1655, Huygens found a way to improve the early telescopes developed by Galileo for his pioneering astronomical observations in 1610. Huygens discovered how to avoid the blurring rainbow images which had so often hampered Galileo's observations. In order to achieve this, Huygens sought the advice of the philosopher Benedict Spinoza, who earned his living as a painstaking lens-grinder. Huygens also received useful suggestions from the superlative amateur lens-grinder Antonie van Leeuwenhoek, who is seen by many as the pioneer of microscopy.†

Huygens's new method involved grinding lenses to a greater precision. This resulted in long, tiring hours of laborious work; and although he was assisted by his brother, the fine glass dust affected an existing respiratory ailment.

---

* Such hindsight inclines us towards a deterministic or teleological (purposive) view of science. This suggests that scientific progress is somehow 'inevitable'. However, science evolves in much the same way as Darwinian evolution, which would not be conceived until two centuries later. Darwin proposed 'the survival of the fittest' as his central idea. Species adapt to ever-changing circumstances, often in quasi-accidental fashion. This is not determinism; it is, so to speak, blind. Scientific concepts evolve in much the same way, i.e. according to how well they explain the observable facts. According to this, the better – or more complete – explanation should supersede the earlier, more limited version. The classic modern example of this can be seen in how Einstein's theories of relativity superseded Newton's central notion of gravity. Newton's idea completely explained the facts, except in certain extreme conditions. An indication of how well Newton's ideas performed in all but the most exceptional circumstances can be seen in the fact that the mathematicians calculating NASA's first flight to the moon used Newtonian gravity, dispensing with the added complications of relativity, which only accounted for miniscule inaccuracies.

† The work of these important figures, as well as that of Newton, will feature in later chapters. Similarly with Colbert and Leibniz, who appear later in this chapter.

Huygens eventually produced a telescope that was twenty-three feet in length and capable of 43 times magnification. (After considerable work, Galileo had managed to produce a telescope of 30 times magnification.) Huygens's improved telescope – the two-lensed 'Huygenian eyepiece' – enabled him to attain an unparalleled level of astronomical observation. Galileo had been the first to observe Saturn with a telescope, and had described it as having two accompanying bulges, which he compared to ears. These caused him to conclude that the planet Saturn was not a single planet, but rather composed of three planets that almost touched each other. It was Huygens who discovered that Saturn was in fact surrounded by a disc-like ring that was detached from the planet. This was so unlike any other phenomenon observed in the heavens that he decided to embark upon a thorough series of observations in order to confirm his unlikely finding. However, in order to establish the priority of his discovery he published the anagram 'aaaaaaaccccccdeeeeeghiiiiiiilllll-mmnnnnnnnnnnnooooppqrrstttttuuuuu'. Three years later he would reveal that this meant *'Annuto cingitur, tenui, plano, nusquam coherente, ad eclipticam inclinato'* ([Saturn] is surrounded by a thin, flat, ring, nowhere touching, inclined to the ecliptic).

Galileo had already discovered four moons orbiting Saturn, but Huygens was able to detect the presence of a further, larger moon, which he named Titan. Unfortunately, even at this stage astronomy still retained an element of its earlier metaphysical associations. (Indeed, such remnants can be seen to this day in our use of the word 'heavens' to describe the sky.) In Huygens's time, astrology remained rife, and Kepler's mysticism and Platonic numerology persisted as strong influences. So much so that at this point even Huygens felt prompted to indulge in speculation beyond his experimental evidence. His discovery of a fifth moon of Saturn was no coincidence, he decided. There were now six known planets (including the earth), and six known satellites (including the earth's moon). This led him to pronounce that there were no further planets or moons to be discovered. Our knowledge of the solar system was complete.

Fortunately, this conclusion did not prevent Huygens from undertaking further astronomical observations and attempting to interpret them.

Not all of his interpretations would prove correct, but they would at least be inferences drawn from evidence. For instance, Huygens noticed that the surface of Mars was pitted with markings. This led him to conclude that its geography was probably similar to that on earth. Consequently, he labelled a V-shaped marking on the surface of Mars as Syrtis Major (meaning 'large bog'). Such mistaken inferences, and their later correction, are the means by which genuine science progresses. Suppositions based upon particular evidence are later rendered redundant by further experimental or empirical evidence. As long as an inference appears to fit the facts, it remains acceptable. The speculative numerology applied to the planets and moons by Huygens is categorically different – technically, it was not backed by experiment. Such difference is subtle and deceptive, and frequently only revealed by hindsight. But the difference is fundamental. Huygens's idea of the complete solar system may have seemed in accord with Galileo's insight that 'mathematics is the language... [of] the universe', but Huygens's numerology would succumb to the test of Baconian experimental induction. On the other hand, Galileo's insight did enable Huygens to calculate, with some accuracy, the length of the Martian day.

Huygens's improved telescope enabled him to make observations of objects far beyond the solar system, such as the large luminescent cloud of gas and dust known as the Orion Nebula. (The brighter interior expanse of this nebula is now known as the Huygenian region.) This led Huygens to undertake his boldest experiment to date, which illustrates both his ambition and the difficulties he faced.

Huygens decided to try to calculate the distance of the star Sirius from our solar system. He assumed that Sirius was itself a sun, and as such was as bright as our sun. He drilled a hole in a metal plate so small that the light shining through it from the sun matched that of Sirius. Using the proportion of the sun's light which passed through the hole, he was able to calculate that Sirius was 2.5 trillion miles away. This is in fact just over one-twentieth of the actual distance. Huygens's mistake had been to assume that all stars, including the sun, were possessed of the same brightness. (In reality, Sirius is far brighter than the sun, and must be correspondingly further away to shine as dimly as it does.) Despite this error, it is clear that Huygens fully grasped the implications of Galileo's concept of a mathematical universe, which could be calculated on a quantitive basis.

So far we have seen that Huygens was attempting to measure space (the distance to Sirius) and also time (the length of the Martian day). It was his further efforts in the latter sphere that would lead to another of his supreme achievements.

Attempts to measure time stretch back into prehistory. Some of humanity's oldest surviving monuments, such as 4,500-year-old Stonehenge, may be regarded as clocks, marking the passing of the equinox and thus the all-important seasons for planting and harvesting. In the third century BC, the Ancient Greek inventor Ctesibius constructed an improved water clock, which came closer to measuring the hour of the day. The mechanical clocks of the medieval era, operated by falling weights, proved highly ingenious but no more accurate. It would be Huygens who brought chronometry (time measurement) into the modern era.

As usual, Galileo had a hand – literally – in this scientific step forward. One Sunday, while bored during a sermon at Pisa Cathedral, Galileo noticed that a lamp hanging on a long wire attached to the high ceiling was swinging like a pendulum. Placing his finger on his pulse he began to measure the time the lamp took to swing through its arc, and found that this time remained constant. Further experiments led Galileo to realize that the constant period of a pendulum's swing was related to its overall length, but appeared to be independent of how far the weight at the end of the pendulum had been displaced from its median position. Unusually, Galileo failed to follow through on this finding; he merely used it for timing intervals in his scientific experiments.

In 1656, more than ten years after Galileo's death, Huygens took the first steps in constructing a pendulum clock. This would provide a constant periodic motion, which could be attached to cog gears turning the arms (minute and hour) on a clock face. In the course of his experiments Huygens discovered that a pendulum did not swing in *precisely* equal intervals. Wide swings took a fraction longer than shorter swings. Also, in order to achieve precision, a pendulum needed to swing in an elliptical arc rather than an unhampered circular one. After innumerable painstaking experiments, he arrived at optimum accuracy. In order to achieve this he made a pendulum which swung through an arc of between four and six degrees. He also incorporated curved metal 'cheeks' (obstructions) on either side of the upper pendulum, causing the bob on the end to swing through an ellipse. Falling weights on pulleys transferred sufficient energy to the pendulum to prevent it coming to a halt from friction and air resistance. Huygens described this clock in his treatise *Horologium* (Clock), which he presented to the Dutch government and also distributed amongst various scientists. He was particularly gratified to receive a reply from the renowned French mathematician Blaise Pascal, who said of *Horologium*: 'I have been among its leading admirers'.

However, when Huygens conducted a series of further experiments, it soon became clear to him that his 'longcase clock' still required further adjustments.* Using meticulous trial-and-error experiments involving two clocks, with long and short pendulums, Huygens at last managed to perfect his mechanism and 'so finely adjusted two clocks in this way that in three days they never had a difference between them even as much as seconds'.† Such was the accuracy of the clocks built according

---

* The longcase clock was the original form of what became known as a grandfather clock. The mechanism of a long pendulum Huygens *horologium* was enclosed in an upright wooden casket in order to prevent draughts and rapid temperature fluctuations disturbing the swing of the pendulum and the free-falling (and rising) weights. At the top of the casket was the clock face driven by the internal mechanism of the pendulum and the rising and falling weights on their counterbalancing pulleys.

† However, such extreme accuracy was not guaranteed. Huygens did not actually construct all Huygens's *horlogiums* himself. After registering his patent, he assigned this to one Salomon Coster, a watchmaker of The Hague. Consequently Huygens was not able to supervise personally the making of all the clocks which bore his name, or those which would later be constructed by foreign makers (often not even under licence). There is the possibility that Huygens's initial claim to the extreme accuracy of his clock may have been a little exaggerated. At any rate, his historical achievement should not be belittled, even if modern sources claim that Huygens's *horologium* 'increased the accuracy of clocks enormously from about 15 minutes per day to 15 seconds per day'.

to Huygens's design that it would be 175 years before they received any significant improvement.

By now, Huygens's achievements had gained him recognition in scientific circles throughout Europe. He travelled to London, where he met the German Henry (formerly Heinrich) Oldenburg, who had become the first Secretary of the Royal Society, recently formed in 1660. Oldenburg and the Royal Society filled the gap left by Father Mersenne after he died in 1648. Such was the growing advancement of science (still known as 'natural philosophy') that its pioneering figures needed to communicate with each other, as well as to circulate their findings and learn of the discoveries of others in their field. Oldenburg was particularly energetic in this sphere, maintaining a wide circle of learned correspondents ranging from Italy and the German states, to Denmark and Holland (Christiaan's father had been one of his earliest correspondents). Like Mersenne, Oldenburg was not above taking sides in the inevitable disputes that arose – not least because he sometimes encouraged them.

Fortunately for Huygens, Oldenburg took a liking to the young Dutchman, and in 1665 he ensured the thirty-six-year-old Huygens's election to the Royal Society – amongst the first foreigners to achieve this exalted position. Huygens also travelled to Paris on various occasions, and he would settle there permanently in 1666 at the invitation of Jean-Baptiste Colbert, first minister to Louis XIV, the Sun King, who was building his vast new residence at Versailles. France was now the major country in Europe, and Louis XIV wished to establish Paris as the most prestigious city on the continent. The French Académie des Sciences was established in 1666 and Huygens became one of its founding members.

By now in his forties, Huygens was already showing signs of middle age. He was described as being rather plump, with a weak chin, and suffering from respiratory ailments. His ill health was compounded by his vulnerability to depression, which would on occasion confine him to bed for days at a time. However, like Descartes, Huygens found that while lying in bed he was able to let his mind wander free, and then pursue his original thoughts to their ultimate conclusion. In his notebooks from this period there are an increasing number of entries to which he would add, when he was particularly satisfied with their content, the word 'EUREKA' (in capitals).*

It was in Paris that Huygens came up with his most important contribution to theoretical physics – namely, his concept of light. Working in England during the previous decade, the great Newton had proposed his own radical theory of optics, suggesting that light consisted of a stream of particles that were emitted by an object and received by the eye. Huygens boldly proposed an alternative wave theory of light. In line with contemporary thought, he assumed that space was filled with an ether of microscopic particles. These could be disturbed, like a stone dropping into a still pond, causing circular waves to emanate across the surface. However, in space this two-dimensional picture became three-dimensional, with spherical waves of light emanating from the light source. Light was not particles, or indeed anything material; it was simply a disturbance in the ether, radiating in waves.

Huygens's theory had its advantages. In a phenomenon known as Huygens's construction, every point on the advancing wave front is a source of secondary spherical wavelets. By this means, Huygens managed to explain the reflection and refraction of light, as well as accounting for why light passes more slowly through a denser medium (which Newton's theory was unable to explain). The chief difficulty with Huygens's theory was that waves – as observed in water – have a natural tendency to bend around obstacles which stand in their path, unlike particles which cast distinct shadows. However, experiments conducted by the Italian physicist Francesco Grimaldi supported Huygens, showing that this 'bending' of light was in fact the case, at least to a degree. When Grimaldi passed a beam of light through two small apertures, one in front of the other, he found that after passing through the second aperture the beam was

---

* Eureka: εύρηκα, in the original Greek, meaning: 'I have found it!' This is of course the legendary exclamation accredited to Archimedes, when he is said to have leapt from his bath on discovering the principle of buoyancy. It is perhaps fitting that Huygens – 'the new Archimedes' – should also use this term.

slightly larger than when it passed through the first. This showed that light did in fact bend, in a process which he named diffraction.*

Huygens would remain in Paris for fifteen years. Apart from his experimental and theoretical researches, he was invited by Chief Minister Colbert to draw up plans for a planetarium, intended to compete with the observatory recently built at Greenwich, outside London. Huygens was also visited by the young Leibniz, who was in Paris on an extended diplomatic mission. It was Huygens who recognized the lacunae in Leibniz's knowledge of mathematics and physics, a common failing amongst German scientists at this time. To help remedy this, Huygens would teach Leibniz the new analytical geometry devised by Descartes. Besides teaching Leibniz, Huygens also set him on a course of study which would eventually result in the exceptional master being outshone by his prodigious pupil. Huygens seems to have accepted this with some equanimity. His character had little of the aggressive ambition often harboured by the exceptionally talented.

Throughout his time in Paris, Huygens wrote frequent letters to members of his large family. His ageing father remained active in his polymathic pursuits – a sometimes domineering presence, he was proud of his son's accomplishments but seems not to have recognized them as superior to his own. In addition, Huygens exchanged letters with his favourite brother, Constantijn, who was in the process of becoming a successful politician and administrator. And Huygens also maintained regular contact with his younger brother Lodewijk, who made up for his lack of intellect by acting as the family joker, but was transformed into the black sheep of the family when he became involved in a duel while at college. (Later,

---

* Newton's particle theory of light would become the accepted version. Not until the twentieth century and the advent of quantum theory would the wave theory of light be resurrected. According to quantum theory, *both* theories – i.e. wave and particle – are needed to explain the behaviour of light. But how can light be both particles (matter) and waves (immaterial)? Various explanations have been put forward to explain this unreasonable state of affairs – ironically, a hangover from the Age of Reason. According to one version, light travels in 'quanta', distinct entities composed of waves. In another version, light travels in waves, but 'collapses' into particles when it is observed.

when their father obtained a post for Lodewijk as a local magistrate in the southern Dutch city of Gorinchem, he brought further shame on the family by accepting bribes.) But most of all, Huygens kept contact with his younger sister Susanna, who held the family together after their mother's death and during their father's frequent absences on missions abroad. She passed on local and family gossip, and was eager to hear of the latest fashions in Paris, imploring Huygens to keep her informed of 'any exceptional Alteration in the dress of the Ladies or in their Hairstyles'. Susanna was a talented musician and spoke French, and even visited Huygens in Paris. It was probably her letters that persuaded Huygens to make a number of return visits to the family home, Hofwijck.

In Paris, Huygens seems to have alternated between bouts of overwork and spells in bed due to ill health and depression. The French Académie des Sciences was established in 1666 and Huygens became one of its founding members. Colbert ensured that Huygens was provided with a constant flow of problems from the academy; and, reluctantly, Huygens was even persuaded to become involved with academy business. However, he felt that the institution would soon destroy itself, 'because it was mixt with tinctures of Envy' and relied upon 'the Humour of a Prince [Louis XIV] and the favour of a minister [Colbert]'. In between times, Huygens pursued his own original work – continuing to make headway with his investigations into theoretical problems of such magnitude as the nature of light, and practical problems such as designing a large-scale planetarium.

It is possible that Huygens's closeness to his family may have smothered his emotions and been at least in part responsible for why he never married. Huygens had dealings with several women throughout the course of his life, especially in Paris. During his early years in the city, he seems to have fallen for a young woman called Marie Perriquet, sending her little gifts – until he was advised by a friend that she was the lover of several 'virtuous old men, long married'.

He also fell in love with Marianne Petit, the daughter of Pierre Petit, who was cartographer to Louis XIV as well as being an important engineer in the royal employ. Petit was in charge of the city's fortifications, and had also been commissioned to draw up plans for a River Seine canal (a forerunner of the present-day Canal Saint-Martin). Petit was particularly interested in Huygens's continuing work on clocks and telescopes, and regularly invited Huygens to his home, where the younger man soon became enchanted by Marianne.

In pursuit of Marianne, Huygens turned to his skill as a painter, and spent long hours painting a portrait of his new beloved. During these sessions they would converse, but on one occasion Marianne informed him that his whole outlook on life was 'heretical'. This remark prompted him to considerable introspection, which only encouraged his tendency to depression. In the end, he became dissatisfied with his portrait of Marianne and destroyed it. However, several haunting drawings of her face appear in his notebooks, amidst his mechanical drawings and mathematical calculations.

Despite all this, Huygens never felt fully at home in Paris. He was a Protestant, and Paris remained very much a Catholic city, with the continuing persecution of Protestants happening throughout the country. Regardless, both Louis XIV and Colbert encouraged Huygens to continue living in Paris – even after France declared war on Holland in 1672. Despite this, Huygens did not finally depart Paris until 1681, when he returned to live in The Hague. He took up residence in the family townhouse, where his father (now in his nineties) was still living.

Huygens brought back with him in his luggage the unassembled parts of the planetarium he had been designing for Colbert. This was intended 'to demonstrate the true paths of the planets by using gear wheels cut with unequally spaced teeth to simulate the planets' varying velocities in elliptical orbits'. He also resumed work with his brother Constantijn. They co-operated in developing lenses for a large telescope to be erected in the garden of the family home. Huygens's ambition was to devise a telescope superior to the ones he had seen in Paris, which had discovered two further moons of Saturn that he had missed.

Huygens's new telescope proved to be of a pioneering, if somewhat unusual, design. For a start, unlike other telescopes it was tubeless. The apparatus consisted of an eyepiece on a tripod at ground level, and a lens mounted on a tall mast. These could be aligned by means of a cord from the eyepiece to the lens on the mast. Gradually, the two brothers succeeded in extending the focal length of this telescope from 34 feet to 210 feet; as they did so the mast grew in height, and the single lens atop the mast went through a series of expansions, the final ones growing to 'the size of dinner plates'. Despite such efforts, Huygens was unable to rival the new telescopes being created in Paris. However, the eccentricity of the tubeless telescope was but the beginning of Huygens's deviation from the scientific norm.

Huygens was dismissive of his rivals in Paris, and he was determined to demonstrate his superiority – even if he was unable to obtain better observational evidence with his latest telescope. This was of no concern, for he felt sure that he understood the nature of astronomy better than anyone since Galileo. So, instead of relying upon telescopic observations, he decided to opt for a more Cartesian approach and build up his epistemology by means of reason alone. From deductive reasoning, he would then move to inference and inductive reasoning. He would use the foundation of his knowledge of the stars, and build upon this to extend his vision to the entire universe.

When Huygens's father finally died at the age of ninety in 1687, Huygens moved out of the city to the family chateau, Hofwijck. Here he launched into writing his final 'masterpiece', which was to be called *Cosmotheoros*. Having wrongly established the distance to Sirius, and mistakenly described the surface of Mars, he now compounded these errors by launching into further speculations. He assumed that such stars as Sirius were similar to the sun, each having its own planets. And although we could not see these planets, he felt sure that they contained life, much like that on earth.

It was less than a century since the Church had sentenced Giordano Bruno to be burned at the stake for promulgating similar ideas. Huygens bravely assumed that by living in Protestant Holland he was safe from Catholic persecution. On this occasion his bravery was matched only by his excessive imagination. On the positive side, Huygens's *Cosmotheoros* has been described by the modern science writer Philip Ball as 'the first attempt to mount a rigorous scientific case for life on other worlds, without doing harm to Scripture'. On the other hand, building upon his observations of the marshes of Mars, Huygens proceeded to extrapolate to 'The Celestial Worlds Discovered' (so the English title of his work would proclaim). As a modern commentary laments, he 'convinced himself that the planets were populated and wrote in detail about shipbuilding and other engineering on Jupiter and Saturn'.

Many of Huygens's fantasies, as well as his explanations, were nothing less than extremely ingenious. For instance, he claimed that God had created the planets and placed them far away from one another so that the beings on each planet could develop their worlds unaware of similar developments on other planets. Unfortunately, God had not foreseen humanity's ability to develop the telescope.

This was all very interesting, but it was not science – merely an early example of science fiction. By this stage, Huygens was a very sick man, and he entrusted the publication of *Cosmotheoros* to his brother Constantijn. Wisely, Constantijn delayed the publication of the manuscript until 1498, some three years after the death of Christiaan at the age of sixty-six. By now, Huygens's work could be neither a danger to himself nor his reputation. Or so Constantijn supposed.

Huygens was a supreme scientist – arguably the greatest of his time. His work provides an illuminating link between the first modern scientist Galileo and the acme of the new science that was later reached by Newton. Unfortunately for Huygens, his work in the many and varied scientific fields in which he made discoveries was destined to become overshadowed by that of his great Italian predecessor and his supreme English successor. By building upon the ideas of Galileo, and becoming a precursor to the ideas of Newton, his contributions somehow became subsumed into both these figures. What had in fact been a vital link was largely overlooked. His place in history was thus ironically eclipsed by his place in historical time.

Yet it was in this very field – time itself – that he made his indelible mark. Huygens's invention of the pendulum clock remains supreme. The introduction of a new precision in the fundamental field of time would prove transformative for all scientists, including Newton, during the centuries to come. And his final extension of his work into science fiction would be but a mere peccadillo compared with the enormity of the transgressions perpetrated by Newton. Even the finest intellects of the Age of Reason, it seems, were not immune from the undercurrents of unreason that continued to muddy the waters beneath its gleaming surface.

CHAPTER 4

THE ENGLISH CIVIL WAR
AND THOMAS HOBBES

THROUGH THE EARLY DECADES of the seventeenth century, offshore England had managed to avoid becoming embroiled in the ruinous Thirty Years' War that so devastated the continental mainland of Europe. However, in 1642 England succumbed to its own version of unreason in the form of the Civil War.

Since the Magna Carta of 1215, which granted certain powers to the individual citizen, English politics had to an extent deviated from the forms of government practised in continental Europe. In reality, these individual powers were extremely limited – nonetheless, the ethos of civil liberty was widely engrained amongst the population.

Following Henry VIII's break with Rome in 1534, tension had persisted between the majority Protestants and the persecuted minority of Catholics. At the same time, a growing conflict arose between the despotically inclined monarchy and the growing power of parliament. The Protestant Charles I, who ascended the throne in 1625, attempted to heal the religious rift by marrying the French princess Henrietta Maria, a member of the Catholic Bourbon royal family. But divisions between the king and parliament were growing increasingly irreconcilable. Charles I was a firm believer in the divine right of kings, which decreed that a monarch ruled by the grace of God. The king's word was sacrosanct, and not answerable to any secular institution.

On the other hand, the elected Parliament of England believed that its members were answerable to the people (in effect the landowning class of voters) whose civil rights were enshrined in the Magna Carta. The king had the power to summon and dismiss parliament as he so chose; yet crucially he depended upon parliament to raise taxes.

These differences finally came to a head in January 1642, when Charles I descended upon the House of Commons and tried to arrest five members of parliament, who managed to flee. The stage was now set for civil war.

The Royalists and the Parliamentarians raised armies, and later that year the Parliamentarian army confronted the Royalist army as Charles I was attempting to march south to London. On 22 October the two armies clashed at the Battle of Edgehill in the English Midlands.[*] The result of the battle was inconclusive and led to an intermittent state of civil war between the so-called Roundheads (loosely, the Puritan Parliamentarians) and the Cavaliers (the dashing Royalists and their co-opted supporters). The English Civil War continued for nine years, and would include a number of savage campaigns, brutal battles, and sieges that ended in wholesale slaughter. Although not as devastating as the Thirty Years' War, it still resulted in the greatest casualty rate in English military history – accounting for the deaths of around one in ten of the male population.[†]

---

[*] During the course of the battle, Charles I entrusted his two sons – the Prince of Wales (his heir) and the Duke of York – to the care of the royal physician, a post at the time held by William Harvey, who had discovered the circulation of the blood. In the words of the contemporary chronicler John Aubrey, who knew Harvey: 'He told me that he withdrew with [the royal princes] under a hedge, and tooke out of his pockett a booke and read; but he had not read very long before a Bullet of a great Gun grazed on the grounde neare him, which made him remove his station.'

[†] This is more than three times the proportion of the population who died during the First World War.

The disciplined New Model Army of the Roundheads eventually prevailed against the exploits of the Royalists, and Charles I was captured by the Parliamentarians. He was then put on trial for high treason. This was the ultimate legal anomaly, as the law of England was enacted in the name of the king (Latin: *rex*). Thus, in a prime example of unreason, the trial of Charles I was officially Rex v. Rex. Either way, Charles I was found guilty, and executed in January 1649. The monarchy was then declared abolished and the Commonwealth of England was set up as a republic.

By now the Parliamentarian cause had come under the leadership of Oliver Cromwell and the Puritans (extreme Protestants). In 1653 Cromwell was declared Lord Protector, and the Commonwealth took on an increasingly militaristic tone, with a notoriously bloody campaign against the Catholics in Ireland. At home in England, Puritan rule intensified, with the banning of such 'Catholic' pursuits as games of all kinds and even the celebration of Christmas. Cromwell was keen to establish a fully functioning and comprehensive religious state, complete with its own laws, institutions, checks and balances. To this end he even contacted Jewish rabbis in Holland, in an attempt to learn how they had managed to integrate their political and religious lives. However, the populace of England soon chafed under Puritan restraint, growing nostalgic for the roisterous celebrations that had for so long marked the passage of the seasons – such as wassailing, Pre-Lent Carnival, Midsummer's Day, Hallowe'en, and especially Christmas.* As a result, in 1660 the son of Charles I, the former Prince of Wales, was invited to return to England, where he was crowned Charles II, thus beginning the period known as the Restoration.

The above is but an outline summary of a series of complex and bitterly contested events. Even so, it is possible to distinguish within this brief description most of the major factors that comprised political philosophy, and continue to do so to this day: revolution, military takeover, fundamentalism (religious or idealistic), and the many

---

* All of these celebrations had long traditions, extending as far back as their origins in pre-Christian seasonal celebrations.

complexities which beset monarchist, democratic, republican and autocratic governments.

Following the Restoration, England entered an age without the divine right of kings, which still prevailed throughout much of Europe. This latter tradition is perhaps best illustrated by Louis XIV's famous declaration '*L'État c'est moi*' ('I am the state'), an article of faith which prevailed amongst monarchs from Habsburg Austria to Habsburg Spain, and from Bourbon France to Tsarist Russia.

Regardless of such medieval traditions (or relics),* there was no denying that Europe was now entering a new era. The turbulent times that accompanied the Age of Reason had begun to raise a number of profound questions. Precisely why these became so prominent in England at this time is difficult to gauge. Revolution, fundamentalist government, fanaticism and stifling absolutism – often combined with an incongruous underlying belief in the uniqueness of the individual or soul – were by no means limited to England. Calvinist Geneva, Savonarola's Florence and his 'bonfire of the vanities', the Spanish Inquisition, the Pilgrim Fathers of New England... these were but a few examples of current politics beyond the norm. However, it was England, home of the four-hundred-year-old Magna Carta,† where the profound questioning raised by political turmoil began to receive serious consideration. And this generality of problems would crystallize around ideas as old as civil society itself, in its Ancient Greek form: What is the nature of the state? Who is it for? What does it involve? How does it work...?

As early as the fourth century BC, Socrates had asked 'What is the good life?' – demonstrating how this question inevitably extended to the

---

* In fact, such ideas can be traced back to the Roman era, when the Republic was replaced by emperors who became gods. Even earlier, the pharaohs of Ancient Egypt derived their authority from similar ideas. However, for the purposes of this discussion, I have disregarded these ancient examples in favour of the more relevant opposition posed by contemporary absolutist rulers.

† The Magna Carta, which King John was forced to sign by his rebellious barons in 1215, restricted regal powers and granted a number of basic civil rights unknown in most European jurisdictions. More pertinently, it meant that the king was subject to the law of the land, like any other citizen.

idea of 'justice' and thence to the establishment of a just society. In the following century, Aristotle took a more collective approach. He assembled the constitutions of city-states throughout Greece, and attempted to compile an ideal constitution, selecting the good points from each. For Aristotle, there were two basic elements: 'the rule of reason' and 'the wisdom of the multitude'. Despite such good intentions, the contemporary British philosopher Jonathan Barnes characterizes Aristotle's political philosophy as 'in parts abhorrent, in parts bizarre... in certain parts surprising'. He sees Aristotle's political theory being 'moulded – and also limited – by the [turbulent] historical conditions of his age'.

Well over one and a half millennia later, the Florentine polymath Niccolò Machiavelli, in his masterwork *The Prince*, would take precisely the opposite approach to Aristotle. In this work, it could be argued, Machiavelli selected the very worst human traits, and used them to demonstrate how a prince could achieve, and hold on to, dictatorial powers to rule a state.

In the following century, during the Age of Reason, the chaotic destruction of the English and continental wars would inspire the English philosopher Thomas Hobbes to set down the formative work of modern political philosophy, in which he describes the state, giving it the ominous title *Leviathan.*

Thomas Hobbes was born prematurely in the English West Country. 'His mother fell in labour with him upon the fright of the Invasion of the Spaniards', i.e. news in 1588 that the Spanish Armada was sailing up the Channel to attack England. Of this he would later remark: 'my mother gave birth to twins: myself and fear'. Hobbes's father was vicar of the local parish – a cantankerous man of little learning who enjoyed playing cards all night. When confronted at his church door about his behaviour by the vicar of the next-door parish, 'Hobs stroke [struck] him and was forced to fly from it and died in obscurity'.

---

* A leviathan was a legendary primordial sea monster of grotesque appearance and savagery that appears in early Mesopotamian literature, the Old Testament and the Book of Revelations in the Bible, as well as gnostic Manicheanism (the duality of God and fallen angels), and even Norse mythology.

In the absence of his father, Hobbes was brought up by a wealthy uncle and educated locally. According to John Aubrey, who knew Hobbes: 'When he was a Boy he was playsome enough; but withall he had even then a contemplative Melancholinesse'. Hobbes proved an exceptional scholar. By his early teens he had translated Euripides's tragedy *Medea* from Ancient Greek into Latin iambic verse. At the age of fourteen he went up to Oxford, but was little enamoured of the university's Aristotelian curriculum. Here he was obliged to study logic, though 'he did not much care for it'; he preferred to visit a local bookbindery, where he pored over atlases. For the most part Hobbes seems to have followed his own intellectual inclinations, picking up a polymathic range of knowledge, aided by his exceptional ability to recall verbatim almost any text which he had studied.

Upon leaving Oxford in his early twenties, he was employed by William Cavendish, future first Earl of Devonshire to tutor his son amidst the splendours of Chatsworth House, one of the grandest stately homes in England. As part of his duties, Hobbes took his charge on the traditional grand tour of Europe, travelling for five years through France and Italy. Here Hobbes came into contact with modern European scientific thought, and also developed an interest in Ancient Greek history. In Venice, he witnessed the struggle between the ruling rich merchant families and the power of the Church, a theme that would later become central to his work.

On his return, Hobbes was befriended by Sir Francis Bacon, who was then at the height of his scientific and literary powers. Although Hobbes was some thirty years his junior, Bacon soon preferred his company to that of his other distinguished friends – maintaining that only Hobbes fully understood his ideas. Bacon now employed Hobbes as his amanuensis.

In 1630 Hobbes returned to Paris, where he once again found employment as a tutor to the son of an English aristocrat. Hobbes would spend seven years in Paris, where he soon gained admission to Father Mersenne's exclusive intellectual circle. This enabled him to read many scientific and philosophical manuscripts before they were published. Later in 1630, he travelled to Italy, where he visited the sixty-six-year-old Galileo, who was living out his final years under house arrest at a villa in Arcetri, outside Florence.

Hobbes now focused on physics – in particular the motion of bodies and their interaction. Unfortunately, his expertise in this subject remained purely theoretical, as he disdained carrying out any actual experiments. On the plus side, the vagueness of his conceptual ideas in physics led him to expand his thought into the study of humanity, and how human beings interact. This led him to propose certain ideas concerning human society and how social interactions prevented humans from lapsing back to the 'brutishness and misery' of their original state. Hobbes's thinking now became directed towards forming his own original philosophy. In this, he sought 'to unite the separate phenomena of Body, Man and State'.

On his return to England in 1637 at the age of forty-nine, he found the country riven with the divisions which preceded the Civil War. Under such troubled circumstances he was unable to concentrate fully on his philosophical enterprise. Despite this, by 1640 he managed to complete a manuscript entitled *The Elements of Law, Natural and Politic*, which he circulated privately amongst his friends. This contained in embryo many of the ideas which would feature in *Leviathan*. However, one particular idea, which he would later disavow, favoured 'Patrimonial kingdoms'. These were countries ruled by an absolute monarch who exercised his power in a paternal manner over the state and its citizens. This was undoubtedly a Royalist sentiment, expressed at a time when Parliamentarian sentiment against the king was beginning to increase throughout the country. Consequently, Hobbes found it prudent to flee back to Paris in 1640.

There he once again became part of Mersenne's circle, even going so far as to write a critique of Descartes's *Meditations*, which was circulating prior to publication. Descartes had requested that Mersenne seek out objections to the ideas he proposed, which would be included (along with his answers to these objections) in the final published version. This was the work in which Descartes rationalized his famous conclusion 'I think, therefore I am'. In his objection, Hobbes pointed out that Descartes's rational doubt in fact only led to the conclusion 'I am; I exist... for as long as I am thinking'. This is a subtle but valid distinction, for as Hobbes pointed out:

It does not seem a valid argument to say, 'I am thinking, therefore I am a thought' or 'I am understanding; therefore I am an understanding'. For in the same way I could just as well say, 'I am walking; therefore I am an act of walking'. Thus M. Descartes equates the thing that understands with an act of understanding, which is an act of the thing that understands.

After the English Civil War broke out in 1642, a large number of Royalists took refuge in Paris. Hobbes was welcomed into this company, to the extent that he was soon appointed tutor to the teenage Prince of Wales (the future Charles II, who had previously been entrusted to his tutor Harvey at the Battle of Edgehill). Hobbes taught the future king mathematics, which had long been one of Hobbes's many interests and was a subject that embroiled him in several controversies.

Hobbes was by nature a retiring character. However, beneath this unassuming exterior he seems to have inherited an element of his father's cantankerousness. This manifested itself in a persistently contrarian attitude towards the ideas of his peers. Consequently, Descartes would become so irritated with Hobbes's obstinately persistent 'objections' that he instructed Mersenne to refrain from passing him any more of Hobbes's letters.

Hobbes had over the years become involved in several such philosophical and mathematical disputes – frequently persisting even when he found himself out of his depth. Two examples will suffice. The first is his controversy with John Bramhall, the Archbishop of Armagh (the senior bishopric in Ireland), which involved the question of free will and determinism. Owing to his clerical position, Bramhall spent much of his time tenaciously defending the English Church against both Catholics and Puritan zealots. Ever original, Hobbes took a materialist approach, arguing that in a world consisting entirely of matter, everything worked according to the laws of physics and thus there could be no room for free will, QED. Bramhall was both a skilled and stylish polemicist,* who

---

* It was Bramhall who coined the phrase 'it is the last feather that breaks the horse's back' – the precursor to the modern phrase 'the straw that broke the camel's back'.

quickly pointed out that Hobbes's argument left him open to a charge of atheism – quite some feat when Britain and the entire continent of Europe were embroiled in vicious conflicts over what *kind* of theology should prevail, rather than arguing that there should be none at all.

Similarly, in mathematics Hobbes declared that he had managed to solve the subject's most ancient conundrum – namely, how to square the circle, i.e. how to construct a square with the same area as a circle, using only the traditional methods involving a compass and ruler. An attempted solution to this problem had first appeared in the so-called Rhind papyrus, the oldest known mathematical document dating from 1650 BC in Ancient Egypt (though some experts believe that this very problem may well date back as far as 3400 BC). The problem is in fact rationally insoluble because the formula for the area of a circle is $\pi \times r^2$. This involves π, an irrational number whose value is 3.1415... – the figures after the decimal point continuing infinitely in random fashion, thus making it impossible to calculate with complete precision. This time Hobbes was corrected by John Wallis, professor of geometry at Oxford, 'who succeeded in making him look silly'.

However, when not diverting himself with such tomfoolery, Hobbes was capable of sustained, profound and original thought. It was in Paris that he settled down to write his masterwork *Leviathan*, which would be published in the summer of 1651. Characteristically, this work succeeded in antagonizing all sides in the political-religious arguments raging through Europe during this period. In the words of Bertrand Russell: 'Its rationalism offended most of the [Royalist] refugees, and its bitter attacks on the Catholic Church offended the French Government.' Even the Calvinists of Geneva were said to have been outraged.

To escape censure, or worse, Hobbes travelled post-haste back to London, where he threw himself on the mercy of Oliver Cromwell – a man whose politics and religion he utterly abhorred. Fortunately for Hobbes, the Puritan Cromwell proved sufficiently broadminded to permit him to live in obscurity in Fetter Lane, amongst the warren of alleyways in the City of London, on condition that he cease from any further political writing.

So what exactly was this work, which had provoked execration on all sides of the political and religious divide? Its full title is *Leviathan or The Matter, Forme and Power of a Common Wealth, Ecclesiasticall and Civil.* This gives an indication of its range and ambition. Hobbes aimed at nothing less than a full description of the fundamental nature of government in society.

In line with his mathematical inclinations, Hobbes originally intended the structure of his work to follow a geometrical pattern, where its irrefutable conclusions could be deduced from a number of self-evident axioms. Fortunately, the power of his thought and style expanded beyond such inappropriate constrictions. Politics may describe itself as a science, but it will always lack the deductive certainty of a 'hard' science such as physics or mathematics. That is, unless it is confined within a 'scientific' form such as Marxism – or a didactic authoritarian formula of the kind which Hobbes sought (fortunately without success) to impose upon it. Hobbes's failure in this aspect is far outweighed by the profundity of the questions he raised, as well as his fundamental analysis of society and government.

Leviathan famously describes mankind's original condition, devoid of social order or statehood, culture or knowledge, commodities or law: 'worst of all, [he lives in] continual fear, and danger of violent death; and the life of man [is] solitary, poor, nasty, brutish and short'. Anything is better than this. Humanity in this state is to be avoided at all costs.

In line with his belief in materialism, Hobbes maintained that life is no more than the motion of limbs, according to the laws of physics. Such determinism makes us automata, and we thus live an artificial life. We submit to live in a 'Common Wealth' – which he calls Leviathan, named after the sea monster who appears in the Bible 'and is a king over all the children of pride'. The Leviathan is a creation of art, and is in fact an artificial contrivance suited to rule over our artificial life. As Hobbes argues elsewhere, in such a materialistic, deterministic world:

> Every Man... calleth that which pleaseth, and is delightful to himself, GOOD; and that EVIL which displeaseth him: insomuch that while every man differeth from each other in

Constitution, they differ also one from another concerning the common distinction of good and evil. Nor is there any such thing as… [the] simply good.

Such a comprehensive (and pessimistic) outlook aligns with Hobbes's earlier expressed view of natural man devoid of society or restraint. This pragmatic morality arguably describes the human condition more perceptively than the dictates of religion, utopia or idealism. But how are we to survive this anarchic morality? Such liberty is surely a fundamental right of nature. Yet alongside this stands an equally fundamental right of law, which both overcomes and nullifies our harmful anarchy. All men acknowledge that they have a right to defend themselves, yet must recognize that they have no right to go beyond this. There is no justification in harming another, unless it is done in the cause of self-defence.

This was the quasi-axiomatic foundation upon which Hobbes sought to build his rational argument for the political state. And such was the powerful reason of his argument that it was bound to be accepted by all, or so Hobbes boldly believed. This state – Leviathan – had sovereign power. But what form was it to take? Monarchy, or republican government? In the view of Harvard political theorist Richard Tuck: 'Hobbes provided some rather low-level arguments in favour of monarchy, but intended his theory to apply to any form of government.' (Under the circumstances of the English Civil War this was hardly likely to win him friends on either side.)

However, although the power of Leviathan was absolute, Hobbes did propose a caveat which undermined such absolutism, introducing an ambiguous element. The power of Leviathan was dependent upon its ability to protect those over whom it was sovereign. In the event of Leviathan's failure to protect its citizens, a state of nature would result, with life once again becoming 'nasty, brutish and short'. For this reason, Hobbes appeared to regard any form of government as preferable to none.

The power of Leviathan, and the protection it afforded, made the ruler and the ruled all part of the same organism. This unity was established by a 'covenant' – which later theorists would call the social contract.

Such theories had been proposed in Ancient Greek times, in particular by Plato. But Hobbes was the first modern thinker to resurrect this valued, if theoretic, notion of a pact between the ruler and the ruled – an implicit agreement under which citizens surrendered their liberty in exchange for protection, civil rights and social order.

However, where Hobbes was concerned this covenant was a very real agreement, with nothing theoretical about it: 'The covenant must confer power on one man or one assembly... it is a covenant made by the citizens with each other to obey such ruling power as the majority shall choose... When the government has been chosen, *the citizens lose all rights*.' (My italics). The only rights a citizen may exercise are those that 'the government may find it expedient to grant'. Most importantly of all: 'There is no right of rebellion, because the ruler is not bound by any contract, whereas the subjects are.' This would seem to contradict Hobbes's ambiguous notion of the sovereign Leviathan's power, where it is obliged to provide protection.

There is but one sleight-of-hand argument which papers over this fundamental divide. When Leviathan ceases to provide protection, it is no longer a Leviathan. But this begs the question as to who judges when this occurs, and at what point another Leviathan is restored.

During the course of his political argument, Hobbes does attack previous thinkers, including Plato, who is dismissed for maintaining that reason is an innate human faculty. For Hobbes, reason is 'developed by industry' – in other words, by living in an ordered, productive state. Indeed, only under such conditions does humanity advance in any way. All human inventions, achievements, rights and laws – our full human potential – can only appear under the Leviathan state.

Hobbes also clings to a narrow definition of rationality: the deductive reason of mathematics and logic alone is acceptable. Inductive reason such as that practised by the new science – as it appears in the works of Kepler, Galileo and even Bacon – was not true reason. For instance, Ptolemy's description of an earth-centred universe was just as valid as Kepler's solar system. Both were derived by deductive reason which fitted the observed facts. Here, it seems, Hobbes was simply returning to his old contrarian self, willing to take on all comers.

The knotty question of how one Leviathan is deposed, and its ensuing restoration in another form, may not have been solved in Hobbes's writings, but it was certainly solved in historical terms during his lifetime. As already mentioned, in 1660 the Commonwealth established by Oliver Cromwell (who had since died) was overthrown. The Restoration took place and Charles II ascended to the throne. To many of the new king's Royalist supporters, Hobbes was by now anathema. However, Charles II and his inner circle of friends proved more forgiving. So much so that Charles II commissioned a portrait of Hobbes, which was hung on the walls of his palace at Whitehall. He even granted Hobbes a pension of £100 per annum (approximately twice the earnings of an Oxford professor), but alas never got around to paying it.

By now Hobbes was in his seventies and very much in need of the king's protection. As the published version of *Leviathan* began to circulate, Hobbes's ideas attracted fierce criticism. His philosophy, known as Hobbism, was denounced both in parliament and from the pulpit. After this, he found it expedient to have his writings published in Amsterdam. The fact that he continued to be so productive into old age was ascribed by Aubrey to his abstemious routine (very much a comparative term during the licentiousness of the Restoration period):

> For his last 30 + years, his Dyet, etc, was very moderate and regular. He rose about seaven, had his breakefast of Bread and Butter; and tooke his walke, meditating till ten; then he did putt down the minutes of his thoughts, which he penned in the afternoon... [He was] generally temperate, both as to wine and women... When he did drinke, he would drink to excesse to have the benefit of Vomitting.

Hobbes continued to play tennis until he was seventy-five: 'In the country, for want of a tennis-court he would walke up-hill and down-hill in the parke, till he was in a great sweat.' He was in the habit of keeping a songbook at his bedside table, and 'at night, when he was abed, and the dores made fast, and was sure nobody heard him, he sang aloud (not that he had a very good voice) but for his health's Sake: he did believe it did his Lunges good'.

He spent an increasing amount of his time in the country, living at Chatsworth House – the residence of the son of his former pupil, who had now become the Earl of Devonshire.

Hobbes was living in the country during 1665–6, when the Great Plague was happening in London, and then began spreading throughout the land – sparing only those able to maintain isolation, such as those living with the Earl of Devonshire at Chatsworth House amidst its extensive Derbyshire estates.

The Great Plague was a major outbreak of bubonic plague which is estimated to have killed some 100,000 people in London, which had previously contained a population of over 400,000. Yet worse was to befall the capital. On Sunday, 2 September 1666, a fire started in a baker's shop in Pudding Lane. This quickly took hold amongst the cramped wooden buildings that surrounded it. By the following Thursday, the Great Fire, as it was known, had gutted most of the city within the ancient walls, including the 400-year-old St Paul's Cathedral and Old London Bridge, whose main thoroughfare was lined with tenement buildings.

In the aftermath of the Great Plague and the Great Fire there was a widespread search for scapegoats upon whom such unprecedented disasters could be blamed. Amidst this outbreak of hysteria, a bill was introduced in parliament against atheism and profanity. A parliamentary committee recommended that the bill 'should be empowered to receive information touching such books as tend to atheism, blasphemy and profaneness... in particular... the book of Mr Hobbes called the *Leviathan*'.

With some justification, Hobbes felt in fear of his life, and began burning any of his manuscripts which he felt could be viewed as heresy. Yet even in this dire situation, he was not one to avoid arguing his case. He produced three short dialogues, which were added as appendices to the Latin version of *Leviathan*. In these he ingeniously argued that since the Court of High Commission (the senior ecclesiastical court in the land) had been abolished by parliament in 1641, there existed no court that could legally charge him with heresy.

Never one to be satisfied with mere empirical argument, he went on to deduce with rigorous logic that nothing could be judged as heresy unless it explicitly contradicted the Nicene Creed, which had been adopted in the fourth century as the fundamental profession of Christian faith. Hobbes stoutly, and correctly, maintained that at no point did *Leviathan* transgress the articles of faith prescribed by the Nicene Creed.

The bill against heresy was duly passed by parliament, but fortunately Hobbes remained under the protection of the Earl of Devonshire. His appendices to *Leviathan* were duly published in Amsterdam, further adding to his widespread philosophical reputation in continental Europe, though to little effect in England.

Hobbes continued writing until well into his eighties, producing an autobiography in Latin verse and finishing a translation into English verse of Homer's *Odyssey* in 1675. He would die four years later at the age of ninety-one. His last recorded words before his death were: 'A great leap in the dark.' Regardless of this agnostic pronouncement, he was buried in the graveyard of a country church in Derbyshire, a few miles from Chatsworth House.

CHAPTER 5

THE NEW WORLD AND THE GOLDEN AGE OF SPAIN

THE SPANISH EXPLORATION AND colonization of South America and the Caribbean in the fifteenth and sixteenth centuries had led to an influx of gold and silver into Europe. This is perhaps best exemplified by the legendary 'mountain of silver' at Potosí, 15,000 feet up in the Andes (in modern-day Bolivia). Here was a mountain that consisted almost entirely of silver ore. The indigenous people there were made to work in the mines and the refining process. The former involved climbing down makeshift mine shafts – some as much as seventy feet deep – by candlelight. The emergence of the miners from the hot shafts into the freezing oxygen-thin air bearing 200-pound sacks of ore was catastrophic to their health. Pneumonia, altitude sickness, disease and sheer exhaustion took a grotesque toll, as did the collapsing of the shafts themselves. Meanwhile the use of mercury in the process of refining the ore accounted for a similar mortality. It has been reliably estimated that 15,000 indigenous people *per year* were press-ganged into working at Potosí, and that by the early seventeenth century it was producing 60 per cent of all the silver mined throughout the world.

The silver was converted into silver dollars ('pieces of eight') that were stamped with the mint mark of Potosí, which had the letters P T S I superimposed on one another (widely thought to be the origin of the $ sign). Silver and gold were transported to Spain in annual convoys of treasure ships, comprising fleets of up to 100 galleons. These brought as much as 170 tons of silver each year into the country, with 20 per cent of this accruing to the Crown, making Spain the richest country in Europe.

Gold and silver flowed into Spain at Cádiz, and out again through the northern ports as it purchased goods and commodities from northern Europe. The distribution of this wealth by Spanish purchasing would bring about an upsurge in mercantile activity which stimulated economies throughout the continent. As is ever the case, such enrichment was soon enabling the recruitment of larger 'defensive' armies whose purpose was to protect this newfound wealth. Inevitably, these armies were soon put to use. The disastrous Thirty Years' War may have ostensibly been caused by religious divisions, but it would not have been fought across the length and breadth of Europe, or for so long, without the support of gold and silver initially imported by Spain from the New World.

Quite apart from its effect on Europe as a whole, the effect of this flood of bullion into Spain would eventually prove disastrous for the Spanish economy and Spanish society in general. The rich benefitted and the economy became hopelessly unbalanced. There was little incentive to produce goods domestically or invest locally in new technologies that were beginning to transform the rest of Europe. The royal family, and their attendant aristocracy, simply bought what they wanted, as well as financing armies to fight their wars. Meanwhile inflation was rampant – as foreign merchants enriched themselves at the expense of Spain, which was soon producing little but the bare essentials.

By the time the supply of gold and silver began to contract, an even more destructive source of income was becoming available. This consisted of the notorious *assientos*, monopoly agreements signed between the Spanish authorities and various merchants (both foreign and Spanish), permitting them to transport slaves from West Africa across the Atlantic to the Americas. What began as limited human trafficking between West Africa and South America soon began to develop into a more regular triangular route. Merchant ships carrying beads and cheap trinkets, cloth, guns and ammunition, set out from Europe for the West African coast. Here these goods were exchanged for enslaved Africans. This human cargo was transported across the Atlantic – the notorious Middle Passage during which many died – and sold for bullion or bartered for molasses, sugar or rum. The goods were then carried on the third arm of the triangle back to Europe. The entire round trip took on average twelve months. By the first half of the seventeenth century, such trade involved more than 10,000 slaves a year; by the end of the century it involved three times this amount. What began with Spain and Portugal would eventually involve northern European countries as far afield as Sweden and Denmark, as well as Columbus's birthplace, Genoa.

English participation in this trade was conducted by the Royal African Company, a monopoly established in 1660 under the auspices of Charles II by his brother the Duke of York (the future James II) and a group of City of London merchants. The profits were considerable; one historian notes that 'in the seventeenth century, the Royal Africa Company could buy an enslaved African with trade goods worth £3 and have that person sold for £20 in the Americas. The Royal Africa Company was able to make an average profit of 38% per voyage in the 1680s.' The money accruing to northern Europe would help finance the transformation of this region from a largely rural medieval economy into the beginnings of the modern era.

By the seventeenth century, northern Europe was also leaving its mark on America, mostly along the eastern shore of the northern subcontinent. At least in the beginning, this enterprise was characteristically different from the Hispanic transformation of South America. The latter had involved the destruction of the Aztec and Inca empires, the mass conversion of the indigenous peoples to Christianity, and the exploitation of gold and silver mines. Instead of organized empires, the first northern European explorers of North America encountered many different tribes of indigenous hunter-gatherers. The first contact between the indigenous peoples and the northern European colonists was characterized by mutual incomprehension. Sometimes tentative contact matured, but frequently mistrust led to hostility.

In 1605, the French established a settlement at Port-Royal (in modern Nova Scotia). Two years later the British established their first permanent settlement, at Jamestown (in modern Virginia), and the explorer John Smith named this region New England. Amongst the early colonists at Jamestown were a number of 'indentured labourers' – mostly petty criminals or daughters of impoverished families transported from the homeland – who served out their time as labourers, after which they were granted freedom and a plot of land. In 1619, the first African slaves arrived at Jamestown. Initially, they too were classified as indentured labour rather than as permanent slaves.

In 1640, three indentured labourers – two white and one black – escaped from the colony. When they were recaptured, the two white fugitives were sentenced to serve out longer periods of indenture. The black escapee, who had been given the European name John Punch, was sentenced to permanent indenture and thus became 'the first official slave in the English colonies'.*

For many, the New World came to be regarded as a land of liberty, especially where religion was concerned. The Pilgrim Fathers, as they would come to be known, originated as several dozen radical Puritans in Nottinghamshire in England; a group regarded as Separatists because they refused to recognize the Church of England. In order to escape persecution they were eventually forced to flee to Holland, where they settled in Leiden. Here they hoped to exercise their right to freedom of worship; but even Leiden proved too oppressive for the Separatists. Their leader, the prosperous merchant John Carver, chartered an English ship, the *Mayflower*, to transport them to the New World. In the autumn of 1620, they set off from the port of Plymouth in the west of England:

---

* In July 2012, DNA evidence revealed that John Punch was a twelfth-generation grandfather of Barack Obama on his (white) mother's side.

102 men, women and children – 'pilgrims' – as well as a crew of more than twenty-five hands, all crammed aboard a ship whose deck was just ninety feet long and twenty feet wide. After a perilous storm-tossed sixty-six-day voyage across the Atlantic, the *Mayflower* arrived at the spot they named New Plymouth.

Here the Pilgrim Fathers prepared to sit out the winter, living off their meagre supplies. By February 1621 half of the settlers had died owing to cold weather, poor shelter and inadequate diet. They then discovered that the seeds they had brought from England would not grow in the local soil. A Native American called Squanto showed the survivors how to plant maize, as well as how to fish the local river and catch eels.

After gathering in their first harvest, the pilgrims held a 'Thanksgiving Day' feast, which was attended by the fifty survivors. They were joined by ninety members of the Wampanoag tribe, who were drawn to the site by the sound of gunfire and celebration. Expecting to take part in a battle, the Wampanoag were pleasantly surprised when they were invited to join the feast.[*]

Despite such apparently auspicious beginnings, relations between the settlers and the indigenous population gradually deteriorated over the years. And as early as the 1630s, Native Americans were being captured and enslaved. So widespread was this practice, in fact, that during the ensuing decades some hundreds of Native American captives were shipped south to be sold as slaves on the plantations of Virginia. In 1675, Benjamin Church, who was a leading figure in the Plymouth colony, forthrightly condemned this practice as 'an action so hateful'. However, despite this enlightened stance, his reason proved capable of an astonishing reversal when it came to black slaves. In common with many of his Puritan brethren, Church owned a number of slaves imported from Africa.

At the same time, other dissensions continued to fester amongst the Puritan settlers. These came to a head in the early 1690s in and around

---

[*] Some now dispute this innocent version of events... even to the point of suggesting that venison was the main dish at the feast rather than the traditional turkey and pumpkin pie, a story which is thought to have been invented by a nineteenth-century American magazine.

the village of Salem, some fifty miles up the coast from New Plymouth. Here an outbreak of mass hysteria in 1692 led to the infamous Salem witch trials, which saw over 200 people charged with witchcraft.

The incidents at Salem appear to have been triggered by, amongst others, a seventeen-year-old orphan called Elizabeth Hubbard, who worked as a skivvy for her uncle Dr Griggs, the town physician. While giving evidence under oath, Hubbard fell into contorted spasms, which Griggs ascribed to supernatural forces. During these fits she is said to have experienced visions and accused a number of women and girls of heretical activities. One of these was a four-year-old child named Dorothy ('Dorcas') Good, who confessed – under (adult male) interrogation – to owning a snake which sucked blood from her fingers. This was seen as the classic behaviour of a witch and her familiar. Under further 'questioning', the child admitted that she had seen her mother Sarah consorting with the Devil. Sarah Good would be sentenced to death, but as she was pregnant this sentence was not carried out until after she had given birth. The infant to whom she gave birth died before Sarah was hanged.

In all, over several months, Dorothy Good testified on several dozen occasions – as a result of which, seventeen people were arrested. These included a local destitute woman, as well as an enslaved South American tribeswoman. Thirteen of the accused would be hanged, and two would die while being held in the local prison.

Amongst the Bible-based societies such as that of Salem, it was a common belief that 'women were inherently sinful and more susceptible to damnation than men'. The Salem trials and the taking of evidence from various witnesses continued over several months – followed by hangings. One of those found guilty, an eighty-one-year-old farmer called Giles Corey who refused to enter a plea, was sentenced to be 'pressed' to death. (After being laid out on the ground, a wooden board was placed over his body; this was then piled with rocks until it crushed him to death.)

Many of the proceedings were a travesty, with evidence including visions of 'spectres', 'touch tests' indicating supernatural powers, and defendants stripped to reveal concealed 'devil's marks' or 'witches' teats' on their body. In the end a total of thirty were found guilty of witch-craft; fourteen women and five men were hanged, Corey was pressed, and a number of others died in the squalid local jail.

Some have seen these trials as having a profound effect on the course of American history. The early Puritan colonists had created Bible-based societies similar to what Cromwell had attempted to establish in Commonwealth England. The difference being that the separate Puritan colonies became virtually a law unto themselves. Yet such was the contro-versy and scandal caused by the witch trials that, in the words of the distinguished early twentieth-century US historian George Lincoln Burr: 'the Salem witchcraft was the rock on which the theocracy shattered'. When the American colonies declared independence some eighty years later, their constitution would grant freedom of worship – but would also incorporate 'separation of powers' between church and state. Others, such as the modern historian Gretchen Adams, have seen the entire Salem affair as 'a cautionary tale about the dangers of isolationism, religious extremism, false accusations and lapses in due process'.

This was no isolated phenomenon, but appears to have been imported from Europe. During the Counter-Reformation and other religious confrontations in the decades around the turn of the seventeenth century, as many as 50,000 people were tried and burned at the stake or otherwise executed by the Inquisition or Protestant authorities. Most of them were older women, accused of 'collaboration with devils'.

Curiously, these trials were seldom the result of interdenomina-tional strife between Catholics and Protestants. Indeed, for the most part they occurred within the separate homogenous religious communities. According to research conducted by US historian H. C. E. Midelfort concerning events in south-western Germany in the century or so between 1561 and 1670, more than 480 witch trials took place during this period. Of these, 317 occurred in Catholic states, with 163 in predominantly Protestant jurisdictions. In all, these resulted in 3,229 persons being found guilty and executed in one form or another. Of these, 2,527 were executed in Catholic states, and 702 in Protestant states. Many of the victims were single older women, widows or spinsters, living on their own within the community. However, a considerable portion of those executed did not fall into this stereotypical category. In some jurisdictions, as many as 25 per cent of those charged were men. And the instigation of such proceedings frequently came about as a result of frenzied accusations or 'fits' (sometimes accompanied by instructive 'visions') made by girls or groups of young women entering puberty.

All manner of sociological explanations have been put forward to account for these traumatic outbreaks of unreason. Feminist interpretations point out that the judges were invariably 'God-fearing' men, with a number suggesting that 'witch figures' stirred up threatening folk memories of ancient pagan priestesses. Some anthropologists see such incidents as releasing social tensions, with scapegoating drawing the community into cohesion.

Meanwhile, in South America, Spain persisted in its Golden Age. Though this was very much a double-edged term – as gold was still contributing both to Spain's riches and to its decline.

The general condition of Spain during this period is epitomized by the idiosyncratic rule of Gaspar de Guzmán, Count-Duke of Olivares, who was the *valido* (favourite and chief minister) to King Philip IV from 1621 to 1643.

Olivares was born in Rome, where his father was the Spanish ambassador to the papal court of Sixtus V, whose main claim to fame was the excommunication of both the Protestant Queen Elizabeth I of England and Catholic King Henry IV of France – the country a previous pope had entitled 'the most Christian nation'. Olivares's mother died sometime around 1600 while he was still a child, and his father ensured that he had a strict academic and religious upbringing. At the age of twelve Olivares voyaged back to Spain, where he was educated at the University of Salamanca, after which he entered the household of the teenage Philip, heir apparent to the Spanish throne. By the time Philip ascended to the throne just before his sixteenth birthday, Olivares had become his avuncular favourite adviser.

Philip IV and Olivares made an odd pair. Owing to inbreeding in the Habsburg family, Philip IV exhibited the prominent 'Habsburg jaw' – a deformity where the lower teeth protruded beyond the teeth of the upper jaw. He had also been over-schooled in the notion of regal dignity – to the point where his public appearances were characterized by an aloof unbending solemnity. Foreign ambassadors to the court frequently reported on his resemblance, in both mobility and facial expression, to a statue.

Olivares, by contrast, was a giant of a man with a small head and a florid bewhiskered face, who was described by a contemporary as an 'extravagant, out-sized personality with a gift for endless self-dramatization'. Despite his evident overbearing ambition, Olivares also had a paranoid element to his character. One aspect of this was his suspicion of Philip IV's young wife, Elisabeth of France, whom he suspected of influencing her husband and surreptitiously plotting against him. In order to distance Philip IV from his wife, Olivares encouraged the king to take mistresses – advice which he seems to have followed with some avidity. (In all, he would produce over thirty known offspring.)

Olivares may have been clumsy and overbearing, but he proved to be an indefatigable worker. He was in the habit of rising at dawn and attending mass and confession, before proceeding to the royal chamber where he would wake the king and sit down with him to discuss the business of the day. He would go on to conduct as many as three meetings a day with the king, before finally retiring to his bed an hour or so before midnight. (As the young Philip IV gradually matured into his regal role, he learned to unbend and enjoy the pleasures of his exalted position, which soon left him with time for but one meeting a day with his industrious *valido*.)

Olivares can hardly be described as a talented statesman, but he knew what he wanted, and he soon mastered the Spanish system of government, bending it to his obstinate will. He reformed the bureaucracy, establishing juntas (small administrative councils) staffed largely by his protégés. This ensured efficient centralized government, which could be harnessed to his central policy: an obsession with establishing Spain as the greatest power in Europe. This would involve the country in a succession of expensive and often disastrous wars, especially in the vain attempt to win back the Protestant Dutch provinces that had won their freedom by ejecting their Spanish colonial masters.

Setbacks in Olivares's policy, combined with his fanatic regime of overwork, soon took their toll. He began suffering from insomnia, and grew notorious for his excessive anger when facing obstacles. It swiftly became clear that he was suffering from a compulsive disorder, which was only exacerbated by the attitude of the royal physicians, with their unvarying recourse to bloodletting and strong purgatives.

Olivares may have subjected himself to a strict regime of overwork, accompanied by a similarly austere lifestyle, but his policy of aggrandizing Spain itself was very much the polar opposite of his private life. Typical of his vainglorious projects was the building of the Buen Retiro Palace on the eastern outskirts of Madrid. Over the years this massive project would expand to include more than twenty large buildings, two vast squares intended for public entertainments, and extensive gardens and ponds. To this palace, Olivares attached a farm of his own, because he knew that Philip IV enjoyed taking walks amidst rural surroundings and marvelling at the sound of birdsong. The extensive aviary he built there led to court gossips ridiculing the entire palace project, nicknaming it the *Gallinero* (Chicken Coop).

By now Olivares's mental vagaries had led to him consulting astrologers before taking policy decisions. This created all manner of irrational anomalies. The endless unsuccessful war to recover the Netherlands was proving so immensely expensive that Olivares was forced to debase the coinage. When this proved insufficient, he took to brokering extensive loans from Genoese bankers. Finally, when he found himself unable to repay these loans, he resorted to declaring the country bankrupt. Meanwhile the austerity of his economic policy at home contrasted with the huge expense of such projects as the Buen Retiro, which eventually provoked uprisings in Catalonia and Portugal. A revolt in Andalusia in 1641 proved the last straw. Reluctantly, Philip IV was forced to dispense with the services of Olivares two years later – but only under the combined pressure of the administration, the queen, and finally even the Inquisition. Indeed, Olivares would probably have ended up in one of the Inquisition's dungeons had he not died in 1645, by which time his mental state had degenerated into full-blown madness.

One beneficial side effect of Olivares's rule was the flourishing of Spanish culture, which was yet another aspect of Spain's multifaceted Golden Age. Indeed, it was Olivares himself who first spotted the talented young artist Diego Velázquez, who would paint an uncannily perceptive early portrait of Olivares. It depicts him clad in the expansive dark robes of the ancient military Order of Calatrava, complete with a large key of office tucked into the belt containing his expansive girth. The portrait succeeds in capturing Olivares's overbearing physical presence and self-confidence, as well as an undermining element of unease in his personality.

Velázquez was but the greatest of the school of painters who emerged during Spain's Golden Age. This cultural flourishing would not be confined to the visual arts, however; music, architecture and literature would similarly thrive. And the early years of this period would witness the emergence of Spain's greatest writer, Miguel de Cervantes.

What little we know for certain of Cervantes's life reads somewhat like the adventure-filled exploits he created for his hero Don Quixote – though in the author's case there would be no leavening element of hilarious absurdity.

Miguel de Cervantes is thought to have been born in September 1547 at Alcalá de Henares, a small city twenty miles north-east of Madrid. Even his name is open to question. In his adult life he would sign himself 'Cerbantes'; though for reasons which remain obscure the printer of his works changed this to 'Cervantes'. Although Cervantes's family had an obscure claim to nobility, it is likely that they were of *converso* origin – that is, of Jewish descent but forced to convert to Catholicism during the 1590s, after being systematically persecuted by the Inquisition. (Ironically, this persecution was led by Tomás de Torquemada, who was himself of *converso* descent, a psychological anomaly which is thought to have contributed to the zeal and sadistic fervour he brought to his role as Grand Inquisitor.)

Cervantes's father, Rodrigo, was a local barber-surgeon.* He seems to have been either feckless or plain unlucky; he was constantly falling into debt, obliging the family to move quickly from one town to the next. On the other hand, Cervantes's mother, Leonor, was a woman of considerable energy and resource, supporting the family and her several children when the law finally caught up with Rodrigo and he spent a spell in gaol.

Further obscurity is added to Cervantes's life by the fact that we don't even know for certain what he looked like: no authenticated portrait of him exists. The minor poet and painter Juan de Jáuregui is known to have painted a portrait of Cervantes, but the unsigned work which some claim to be a lost portrait was only inscribed with the name Cervantes some centuries after the artist's death. As such it has entered the public imagination. For what it is worth, this portrait depicts a long-faced man with a well-trimmed beard and a long thin drooping moustache. He is wearing a prominent white ruff and his facial expression is austere but otherwise impenetrable. (The gentlemanly portrait of Cervantes dating from two centuries later which appears on commemorative stamps, banknotes, coins and so forth is a work of pure imagination.)

The Cervantes family ended up in Madrid, where in 1569 the twenty-two-year-old Cervantes was arrested for wounding his opponent in a duel. Some years later we find Cervantes in Rome, working in the household of an Italian bishop. When war broke out between Venice and the Ottoman Empire in 1570, Cervantes travelled to Naples (which was then Spanish territory) and was commissioned in the navy that

---

*This was the most common form of medical practitioner throughout the medieval era and beyond. The tools of the barber's trade – razors, scissors and so forth – were adapted to the basic surgical requirements of the time. These included amputations, bloodletting, and pulling teeth. They were also known for mixing medicinal elixirs as well as ointments of doubtful provenance and little positive effect. Though this aspect of their activities was usually practised in clandestine fashion, as medicines and the like were officially the provenance of professional physicians – who regarded themselves as superior to mere barber-surgeons. A legacy of this prejudice remains to this day in the fact that physicians and other medical doctors are permitted to entitle themselves 'Dr', whereas surgeons have no such distinction and remain mere 'Mr', 'Mrs' or 'Ms'.

had joined the Holy League assembled by Pope Pius V to aid Venice. Cervantes was present in 1571 at the great naval Battle of Lepanto off the west coast of Greece, which saw the defeat of the Ottoman fleet. Unlike his future protagonist Don Quixote, Cervantes was not given to exaggeration, and his account of his heroism in the battle has the ring of truth – as well as being backed by the evidence of his wounds. Despite suffering from malaria, Cervantes led an assault on an Ottoman galley, receiving two wounds to the chest and a further blow which badly maimed his left arm. His later comment on this event was that he 'lost the movement of the left hand for the glory of the right'.

After this, he spent six months in a hospital in Sicily, before being discharged. In this, he was extremely fortunate. At the time, those who suffered wounds in battle often had little chance of survival – infection, medical ignorance and misguided treatments all took their toll. Cervantes was even able to return to naval duties, and around this time he was joined by his younger brother Rodrigo. While the two of them were serving aboard the Spanish galley *Sol* in 1575, it was intercepted off the coast near Barcelona by Ottoman corsairs (Barbary pirates). The crew of the *Sol* were taken to Algiers to be held for ransom. The Cervantes family was able to raise the ransom for Rodrigo, but as no ransom was forthcoming for Cervantes himself he was sold into slavery.

During this period Cervantes is known to have gained the Arabic nickname *shaibedraa* (one-handed). Ottoman documents note that he was transported to Istanbul, where he took part in the building of the Kiliç Ali Pasha mosque. This was designed by the renowned architect Mimar Sinan, who was by then in his nineties. Owing to Cervantes's disability, he may well have acted as a foreman, translating orders for other Spanish slaves employed as labourers. After four years of captivity (and four unsuccessful attempts to escape), Spain signed a treaty with the Ottoman Empire and Cervantes was released, returning to Madrid.

The Spanish economy was by now sinking into recession, and Cervantes was lucky to gain employment as a tax inspector. Such low-paid work required skilful navigation between bribery and embezzlement simply to make ends meet, and on more than one occasion Cervantes found himself in gaol. During this period he is known to have fathered an illegitimate daughter, whom he would later ensure was educated in a convent at his expense. In 1584, at the age of thirty-seven, Cervantes married Catalina, the teenage daughter of a propertied widow.

Cervantes had long dreamed of becoming a writer, and some of his early attempts at drama were successful enough to attract the attention of the Count of Lemos, who afforded him modest support. For a few years Cervantes lived in Seville, but in 1606 he returned permanently to Madrid. By now he was deeply into composing the second volume of his vast masterwork *El Ingenioso Hidalgo don Quijote de la Mancha* (The Ingenious Gentleman Don Quixote of La Mancha).

This is viewed by many as the first, and certainly one of the greatest, modern European novels. It is comic in aim – as well as being satirical, psychologically observant, and commonsensical in its realism. Comedy does not always last beyond the age of its creation, seldom fully transcends national boundaries, and frequently faces difficulties in translation. Astonishingly, *Don Quixote* manages to clear all these hurdles. For those who appreciate the subtleties and breadth of its telling, this tale remains as vividly alive as it must have been to its creator. Here, it is the readers' reason that is subverted, as their unreason is awoken to hilarious appreciation. This is an epic of madness in a world of fragile sanity.

Cervantes's vast and varied novel features the many adventures of the self-styled Don Quixote, a *hidalgo* ('son of someone', i.e. the lowest rank of Spanish nobility) whose mind has become unbalanced by the excessive reading of chivalric romances. Approaching the age of fifty, he decides to leave his home amidst the wide plains of La Mancha and embark upon the adventurous life of a knight errant. This medieval age of chivalry, if it ever existed beyond the bounds of troubadour poetry, has definitively passed – and its inherent absurdities are cruelly mocked. Having donned his armour, and given himself the resonant title Don Quixote (his real name is Alonso Quijano), our hero sets off on his old nag Rocinante, who echoes many of the qualities of his master: he is difficult, aged and barely up to the task he is set.

The early scenes of Don Quixote's adventures hint at the tenor of his many 'exploits' to come. Convinced that in true chivalric tradition a knight errant must have a lady love, 'a princess of... beauty superlative... [beyond] compare', Don Quixote bestows this role upon a local farm girl, calling her Dulcinea del Toboso, though she remains unaware of this honour. Intent upon impressing his golden-haired well-born Dulcinea with heroic deeds, he sets out on his quest. He arrives at an inn, but in his deluded state he decides that this must be a castle. The prostitutes he encounters there he greets as *doncellas* (maidens of the court), and he assumes that the innkeeper is lord of the castle, requesting that he dub him as a knight. Through the hours of darkness, Don Quixote holds a vigil over his armour, which he has placed in a horse trough. Consequently he becomes involved in a brawl with some muleteers who attempt to remove his armour from the trough so they can water their mules. In order to get rid of Don Quixote, the innkeeper performs a mock ceremony in which he dubs him a knight.

After yet another farcical mishap, Don Quixote meets some traders from Toledo, whom he deems to have insulted his imaginary Dulcinea. To protect her honour, he attacks the traders, who proceed to beat him up, leaving him lying in a sorry state at the roadside. Here he is found by a local peasant, who ensures that the wounded Don Quixote returns home.

Further mishaps ensue. As Don Quixote lies unconscious in bed, his niece, his housekeeper and the local priest decide that in order to protect him they should burn the injurious and immoral books in his library that have inspired his delusions. This scene allows Cervantes to inject his own ironic views on various works of literature, as well as casting aspersions on the priest's views. (How come he knows in such detail where to find the immoral passages in the books he chooses?)

Pretending that he is fully recovered, Don Quixote now persuades his neighbour, an illiterate labourer called Sancho Panza, to be his squire and accompany him on a second chivalric quest. In return for being his squire, Sancho is promised that he will be made governor of an island.

Their adventures begin with Don Quixote's celebrated encounter with the windmills. Convinced that these windmills are in fact 'thirty or forty' ferocious beasts, Don Quixote bravely charges at them on Rocinante. Whereupon his lance becomes entangled in the sail of one of the windmills, he tumbles off Rocinante, and Sancho Panza is forced to come to his rescue.

Such would be the impact and popularity of this scene that the phrase 'tilting at windmills' has entered the language as a synonym for doing battle with imaginary enemies. Indeed, the very word 'quixotic' would also become a byword for an impossibly idealistic but impractical act.

The frail and spindly 'knight' Don Quixote on his nag Rocinante, followed by the rotund 'squire' Sancho Panza on his donkey, has formed one of the great comic double-acts of literature. The earthy realism (and native intelligence) of Sancho Panza provides a perfect foil for the self-deluded idealism of Don Quixote. Cervantes gives full range to Sancho, allowing him to comment on his master's chivalric deeds in colloquial fashion. Though ironically, by the end of their long succession of picaresque exploits, Don Quixote has begun to take on some of Sancho Panza's characteristics, and vice versa. Thus, as the book eventually draws towards its close, with Don Quixote on his deathbed, he is trying to persuade Sancho Panza that they should embark upon a life as pastoral shepherds.

So what should we make of all this tomfoolery? Cervantes's tale is fantastic yet also grounded in reality. As such, it is open to all manner of interpretations – or none! It can simply be enjoyed as a farcical tale involving the exploits of two disparate characters in the world of seventeenth-century Spain. At the same time, like so much humour, it is irrepressibly subversive. Cervantes makes a mockery of the exaggerated conceits of yesteryear – a fabulous age which forever overshadows the banality of contemporary life. The preceding era of knightly virtues reduces the Age of Reason to a paltry shadow of former greatness.

Don Quixote is a mirror of his times. Despite Spain's grandeur – still kept alive by silver and gold from the New World – the country was lapsing into a state of stasis. As treasure continued to flow into Spain, its very plentifulness led to a decline in its value. This bullion could seemingly buy anything, yet it created nothing. Spain was sinking into its past, while the rest of Europe progressed. Don Quixote can be seen as epitomizing this: he both lives in the past and in effect *is* the past, yet he is of necessity forced to live in the present — a reality which does not share his ancient pretensions. The unreason of his delusions is forever running up against the reason of the real world.

CHAPTER 6

TWO TRANSCENDENT ARTISTS

Spain's Golden Age would see the emergence of two major artists, each unique in his own characteristic fashion.

The artist we know as El Greco was born in the remote village of Fodele in the mountains east of Candia (modern Heraklion) on the Greek island of Crete. His birth name, Doménikos Theotokópoulos, would prove impossible for the Spanish to pronounce, hence the nickname *El Greco* (The Greek), which he acquired when he moved to Spain. His birth date was 1 October 1541 – a Saturday – indicating that he was probably baptized on the following Sunday (*Domenica* being the Italian for Sunday). For over three centuries Crete had been a Venetian colony, and it would remain so for another century. Italian was the adopted language of the upper classes, to which El Greco's merchant father belonged. It is also known that his uncle was an Orthodox priest, making it very likely that he was brought up in the Greek Orthodox faith. El Greco's birthdate makes him an almost exact contemporary of Cervantes, though it is all but certain that the two never met. However, it is worth bearing in mind that the Spain which El Greco would paint was the locus of Cervantes's great work.

Despite being a Venetian colony, Crete retained a strong Byzantine tradition, and El Greco's earliest artistic instruction was certainly influenced by his religion. Evidence for this was recently discovered on the Aegean island of Syros, where a very early work in the form of an icon signed Χείρ Δομήνιχου (Created by the hand of Doménicos) was discovered in 1987. There was a thriving school of post-Byzantine art in Candia, and by the age of twenty-two El Greco had qualified as a member of the local guild, which contained more than a hundred *maestros*. Another of El Greco's paintings from this period shows a curious blend of Byzantine iconography and contemporary Italian mannerism (as practised by the likes of Michelangelo, whose exaggerated realism invested his figures with dramatic effect).

However, for any ambitious young painter there was no denying that Candia was something of a provincial backwater. Consequently, El Greco left to pursue his career in Venice around 1567, when he was in his mid-twenties. Here his style was transformed, as he quickly absorbed the profound realism of the ageing Titian. During his three-year stay in Venice he developed the mannerist trait of elongating his figures, twisting their forms to give them life and gesture. He also learned how to capture the changing light of the apparently waterborne city, lending drama to his painted skies and violent perspectives. Such was the improvement and originality of El Greco's style that he attracted the attention of the seventy-year-old Giorgio Clovio, a renowned miniaturist and illustrator lauded by Vasari as 'the Michelangelo of miniatures'. Giorgio befriended El Greco, declaring that he had 'a rare talent for painting'. On Clovio's suggestion he travelled to Rome, bearing a letter of recommendation to Cardinal Alessandro Farnese, a wealthy patron of the arts for whom Clovio had worked as a court painter.

By now El Greco had grown sufficient self-confidence to follow his own idiosyncratic instincts, harking back to his alien Greek roots and imbuing his mannerism with an elusive Byzantine quality. When Clovio visited his friend in Rome, he found El Greco working in a darkened room. According to Clovio, he explained that the darkness inspired his thoughts, while daylight only disturbed his 'inner light'. Although El Greco would not admit it to himself, the grandeur of Rome and the sheer magnificence of its many artworks threatened to overwhelm him. His instinct drove him to express this inner conflict in the drama of his own work.

This is superbly caught in a portrait he painted of his friend and mentor Clovio. The aged painter's lined grey-bearded face is all but expressionless, its feelings contained. But these are given consummate expression in other elements in the painting. First, Clovio's gnarled hand, with its wrinkled skin, its large forefinger pointing towards the open pages of a leather-bound volume – Clovio's masterwork of biblical illustrations *Il Libro d'Ore della Vergine* (The Book of Hours of the Virgin), often known as the *Farnese Hours*. Above the book, completing the composition, is an open window revealing a storm-scape of dark clouds and wind-blown trees. These disparate elements balance the composition, leading the eye from one element to the next. Only gradually does one realize that the painting has not fully coalesced. This is a young artist whose ambition still outruns his burgeoning talent.

We now come to El Greco's vexed relationship with the works of Michelangelo. Although the young painter was undoubtedly influenced by Michelangelo's mannerism, he remained reluctant to acknowledge this. When questioned about Michelangelo, El Greco replied that 'he was a good man, but he did not know how to paint'.

Michelangelo had died some years earlier, in 1564, but although his work was widely admired it was not without its controversial aspect. Most notably, his later painting of the Last Judgement, a fresco which covered an entire wall of the Sistine Chapel, was criticized for its widespread portrayal of male, and some female, nudity. Pius V, who had ascended to the papal throne in 1566, was now of the opinion that these figures should be partly painted over, their nudity obscured by clothes and loincloths. El Greco caused a furore when he dismissed Michelangelo's *Last Judgement* and suggested to Pope Pius V that the entire mural should be overpainted; whereupon he would paint a better work in its place.

Such was the uproar caused by El Greco's arrogance that the architect Pirro Ligorio was prompted to dub him a 'foolish foreigner', and Cardinal Farnese even went so far as to expel El Greco from his palazzo.

It was El Greco's continuing unpopularity in Rome which is said to have prompted him to leave for Spain in 1577, where his career would finally come into its own. El Greco would find many aspects of Spanish life congenial to his character. Most importantly, the Spanish took their religion seriously. This was hardly the case in Rome, which had become notorious for the laxity of its morals, especially amongst the wealthy cardinals.* The austerity of Spanish Catholicism chimed with El Greco's Greek Orthodox upbringing. (Whether or not he converted to Roman Catholicism remains open to question. Though he outwardly participated in regular Catholic observances, many suspect that his faith remained at heart Greek Orthodox.)

El Greco travelled to Madrid, but was unable to find satisfactory work there, so he settled in Toledo, some forty miles south of the capital. Clovio had provided El Greco with a letter of recommendation to the resident humanist scholar Benito Arias Montano, who also acted as agent for Philip II.

Toledo was the religious capital of Spain, and El Greco found the city congenial, receiving a number of commissions through Montano. His portraits of aristocrats and local worthies during this period are particularly memorable. Even so, El Greco had no intention of settling there permanently. His aim was still to establish himself in Madrid, and become a court painter to Philip II. Despite this, El Greco would remain in Toledo for several decades, during which his style matured in its own consummate and utterly original fashion. However, such was the unmistakable nature of his style that his works did not attract universal approval. The vivid drama, often distorted figures, and frequently 'unfinished' aspect of his style were not acceptable to those of more conservative

---

* Despite being an able and active papal diplomat, as well as a renowned patron of the arts, Cardinal Farnese found time to father a daughter with a lady-in-waiting. The Farnese Gardens (Orti Farnesiani sul Palatino) in Rome are named after him. Here, he established the first private botanical gardens in Europe.

tastes. Static scenes of detailed, fully finished figures were the order of the day – and in a very literal sense, too. The Counter-Reformation had led to specific requirements for Catholic art. The portrayal of religious scenes was expected to stress the exemplary content of the paintings, without the distraction of stylistic innovation.

When El Greco did finally receive a commission from Philip II, it was for an *Allegory of the Holy League* (often called the *Adoration of the Holy Name*). For this, El Greco painted portraits of the main signatories of the Holy League: Philip II, Pius V, the Doge of Venice and Don Juan of Austria (the victor of the Battle of Lepanto). These all appear in the lower half of the painting, which also includes the Entrance to Hell in the form of the large open mouth of a leviathan consuming a mass of naked writhing bodies (clearly inspired by the nightmare scenes of the Dutch artist Hieronymus Bosch). Above the clouds in the upper half of the painting, a group of angels is worshipping the name of Christ. The swirling host of angels above the surging white clouds invests the overall scene with a dramatic effect, which is heightened by the huge gaping toothed jaws of the leviathan.

But the finished *Allegory of the Holy League* did not find favour with Philip II. For a start, the overall drama of the scene far outshines its allegorical content. Also, Philip II is said to have objected to the inclusion of recognizable living portraits in a religious scene. The king's taste was for a more serene art.

Thus ended El Greco's hopes of becoming a court artist and receiving a steady (and lucrative) stream of commissions to decorate the interior of El Escorial, the vast monastery-palace Philip II was building north-west of Madrid. And so El Greco was forced to resign himself to life in provincial Toledo. Yet this was to be a blessing in disguise: here he would be allowed the comparative freedom to develop further those aspects of his style and vision that so appeal to the modern eye.

For the more advanced taste of his own era, El Greco's masterpiece was undoubtedly *The Burial of the Count of Orgaz*. Like his *Allegory*, painted ten years previously, this is a vast work (approximately fifteen feet by twelve feet), and it is similarly divided into an upper vision of the heavens and a lower terrestrial scene. The overall image was inspired by a local legend – according to which, Count Orgaz, a descendant of Byzantine emperors, lived such a pious and philanthropic life in the nearby small town of Orgaz that at his funeral St Stephen and St Augustine themselves descended from Heaven to bury him with their own hands. El Greco depicts the two saints in their golden robes tenderly lowering Orgaz's armour-clad cadaver into the grave. Witnessing this event is a row of eminent citizens of Toledo, attired in black mourning clothes and white ruffs. Each face is a masterful portrait in its own right, and amongst them is a self-portrait of a serious high-browed man with a neat brown beard and penetrating eyes. El Greco's young son Jorge is painted in the lower left-hand corner of the scene. Meanwhile, in the large domed upper half of the painting, the curiously solid pearly clouds part to allow the soul of Orgaz to ascend towards the figure of Christ in all his glory, clad in a pure white robe, a sea of saintly faces peering up at him.

The painting as a whole contains mannerist and Byzantine elements: iconic Orthodox influences blend with post-Renaissance realism. This is El Greco's conscious summation of all that he was capable of expressing. Though in no way a humanist work, it could not have been achieved without the humanist revolution which had broken the mould of medieval culture. It is both profoundly devout and yet somehow severely joyful, expressing the faith of a devout artist at the height of his powers.

El Greco received a regular stream of commissions while he was in Toledo, and is said to have lived in some style. He rented accommodation belonging to a local aristocrat, the Marquis de Villena, occupying three apartments containing some twenty-four rooms. He also used some of these rooms as his studio and accommodation for his assistants. Musicians played to him and his guests when he invited friends to dine with him. He also had a Spanish female companion; it was she who had given birth to Jorge. El Greco's companion has been identified as one Jerónima de Las Cuevas, but it is thought that they never married.

Between 1585 and 1609, while El Greco was resident in Toledo, the city witnessed the expulsion of the Jews and the Moriscos (Muslims who had been forced to convert to Christianity). This came about as the

Counter-Reformation gathered momentum and the Spanish Inquisition took on a more central role in society. The expulsion of the Jews and the Moriscos resulted in an economic downturn in the city, with entire districts becoming deserted, grass growing between the cobbles of their streets and squares.

Such circumstances may well have contributed to El Greco's late work known as *View of Toledo*, a masterpiece of troubled brilliance. However, the main impetus behind this painting was undoubtedly spiritual. El Greco was now in his late fifties and his faith had taken on a strong mystical element. *View of Toledo* is a portrait of the city high on its distant hillside above the River Tagus, featuring the main landmarks such as the cathedral and the Alcázar (a castle dating from the Muslim era). Yet these are as nothing beneath the vast threatening sky which occupies a large upper portion of the painting. This is a sensationally dramatic rendering of light and darkness – the like of which had never been seen before in European art, and remains unique in its originality.

El Greco's use of unexpected contrasting colour and elongated limbs in his figurative paintings imbues them with a tension, giving an almost flame-like quality to their shape. However, in his depiction of the sky above Toledo the tension is achieved with a more limited palette of harsh dark colouring and contrasting light suffused with unexpected red tones – from pink to blackened scarlet. The surface of the sky is rent apart by its glimpses of background light.

The rarity of the style in the painting is echoed by the rarity of its subject matter. The Counter-Reformation agenda adopted after the Council of Trent in 1563 had in fact banned the painting of landscapes – stigmatizing this as a Protestant and secular travesty of art. El Greco's mystical and dramatic *View of Toledo* can hardly have been accused of such anti-Catholic intention, but it was contrary to doctrine nonetheless. So why did El Greco choose to paint this scene? As more than one critic has pointed out, this is very much a 'city of the spirit'. It may indeed be seen as a final testament to his faith. El Greco would die in 1614 at the age of seventy-two, just a few years after he had completed this work. During the ensuing centuries, his 'unfinished' style, contrasting tones and distorted figures would fall from favour. It would be some 250 years before the British artist J. M. W. Turner at last understood the realistic originality of his stormy sky over Toledo. Later, the intensity of El Greco's observation would appeal to Cézanne, and his figurative distortions would inspire Picasso and the Cubists.

The ever-ambitious, ever-competitive Picasso may have been inspired by El Greco, but the object of his deepest envy was undoubtedly Diego Velázquez, generally regarded as the consummate Spanish artist of his age. Towards the end of his life, Picasso returned again and again to Velázquez's masterpiece *Las Meninas* (The Ladies-in-Waiting), creating a series of no less than fifty-eight works as he attempted to copy, analyse and tease out the secrets of this complex work in his own perceptive modernist shorthand. *Las Meninas* more than deserved such intense scrutiny.

The authoritative *A World History of Art* characterizes *Las Meninas* as 'Velázquez's supreme achievement, a highly self-conscious, calculated demonstration of what painting could achieve and perhaps the most searching comment ever made on the possibilities of the easel painting'.

Velázquez's extravagantly mysterious masterpiece is centred upon the five-year-old Infanta Margaret Theresa, the first child of Philip IV of Spain by his second wife, his Habsburg niece Mariana of Austria. The golden-haired child is dressed in an extravagant white farthingale (hooped skirt), her head turned as she gazes obliquely at the viewer. She is attended by two ladies-in-waiting, one of whom is kneeling attentively at her side, offering her a drink. Other figures include a chaperone, a recumbent mastiff, two palace dwarfs (as people of small stature would have been known). To the left of the picture is a self-portrait of a moustachioed Velázquez, easel in hand, standing before a large canvas, also focusing his gaze on the viewer. In the background is a lighted open doorway with the silhouette of Don José Nieto Velázquez, the queen's chamberlain (and possibly a relative of the painter). To the left of the doorway is a mirror, in which we can just distinguish the figures of Philip IV and Mariana. This solves the puzzle of why the Infanta and the artist are both looking out of the painting. Velázquez is engaged in painting a portrait of the king and queen, and the figures are gathered in his studio, watching him at work. The viewer is standing in the place occupied by Philip IV and Mariana, making those who see the painting both spectators and participants.

Quite apart from the subtlety of perspectives and reflections, the figures themselves are rendered with masterful realism. The group in the foreground is skilfully animated by juxtapositions and gestures. The smaller, male Italian dwarf to the extreme right is prodding the dog with his foot in an attempt to rouse him. Beside him, the forthright distortions of the female dwarf's darker face provide an illuminating contrast to the innocent fair-skinned features of the child Infanta.*

The renowned twentieth-century art critic Ernst Gombrich provides perhaps the best response to this work, combining both common sense and imaginative insight:

> What exactly does it all signify? We may never know, but I should like to fancy that Velázquez has arrested a real moment of time long before the invention of the camera. Perhaps the princess was brought into the royal presence to relieve the boredom of the sitting and the King or Queen remarked to Velázquez that here was a worthy subject for his brush.

In the Spanish court, when the sovereign made some remark, be it ever so trivial, it had the power of a command. So it may well be that

---

* Ironically, as the little Infanta Margaret Theresa grew up she would develop an ever more pronounced Habsburg jawline, reducing her youthful beauty to a lantern-jawed plainness. With the benefit of hindsight, it is possible to detect a hint of this incipient distortion in the childish features captured by Velázquez. Margaret Theresa was destined to live a tragic life. The Spanish and the Austrian Habsburgs were intent upon uniting against powerful France. In pursuit of this aim the fifteen-year-old Margaret Theresa was married to the Holy Roman Emperor Leopold I, a Habsburg from the same Austrian branch of the family as her mother. Six years later, her body 'weakened due to four living childbirths and at least two miscarriages', she died in 1673 at the age of just twenty-one.

this painting, regarded by many as one of the most significant in the history of western art, was prompted by nothing more than a 'passing wish'. Velázquez's overwhelming response to this offhand remark would result in a work of such transcendent brilliance that it has been described as 'the theology of painting' and also 'the true philosophy of art'.

Diego Velázquez (often pronounced 'Veláthkweth') was born in Seville in 1599. His father was a notary and his family were shopkeepers of Portuguese origin, possibly Jewish *conversos* (though he would later claim to be descended from lesser nobility). Beyond this, little is known of his childhood – and not only his childhood. Not for nothing has his biographer Laura Cumming remarked that 'Velazquez is sometimes said to be the most distant of artists, remote and inscrutable as a star in outer darkness. His life is unknowable, his mind unfathomable, his genius for creating illusions of living people almost beyond comprehension, as if he were not quite a real human being himself.'

We know that Velázquez grew up in the thriving city of Seville, in south-west Spain. At the time this was one of the largest and most prosperous cities in Europe, with a population of 150,000.* Although Seville was situated some fifty miles up the River Guadalquivir, it held a monopoly on all Spanish trade with South America. Here was where the treasure ships unloaded their cargoes of gold and silver. Only after the 1620s, when the Guadalquivir began to silt up, was this trade transferred to the coastal port of Cádiz.

Seville was also a cosmopolitan city, attracting merchants from all over Europe who wished to exchange their wares for pieces of eight and the like. Amidst such flourishing trade the arts thrived, with the city boasting more than a dozen artists' studios. At the age of thirteen, Velázquez was apprenticed to the studio of the important but undistinguished artist Francisco Pacheco. In 1618 Pacheco would be appointed Censor of Paintings to the Inquisition, and he is known to have visited El Greco at Toledo in 1611. (This was around the time that El Greco painted his

---

* Making it more than twice the size of Madrid, Rome or Amsterdam. Only London (200,000) and Paris (400,000) were more populous in Europe.

View of Toledo, but before Pacheco became Censor.) Pacheco would also write *The Art of Painting*, regarded as 'perhaps the most important treatise on Spanish painting'.

More importantly where Velázquez was concerned, Pacheco is known to have had a large collection of engravings by the likes of Michelangelo, Dürer and Veronese, meaning that Velázquez would have been exposed to the work of these masters at an early age. In 1618, the nineteen-year-old Velázquez married Pacheco's daughter Juana, by whom he would have two daughters, Francisca and Ignacia.

By nineteen, Velázquez was already painting works of exceptional quality. Amongst these was *The Waterseller of Seville*. In this painting, Velázquez depicts the lean gnarled features of a local waterseller, subtly suggesting how his life of poverty has aged him before his time. (His features are deeply lined, yet he has a full head of short dark hair, with just a few flecks of greyness on his bearded chin.) This contrasts with the bright smooth face of the young boy to whom he is handing a glass of water. The waterseller rests his right hand on his large rotund clay water pot. Above this, to the left, our eye is led to a smaller jug with indentations (almost as if it is unfinished), which rests on the table beside the boy with a cup placed above its mouth. Velázquez manages to lend the simple giving of the clear glass of translucent water a sacramental quality: dignified age passing on an almost-living liquid to callow youth. The entire scene is rendered with an almost hallucinatory realism, showing what appears to be the unmistakable influence of Caravaggio, who had died (or been murdered) some eight years previously.

This leads to an anomaly. It has been suggested that Velázquez was influenced by Caravaggio when he saw some of his paintings in Italy. But at this early stage Velázquez had certainly not travelled abroad. Indeed, he seems not yet to have left Seville. Also, the circumstances of Caravaggio's death had left his reputation under something of a cloud; this was hardly the type of painter whose works were liable to be well received in the home of the Spanish Inquisition. So how could Velázquez have so evidently been influenced by Caravaggio in this early work? We can only assume that Pacheco, in the years prior to his appointment as Censor of Paintings to the Inquisition, had amongst his collection of etchings a painting by Caravaggio of sufficiently dramatic chiaroscuro to influence the young Velázquez. This is not as unlikely as it might seem, for Caravaggio spent much of his last years in Naples, which was at the time ruled by Spain and would certainly have traded regularly with Seville.

The Waterseller is just one of a number of similar paintings completed by Velázquez during his early years in Seville. These include similarly realist paintings of everyday scenes, such as a woman frying eggs, maidservants in a kitchen with fish, and the like. The 'breathtaking veracity' of these scenes was the object of widespread local admiration. However, they were also criticized by some for their lower-class subjects: why wasn't this prodigy painting religious subjects? In one of the few recorded remarks attributed to Velázquez, he is said to have replied: 'I would rather be the first painter of coarse things than the second in high art.' An understandable reaction in an ambitious young painter. There was still novelty and unexplored possibilities in secular scenes, whereas the plethora of religious paintings from the medieval era, through the Renaissance to the new Age of Reason, had covered almost every possible aspect of originality. However, if Velázquez was to go on painting such scenes, or indeed avoid the religious art prescribed by the Inquisition – to which he seemed to be averse – he was going to need the protection of a powerful patron. Velázquez seems to have been well aware of this from the outset, and he set his ambitions accordingly.

Judging from a hagiographic memoir written by his father-in-law Pacheco, Velázquez could do no harm in his eyes. Thus Pacheco's appointment as Censor of Paintings to the Inquisition would seem to account for the initial freedom of subject matter in Velázquez's work. However, his disinclination to paint religious scenes seems to have been an integral part of his character. During the course of his life he would paint surprisingly few such scenes. Fortunately for Velázquez, his powerful patrons would prove more interested in having their portraits painted than sponsoring works that demonstrated the profundity of their religious faith.

In 1623, Velázquez set off for Madrid, the home of the royal court, in the hope of finding a rich patron. He took with him a letter of recommendation to Don Juan de Fonseca, chaplain to the young Philip IV. As evidence of his artistic talent he also carried an example of *The Waterseller* (such had been the popularity of his original painting that he had made two copies).

According to Pacheco's version of events, Velázquez arrived early one morning at the door to Fonseca's residence and was immediately invited in. When Fonseca was shown Velázquez's painting he was so astonished by its sheer artistry that he purchased it at once. At the same time, he demanded that Velázquez should paint his portrait. Astonishingly, Velázquez managed to complete this task by the end of the day, whereupon Fonseca rushed off to the Alcázar taking the picture with him. Pacheco wrote that: 'Within the hour everyone in the palace saw it, the Infantes [heir to the throne] and the King himself, which is the greatest distinction it could receive. It was decided that the artist should paint his majesty.'

There is one particular anomaly in this story. Philip IV was only eighteen at the time; he had been married to Elisabeth of France at the age of ten – hardly the age to have been any judge of fine art. Surprisingly, the rest of the story appears to have been true. Within just a few days, Philip IV was sitting for his first portrait by Velázquez. This would prove to be a highly realistic likeness of the king: 'Puffy, adenoidal, so pale the blue veins are visible beneath the clammy white temples, with no sign yet of the famous upturned moustache that will attract attention away from the protuberant lips and long Hapsburg jaw.'

Despite this, it was generally agreed that this was by far the finest portrait yet painted of Philip IV. More importantly, Velázquez had caught the eye of Philip IV's all-powerful *valido*, the Count-Duke of Olivares, who noted how moved Philip IV had been by the portrait. He also noted the rapport which had sprung up between the artist and his royal sitter, even during the short periods Velázquez had been granted to work on his portrait. Olivares took it upon himself to decree that from now on no other artist would be permitted to paint Philip IV's portrait.*

---

* Over the coming four decades Velázquez would regularly paint portraits of Philip IV. And Olivares would see that his decree regarding Velázquez's unique right would be upheld – with but one notable exception.

This decision certainly pleased the king, but was not so well received by the other court painters, several of whom had been in royal service for many years during the reign of Philip IV's father, Philip III. Olivares also awarded Velázquez fifty gold ducats from the royal purse so that he could bring his family from Seville to Madrid.

The year 1623 would mark the start of Velázquez's meteoric rise at court. He was given an apartment at the vast Alcázar palace and awarded a regular court salary – with an additional sum for every portrait he painted of the king. Within a matter of months after his first portrait, Velázquez was commissioned to paint a second, grander portrait of the young ruler seated astride his horse. This has now been lost, as has another royal portrait he painted that year – this time of the visiting Prince of Wales, who would later become Charles I of England. The following year would see the completion of Velázquez's penetrating portrait of his bulky, overbearing patron Olivares.

Owing to the meticulous bureaucracy which prevailed at the Alcázar, we can glean the details of Velázquez's life – how he originally occupied rooms in the east wing of the palace, then the west wing, and later was granted an apartment that occupied two floors. We even know the books he possessed: Herodotus, the Ancient Greek 'father of history'; the inevitable treatises of Aristotle; and more surprisingly a work of modern philosophy by Descartes. Other works on astronomy, geometry and poetry reveal the breadth of his interests. We also know that his daughter Ignacia died in infancy. But we know nothing of the man himself. How deeply affected was he by the death of his daughter? Was the philosophy he read a consolation or an inspiration? There is no doubting the fact that his work was deeply imbued with geometric knowledge, but quite how he absorbed this remains unclear. Another fact gleaned from the records is that Velázquez was granted unprecedented three-hour sittings for his portraits of Philip IV, suggesting that the young king found his company congenial (or perhaps that it enabled him to have three hours of peace, away from the pestering distractions of Olivares).

However, not all were so utterly convinced of the superior talent of the new arrival at court. Though Velázquez struck up friendships with some of the court painters, others of the old school, who had served under Philip IV's father Philip III, were less convinced of his abilities. They resented being denied the opportunity to paint portraits of the king, and found themselves relegated to creating canvases to cover the walls of the Alcázar, and later Olivares's white elephant project Buen Retiro.

When Philip IV was made aware of this discontent, he decided to resolve the matter once and for all. A competition was announced to find the finest artist in Spain. Painters who entered the competition were asked to create a work marking the great event which had led to the founding of modern Spain: the expulsion of the Moriscos.

After a thorough examination of all the paintings entered for this competition, Velázquez's work was judged the winner. Unfortunately, his work would be destroyed by a fire at the palace during the following century, so all we have is a prosaic contemporary description of his victorious entry, saying that 'it depicted Philip III pointing with his baton to a crowd of men and women being led away by soldiers, while the female personification of Spain sits in calm repose'. As a reward, Velázquez was appointed to the rank of Royal Usher, with a further addition to his daily allowance.

In 1628, Spain received a visit from the Flemish painter Peter Paul Rubens, who was attached to a diplomatic mission to the Spanish court. Rubens was a master of the baroque style, and he would be the one exceptional painter who was granted the privilege of painting Philip IV's portrait. The fifty-one-year-old Rubens was at the height of his fame, his work renowned throughout Europe, whereas Velázquez was not yet thirty years old, and news of his talent had barely spread beyond the confines of the Spanish royal court.

Rubens was an astute judge of character, and we know from his private writings what he thought of Philip IV: 'hesitant, under-confident, too easily led by his politicians'. Of Velázquez he remarked that he was 'modest'. However, the fact that Velázquez did not resent the flamboyant middle-aged maestro (who even had his own castle outside Antwerp) usurping his position as sole royal portraitist would seem to speak louder than Rubens's assessment of his character.

Rubens's resplendent overblown style was very much the polar opposite of Velázquez's meticulous profundity, yet Velázquez was quick to appreciate some of the less-evident subtle touches of the old master. And Rubens for his part recognized that Velázquez should be given the opportunity to expand his talent, and made representation to the king accordingly. In Rubens's view, Velázquez could only fulfil his potential as an artist if he was granted leave to visit Italy, where he could study first-hand the works of the Renaissance masters, as well as more recent artists such as Caravaggio.

Rubens would remain at the Spanish court for seven months, and by the end of this time he had managed to persuade Philip IV to grant Velázquez an extensive leave of absence to visit Italy, funded by his majesty. In 1629, Velázquez set out on a tour of Italy which would last one and a half years.

Although this trip would prove instrumental in Velázquez's artistic development, little is known of his personal reactions to Italy. Once again, the artist remains elusive – except in his art. He is known to have visited half a dozen cities, including Venice and Rome. In Naples, he painted a portrait of Maria Anna, sister of Philip IV, who was married to the Holy Roman Emperor Ferdinand III, who was also King of Bohemia, Hungary and Croatia as well as Archduke of Austria. In Velázquez's own unfussy way, his portrait of the twenty-four-year-old empress captures her red-headed beauty, as well as giving an indication of the self-possession and ability that would enable her to govern Naples during her husband's frequent absences in Bohemia, Hungary and Austria. She would also be instrumental in maintaining Naples's important link to her native Spain.

Although we know next to nothing of Velázquez's personal development during this period, his artistic development speaks volumes. Certain elements – such as luminosity and subtle variations of composition – are evident in his larger paintings. These would culminate in his magnificent *Surrender of Breda*, painted on his return to Spain. This large canvas depicts one of Spain's rare successes in the Dutch Revolt. It would be commissioned by Philip IV – unsurprisingly encouraged by Olivares, who was persisting with his disastrous war in the Netherlands. (Aptly, the painting itself would adorn the walls of Olivares's other ruinous project, the Buen Retiro Palace.)

In the central foreground of the *Surrender of Breda*, the Dutch leader

Justinus van Nassau bows as he hands the key to the city of Breda to Ambrogio Spinola, the general of the Spanish forces. The forest of raised Spanish lances behind Spinola far outnumbers the few beflagged remnants of the Dutch army, while in the background is a superbly rendered vista of the flat, war-ravaged countryside of Holland. The soft palette employed by Velázquez indicates a Venetian influence, while many other aspects, including the figures of the soldiers, show how much he had learned from the Renaissance masters during his trip to Italy.

On his return to Spain, Velázquez would also resume his royal portraits of Philip IV. In the opinion of his biographer Laura Cumming, these paintings of Philip IV 'are the most remarkable biography of a monarch in all art'. They trace his life from the uncertain teenager who prematurely inherited the throne, through his forty-four-year reign, 'to the melancholy disillusion of old age. The lugubrious face thickens, the eyes sag, the dangling jaw takes on a foolish pathos. Only the moustache, whose upswept prongs were imitated by Salvador Dalí, remains forever vital.'

Thus Velázquez charted the arc of Philip IV's reign, which saw Spain through the end of its Golden Age and the beginning of its ensuing decline. Yet as a portraitist Velázquez was so much more than just a painter of kings and queens. He was equally adept at painting all manner of people – from dwarfs to ladies of the court, the king's jester, an ageing tramp,* and even Pope Innocent X (on a second visit to Italy). How did

---

* Portrayed as a bulky figure whose poverty-ravaged features gaze out at the viewer with an expression that is both provocative and inquisitive. He is seemingly naked beneath his full-length ragged brown coat, his tattered boots worn down unevenly, suggesting he has a limp. Incongruously, he is clutching an old book in his right hand. This is explained by the name Velázquez bequeaths on him. He is *Aesop* in modern guise: the legendary fabulist of the ancient world, whose tales often anthropomorphize animals to illustrate instructive parables, or simple proverbial wisdom – such as 'killing the goose that laid the golden egg'. Passing references to Aesop in works ranging from Herodotus to Plato suggest that he may have been a Phrygian, or an African slave, who lived in the sixth century BC on the Aegean island of Samos. Velázquez's tramp is an emblem of all such people: condemned by society, yet potentially capable of achieving legendary status. As Velázquez portrayed him, he challenges us all and our complicity in his fate.

Velázquez manage to capture such a wide range of humanity with such unerring accuracy and penetration? The key seems to lie in the fact that he viewed all his sitters as peers – in his regard they became essentially equal to each other, as well as to the artist himself. This was humanity in all its bewildering, and sometimes bewildered, vanity. The expression of Philip IV's court jester is both fleetingly pitiful and fleetingly playful. On the other hand, Pope Innocent X has a hard face, stern of expression, with the sly perspicacity of a manipulative diplomat; a man trapped in the vestments of his spiritual office, yet somehow devoid of spirituality.[*]

And what do Velázquez's depictions of himself reveal? For all the clarity and reason of his other portraits, his self-portraits remain enigmatic and elusive, somehow stepping back from the light of reason – as subtly shape-shifting as the variations of his goatee beard and the length of his twirled moustaches. Contrary to Rubens's suggestion of modesty, Velázquez's views of himself contain an inner pride. The image varies – from the haunted young thinker of the 1630–5 self-portrait to the dashing figure standing beside the victorious Spanish officers at the *Surrender of Breda*, looking slightly ridiculous in an outsized fashionable hat, his wry expression hinting at his awareness of this. Then there is the stern figure behind the canvas emerging out of the dimness in *Las Meninas*, leaning back, brush in hand, as he assesses the spectator (or implied royal couple). It seems that, like the work of his near-contemporary Shakespeare, Velázquez's art has consumed his personality until only a shadow is left. For both these figures, after all the magnificent yet self-doubting impersonations – the Hamlet, the intense-eyed young man who read Descartes, the foolish Lear, the soldier in his absurdly fashionable hat – little of the merely personal is left. But despite this, Velázquez succeeds in throwing down his challenging talent, like a dueller's glove, across the centuries to the likes of Picasso, Dalí and Bacon…

---

[*] This was the portrait which inspired the twentieth-century Anglo-Irish painter Francis Bacon to paint his 'screaming popes' series.

René Descartes was a central figure in the emergence of modern philosophy and science.

Peter the Great's Enlightenment ideas, which contrasted with his harsh and autocratic rule, typify the duality of the Age of Reason.

Depiction of René Descartes (*second from right*) and Queen Christina (*seated, opposite him*) discussing philosophy. After becoming tutor to Queen Christina, Descartes was horrified to learn that she expected him to arise at 5 a.m. for her lectures.

Caravaggio's art was often in conflict with the spirituality of his patrons, typified by his depiction of St Paul's conversion to Christianity on the route to Damascus.

Above: Caravaggio sought to achieve a very precise realism of expression, heightened by his use of chiaroscuro, as evidenced in this second iteration of *The Fortune Teller* (c. 1595).

Left: *Judith Slaying Holofernes* (c. 1620). The raw violence of this scene is said to reflect Artemisia Gentileschi's feelings regarding the rape she suffered.

Artemisia Gentileschi was the first woman to become a member of the Florentine *Accademia delle Arti del Disegno* and fulfilled commissions for patrons as diverse as Charles I of England and Philip IV of Spain.

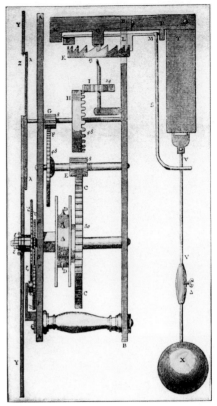

Above: As a physicist, mathematician, astronomer and engineer, and inventor of the pendulum clock (*right*), Christiaan Huygens was one of the Age of Reason's first great scientists.

Cromwell at the Battle of Naseby, which was fought in 1645. The chaos of the English Civil War inspired Thomas Hobbes to write his great political tract *Leviathan*.

Above: *Examination of a Witch* (1853). It is suggested that outbreaks of witchcraft in the Early Modern world were the result of socio-political turmoil, with scapegoating drawing communities into cohesion.

Left: Portrait of Gaspar de Guzmán, Count-Duke of Olivares, who became *valido* to Philip IV, painted by Velázquez (1624).

Many regard *Las Meninas* by Velázquez as one of the supreme works of European art. Despite this, its many visual complexities continue to defy analysis.

The *Semper Augustus* gained notoriety for being the most expensive tulip ever sold during the seventeenth-century Dutch 'Tulipmania'.

The Amsterdam Stock Exchange, the world's first, officially opened in 1611.

El Greco's masterpiece, *The Burial of the Count of Orgaz*, depicts St Stephen and St Augustine descending from heaven to bury the pious Count Orgaz themselves.

CHAPTER 7

THE MONEY MEN
AND THE MARKETS

THE AGE OF REASON also saw the beginning of a new financial era, with the emergence of capitalism as we know it today. Basically, to start off with, this involved the private or joint investment of capital (money) in commercial enterprises. The joint sponsoring of galleys engaged in trading expeditions initially emerged in Venice during the fifteenth and sixteenth centuries. By 1600, this method was also being adopted by the British and the Dutch, who had begun despatching trading ships around the Cape of Good Hope to India and the East Indies. There they purchased (or otherwise obtained) such goods as nutmeg, mace, pepper and other spices – easily transported rarities that fetched high prices in Europe. The profits made by such voyages were eye-watering: when all costs were deducted, a profit of 400 per cent was not uncommon. On the other hand, it was not unusual for a flotilla of a dozen ships to set out and less than half of them return. Piracy, shipwreck and other misadventures were frequent.

Previously, Spanish royalty, Venetian oligarchs, Italian bankers, and rich merchants were the only ones who could afford to invest in (or be bankrupted by) such expeditions. It was the newly independent Dutch who were the first to democratize this form of trade. In 1602, the government of the United Provinces of the Netherlands came up with a means of rationalizing this lucrative but risky business. The government created a monopoly company, which would carry out all Dutch trade with the Far East. This was named the Vereenigde Oostindische Compagnie – a tongue-twister that translates as the 'United East India Company' and became known as the VOC for short.

According to the company charter: 'All the residents of these lands may buy shares in this Company.' This meant that a large number of people could buy moderate or small amounts of shares in the VOC, with this capital being invested in all Dutch trading expeditions to the East Indies. This not only expanded the ownership of these risky expeditions, but also eliminated a large element of risk for investors, by simply spreading the risk throughout the many investors. As Jacob Goldstein notes in his book *Money*: 'A huge range of people invested in the VOC – over 1,000 people in Amsterdam alone, including the maid of one of the directors of the company, who put in ten months' salary.' Here, the link between capitalism and democracy begins to become evident.

The government initially granted the monopoly charter to the VOC for twenty-one years. After that, the company would be wound up and the shares of the profits divided accordingly. But investors were also given the opportunity to cash in their shares after just ten years, if they so wished. More importantly, a line was added to the charter allowing shareholders who could not wait this long to sell their shares to anyone who was willing to pay for them. At a stroke, a market had been created for the exchange of stock in the company.

In no time, the market itself became a self-perpetuating entity. People began buying VOC shares on spec, and sometimes attempting to sell them even before the ships of the latest expedition had set sail from harbour – an event which often inspired optimism, and a subsequent rise in the price people were willing to pay for shares.

In time, people who wanted to sell their shares, along with those who wished to buy them, took to gathering on Nieuwe Brug (New Bridge), the bridge over the canal linking Amsterdam harbour to the city centre. This was the route used by captains delivering their ships' mail, and thus was the best place to learn news of the latest arrivals in port, and the success or failure of their expeditions. On rainy days (a frequent phenomenon in waterlogged Holland), the dealers would retire to shelter in the nearby Oude Kerk (Old Church).

Soon, Nieuwe Brug became so crowded that the city authorities decided to construct a building on nearby Warmoesstraat, one of the oldest streets in the city, where the dealers and their clients could conduct their business without stopping traffic. The result was an impressive building, behind whose façade was a large open courtyard surrounded by a covered colonnade with forty-two numbered pillars, where dealers would set up their pitches. This building opened in 1611, becoming the world's first stock exchange.

From the outset, the Amsterdam Stock Exchange was only open at certain times of day: from 11 a.m. until noon, and later for an hour before dusk (limited to half an hour in winter, when the evenings drew in). This sensible move concentrated the activities of the buyers and sellers, so that sellers would not have to wait around all day for buyers, and vice versa. It also overcame another, more psychological difficulty. Sellers inevitably entered the market with high expectations; while buyers had expectations of lower prices. Such concentrated hours focused the minds of both parties, making them more willing to compromise, reach an agreed price, and close a deal before the market itself closed. An exchange clerk was appointed, with the task of ringing a bell to start and close business. Any dealers who arrived late were liable to a fine. People bought shares by taking what became known in the jargon as a long position. That is, they expected that at some time in the future their shares would rise in value so that they could sell them at a profit.

In the early days of the VOC, one of its directors, a wealthy merchant called Isaac Le Maire, fell out with his fellow directors, and was pressurized into resigning his directorship. Such was the enmity of this dispute that when Le Maire left the company he was made to sign an understanding that from now onwards he was barred from all involvement with trading beyond the Cape of Good Hope or the Straits of Magellan (the two trading routes to the Far East). Le Maire was outraged at this treatment, and vowed to have his revenge. Being a man of reason, he ingeniously deduced that if it was possible to hold a 'long' position on shares, it would also be possible to hold a 'short' position, by which money could be made from shares *falling* in price. And he soon devised a method for doing this.

Le Maire now joined with nine of his wealthy friends and set about 'shorting' the market for VOC shares. To do this, they contracted to sell VOC shares to a group of buyers for future delivery at a given price somewhat above the present market value. As the market rose, and sometimes fell, at a variable rate, this looked like a good offer. It appeared to guarantee a moderate but risk-free profit – and thus attracted a good number of future buyers. Note that at this time Le Maire and his cronies did not even need to own their promised shares; they had simply agreed on a future date and a future price.

Having entered into a good number of such 'futures' agreements, Le Maire and his friends then began a clandestine whispering campaign, spreading rumours that, contrary to impressions, VOC was in fact running into financial difficulties. Confidence in the company began to wane, and a number of shareholders began selling their shares. As word of this circulated, it had a multiplying effect, and soon the value of VOC shares started a serious decline.

By the date on which the buyers had agreed to purchase Le Maire's VOC shares, the actual value of these shares had sunk far below the price agreed. Le Maire and his cronies then bought up the contracted amount of shares on the market at the new low prices, and exchanged them with the buyers, who were obliged to pay the high price to which they had agreed. Le Maire had shorted the market.

After Le Maire made his 'killing' on the market, the VOC soon got wise to his methods and banned shorting. (Shorting the market has continued – and on several occasions been banned – to this day.) The trouble with banning such 'futures' trading was that it soon became clear that this method of trading had a useful and popular place in share markets, especially in commodities such as seasonal crops. When farmers planted their crops, they often sought a 'guaranteed' future minimum price. This way, they were insured against bankruptcy if the market price for their crop failed. The buyers of the futures contracts were relying upon the likelihood of the market rising. Thus all sides were satisfied with the mutual reassurance guaranteed by such agreements.

Le Maire's shorting episode proved little more than a hiccup for the Amsterdam Stock Exchange, as well as the trading fortunes of the VOC, which continued to flourish. An indication of the sheer size of the markets in rare spices and pepper can be seen from the figures for pepper holdings throughout the Netherlands. By 1635, warehouses in Amsterdam and other Dutch ports handling VOC imports held no less than 2 million kegs of pepper. The following year, this had increased to 3 million kegs. Canny warehousing of such products by the VOC ensured that the markets were not flooded. Also, when the imports experienced a shortfall of pepper, these reserves could be tapped to ensure that the price remained steady. Too high a price would simply have priced pepper out of the market.

Such simple market practices were in their infancy, however, and would continue to be tested by unforeseen circumstances in the new business of finance. As already indicated, financial markets soon extended beyond VOC shares into all manner of commodity markets – from necessities such as wheat and the financing of canal-building projects, to luxuries such as coffee and spices, and even to exotica such as tulips, the flowers for which the Dutch are famous to this day.

The first tulips to arrive in Europe came from the Middle East during the sixteenth century. It is said that the ambassador of the Holy Roman Emperor at the court of the Ottoman sultan sent the first tulip bulbs to Vienna in 1554. The hitherto-unknown colourful blooms caused a sensation, and word of this wonder soon spread throughout Europe. However, it was thought that such a bulb could not flourish in the cold damp climate of the Netherlands. This all changed with the arrival of the pioneering botanist Carolus Clusius from the French-speaking southern Netherlands (now southern Belgium). Clusius took up a post at the University of Leiden, where he began successfully cultivating tulips, whose vibrant petals soon made them popular amongst the merchant classes.

Following the success of single-hued tulips, a further sensation was sparked by the arrival from Constantinople (Istanbul) of a consignment of tulips with 'broken-hued' petals. (This rare effect was in fact caused by a virus that broke up the solid colours, allowing a paler undercolour to emerge in florid striations.) The price of tulips with ordinary single-hued petals had already begun to rise, and the arrival of the rare broken-hued variety only added to this impetus. The broken-hued variety, especially the rare Semper Augustus variant, soon became a much-coveted status symbol, and merchants began bidding ever-higher prices for this luxury item. The price rise for tulips of all kinds was then given further impetus when French-speaking traders from the southern Netherlands got wind of the market. Speculators, who had no intention of growing the bulbs, entered the market around 1634, with prices soaring still further as bulbs rapidly changed hands at ever-increasing prices. According to Goldstein, these new speculators extended across the social scale: 'Nobles, citizens, farmers, mechanics, seamen, footmen, maidservants, even chimney sweeps and old clotheswomen, dabbled in tulips'.

By now the prices which bulbs were fetching had become so high that innovative techniques in speculation began to appear. The futures market remained banned on the Amsterdam Stock Exchange, but as most of the trading in bulbs was done elsewhere, a new futures market began to emerge. For the down payment of a relatively modest sum, one could obtain the option to buy a tulip at a future date at a predicted price. If by that date the price of the tulip had risen higher than that price, profit was guaranteed without the need for any heavy initial outlay. This method was soon reaping huge dividends. An ordinary single-hued bulb which had cost just 20 guilders in 1634 was sold three years later for an astonishing 1,200 guilders. Meanwhile, a single bulb of the exotic bloom Semper Augustus changed hands for 3,000 guilders. (This at a time when a skilled artisan was lucky if he earned more than 300 guilders a year.)

Things soon reached such a pitch that in the French-speaking southern Netherlands a bulb was exchanged for a small brewery (*brasserie*), prompting this variety to become known as Tulip Brasserie. A sailor who returned home from a long voyage happened to call in at the home of his brother, a merchant. Here he found what he thought was an onion on the table and ate it. In fact, it was a highly valuable tulip bulb. When the merchant arrived home and discovered what had happened, he was so furious at his loss that he had his brother arrested and flung in jail.

'Everything has a price' had now reached the point where 'the price is everything'. The market had been transformed into what would become known as a bubble. Evidently such rises in prices could not go on forever; one day the bubble would have to burst. But how would this happen? What would it take to bring about a return to reason?

Appropriately, the beginning of the end is said to have occurred due to a misunderstanding, when buyers refused to travel to Haarlem for a bulb auction. In fact, the buyers stayed away owing to a rumour that there had been an outbreak of bubonic plague in the city. However, word began to spread that there was no longer a market for tulip bulbs. Buyers of bulbs started to have their doubts, and bulb-owners began selling, with multiplying effect.

The bubble burst in February 1637. During this month prices tumbled to just 5 per cent of their previous valuation, with some of the cheaper varieties falling as low as 1 per cent. All over the country, future options were called in at previously agreed prices, and investors were bankrupted. Wealthy respected citizens were wiped out overnight, great merchant houses ruined, and countless small investors returned to the poverty from which they had only just emerged. In some of the bulb-trading towns, such as Haarlem and Alkmaar, practically the entire population faced financial ruin.

This episode – and indeed the entire conduct of the Amsterdam share market – appeared to many to be the very embodiment of unreason. The first man to describe the activities of the stock exchange was a Jewish Portuguese merchant called Joseph de la Vega, who wrote a fittingly titled work called *Confusion of Confusions*. His description of business on the floor of the exchange has a ring of truth that echoes through the centuries:

A member of the Exchange opens his hand and another takes it, and thus sells a number of shares at a fixed price, which is confirmed by a second handshake… The handshakes are followed by shouting, the shouting by insults, the insults by impudence and more insults, shouting, pushes, and handshakes until the business is finished.

Joseph de la Vega certainly knew what he was talking about, being not only a wealthy merchant and share-dealer, but also a successful poet and a philosopher. While such a combination of professions seems very much of its era, history would prove his outrage at the unreasonable disorders of the market to be timeless.*

The English version of the VOC was in fact founded prior. On 31 December 1600, Queen Elizabeth I granted the East India Company a monopoly on all English trade with countries to the east of the Cape of Good Hope and west of the Strait of Magellan. Any who attempted to circumvent this monopoly were liable to forfeiture of their ships and cargo, which would be divided equally between the company and the Crown. Those responsible for the misdemeanour would be imprisoned at the 'royal pleasure' (an English legal term for an indefinite sentence, often used for insane, out-of-favour aristocrats or incorrigible malefactors).

---

* Tulipmania may have been the first speculative bubble, yet its instructive elements have yet to be absorbed – by financiers, speculators and gamblers of all hues. Such bubbles have become an all-too-regular feature of financial markets. Less than a century after Tulipmania, London would see the South Sea Bubble – with bubbles recurring at regular, though more frequent intervals throughout the ensuing centuries. The greatest bubble of the twentieth century would of course be the Wall Street Crash of 1929; the present century would begin with the NASDAQ exchange experiencing the dot-com bubble. Many economists of varying expertise, from J. K. Galbraith to Alan Greenspan, have entertained themselves and their audiences by describing such instances of 'irrational exuberance' – yet found themselves unable to give any satisfactory explanation of such phenomena. When they will occur, and why they occur, remain the province of the sages of hindsight. Many suspect that the next bubble will occur in Bitcoin. Nout Wellink, former president of the Dutch Central Bank, has described Bitcoin as 'worse than the tulip mania… at least then you got a tulip, now you get nothing'. Such prophets of doom have throughout the centuries been as widespread a phenomenon as the sages of hindsight – both proving to be of equal social and financial utility. Financial bubbles are thus a heritage from the Age of Reason, exhibiting the unreason which also characterized this age.

The East India Company's first major voyage took place in 1601 with a flotilla of three ships and an investment of £60,450 (more than £8 million in modern terms). The financial structure of the company was less democratic than the stock exchange that financed the voyages of the VOC. In London, the Royal Exchange had been opened by Elizabeth I as early as 1571, but this was in reality a market for various goods and commodities, such as alcohol and luxury items. According to a modern historian of the Company: 'Stockbrokers were not allowed into the Royal Exchange because of their rude manners, hence they had to operate from other establishments in the vicinity, such as Jonathan's Coffee-House.'

Manners would seem to have been the least of it: Joseph de la Vega's observations concerning the stockbrokers of Amsterdam were equally applicable to their London colleagues. Here again, the reasonable construct of the stock market appears to have been undermined by the unreasonable behaviour of its operators:

> The best and most agreeable aspect of the new business is that one can become rich without risk. Indeed, without endangering your capital, and without having anything to do with correspondence, advances of money, warehouses, postage, cashiers, suspensions of payment, and other unforeseen incidents, you have the prospect of gaining wealth if, in the case of bad luck in your transactions, you will only change your name. Just as the Hebrews, when they are seriously ill, change their names in order to obtain relief, so a changing of his name is sufficient for the speculator who finds himself in difficulties, to free himself from all impending dangers and tormenting disquietude.

Little wonder, then, that the financing of the East India Company was raised amongst those to whom Elizabeth I granted the original charter – namely 'George, Earl of Cumberland, 415 Knights, Aldermen and Burgesses'. Of these, 125 became shareholders, raising a total of £72,000. Initially, these shares remained in the hands of what has been called a 'coffee house clique'. However, owing to the vicissitudes of fortune and trade, shares soon began to fall into the hands of the dreaded stockbrokers.

By this stage the VOC had arguably become the first great multinational company. Amongst its shareholders were men (and some women) of various different nationalities – from Dutch to Portuguese, from French to German. And although its headquarters was in Amsterdam, it was beginning to establish trading forts and monopoly spice islands from India to Indonesia.*

From the outset, the East India Company had to compete with the VOC for trade in Java and the Spice Islands (in the Indonesian archipelago). The VOC proved more adept as traders, causing friction between the two. This led to various incidents that eventually sparked the First Anglo-Dutch War, which resulted in a number of naval battles between 1652 and 1654. By then, the Dutch had a merchant fleet consisting of more ships than those of all the other European nations combined, and this was conducting trade from the East Indies to the Baltic, as well as the Americas. (In 1624, the VOC's sister company the Dutch West Indies Company had established a settlement on the southern tip of Manhattan Island named New Amsterdam. Not until forty years later, at the end of the Second Anglo-Dutch War, would this be ceded to the English and renamed New York – in exchange for the tiny remote Indonesian island of Run, which was renowned for its nutmeg trees.) During the First Anglo-Dutch War the English navy prevailed in most of its encounters with the Dutch fleet; however, their only real success was in establishing control of the sea around the English coast, with little protection being afforded to English merchant ships in the East Indies.

---

* The VOC used the remote South Atlantic island of St Helena as a staging post, where ships could replenish their supplies of fresh water and such fruit as they could find. They did not settle the uninhabited island. Instead they inscribed a stone laying claim to the territory – which had in fact first been discovered in 1502 by the Portuguese. By the mid-1600s the VOC had established the Cape Colony which became the company's first permanent settlement that was not a trading post, and this largely superseded St Helena. The Dutch introduced Huguenot farmers there who produced victualling for the passing VOC ships.

Partly as a result of this setback, the East India Company concentrated its commercial activities on the subcontinent of India. Initially they began trading in cotton, sugar, tea, spices and saltpetre (for gunpowder). Later they would make forays into the Madagascar slave trade and the opium trade with China. In this way, the East India Company would eventually grow into the greatest private commercial enterprise the world had ever seen. Indeed, the East India Company would become virtually a nation within a nation. It had its own trading ships and its own warships, which flew its own flag. It recruited its own army, which gradually began a war of conquest over India; and at its height this army boasted 260,000 men, more than twice the size of the British army at the time.[*]

Commerce was beginning to transform the world as never before. And it was the Age of Reason that produced some of the earliest modern thinkers who attempted to analyse the mechanics of this transformation. How did commercial interaction work? What, if any, were its guiding principles? Here was a vast field of human thought which had virtually lain fallow since classical times. Aristotle was probably the first to use the word οἰκονομικά (economics) as we know it. In Ancient Greek, this meant 'household management'. Aristotle discerned one central principle: expenditure should not exceed income. In line with much Ancient Greek thought concerning individual behaviour, this led him to ask: 'How can we lead the good life?' So economics became linked with individual morality – or, on the larger scale, politics.

Thus it comes as little surprise that the first modern thinker to write on the subject, a Frenchman named Antoine de Montchrestien, should name his work *Traité de l'Économie Politique* (Treatise on Political

---

[*] Not for nothing is the East India Company regarded as the driving commercial enterprise which set Britain on course for establishing the largest empire the world has ever seen. At its height, some two centuries later, the British Empire would extend over 13 million square miles, covering a quarter of the world's land mass and ruling over 500 million people, which was approximately a quarter of the world's population at the time. The acknowledged 'jewel in the crown' of this empire was India, which was removed from East India Company control in 1858, with Queen Victoria being declared 'Empress of India' some twenty years later.

Economy). Although the ideas contained in this work were hardly of startling insight, Montchrestien's choice of name for his subject stuck. For some centuries to come, the field of study we know as economics would be called political economy. And the first truly original thinker in this subject would be the Englishman Sir William Petty, a polymath of considerable theoretical and practical expertise whose rational acuity was sadly blemished by a life of unscrupulousness far beyond the bounds of reason.

William Petty was born in 1623, the son of a haberdasher in the southern market town of Romsey. He seems to have been a precociously quick-witted but difficult child, with little or no knowledge to sustain his insuperably high opinion of himself. At the age of fourteen he ran away to sea, becoming employed on a ship in the cross-Channel trade with France. Petty's character ensured him such unpopularity amongst his shipmates that when he accidentally broke his leg falling from the rigging he was abandoned in France. According to the chronicler John Aubrey, Petty claimed that this was 'the most remarkable accident of [my] life'.

After recovering from his broken leg, Petty taught himself French, Latin and Greek, supporting himself by acquiring a post as a tutor (a considerable achievement considering his previous lack of education). If his word is to be believed, and the evidence appears to support this unlikely claim, he also taught himself astronomy and mathematics to the highest level. He then 'began to merchandize' so successfully that he acquired sufficient funds for him to finance his studies at the renowned Jesuit college at La Flèche (where Descartes had studied two decades previously).

Despite his high opinion of himself, Petty was of unprepossessing appearance: physically weak, of extremely short stature, and so short-sighted as to be almost blind. Upon leaving La Flèche at the age of eighteen, he set out for Paris, determined to fulfil his overweening – but as yet unfocused – ambitions. Here he quickly fell on such hard times 'that he lived a weeke on two penniworth... of Walnutts'. His luck changed when he met the exiled William Hobbes, who was so delighted with his company that he introduced him to Descartes and Father Mersenne.

Petty then travelled to Holland, where he briefly studied medicine at the University of Leiden, then the most advanced medical school in northern Europe. After this he returned to England, where he presented himself at Oxford with such self-confidence that he managed to become a don at Brasenose College, where he taught anatomy (an unusual choice of subject for one so short-sighted). It was here that he participated in a miraculous act that would appear to be another of his characteristic exaggerations, had it not been observed by a multitude of witnesses.

A twenty-two-year-old servant girl named Anne Greene had been seduced by the seventeen-year-old son of her master: She was not aware of her pregnancy until she miscarried in the privy after seventeen weeks, whereupon she tried to hide the remains of the foetus but was discovered, charged with infanticide and sentenced to be hanged on 14 December 1650. At her own request, several of her friends yanked on her swinging legs, and a soldier struck her several times with the butt of his musket to expedite her death and 'dispatch her out of her paine'. Anne Greene's body was then cut down from the scaffold and given to Petty for anatomical research.

The next day, when Petty was about to begin dissecting Greene's body, he discovered that it still had a slight pulse. He and some colleagues immediately set about attempting to revive her using a variety of techniques, ranging from ancient bloodletting with leeches to the most modern European practice that involved 'heating odoriferous Clyster to be cast up in her body, to give heat and warmth to her bowels'. (Petty had presumably learned at Leiden of this European innovation, which involved 'an insufflation of tobacco smoke into the rectum by enema'.) After fourteen hours of such treatment, Anne Greene staged an unlikely recovery, whereupon she was pardoned and set free.

This widely broadcast 'miracle' established Petty as one of the leading physicians in the country. He was now just twenty-seven years old, and the world lay open before him. Petty soon left for London, where he met such medical luminaries as William Harvey – whose discovery of the circulation of the blood would have a formative effect on Petty's economic ideas. At the same time, Petty also managed to talk his way into a prestigious and well-remunerated professorship of music at Gresham College, without any apparent qualification. But Petty had set his sights on higher things. Despite his reputation as a bumptious and somewhat unpleasant man he managed to ingratiate himself with none less than Oliver Cromwell, who was on the point of becoming Lord Protector of the Commonwealth of England, Scotland and Ireland following the execution of Charles I.*

At the time when Petty encountered Cromwell, the Puritan leader was conducting a vicious military campaign to subdue Catholic Ireland, which was regarded as the back door to England for any Catholic European invader. Petty managed to convince Cromwell to appoint him as chief physician to his army in Ireland. Following Cromwell's victory, Petty saw to it that he was appointed by Cromwell to conduct a land survey of Ireland. This had a similar aim to the Domesday Book, which William the

---

* England had, and still has, no written constitution. Instead it has a body of laws, passed by parliament and approved by the monarch, which evolves a constitutional rule according to precedent. In the absence of a monarch, after the execution of Charles I, England entered a constitutionally unprecedented era. Oliver Cromwell was chosen by parliament to become Lord Protector in 1653, meaning he was head of state (i.e. with the powers of a monarch) and at the same time leader of the government, as well as being a principal commander of the New Model Army, the Protestant force which had defeated the Royalists in the Civil War. As a Protestant, Cromwell was opposed to Catholics; yet he also refused to recognize some Protestants such as Quakers and other 'dissenters' who would not join the Church of England. At the same time, the Church of England was 'purified' of all supposed Catholic influence, including monastic orders as well as idolatry in the form of statues and religious art in churches. Thus the Puritan Oliver Cromwell effectively held the power of a monarch, chief minister of the government, religious leader – and, most significantly, head of the army. In other words, he held the power of a supreme dictator. The Commonwealth ended after the death of Cromwell, when parliament invited Charles II to return as king, and the country once again reverted to a constitutional monarchy. Consequently, it became a tradition amongst the landed gentry for the first son to inherit the family estates, the second son to purchase a commission in the army (or the navy), the third son to become a lawyer, and the fourth son to enter the Church of England. This was intended to ensure that the landed gentry were represented in all institutions of power, and that the country could never again be vulnerable to a military or religious coup establishing a dictatorship.

Conqueror had commissioned for England after the Norman Conquest in 1066. All properties, estates, possessions and inhabitants throughout the land were to be surveyed and accounted for. Indeed, this assessment of the entire economic structure and extent of Ireland can be seen as the epitome of the then current term for economics: 'political economy'.

Despite having no previous cartographic expertise, Petty managed to complete this mammoth task in just over a year (1655–6). His efficiency and motivation appear to have been encouraged by the opportunity he took to claim for himself the many deserted estates from which their Catholic owners had fled. According to Aubrey, by the end of his survey Petty could 'from Mount Mangorton in the county of Kerry behold 50,000 acres of his own land. He hath an estate in every province in Ireland.'

Naturally, this won Petty few friends in Ireland. At one point he was challenged to a duel by Sir Hierome Sanchey, a 'ruthless' cavalry commander in Cromwell's army who was 'noted for his bravery'. Petty's response was precise and characteristic. Owing to his near-blindness and shortness of stature, he knew that he had no hope of winning any such duel, yet he also realized that to refuse such a challenge would leave him open to public mockery and probably end his chances of any official appointment. So Petty decided to exercise his right, as the recipient of the challenge, to name both its place and the weapons to be used. He chose 'a darke Cellar, and the weapon to be a great Carpenter's Axe'. This reduced the entire proceedings to a farce, and Sanchey withdrew in disgust.

However, it was during this most ignominious and unscrupulous period of his life that William Petty was able to develop the original ideas for which he remains known to this day. Amongst his many actual (rather than claimed) accomplishments, he is known to have read and absorbed the works of Sir Francis Bacon, with their insistence that all science must be based upon empirical evidence. Petty's meticulous and comprehensive survey of Ireland led him to develop an ad hoc but undeniably empirical theory of political economy. Indicatively, he chose to refer to his method as 'Political Arithmetick' – for, like Galileo, he understood that 'mathematics is the language in which God has written the universe'.

Not for nothing is Petty considered by many as 'the true father of economics'. Here was an ambition and originality typical of the Age of Reason: an attempt to organize a new field of human thought on a comprehensive scale such as had never before been attempted. Petty's combination of experience and scientific measure is in many ways utterly modern. Despite the flaws and oversights in his thought, here we can recognize the beginnings of a new science. However, as the subject matter of this new science was nothing less than humanity itself, it is understandable that early simplifications could often appear clumsy or even brutal.

Petty's experience was gained from surveying Ireland and later running his large ill-gotten estates. And as such he often describes his motives in the bluntest manner:

> To express myself in Terms of Number, Weight or Measure; to use only Arguments of Sense [i.e. Reason], and to consider only such Causes, as have Visible Foundations in Nature; leaving those that depend upon the mutable Minds, Opinions, Appetites and Passions of particular Men, to the Consideration of others.

This was to be pursued as a science, rather than as a moral endeavour. And as such, Petty's prescriptions bear an unpleasant similarity to Machiavelli's notorious political treatise *The Prince*, and its ruthless advice on how to achieve, and maintain, political power – regardless of all morality or principle. But in Petty's case, instead of realpolitik we have what might be termed 'realeconomik'. What Petty described was how the world works, not how we would like it to work (though he was not above inserting his own original rational insights). However, as already noted, the use of reason frequently overlooks the human, or humane, element – from Descartes's forays into vivisection to the establishment of the Amsterdam Stock Exchange and the crashes that followed in its wake.*

---

* Two centuries later, the Scottish writer Charles Mackay would document such outbreaks of collective unreason in his perceptively titled work *Extraordinary Popular Delusions and the Madness of Crowds*.

Petty's survey of Ireland would inspire many of his most original economic ideas. From the outset, he viewed the economy in a similar way to Harvey's description of how the heart accounts for the circulation of the blood, though he applied this medical analogy in heartless fashion: 'As Students of Medicine practice their inquiries upon cheap and common Animals... I have chosen Ireland as such a Political Animal.'

However, beneath such egregious racism Petty was laying the foundations of modern economic thought (and this over a century before Adam Smith, who is generally recognized as the father of economics). Petty set out 'to make a Par and Equation between Lands and Labour so as to express the value of any thing by either alone'. He did this by calculating the value of labour in the same way as had traditionally been used to calculate the value of land. Just as land was valued at twenty times the value of what it produced each year, so a labourer should be valued at twenty times his annual income. It was thus possible to calculate the loss to a nation of the deaths of its working inhabitants – especially during war or plague. In the same way, the fields, farms and towns of a nation could now be reduced to a common figure: their monetary value.

Here lay the true yardstick. The value of money was not anything intrinsic; it lay in what it could purchase or be exchanged for. Money was the blood which circulated through the economic body.

Extending his medical metaphor still further, Petty pointed out that it was essential for the blood to circulate through every limb of the body politic if the nation were to remain healthy. This led him to several radical suggestions. If unemployment resulted in labourers being reduced to idleness, no money circulated through this part of the economy, which simply atrophied. For the public good, it was necessary to hire unemployed labourers on public work projects – or indeed even in fruitless tasks – so long as they earned money and spent it, keeping the currency flowing through all parts of the nation. (The wisdom of this idea would not be fully realized until the advent of John Maynard Keynes in the twentieth century.)

In pursuit of such thought, Petty came up with all manner of central ideas way ahead of his time. In the previous outline of his thinking it is not difficult to discern the notion of gross domestic product, and how the economy could be controlled by the quantity theory of money (as would be championed by another twentieth-century economist, Milton Friedman).

However, it must be admitted that not all Petty's ideas were entirely selfless. A central plank of his economic argument was that landowners were unfairly overtaxed; and indeed owners of vast estates (such as himself) were vastly overtaxed. Why? Petty argued that such taxation belonged to a bygone era, when feudal lords pledged their allegiance to the king, paid taxes to him, and were duty-bound to raise an army from amongst their serfs in times of conflict. But now there was no king, and instead estates should be recognized as economic enterprises within the nation-state.

This meant that landowners ought not to be taxed according to the acreage of their land, but rather their tax burden should be balanced against the income gained from their estates. (It is worth noting here that much of Petty's commandeered property consisted of barren mountainsides and unproductive bogland.)

Petty may have chosen to omit his personal interest in such an idea, but he could not resist pointing out the revolutionary implications that could be drawn from his understanding of monetary policy. If money was the measure of society, then money could be used to control that society. What was the need for government, when money could be used as the instrument for running the country?

Here Petty's Machiavellian streak came to the fore. If a country could be controlled by money, it had no need of a monarchy, religion, or even many departments of government. Money could exercise power, it could be used to promote moral qualities, and it could certainly make the body politic not only healthier and happier, but also more prosperous.

Fortunately, few paid any attention to these subversive ideas buried deep in Petty's texts; either that, or they simply did not understand the implications of what he was talking about. Ironically, if Petty had been given credit where credit was due, he would certainly have ended up in the Tower of London on a charge of high treason, where his ultimate fate was unlikely to have been so fortunate as the miraculous outcome of his patient Anne Greene.

On the other hand, Petty's ability to survive the political vicissitudes of his age is almost as astonishing as his customary behaviour. Despite his services to Cromwell, Petty somehow managed to survive the fall of the Commonwealth. Following the Restoration and the coronation of Charles II, he achieved the remarkable feat of ingratiating himself with the new order, and even thriving under its auspices. (This, at a time when vengeance was the order of the day, with many of the regicides who had signed and sealed Charles I's death warrant being hunted down and executed. Those who had already died had their cadavers exhumed and were 'posthumously executed', i.e. beheaded, or hung, drawn and quartered.)

Petty's switching of allegiance was accomplished with such success that in 1661 he was even knighted by Charles II. Whereupon he returned to Ireland to live out his days on his vast ill-gotten estates. Despite his unscrupulous self-serving and generally offensive demeanour, contemporaries described him as 'humorous, good-natured and rational'. Such an opinion would seem to be a fair reflection of the tenor of the Age of Reason.

CHAPTER 8

TWO ARTISTS OF THE DUTCH GOLDEN AGE

S UCH ADVANCES IN FINANCE and political economy marked the extension of reason into new spheres of life that had begun to evolve after
the Renaissance. Such reason (and bouts of unreason) were all part of
a new social self-understanding. And the riches accumulated by these
evolving enterprises resulted in the emergence of a modern middle
class. Here, symbols of status and mannerly behaviour were often more
significant indicators of social standing than mere money. This new class
consisted of burgers, bourgeois, burgesses, merchants, and businessmen
involved in all kinds of new manufacture, from lens-grinding to clock-
making. There was money to spare, and this was spent on all manner
of adornments and luxuries, including clothing, jewellery, spices and the
like. But homes needed something more than mere furniture, carpets and
spiced food; they required something to indicate the aspirant taste of the
owner, something to set the seal on their personality. It was here – amidst
the blossoming of this new self-confident individuality – that secular
domestic art came into its own.

Amidst the emergent democratic society of the Netherlands, artists began to flourish as never before. They still remained subservient to their sponsors when it came to fulfilling commissions – subjects were chosen for them, their very realization often dictated to a constricting degree. The scene was to be religious, domestic, a landscape or a portrait, but the artists soon developed their own way of interpreting their masters' wishes. Artists also developed an individuality of style, and this became typified by the word 'baroque'.* This ornate, often extravagant style very much reflected a new self-confidence within the artists themselves, as well as their masters. Of all the Dutch and Flemish artists who typified this style, two stand out – both in their immediately recognizable idiosyncratic interpretations, and the new self-understanding with which they imbued their art.

We have already come across Rubens, who so dazzled Velázquez when he arrived amidst all his pomp at the Spanish royal court. By that time, Rubens had become a larger-than-life figure whose interests extended far beyond his role as an artist – diplomat, adviser to royalty, businessman in charge of a factory of artists who produced his works on an almost industrial scale… There seemed to be no end to his talents and activities.

Peter Paul Rubens was born in June 1577 in the German city of Siegen in Westphalia, where his Calvinist parents Jan and Maria had

---

* The baroque characterized a widespread outlook in European life of the period. Its influence extended far beyond painting, permeating the entire culture of this era, and can be seen in every sphere from music to architecture, from poetry to sculpture. Its flamboyant attitude appealed to Catholic tastes, and became prevalent during the Counter-Reformation. However, the baroque was not exclusively a Catholic phenomenon. Where the Catholic baroque tended to expand into visually impressive imagery intended to evoke emotions and wonder in the audience or viewer, the Protestant baroque was inclined to imbue its subject matter with the creator's personal emotions. Whereas finance and the development of political economy had reflected the material evolution of society, it was art that mirrored its psychological (or spiritual) evolution. As for explanations of the etymology of the word 'baroque', these are as complex and varied as its many manifestations. One possible explanation suggests that the word is derived from *baroco*, a mnemonic for a complex variety of Aristotelian syllogism.

fled from their home in Antwerp in the Spanish Netherlands to escape Catholic persecution. Jan was a magistrate, descended from a locally important family, and there are indications that Maria was a woman of some education. She was able to speak and write Latin, an accomplishment unusual in women of all but the highest families. In Siegen, Jan became legal adviser to Anna of Saxony, wife of the ruler William I of Orange. Jan became the lover of Anna of Saxony, and fathered a daughter with her in 1571. Consequently, Jan was imprisoned, but his wife stuck by him, and gave birth to Peter Paul and other children after Jan's release. (When Jan died some years later, she composed the Latin epitaph for his gravestone, which included the information that his wife had borne seven children 'all by him'.)

When Peter Paul was twelve, his mother and the family returned to Antwerp, where he was brought up a Catholic. Little wonder, with such a background, that the young Rubens developed a complex personality. In Antwerp he briefly continued with his humanist education, reading classical works and learning Latin at the local academy. But money was tight, and at fourteen he became a page at the court of a local aristocrat. He only remained there for a year, but the court's atmosphere would leave a lasting impression on the observant teenager. Manners and good presentation were essential if one wished to be accepted. Yet in order to succeed, this could be no empty display; talent, culture and learning played an even greater role in gaining the respect of one's peers. Rubens would never forget these early lessons. (It seems likely that these social graces may have been impressed upon him by a father figure in the form of a sympathetic chamberlain at the court.)

After his spell as a page, Rubens made a vital life decision. Despite his mother's disapproval he became apprenticed at a local artist's studio. There was a thriving artists' community in Antwerp, and during his apprenticeship Rubens moved from one studio to another, thus exposing himself to a variety of artistic styles. From one artist he learned of the woodcuts of Hans Holbein, by another he was instructed in landscapes, but he finally ended up at the studio of Otto van Veen, a talented court painter who had studied Renaissance art in Italy. Rubens spent four years at his studio, finally graduating and being admitted to the guild of local painters at the age of twenty-one. By this time he had already painted his *Portrait of a Man* (1597), depicting a pensive youthful figure in a white ruff, who is holding a pair of dividers and a closed gold watch between the ink-stained nails of his hands. The man's stylish clothes and ruff indicate that he is a professional, the dividers suggest measurement, the dirty nails come from drawing up plans in pen and ink, and it is thus usually assumed that the sitter was an architect. The gold watch was a common memento mori.

This is a fine, but not exceptional work. With hindsight, we can see that Rubens's talent needed exposure to greater artists, who would spur his ambition, goading his competitive streak, and teach him the full range of what could be achieved with oil paint. And just three years later, Rubens set out south across the Alps to Italy.

His first sight of Venice was a revelation. The Mediterranean light shimmering on the milky-blue waters of the canals, the bustling traffic of gondolas, the sheer novelty and extravagance of the city's palazzos and churches. Van Veen had given Rubens a letter of introduction to Vincenzo I Gonzaga, Duke of Mantua, who was sufficiently impressed to take on the twenty-three-year-old artist as a court painter. Gonzaga was a connoisseur of art and took a personal liking to Rubens. He made it his business to escort his new painter through his gallery of paintings, indicating the subtlety of their techniques and effects, the various tricks of light and perspective they employed, and the sheer daring and novelty of Renaissance art. Thus Rubens was exposed to Titian, Veronese, Tintoretto and other Venetian painters. Better still, Rubens's new master allowed him to extend his technique by painting copies of some of these works.

The thirty-eight-year-old Gonzaga was very much a Renaissance man, and his court entertained such luminaries as the poet Torquato Tasso, the finest poet in Italy at the time; the astronomer Giovanni Magini, who was tutor to the duke's two sons, and even Galileo Galilei, who would have been appointed to a court position if he had asked for less money. But the duke also had a dark side. As a young man he had murdered one of his father's courtiers, a brilliant young Scottish scholar, in a dispute over a woman. Whether or not Rubens knew of this dark secret, the portrait he painted of his friend and mentor the duke certainly depicts a powerful character capable of such an act.

Later that year, Gonzaga despatched Rubens to Rome, by way of Florence. Rubens's brief was to paint precise copies of the great works of art he saw on this trip, so that his master could add them to his own collection. This journey enabled Rubens to study at first hand masterpieces by leading Renaissance artists such as Michelangelo and Leonardo da Vinci. He was particularly intrigued by Michelangelo's mannerist style, which gave his paintings the sculptural aspect that he exploited to the full in many of the figures adorning the ceiling of the Sistine Chapel. Rubens was also able to study the remarkable statue *Laocoön and His Sons*, the finest extant work of the Roman classical era, which had been unearthed in a Roman vineyard in 1506.

This sculpture depicts the muscular naked figure of Laocoön (a Trojan priest) together with his sons, who are being attacked by two large serpents encircling their bodies as they writhe and struggle to free themselves from the lethal entanglement. It was tellingly described by the Renaissance writer Pietro Aretino: 'the two serpents, in attacking the three figures, produce the most striking semblances of fear, suffering and death. The youth embraced in the coils is fearful; the old man struck by the fangs is in torment; the child who has received the poison, dies.' This is a work of immense three-dimensional complexity, and the pain-contorted expressions of the three faces have led to it being described as 'the prototypical icon of human agony'. Rubens made a detailed drawing of this work, absorbing techniques which would have an indelible effect on his later style.

Word had begun to spread of the young artist's remarkable talent, and it was now that Rubens received his first major commission. This was from Albert, the Habsburg ruler of Rubens's native Spanish Netherlands, and was for a panel depicting the Mocking of Christ in the Roman church of Santa Croce in Gerusalemme. In this work Rubens demonstrated both the facial expressions he had absorbed from *Laocoön* and dramatic chiaroscuro effects he had learned from various Roman works by Caravaggio. There is no doubting the mastery and mystery of this complex and shadowy first commission, yet it also shows how the heady influences which informed this work had not yet been fully absorbed by Rubens. He remained overwhelmed by what he had seen and learned.

In 1603, Gonzaga sent Rubens on a diplomatic mission to Spain to deliver a number of paintings as a gift to the Spanish monarch Philip III.[*] This mission had all the makings of a disaster. During the thousand-mile journey from Mantua across the Alps, southern France and the Pyrenees to the northern Spanish city of Valladolid (then the current location of the royal court), Rubens's party encountered a number of fierce storms. This had the effect of badly damaging some of the paintings they were transporting, and entirely destroying others. Then, on arrival in Valladolid, Rubens found that Philip III was away. Rubens took this absence as an opportunity to try to restore some of the damaged paintings, overpainting them with his own memory of their original appearance. The paintings that had been destroyed beyond repair he simply substituted with works of his own. The king's first minister, the Duke of Lerma, was so impressed with the speed and facility with which Rubens reworked the mutilated paintings that he gave Rubens a generous commission to paint a portrait of him on horseback.

This work is remarkable from a number of aspects. It was Rubens's first portrait on horseback, and is unmistakably modelled on Titian's 1548 *Equestrian Portrait of Charles V*, which was in the Spanish royal collection.[†] At the same time, the radiant cloud effect behind the mounted figure of the Duke of Lerma bears an uncanny resemblance to that found in El Greco. Both of these influences he can only have seen for the first time on his visit to Spain. When Rubens learned, he learned fast. And it was now, at the age of twenty-six, that all the many and varied styles he had encountered – and copied – began to coalesce into

---

[*] This was Rubens's first diplomatic mission, and should not be mistaken for his mission to Madrid in 1628 which so impressed the young Velázquez.

[†] Charles V was Holy Roman Emperor, and also King of Spain.

Rubens's early mature style. (This was but the beginning of an evolution that would continue in various forms throughout his long career.)

After his mission to Spain, Rubens returned to Italy. Four years later, he learned that his mother was ill and hastened back to Antwerp; but she had died before he could reach home. The following year, at the age of thirty-two, Rubens married Isabelle Brant, the daughter of a leading citizen of Antwerp. That same year, Rubens painted a double portrait of himself and his young bride. The self-image he presents is of a young gentleman in fashionable attire, including striking saffron-coloured stockings. Isabella is seated beside him, in equally fashionable but only slightly more subdued clothing. The way her right hand is lightly placed on his, and the way their bodies are inclined towards one another, suggests a loving couple.

Despite being a major port, Antwerp is situated some fifty miles up the Schelde estuary. This had been blockaded for some years by the Dutch fleet, restricting the port's sea trade. But in 1609 a truce was signed between the Protestant Dutch Republic in the north and the Habsburg-controlled Spanish Netherlands in the south. This opened up the city once more, and Antwerp soon returned to its former prosperity. Albert, the Habsburg ruler of the Spanish Netherlands, now gave Rubens another commission, which was the most important he had yet received. He was to paint a large-scale work to commemorate the truce, which would be hung on the vast wall of the Statenkamer (State Chamber) where the treaty itself was signed.

Rubens's painting portrays the Adoration of the Magi – deemed a suitable subject to symbolize the reconciliation between the two sides. He succeeds in making this scene highly complex in its realization, yet immediately simple in its subject – a remarkable feat. On the left is the focus of attention: Mary and the infant Jesus. The three wise men (the Magi) are depicted along with a large number of background figures. The Magi stand out, but the host of background figures each somehow achieve their own originality amongst the muted chiaroscuro of the overall scene. This is, if anything, a summary of all that Rubens had learned during his years in Italy, as well as being an expert demonstration of how he had absorbed these influences and made them his own.

An indication of Rubens's new status in his home country can be seen in the fact that he was appointed court painter to the governor Albert VII, Archduke of Austria, yet allowed to go on living in his native Antwerp – despite the fact that the imperial court was some twenty-five miles south, in Brussels. Rubens was also granted exceptional permission to accept commissions from other patrons, which considerably added to his income.

Rubens was quick to capitalize on his newfound status and wealth. He designed a superb baroque villa for himself in the centre of Antwerp (now known as the Rubenshuis, it can still be visited). This was set amidst a fine garden, and also included a large library that reflected the artist's widespread reading. Besides being a superb artist, Rubens prided himself on being a sophisticated man of considerable culture. He was an avid reader, who according to the twentieth-century art critic E. H. Gombrich 'exchanged ideas with the leading scholars of his age'. Many of these he would meet during the course of his travels as a diplomat.

The days of a Renaissance man such as Leonardo da Vinci had passed; science and art had now diverged too widely. However, it was still possible for an exceptional man to combine deep learning, courtly talents and artistic genius. Rubens was just such a man. Though, unlike the Renaissance incarnations, who had a tendency to be solitary or scholarly, Rubens inclined more towards an extrovert public personality, and was sufficiently versed in the ways of the world to involve himself in the political diplomacy of the day. It is difficult to imagine a Leonardo, or certainly a Caravaggio, taking up public office. Rubens was one of a new breed of men, gifted with both public and private talents, who emerged fleetingly in the Age of Reason and have appeared seldom since.*

---

* Benjamin Franklin, who was an original scientist and inventor as well as being an active statesman, and Thomas Jefferson, who was a gifted architect and philosopher as well as becoming the third president of the United States, both fall into this category. In the twentieth century, Ignacy Jan Paderewski, the concert pianist of international renown who ended up becoming prime minister of Poland, is another rare example of this exceptional type.

The Rubenshuis also had an extensive studio attached, which Rubens soon began filling with talented young artists who sought to become his apprentices. From now on, many of Rubens's paintings were completed with the help of his apprentices, and in time he would have more than twenty skilled assistants working there. Like Rubens himself, they had to learn to paint quickly, skilfully, and strictly within the parameters of his style. Despite such restrictions, Rubens was unusually generous, in that he often described these works as collaborations, naming the assistant who had helped him most. Amongst his collaborators and apprentices were some of the finest artists of the coming generation. Most notable of these was Anthony van Dyck, who would go on to achieve fame as court painter to Charles I in England.

Amazingly, despite the vast output of Rubens's studio, he also found time to undertake a series of diplomatic missions. These took him all over Europe – from London to Madrid, from Paris to Rome. Many at the courts he visited snobbishly regarded him as little better than a tradesman, because he worked with his hands and did not live the life of leisure expected of a gentleman. Others of more discernment looked upon Rubens as the exceptional man he was: an accomplished diplomat and man of culture, and one of the finest artists in Europe.

While in Paris in 1622, Rubens was befriended by the powerful Marie de' Medici, the widow of King Henry IV of France. Marie was a difficult woman, much given to meddling in French politics, and had become Regent of France during the childhood of her son Louis. However, when he came of age she had high-handedly refused to hand over power. In 1617 she was placed under house arrest at the Château de Blois, from which she managed to escape down a rope ladder thrown over the walls. Whereupon she instigated an uprising against her son, now King Louis XIII.

Despite Marie's faults (and they were many, especially in her choice of advisers, lovers and her ability to make enemies), Marie de' Medici had inherited the exceptional artistic taste of the ancestors who had come to rule Florence during the Renaissance. Over the years she would hire many fine artists, but it was to Rubens that she entrusted the major commission of her life. This was intended to be nothing less than a supreme glorification of her life and family, and would consist of some twenty-one paintings to adorn the walls of the large gallery in the Luxembourg Palace.

Regardless of the somewhat severe constrictions of this commission, it would inspire Rubens to create some of his finest work. One of the paintings in this series, entitled *Reconciliation of Mother and Son*, may feature an imaginary scene depicting an apotheosis of wish fulfilment on Marie's behalf, yet its sheer artistic power is unmistakable. Amidst the swirling robes and clutched lightning, as the figure of Divine Justice slays the multi-headed hydra of conflict, we see the forgiving features of Louis looking down at his mother. The painting diplomatically defuses the actual circumstances of the conflict by placing the reconciliation in a mythological setting. It also depicts a suitably uplifted Marie, viewed from an angle which deftly softens her portly middle-aged figure and fading charms as she gazes lovingly up at her son.

During his later years, Rubens became more adept than ever at painting fleshy nudes that in fact depicted a more realistic version of the northern European women of the period than had hitherto been the case. These were not the sylph-like angels of the Italian Renaissance; they were solid, secular, Dutch and utterly real. Rubens's uncanny ability to depict plump, spilling naked flesh, in all its visceral glory, would inspire his great successor Rembrandt, as well as a string of gifted artists throughout the ensuing centuries. Most recently, Francis Bacon and Lucien Freud both had their own take on Rubens's ability to render human flesh – the very substance of what we are.

In his later years, Rubens suffered increasingly from the painful gout which would contribute to his death at the age of sixty-two. During his final year, despite the crippling pain and physical limitations imposed by his illness, he managed to complete a final self-portrait. Here, the former larger-than-life figure gives himself a solemn, somewhat sad dignity. Just months later he would be buried beneath an epitaph which proclaimed that he 'deserved to be called Apelles for all time, who made a pathway to the friendship of kings and princes'.*

Just as Rubens had a supreme penchant for conveying in visceral actuality the mortal garment which we all inhabit, his successor Rembrandt enables us to see beneath the skin of the characters he depicts, glimpsing their very soul – or so it seems. And the character he most frequently subjected to this introspective interrogation would be none other than himself. Time after time we see Rembrandt's face staring back at us: from the self-confidence of his proud young manhood, through the varied stages of his long life, to the humiliated blemished features and chilling self-realization of his final years.

Rembrandt van Rijn was born in Leiden in the Dutch Republic in 1606. His father was a miller, his mother the daughter of a baker – both from moderately prosperous families. Though his father was a Protestant and his mother a Catholic, there appears to have been no religious conflict at home – merely the nurturing of a deep Christian faith, which remained an integral part of his psychology to the end of his days.

Having been educated in Latin, Rembrandt entered the University of Leiden at the age of thirteen, but his obsession with painting meant that he soon left to become an apprentice in the studio of Jacob van Swanenburg, a local historical painter who had spent much of his early life working in Italy. Like Rubens, Rembrandt then passed through several artists' studios, absorbing the different styles prevalent in each, and ending up at a studio in Amsterdam. Yet unlike Rubens, Rembrandt did not then leave for Italy. Indeed, he would remain for the rest of his life within the confines of the Dutch Republic. And this would be no limiting experience; at the time the Dutch Republic was in the process

---

* Apelles of Kos who lived during the fourth century BC, had long been regarded as the finest artist of the ancient world, and as such he took on legendary status during the Renaissance and its enthusiasm for all things classical. However, as the twentieth-century English art critic Percy Gardner put it, 'Fewer things are more hopeless than the attempt to realise the style of a painter whose works have vanished.'

of becoming one of the most cosmopolitan nations on earth. The VOC was establishing a global empire, making citizens of the Dutch Republic cognizant with countries around the world, its cities displaying materials and even inhabitants of many far-flung lands.*

Rembrandt was something of a prodigy. In 1624, at the age of just eighteen, he set up a studio in Leiden with his seventeen-year-old friend and fellow artist Jan Lievens, which soon began attracting apprentices. By now Rembrandt had developed a penchant for painting aged scholars, biblical scenes, and portraits that according to contemporary sources bore an uncanny likeness to their sitter. He also developed a considerable skill in prints and etchings, many of which made original use of the contrast between light and darkness. This was something more than the sensational chiaroscuro pioneered by Caravaggio; in Rembrandt's hands the contrast between dark and light took on a more profound, spiritual aspect.

Rembrandt's first big break would come in 1629, when he was 'discovered' by the polymath secretary to the Prince of Orange, Constantijn Huygens, the well-connected father of the great scientist Christiaan Huygens. Consequently, Rembrandt soon began receiving commissions from the current ruler of the Dutch Republic, the stadtholder Frederick Henry, Prince of Orange. In 1632, Rembrandt returned to Amsterdam, and it was here that he painted the work which made his name: *The Anatomy Lesson of Dr Nicolaes Tulp*. This is a superb group portrait of eight members of the Amsterdam Guild of Surgeons. Astonishingly, it was Rembrandt's first large group portrait – a notoriously difficult genre that required the artist not only to paint accomplished likenesses of the figures portrayed, but also somehow to focus them into a group. Rembrandt achieves this by depicting Dr Tulp demonstrating the anatomical detail of a partly dissected corpse, with his fellow guild members craning forward, intent on what he is saying and doing. Yet this is so much more than a well-achieved group portrait, with the intent faces peering forward out

---

* In Rubens's *The Adoration of the Magi*, he follows the tradition that one of the three wise men, Caspar, was black. The artist also includes the face of what appears to be Caspar's small black child. Both of these faces have sufficient verisimilitude and character to suggest that they were painted from life.

of the gloomy background into the lighted foreground of the anatomy table; it is also a lesson in science. Dr Tulp is holding a set of forceps in his right hand. This is lifting the muscles of the dissected arm, showing how they make the fingers at the end of the arm curl – a movement he is illustrating with the fingers of his raised left hand. Such is the painting's realism and scientific understanding that we might be reminded of Descartes conducting his vivisections of various animals. Here is an archetypical artwork of the Age of Reason, and it was the work which made Rembrandt's name, winning him a succession of commissions from rich clients.

In 1634, Rembrandt married Saskia van Uylenburgh, the daughter of a well-connected and wealthy government administrator in the northern province of the Republic. The double portrait that Rembrandt painted of himself and his new bride is a romp of celebration. The seated Rembrandt turns towards the viewer with a triumphant expression, a large glass of wine held aloft in his right hand. His left hand is cupped around Saskia, who is sitting on his lap. Both are dressed in sumptuous attire. Rembrandt's wide black hat is tilted at a rakish angle, its large white feather spilling over his head. We can only see the back of Saskia's dress, but this is enough to suggest the intricacies of its fashionable bustle and flares. Unwittingly, according to some, Rembrandt is here demonstrating the first stage in the parable of his coming life. He even named the painting *The Prodigal Son in the Brothel*.

Rembrandt now began to live the high life, spending well beyond what had become his considerable means. In the year following his marriage to Saskia, he rented a large new house. To furnish it he took to visiting auctions, but soon became more interested in bidding for all manner of exotica that caught his fancy (even, on occasion, covertly bidding up the price of his own paintings). Two years later, he moved once more, this time into an extensive building known as the Sugar Refinery. This was large enough to house his family, and also had space for his prospering studio and his assistants. Amsterdam was thriving, and Rembrandt was intent on thriving with it. In the course of his many commissions, Rembrandt began using his wife Saskia as his model.

This was the late 1630s. Twenty years previously, the Amsterdam Exchange Bank (*Wisselbank*) had been founded – the first genuine central bank – which established the value of the guilder, maintaining the first-ever reserve currency. This not only helped finance VOC expeditions, but initially also maintained 100 per cent cash reserves to cover its loans. On top of this, it was backed by the City of Amsterdam. The currency was literally as safe as houses, and the VOC had by now established a monopoly on the trade of nutmeg, mace and cloves, which were selling at around fifteen times their cost price in Indonesia. Everyone had money to spare in Amsterdam, and the first tulip bulbs were beginning to appear on the market.

Despite Rembrandt's high living, he never lost his profound faith. As the years passed, he became increasingly immersed in the biblical stories of the Old Testament. According to the twentieth-century English art critic Kenneth Clark: 'His mind was steeped in the Bible – he knew every story by heart down to the minutest detail.' These stories became in many ways psychological reference points in his life. He wished to absorb and reproduce every story down to its most telling image, even going so far as to search out equivalents in his own life. When had he experienced anything like this? How had it affected him? And thus we must conclude that, even from the beginning, when he portrayed himself as the Prodigal Son he knew what he was doing. He sensed that such giddy good times could not last forever. The day would come when he would suffer a reversal of fortune.

Rembrandt's wish to depict and inhabit the details of the biblical stories that so influenced his self-understanding led to him making friends amongst the sizeable Jewish population of Amsterdam, who inhabited the Jodenbuurt (Jewish district). Rembrandt is said to have frequented the synagogues in his pursuit of further interpretations and details of biblical events, at the same time closely observing the faces of those who passed on this knowledge, and often reproducing them in his paintings. One of the finest amongst these is *Jacob Blessing the Sons of Joseph*, taken from the Book of Genesis, which depicts a family scene where the aged, dying Jacob – with Joseph and his wife at his bedside – lays his hands on his two grandsons, Ephraim and Manasseh. As the art critic Michael Kitson describes it: 'The mood is neither tragic nor tender, nor serene but what can only be called sublime.' Yet here is a moment whose repercussions would be legendary – according to tradition, Ephraim symbolizes the future coming of the Christian faith.

Rembrandt's paintings of biblical scenes, infused with both theological and spiritual knowledge, would become an ever-deepening element of his artistic life. In many ways, this can be seen as an outward manifestation of his own self-understanding. The other strand that persisted throughout his life and art came in the form of self-portraits. It is known that Rembrandt created over a hundred self-portraits during the course of his life – some drawings, many etchings, and as many as fifty full oil paintings. He was never good-looking in the generally accepted sense of the word, but there is no denying that he had an intriguing face. Or at least, so he made it appear in his self-portraits, as the ravages of time – from the high-living dandy of his youth to the near-despair of his old age – left their mark on his features. In knowing himself, he also came to know the characters of his biblical scenes, understanding their inner emotions, as well as being influenced by the appearance and habits of the Jews he befriended.

None of us are saints all the time – even those who appear in the stories of the Old Testament. And Rembrandt was only too aware of his failings. Indeed, despite his greatness and the profundity of his later work, we can still recognize that, despite his genius, 'you were silly like us'. And he knew it. From the carefree abandon of the Prodigal Son to the low cackling self-portrait of his approaching senility, he was never afraid of self-exposure. In life, he couldn't help himself from himself. It is the contrast of these human frailties with the chastened despair which arose from his suffering that made him and his art complete. As the English art critic John Berger put it when describing Rembrandt's final self-portraits: 'All has gone except a sense of the question of existence, of existence as a question'.

The tale of Rembrandt's actual life is in many ways an unedifying parable. After his initial fame, things still went well – at least for a while. In 1639, his commissions seemingly unaffected by the financial ravages of the Tulipmania bubble, he moved into a grand house in Sint Anthonisbreestraat, borrowing money to complete the sale. Here in 1641, after having a number of children who died in infancy, Saskia bore him a son, Titus. At the same time, Rembrandt was commissioned for a vast group portrait, which has come to be known as *The Night Watch*, for which he was paid the unheard-of sum of 1,600 guilders – with each figure depicted contributing on average 100 guilders, dependent upon his prominence in the painting.

Even in its modern 'cleaned' version, this is still a dark painting – though it is meant to be of a daylight scene, despite its name. According to Kitson: 'The group portrait is here transformed into an action picture: a work of dazzling inventiveness and splendour or, as some nineteenth-century critics maintained, a wildly over-inflated view of a very ordinary event.'

According to a persistent legend, this work was so dark that the commissioners were outraged at Rembrandt's idiosyncratic interpretation of his brief. More recent research suggests that this was not the case. Either way, this work marked a tipping point in his life and career.

In 1642, Saskia died. Rembrandt's debts caught up with him. At the same time, the demand for large lucrative group portraits ceased. Even his portraits were now regarded as old-fashioned. A nurse called Geertje Dircx was hired to look after Titus. Rembrandt had an affair with her which broke up acrimoniously. She took him to court for 'breach of promise' because he wouldn't marry her; Rembrandt was ordered to pay her a small regular income. Later he discovered that she had stolen and pawned Saskia's jewellery, and he sought to have Dircx committed to the poorhouse.

As if things weren't bad enough, he then had an affair with his maidservant, Hendrickje Stoffels. From her many moving appearances as a model in his paintings, it appears that he loved her. But he couldn't, or wouldn't, marry her – this would have cut him off from access to the trust set up for Titus by Saskia's family. And so it went on… Rembrandt's profligate spending landed him further in debt, and he was forced to sell the house (which he hadn't even yet paid for) at a highly reduced price.

Hendrickje died in 1663. Rembrandt's painting remained out of fashion, and even when he completed one of his rare lucrative commissions, this was rejected. In 1668 Titus died at the age of twenty-six. But, despite Rembrandt's impoverishment, his fame had spread. When Cosimo III de' Medici, Grand Duke of Tuscany, visited Amsterdam in 1667, he asked to meet Rembrandt. Two years later, aged sixty-three, Rembrandt died and was buried in a pauper's grave.

The Age of Reason had lost its finest artist; his life, but not his art, had been undermined by his inability to curb the irrational extravagances of his nature. Ironically, it was his self-understanding derived from these very failings which lent his art its transcendent realization of our humanity.

CHAPTER 9

THE SUN KING
AND VERSAILLES

THE DUTCH REPUBLIC AND England were now becoming driving forces in Europe, acquiring wealth and overseas colonies, as well as large mercantile and armed fleets. Nevertheless, they remained – territorially speaking – small nations at the northern periphery of the continent. Despite the ravages of the Thirty Years' War, Habsburg Austria – along with its German 'electorates' and other eastern European possessions – remained the main territorial power in central Europe, while its independent Spanish branch continued its slow decline. However, the largest, wealthiest and by far the most powerful nation in Europe was France. It was ruled by Louis XIV, the Sun King, so-called because the entire realm orbited about him. He would rule France for seventy-two years – the very embodiment of the divine right of kings. When he famously declared '*L'État, c'est moi*' ('I am the State') this was scarcely an exaggeration, although during the course of his reign he would be advised by a series of able first ministers.

Louis XIV established his residence and his court at the vast Palace of Versailles, some twelve miles south-west of Paris, thus establishing it as the nation's capital. The palace not only contained the royal household, but also extensive wings of lesser apartments inhabited by the leading aristocrats of France. This not only made them closely attendant upon the king's favour, but also restricted them from defying royal rule or hatching plots in their provincial estates. (In the light of France's centuries of disputed and divided royalty, and similarly disunited territories, this was not only a wise policy but a necessary one.)

The Palace of Versailles was, and remains, the largest royal residence in Europe. A few simple facts indicate its enormity. The palace itself has over 720,000 square feet of floor space, corridors and staircases. Despite this, living space was cramped, as the building – with its two long wings – had to house more than 10,000 people. These included the royal household, aristocrats and their families, government administrators, and servants. The architects had made no allowance for plumbing, so silver chamber pots were placed at intervals along the passages. Apart from in the royal suite there was no privacy in the use of lavatorial facilities, and of necessity all residents carried nosegays to numb their olfactory senses whenever indoors. (The Sun King was in the habit of holding audiences with chief adminis-trators or aristocrats while he sat astride his regal lavatory 'at stool'.)

The crowning glory of the palace is the Hall of Mirrors, a gallery which extends more than 200 feet along the first floor, overlooking the gardens. It contains no less than 357 mirrors, and during Louis XIV's reign it was furnished with solid silver chairs and tables. (At the time, the Venetians held a closely guarded monopoly on the making of mirrors, but Louis XIV's enterprising chief minister Jean-Baptiste Colbert found a way to circumvent this restriction.) The immediate gardens were laid out in strictly symmetrical patterns 'in the French style', and contained some 1,400 fountains and 400 sculptures. The outer walled hunting park extended over more than fifty square miles.

Louis XIV was born in 1638, and acceded to the throne at the age of four. A regency was established by his mother, the Habsburg Anne of Austria, who despite her name was Spanish, being a sister of Philip IV of Spain. Anne was aided in her regency by Cardinal Mazarin, who had served as a skilled chief minister to Louis XIV's father, Louis XIII, and continued in this role during the early years after Louis XIV took full powers. During the regency, Anne and Mazarin managed to overcome a civil war known as the Fronde, during which the feudal aristocracy attempted to reassert their traditional power against that of the centralized government.

In 1651, Louis XIV was adjudged to have come of age (at thirteen), and ascended to the throne in his own right. However, two years later, when he fell in love with Mazarin's niece Marie Mancini, his mother Anne put a stop to it. She had plans of her own, and ensured, in true Habsburg fashion, that her son instead married her niece Marie-Thérèse, a daughter of Philip IV of Spain, thus hoping to seal peace between the two countries.

In fact, such was the complexity of European politics at the time, precisely the opposite was the result. When Marie-Thérèse married Louis IV she was made to renounce her claim to any Spanish territory, and instead would be provided with a massive dowry of 500,000 écus. However, when Philip IV died five years later, this dowry remained unpaid. By now Louis XIV's mother was on her deathbed and the twenty-seven-year-old monarch had become more confident in his position. He thus decided to use this non-payment as an excuse to invade the Spanish Netherlands in what became known as the War of Devolution. This ensured that a large part of the Spanish Netherlands now 'devolved' into France.

One of the main aims of Louis XIV's rule became the further aggrandisement of France. This meant that during his long reign the country became involved in a series of costly wars, many of which extended the nation's borders to include new cities and provinces. These included Artois in the north and Roussillon in the south-east (both formerly Spanish). Further additions included Alsace (1675), Franche-Comté (1678) and Strasbourg (1681). Meanwhile France was in an almost continual state of war with England before, throughout and after the reign of Louis XIV, though much of this consisted of disputes over North American territory, especially in Canada. In between campaigns, Louis XIV never entirely disbanded his armies, instead employing many soldiers on extensive building, drainage and other projects at Versailles.

These wars placed an increasing burden on the nation's exchequer, resulting in the population having to bear ever-more oppressive increases in taxes. Thus, over the ensuing decades of his reign, the initially popular young monarch gradually transmogrified into a much-hated tyrant, a progenitor of the greatest revolution Europe had ever witnessed.*

Echoing the troubled times that saw the cultural flowering of Ancient Greece, as well as the remarkably similar constant city-state wars which provided the backdrop to the Italian Renaissance, Louis XIV's continuous expansive campaigns along France's borders coexisted with an unparalleled cultural efflorescence within France itself, especially (but not exclusively) at Versailles.

The king and his aristocrats vied with each other to patronize the arts at Versailles, a circumstance which naturally attracted all manner of ambitious artists, poets, intellectuals and performers. Cardinal Mazarin, for instance, is known to have accumulated a collection of some 500 paintings, which he housed at his private residence in Paris (now the Institut de France, home of the Académie Française).

Mazarin's favourite artist was Nicolas Poussin, who was born in 1594 amidst the northern French countryside of Normandy. Here he received an education in Latin, which led him to a deep appreciation of all things classical. This in turn inspired him to try to picture the scenes described in the works of the Ancient Roman poets. As a young man, he roamed the countryside 'busy without cease filling his sketchbooks with an infinite number of different figures which only his imagination could produce'.

---

* The French Revolution, which occurred some seventy-five years after the death of Louis XIV, would become increasingly inevitable. The political situation in France, epitomized by the absolute rule of the Sun King – who famously understood himself to be the very state itself – was so far beyond remedy that meaningful reform became impossible. His grandson Louis XV would recognize this with his perceptive admission of despair: 'Après moi, le déluge' (Loosely: 'When I am gone, all this will be swept away'). During the French Revolution, his son Louis XVI would be executed on the guillotine: the final nail in the coffin of the divine right of kings.

Poussin's sketches attracted the attention of the baroque artist Quentin Varin, who lived nearby. Poussin's parents forbade him from becoming an apprentice in Varin's studio, so at the age of eighteen Poussin ran away to Paris. Here his evident talent gained him access to a number of studios, but Poussin was temperamentally averse to such mass-produced collective art. He chose to work on his own, and at his own more measured pace. By shunning the studio system, which ensured entry into the painters' guild that maintained a monopoly on the profession, Poussin must have come close to starvation. Law court records indicate that he regularly incurred small debts he was unable to pay.

However, Poussin was lucky enough to become friends with Alexandre Courtois, the *valet de chambre* to the difficult Marie de' Medici, who was at the time Regent of France during the childhood of her son Louis XIII. Marie was a woman of renowned artistic taste, and Poussin's friendship with Courtois enabled him to gain access to the Royal Collection. Poussin became entranced by the restrained classical beauty of the Italian Renaissance artist Raphael, whose paintings he meticulously copied. When Marie's court poet Giambattista Marino saw Poussin's works, he was so impressed that he commissioned him to produce an extensive series of drawings illustrating classical poems by the first-century Roman poet Ovid.

After two unsuccessful attempts, Poussin finally managed to make it to Rome. Here he found that his love of classical restraint clashed with the fashionable excesses of the new baroque style. Despite this, he soon began to attract a regular succession of commissions. Most importantly, his works were highly admired by Cardinal Richelieu, who became long-term chief minister to Louis XIII and would later become mentor to his own successor, Cardinal Mazarin.

Poussin favoured classical and biblical scenes, which were rendered with severe rational restraint, even when they depicted scenes of violence such as the Rape of the Sabine Women. A simulacrum of violence is achieved by the dramatic poses and gestures of the figures, rather than sensational detail. His effect is thus theatrical, rather than brutal. As one modern critic has aptly observed: 'His work predominantly features clarity, logic, and order, and favours line over colour.' Likewise, the often-muted tones he uses to depict the facial features of his figures can be suggestive of an interiority, rather than a more blatant expression.

It was this very lack of indulgence that would prove so influential to his French artistic successors – such as the great artist of the revolutionary period Jacques-Louis David, and the formative impressionist Paul Cézanne. It is the latter, in particular, who appears to have understood the core of Poussin's classical intentions: 'Imagine how Poussin entirely redid nature, that is the classicism that I mean. What I don't accept is the classicism that limits you. I want that a visit to a master will help me find myself. Every time I leave a Poussin, I know better who I am.' Here was a reason and restraint which reflected in upon itself; an introspection whose rationality was a foil to the subjective unconscious irrationality of many of Rembrandt's portraits.

Yet the flourishing culture which grew up around the court at Versailles was not limited to art. Indeed, its finest ornaments were undoubtedly literary. With the advent of Racine and Molière, French drama achieved a prominence unmatched throughout Europe.

But first this must be put into context. The classical restraint and formalism of French drama was in many ways the embodiment of the Age of Reason. It eschewed any attempt at vulgar realism; the intention was to enact a wholly artificial performance. Even the acting was intentionally unreal. Such action as took place would come to a halt as the leading characters declaimed their lines to the audience, their words reinforced with traditional rhetorical gestures. There was no attempt to enact crass or unseemly behaviour. This accounts for why Shakespearian drama, during this period and for some centuries to come, was regarded by the French as little more than barbarism. Compared with the artificiality of French declamatory drama, it had no formal rules. For this reason, French drama was seen (by the French, the most civilized nation in Europe) as utterly superior to the realistic blunderings and ravings of their English counterparts.*

---

* Not until the early nineteenth century would Shakespeare achieve recognition in France. This was inspired by an event which took place on 11 September 1827, when the twenty-three-year-old French romantic composer Hector Berlioz attended a performance of *Hamlet* by a troupe of English players at the Odéon

The playwright we know by the stage name Molière was in fact born Jean-Baptiste Poquelin in 1622 in Paris. Such was his popularity as an actor, poet and especially playwright, along with the widely admired felicity of his style, that French would become known as 'the language of Molière'.

Prior to Molière, French was spoken in all manner of regional dialects, and in a wide variety of provincial usages. It was Molière's influence that helped it begin to coalesce into a necessary classic form, which could be officially used throughout the realm. (Some three centuries previously, the poet Dante had achieved a similar influence over Italian. By writing his *Divine Comedy* in the Tuscan dialect of Florence, he made this the universally recognized form of Italian.) However, the French passion for rationality gave 'the language of Molière' a double-edged effect. It formalized French, yet at the same time attempted to restrict it to a permanent standard, working against any natural evolution of the language and the introduction of modernisms and foreign words.*

---

theatre in Paris. Despite speaking no English, he was overcome by the drama being enacted on stage, and immediately fell in love with Irish actress Harriet Smithson, who was playing Ophelia. From that day on, he was inspired by two ambitions: to marry Harriet, and to compose music inspired by Shakespeare. Amongst Berlioz's works, his *Symphonie Fantastique* and *Roméo et Juliette* fall into the latter category. After years of ardent pursuit of Harriet – who spoke no French, while he still spoke no English – she was finally persuaded to marry him in 1833.

* The legacy of this attempt to maintain the 'purity' of the French language remains to this day. When new words from other languages start to appear in French, the Académie Française seeks to deter their public usage on signs, adverts and official documents, as well as in everyday speech – at the same time creating a French equivalent. For instance, instead of the English word 'email', the Académie coined a French equivalent, *courriel* (pronounced 'koo-ryehl') from an amalgamation of *courrier* (mail) and *electronique* (electronic). Other European languages have largely persisted in living form without such 'protection'. One of the many reasons why English has survived to become the 'world language' is that it has constantly been forced to absorb strong influences – both verbal and vocal – from North America, Australia, Africa, the Caribbean and elsewhere. These have obliged it to evolve constantly, discarding outmoded usages along the way, and thus remain a living adaptive means of communication. For example, the English generally spoken in England now, almost a quarter of the way through the twenty-first century, is already recognizable as different from that spoken even during the last decades of the previous century.

Molière came from a wealthy background and was educated at the college now known as the Lycée Louis-le-Grand, where many of his fellow pupils would have been the sons of aristocrats. Here he underwent a rigorous formal study of the classics; and, significantly, would also have taken part in enactments of ancient dramas. After this, his father purchased for him a post at the court of Louis XIII as *valet de chambre ordinaire et tapissier du Roi* (common valet and keeper of the royal carpets). Despite its somewhat humdrum title, this was little more than a sinecure which gained one social access to members of the royal household. His father wished to ensure him entry into prestigious circles, with the aim of eventually attaining high office.

But Molière had other plans. He had secretly fallen in love with the stage. In 1643, at the age of twenty-one, he abandoned his class along with all thought of a public career, and joined the well-known actress Madeleine Béjart. Together they formed a theatre company; but although they both knew how to act, they had not yet acquired sufficient expertise in the finance and administration of such an enterprise. Two years later the company went bankrupt, and Molière was marched off to a debtors' prison. Fortunately, word of this quickly reached his father, and within twenty-four hours Molière had re-joined Madeleine. Together they decided upon a new plan. They would form a group of travelling players, which would tour the provinces (thus, if necessary, keeping one step ahead of their creditors). This new group would go on to tour for more than a decade, achieving some success. And it was during this period that Molière began writing his first plays.

At the time, European theatre was heavily influenced by the standard enactment of Italian *commedia dell'arte*. This involved a wide group of stereotyped, somewhat exaggerated characters. These invariably included a clownish servant, Arlecchino (Harlequin); a rich old man called Pantalone; the essential *innamorati* (usually two young upper-class lovers); an impossible braggart who pretended to the title Il Capitano; and the ever-popular butt of many a joke, the roguish Scaramouche, who is frequently beaten by Harlequin for his overweening behaviour or abject cowardice. The cast might also include a number of other pantomime figures whose characters echoed their simple grotesque masks. The actors' entrances, and exits, were scripted. However, between these prompts they were required to improvise, making up jokes or preposterous mishaps as they went along, following the vague outline of the plot. (A good company of actors always had a wide repertory of such routines, into which the stock characters fitted seamlessly – prompting the expected roars of laughter, shrieks of fear or cries of horror amongst the audience.)

The plays which Molière wrote sought to break away from the knock-about and often hackneyed improvisations of *commedia dell'arte*. Instead he sought to impose a fully realized and memorized script upon his actors. Although elements of the old methods remained, his characters tended to be more subtly mocked, exposed as hypocrites, or satirized. His early titles, such as *The Doctor in Love* and *The Bungler*, give an indication of this.

After twelve years of touring, Molière's troupe was at last given permission to perform in Paris. Here they staged a series of performances in front of the young Louis XIV and his court in the theatre hall of the Louvre. This proved such a success that Molière's troupe were taken under the patronage of Philippe I, Duke of Orléans, the king's younger brother. By this time Molière had begun to write tragedies, though performances of these were usually followed by short single-act farces, so that the audience left the theatre feeling fully entertained.

Molière's company was now permitted to share the prestigious large hall of the Petit-Bourbon, a Parisian royal palace, with the hugely popular *commedia dell'arte* company. The latter was run by the Italian Tiberio Fiorillo, who was renowned for his performances of Scaramouche. The initial rivalry between the up-and-coming young Molière and the estab-lished fifty-year-old maestro Fiorillo soon evolved into a close friendship. Fiorillo passed on to Molière many of the subtleties of his art, which he had developed during his long career. This led to Molière becoming a superior dramatist, both skilled and prolific, especially in plots unfolding around dramatic mockery.

The Parisian audiences tended to prefer farces, which were often little more than reworkings of *commedia dell'arte*. This irritated Molière, who decided to branch out into musical comedies, incorporating elements of both the old and the new. The drama would unfold, and then pause to allow an actor to sing an aria, or the troupe to perform a ritual ballet. Molière's plays also developed his penchant for mockery, as well as satirical aspects of social behaviour. Possibly as a result of his involvement with actresses, he held a pessimistic view of fidelity. This resulted in another masterpiece, *Sganarelle ou le Cocu Imaginaire* (The Imaginary Cuckold).

In 1662, Molière married Armande Béjart, whom he believed to be the young sister of his old friend Madeleine. In a parody of classic French farce, she was nothing of the sort – in fact, she appears to have been the illegitimate daughter of the Duke of Modena. Later that year, Molière would produce another masterwork, *The School for Wives*, which mocked the tradition of leaving aristocratic women uneducated – which certainly echoed his feelings at the time.

Molière's satirical treatment of such subjects began to earn him a number of powerful enemies, especially amongst the Church and more traditional authorities, who attacked his 'realism'. In particular, his *Tartuffe* was criticized for holding the Church up to ridicule, while *The Doctor in Spite of Himself* drew the wrath of the medical profession and indeed all scientists, whose crude practices and overweening pretensions were mercilessly pilloried. But by now Molière had the patronage of the Sun King himself, who allowed him to name his company the King's Troupe.

In 1670, Molière staged before Louis XIV and his court at the Château de Chambord a performance of *Le Bourgeois Gentilhomme* (loosely: 'The Would-be Nobleman'). This is perhaps his best-known work outside France. It satirizes the pretensions of a certain Monsieur Jourdain, son of a wealthy cloth merchant, who wishes to rise above his middle-class origins and become an aristocrat. To this end, he hires a number of teachers to coach him in the ways and manners of the nobility. The quintessence of this process takes place during a philosophy lesson, when he seeks to learn how to speak prose:

MONSIEUR JOURDAIN: Oh, really. So when I say 'Nicole, bring
    me my slippers and fetch me my nightcap' is that prose?

PHILOSOPHY MASTER: Most clearly.

MONSIEUR JOURDAIN: Good heavens! So for forty years I've
been speaking prose without realizing it.

Molière himself took the lead in this performance, as well as writing
the entire script. (Only the musical and ballet 'interludes' were produced
by collaborators.) By this stage, Molière was producing a steady stream
of masterpieces, almost annually. But as he reached his late forties, the
constant writing, acting and supervision of productions – involving
dealings with temperamental and jealous actors – began to take its toll.
When Madeleine died in 1672, the loss affected him deeply despite
characteristic attempts to mask his grief. And in a supreme irony, he too
would fall victim to biting satire. While performing in his latest work *The
Imaginary Invalid*, he collapsed into a coughing fit on stage. (It is said
that the audience initially thought that this was all part of the act, and
laughed heartily at the veracity of his performance.)

With typical stoicism, Molière insisted upon completing the performance. Afterwards he suffered a haemorrhage, and died a few hours later.
(Some sources have suggested that this illness might have been tuberculosis, which he had picked up during his brief spell in gaol several decades
previously.) The manner of Molière's death would leave a lasting legacy;
for years French actors have maintained a superstition about wearing
green on stage, the colour of Molière's costume in his final performance.

Despite the disparity between French and English stagecraft and
dramatic performance, many of Molière's works were translated and
staged in London, attracting enthusiastic audiences. But it never matched
the acclaim he retains in France. However, there is an irony here that
would certainly have been appreciated by Molière himself. Despite French
being seen as 'the language of Molière', his use of language in his plays
was frequently inconsistent – even ungrammatical on occasion – as well
as containing mixed metaphors and many an empty rhetorical flourish.

Yet in the eyes of the twentieth-century US drama critic Martha
Bellinger, these are as nothing 'in comparison to the wealth of character
he portrayed, to his brilliancy of wit, and to the resourcefulness of his

technique'. Although Molière despised precious over-refinement, hypoc-risy, fraudulent pretension and sentimental pathos, he was capable of suggesting the full range of genuine human feeling. In rendering sadness, he could paradoxically convey 'a puissant and searching melancholy, which strangely sustains his inexhaustible mirth and his triumphant gaiety'.

Molière's skill as a playwright was only matched by that of his young friend and fellow court dramatist Jean Racine, whose speciality was tragedy. This he composed in alexandrines – the dodecasyllabic (twelve-syllable) French verse form. His works often featured Ancient Greek topics, at the same time obeying the 'dramatic unities' – the classic rules of drama laid down by Aristotle. Not for nothing have his works been regarded as 'examples of neo-classical perfection'.

As if such restriction were not enough, he also limited himself to a vocabulary of just 4,000 words, eschewing all anachronistic modernisms. But instead of limiting his writing, such strictures served to concentrate his talents, giving his verse a diamond edge and allowing his dramas to express emotions – from wit to rage – with utter clarity. Such discipline also enabled him to instil in his characters precise but profound psychology, allowing the tragedy to unfold with complex yet compelling motives.

Jean Racine was born in rural Picardy in 1639. By the age of four, his mother and his father had died, and he was taken into the home of his grandfather. When Racine was ten, his grandfather died and his grandmother retired to the convent of Port-Royal, south-west of Paris. This was run by the Jansenists, a strict theological movement within the Catholic Church. Their teachings emphasized original sin, thus deploring all human desires and insisting upon a life dedicated to striving after grace. Illogically, their most notorious belief was in the predestination of the human soul. God's omniscient power overrode all the apparent free will we experience. One's soul was thus predetermined to enact its fate, which resulted in inevitable damnation or salvation. So strict were the teachings of the Jansenists that many in the Catholic Church regarded them as little better than the strict Protestant Calvinists.*

---

* Jansenism would ultimately be banned by Pope Clement XI, in 1713.

Racine was educated at the Jansenist school at Port-Royal, which would remain a formative influence throughout his life. Here he excelled in classical studies, thus ensuring that Ancient Greek and Latin mythology would play a central role in his plays. Racine was then sent to complete his education by studying law in Paris, but he was soon attracted to the literary circle of the poet and critic Nicolas Boileau instead. Racine's knowledge of classical drama, and his facility in recounting these works, quickly became evident. Boileau persuaded Racine to write down his own versions of these classic tragedies, and encouraged him with suggestions on how to tighten his plots and manipulate them for dramatic effect.

Eventually, Boileau showed Racine's work to Molière, who was more than impressed. Thus Racine's first dramas on classical themes – *The Thebans* and *Alexander the Great* – were staged by Molière's company. These achieved such success that they quickly led to Racine breaking with the Jansenists of Port-Royal. Racine had been befriended by Molière, who ensured his entry to the royal court.

Racine's tragedies soon became the fashionable counterpart to Molière's comedies. The strictness of Racine's formal style and the ruthless, inevitable denouement of his plays undoubtedly owed a great deal to his psychology: the heritage of his education and his break with the Jansenists. By now in his thirties, his life was untroubled. He had the king's favour, a place at court, and his friendship with Molière, who helped him set up his own troupe of players to perform his tragedies.

However, this friendship would eventually come to an abrupt end when Molière tricked Racine by putting on one of his plays with a rival company. Racine retaliated by seducing Molière's leading actress at the time, Thérèse du Parc, and making her the leading lady in his own company. Then, at the height of his fame, Racine fell from grace when he married the Jansenist Catherine de Romanet, and under her pious influence abandoned writing drama. In 1672 he was elected to the Académie Française, but he eventually became tired of this distinguished administrative role. He longed to return to his former life as a dramatist, and became consumed by his ambition to regain his previous eminence at court. Eventually, the king's morganatic wife, Madame de Maintenon, was instrumental in his restoration to royal favour – whereupon he once again began composing tragic dramas, this time on biblical themes. Both Molière and Racine came to rely upon the talents of Jean-Baptiste Lully, the king's favourite musician. Lully not only composed music, but also exhibited great expertise as both an instrumentalist and a ballet dancer – earning him the accolade 'prince of French musicians'.

High art was not the only beneficiary of the revolution in French taste and manners that took place during the reign of the Sun King. Until the early years of the previous century, medieval French cuisine had been heavy on spices, often used to mask spoiled meat. This was a commodity that was all but impossible to preserve fresh in an age where ice was not readily available. Thick rich sauces often gave a sweet-sour flavour to dishes, or made them hot like curry.

This style of cuisine underwent a transformation with the arrival in 1533 of the Florentine Catherine de' Medici, who married the prince destined to become King Henry II. (Her younger cousin, the aforementioned Marie de' Medici, would marry into French royalty in 1600.) Amongst Catherine's entourage were a number of skilled Italian cooks.* After initial resistance, their methods soon won over many of the court cooks and transformed French cuisine. The Italian cooks insisted upon fresh meat and fish, gently cooked with delicate sauces intended to enhance the flavour of the main ingredient rather than mask its taste.

Meanwhile, in France's outer provinces, the cuisine was often influenced by neighbouring culinary dishes from places such as Flanders, Alsace, Switzerland, Italy and Spain – and even Moorish cooking from North Africa. At the same time, new foods such as tomatoes, peppers, maize and potatoes began to arrive from the New World. These inspired a number of classic dishes, e.g. haricot beans became central to the cassoulet of Toulouse, and potatoes and cayenne pepper became ingredients in the

---

* The word 'chef' was not used until the mid-1800s, when it originally appeared as *chef de cuisine*, loosely meaning 'chief of the kitchen'.

bouillabaisse of Marseille. The import of turkeys was particularly popular. On one occasion, Catherine de' Medici presided over a festive dinner that included more than sixty turkeys.*

The French still insisted that a meal should be presented as a spectacle, with all the dishes served simultaneously – forming a spectacular tableau to greet the guests as they entered the dining salon. This was aptly named *service en confusion*. However, this was far from being the only confusion in French cuisine. Cooks would develop their personal method for preparing a dish, hoping that their own secret ingredient would win them favour. Such lack of agreed preparation and ingredients was in desperate need of formalization, if named dishes were to be standardized. The man who introduced this rationale into the confusion of French cuisine was François Pierre La Varenne, who was born in 1615, possibly in the rich culinary region of Burgundy.

It is thought that he first learned his trade in the kitchens of Marie de' Medici, which he entered as a general pot-boy before graduating through the various speciality sections that prepared soups, meats, fish, pastry and so forth. He must have shown exceptional talent, for at the age of just twenty-six he was hired as 'chief of the kitchen' to the Marquis of Uxelles, the powerful general who became foreign minister to Louis XIV. Here La Varenne invented for his master the dish known as duxelles (pronounced 'duck-SELL'), a concoction of finely chopped mushrooms, shallots and herbs, sautéed in butter and reduced to a paste that can be used as stuffing for meat or baked in pastry.

In 1651, at the age of thirty-six, La Varenne published *Le Cuisinier François*, the first generally recognized book on French cuisine. This set about codifying the preparation of dishes in a systematic fashion. In

---

* The origin of the name turkey for this new bird introduced from the New World resulted from a series of confusions. For unknown reasons, the first live animals of this sort to arrive in Spain were thought to have come from Turkey, and were initially known as *turquia*. On the other hand, in Turkey it was assumed that these animals came from India, which is why they became known as *hindi*. An echo of this mistake appears in French, where this bird was known as *dinde* (d'Inde meaning 'from India').

other words, he set down the rules for how each particular dish should be cooked and served to maximum effect.

The remnant medieval taste for spices such as cinnamon, cumin and ginger was transformed by the introduction of local herbs such as fresh parsley, thyme and tarragon. La Varenne adopted many of the Italian innovations introduced by Catherine de' Medici during the previous century, but here again he sought to impose order. Savoury dishes were to be served separately from sweet dishes or puddings. Salted dishes should always precede sugared or honeyed concoctions.

La Varenne was also instrumental in systemizing the ingredients and preparation of various sauces. Indeed, it is this work which introduced the names, as well as the recipes, for such standard items as béchamel and hollandaise sauces, as well as bisque (fish soup). Dishes requiring several herbs would be cooked with a *bouquet garni* (another Varenne coining). He also introduced the term *fonds de cuisine* (stock) as well as reductions (for intensifying flavour), and the use of egg white to clarify a clouded broth into a more refined and flavoursome consommé. This clarification process could also be used to render cloudy red wines clear.

La Varenne's masterwork was followed two years later by *Le Pâtissier François*, which also broke new ground, being the first comprehensive guide to the creating and baking of French pastries. Although both of La Varenne's' works were quickly pirated – with unauthorized editions appearing in various European languages – they soon became the standard authority on French cuisine, and would remain so for years to come.

This period also saw the proliferation of champagne, the wine originating in the vineyards around Reims, site of the coronation of the kings of France during the Middle Ages. Vineyards planted in the chalky soil of the Champagne region had been producing wine since Roman times. (The very name is thought to derive from the Roman Campania, the similarly wooded hilly region around Naples in southern Italy.) Being in northeast France, the district had a cooler climate than other wine-growing regions, and this resulted in an unusual phenomenon. During winter, the wine in the cellars would cease fermentation; with the coming of spring, the yeast cells would continue fermentation. A side effect of this second fermentation was the production of carbon dioxide, which caused bubbles to form in the wine.

Ironically, this was initially considered a defect. Dom Pérignon, the seventeenth-century Benedictine monk often credited with the perfection of the *méthode champenoise*, was in charge of the wine cellar at Hautvillers Abbey, some fifteen miles south of Reims. He in fact spent most of his career attempting to eliminate bubbles from the wine, whose excess pressure often caused the bottles in his cellar to explode. Despite this, a statue of the 'founder of champagne' now stands in the heart of Champagne, depicting Dom Pérignon in his monastic robes holding a bottle of overflowing champagne.

But while the court at Versailles lived in luxury, the common people of France were being reduced to ever-more abject poverty, forced to pay the ruinous taxes needed to finance Louis XIV's perpetual wars. During the previous centuries the peasantry had been reduced to eating frog legs and snails – which had not been regarded as food since Roman times. But now the peasantry were deprived of even this meagre fare, as these items were transformed into fashionable delicacies to accompany the feasts at Versailles.

CHAPTER 10

ENGLAND COMES OF AGE

Throughout the Age of Reason, England continued to emerge as a major power in Europe. Its Royal Navy, built up by Henry VIII in the sixteenth century, became a major defender of the 'island nation' when it defeated the might of the Spanish Armada during the reign of Henry's daughter Elizabeth I. It also enabled England to expand its imperial ambitions in North America and the Caribbean, mainly at the expense of Spain. With the establishment of the East India Company in 1600, England's empire began to expand into the Far East, competing with some success against the Dutch VOC.

Meanwhile, at home, post-Shakespearian England continued its cultural evolution – to such an extent that the court of Charles I attracted the Flemish baroque artist Anthony van Dyck, who was seen by some as the only painter in Europe to rival Velázquez.

Van Dyck was born in Antwerp in 1599, and soon exhibited a precocious talent. By the age of fifteen he was working in Rubens's studio, one of the select team permitted to 'finish' the works of the master. Rubens declared that Van Dyck was 'the best of my pupils'.

As early as 1620 Van Dyck was invited to England, where he was employed by Elizabeth I's successor James I, as well as various important figures at the royal court. Van Dyck was just twenty-one years old and his style was far from fixed. In England his exposure to the art collections of various aristocrats opened his eyes to the possibilities explored by the Italian Renaissance painters. In particular, the works of the Venetian artist Titian in the collection of the Earl of Arundel indicated to him how it was possible to use shades of colour to add new complexity to the modelling of figures, especially in portraits.

Van Dyck left London after four months, and soon made his way to Italy. Here he travelled extensively, viewing a wide variety of Italian art, all the while supporting himself as an increasingly skilled portraitist. Most famously, his rendering of St Rosalia, often invoked against the plague, would become 'the standard iconography of the saint from that time onwards'. Van Dyck would initially paint Rosalia as standing on a rocky ledge interceding with the heavens on behalf of the city of Palermo far below. This was but the first of many portraits of the saint.*

Van Dyck would later form a lasting attachment to the English court of Charles I, who was intent upon establishing for England – and himself – a leading role in European art. (Indeed, such was his informed knowledge of contemporary art, as well as the depth of his pocket, that he even managed to attract Orazio Gentileschi, and later his daughter Artemisia, to his court.) In his portraits of Charles I and many of his courtiers, Van Dyck would bring a new elegance to the art of portraiture, while at the same time investing his work with an element of intimacy. It was Van Dyck, more than any other, who caught the Cavalier spirit of this English era.

Van Dyck's best-known work from this period is probably his *Triple Portrait of Charles I*. This depicts the king's head from three different angles, dressed in three different costumes. The central face-on portrait is particularly characterful and poignant. This is a man who saw himself as the personification of the divine right of kings; yet for all his inherent

---

* Four hundred years later, the city of Palermo would turn to St Rosalia for protection against the Covid pandemic. As the city was in lockdown, these prayers for the saint's intercession were posted on social media.

pride what is depicted is also a recognizably fallible human character. Ironically, this masterpiece was intended as a mere reference work, to enable the sculptor Gian Lorenzo Bernini, who lived in Italy, to create a lifelike marble bust of the king without actually travelling to see him. On seeing Van Dyck's triple portrait, Bernini was so struck by its psychological insight that he is said to have claimed it to be 'the portrait of a doomed man'. (Charles would be plunged into the Civil War seven years later, and beheaded in 1649.)

Such was Van Dyck's success in England that he set up a large studio-cum-workshop in the style of his master Rubens, where artists would follow his initial drawings and detailed instructions to produce 'virtually a production line of portraits'. However, Van Dyck would invariably execute the faces in these portraits himself, imbuing them with his own unique painterly qualities. In the manner of his contemporaries, such as Rubens and the Gentileschis (father and daughter), he also produced a number of biblical scenes. As in his earlier portrait of St Rosalia, these eschew the surface element of elegance, adopting the more raw and turbulent veracity of Titian and Rubens (as in his *Samson and Delilah*) or a dramatic spirituality (as in his *Lamentation of Christ*).

In later life, Van Dyck was stricken with illness. His health deteriorated, and he died prematurely in London at the age of just forty-two. This took place in the year preceding the outbreak of the English Civil War, during which the Cavalier world that he had depicted with such panache would be swept away, to be replaced by the victorious Puritan austerity.

According to a long-held tradition, there has always been at least one great poet writing in the English language since the time of Chaucer in the fourteenth century. This was arguably the case before Shakespeare filled this role, and remained so after his death in 1616 – with the succession passing on, if not to his loyal young friend Ben Jonson (1572–1637), then to the amorous and meditative cleric John Donne (1572–1631).* They

---

* Donne is responsible for the indelible lines, today usually remembered as: 'No man is an island, entire of itself... Ask not for whom the bell tolls; it tolls for thee.'

would in turn be succeeded by John Milton, who was born in London in 1608 and grew up amidst the decades of religious and political turmoil which preceded the Civil War.

There was never any doubting Milton's position with regard to this vital upheaval that divided England into two bitterly opposed camps as never before. (Previous civil wars, such as the mid-fifteenth-century Wars of the Roses, had involved royal succession. The seventeenth-century Civil War that erupted during the Age of Reason involved the very way of life of citizens throughout the land.) Milton was from the outset a stanch Protestant, and would become a convinced Parliamentarian. His father, also named John Milton, was disinherited by his prosperous Catholic father when he turned Protestant. However, the poet's father managed to earn a good living in London as a scrivener, writing out court and legal documents, including wills, for those not versed in composing such formal language, as well as contracts for illiterate traders.

The biographer John Aubrey, who knew Milton, said of him: 'When he was young, he studied very hard and sat up very late continuing till twelve or one o'clock at night.' By the time Milton went to Cambridge at the age of sixteen, the lack of daylight – or participation in the more robust pursuits of his age – had given him a pale, somewhat effeminate appearance: 'His complexion exceeding faire – he was so faire that they called him the Lady of Christ's College.' Despite this, Milton was such a determined and opinionated scholar that he quarrelled violently with his tutor, Bishop William Chappell.

At Cambridge, Milton acquired a wealth of learning, including proficiency in Latin, Greek, Hebrew, French, Spanish and Italian (furthermore, he would later learn Dutch). He also began composing verse with 'a lofty and steady confidence in himself, perhaps not without some contempt of others'. Amongst his early poems was 'An Epitaph on the Admirable Dramaticke Poet, W. Shakespeare', which some have seen as an indication that Milton's ambition was nothing less than to emulate his illustrious predecessor. (Indeed, in the opinion of his first biographer, William Hayley, Milton was 'the greatest English author', and Hayley is not alone in this opinion.)

Reading between the lines in the description above, it is clear that Milton was hardly a sympathetic character, preferring to voice his own opinion rather than court popularity. From the outset, he was not above inserting his strongly held Puritan beliefs into his poetry. In his early work *Comus*, a masque he composed after leaving Cambridge, his opinions on morality are plainly expressed: 'Love virtue, she alone is free.' Although this dramatic entertainment features Comus, the Ancient Greek god of revelry, it is widely seen as 'a masque in honour of chastity'. The lead character, named simply The Lady, uses her right reason (*recta ratio*) to resist the blandishments of Comus.

Despite the Puritan narrowness of Milton's views on morality (and politics) throughout his life – 'Licence they mean when they cry Liberty' – there is no denying the breadth of his talent and his learning. At the age of thirty he set out on a journey to Europe with the express intent of increasing both these qualities still further. His grand tour took him through France and Italy. In Florence, his knowledge of science led him to seek out Galileo, who was under house arrest on orders of the pope. He also met and conversed with others in Florentine intellectual circles, where he would have become conversant (if he was not already so) with the latest scientific ideas of Copernicus, Kepler, Torricelli and the like.

During his travels, Milton seems to have reined in his high opinion of himself and his strict moral outlook, to the extent that he cut quite a figure in such circles. He enjoyed Florence, 'which I have always admired above all others… not just of its tongue but also of its wit'. He frequented the academies, which deserved 'great praise not only for promoting humane studies but also for encouraging friendly intercourse'.

In Rome he even relented to the extent of enjoying the company of resident English Catholics, cardinals and the Vatican librarian, going so far as to attend convivial dinner parties and visits to the opera. However, eventually he was forced to interrupt his travels on account of 'sad tidings of civil war in England'.

Back home in June 1642, the thirty-three-year-old Milton married the seventeen-year-old Mary Powell. This was presumably an arranged marriage, rather than an affair of the heart, for Milton soon found himself offended when Mary refused to conform to his austere lifestyle. Similarly, he took umbrage at what he considered to be her mental vacuity, to say nothing of the Royalist views she had inherited from her family. It appears that the marriage was not consummated, and within months Mary returned to her family.

Indicatively, Milton at once began writing and publishing a series of polemical pamphlets on the subject of divorce – arguing that grounds for this should be extended beyond adultery to include all manner of misdemeanours, especially incompatibility. These pamphlets succeeded in gaining the opprobrium of all sections of society, from Catholics to Protestants, from Parliamentarians to Royalists – a unique achievement at this time. Even Milton himself would quickly come to regret these intemperate outbursts. Surprisingly Mary would return to her marriage, which would soon produce two daughters.

Milton benefitted from the Roundhead victory in the Civil War, and served as a government official for Oliver Cromwell's Commonwealth. He may have been an incongruous blend of Renaissance humanist and Protestant Puritan, but he was also a convinced Parliamentarian, and would remain so even after the collapse of the Commonwealth led to the Restoration of Charles II. Moreover, he was not afraid to voice his opinions. This was a brave, if not foolhardy, gesture.

It was during these times of political turmoil and even personal danger that Milton composed his finest work, the epic poem *Paradise Lost*, which originally consisted of ten books containing in all more than a thousand lines of superlative blank verse. According to Aubrey, Milton wrote this work between 1658 and 1664, but subsequent scholarship has revealed that parts of *Paradise Lost* were composed verbatim some years earlier for altogether different works. He would go on to write a sequel in the form of *Paradise Regained*; it seems evident that this was a great project, which he had been mulling over for some years.

Milton's politics would remain those of an 'acrimonious and surly republican', and his continuing support for the defeated Commonwealth would force him into hiding, while his works (both poetic and polemic) were ordered to be burned. On top of this, he was reduced to poverty and became blind – much of *Paradise Lost* was dictated to his daughters.

The central theme of *Paradise Lost* is the Fall of Man. At the outset we see Satan (Lucifer) and his Fallen Angels: Beelzebub, Belial ('And when Night / Darkens the streets, then wander forth the Sons / Of Belial, flown with insolence and wine'), Moloch and Mammon (to this day, recognized as a synonym for greed, money and excessive material wealth). They have all been cast down into Tartarus (Hell) for rebelling against God in Heaven. 'O Sun, to tell thee how I hate thy beams / That bring to my remembrance from what state / I fell, how glorious once above thy sphere'.

Lucifer and his fallen angels are in chains amidst 'the burning lake… whose waves of torrent fire inflame with rage'. But they manage to free themselves and build the city of Pandemonium (from the Greek *pan* meaning 'all', and *daimon* meaning 'demon'). They are motivated: 'All is not lost, the unconquerable will / And study of revenge, immortal hate / And courage never to submit or yield'. The poem is also studded with psychological insight: 'The mind is its own place, and in itself / Can make a Heav'n of Hell, a Hell of Heav'n'; 'Neither man nor angel can discern / Hypocrisy, the only evil that walks / Invisible, except to God alone'.

Meanwhile, God has created Earth, and peopled it with his most favoured creation: mankind. Satan schemes to travel from the Abyss (the depths of Hell), through Chaos, up into God's creation, where he enters the Garden of Eden: 'Long is the way / And hard, that out of Hell leads up to light'.

This is the place God has given to Adam and Eve, who live in total freedom, ruling over the paradise of God's creation. ('Paradise' derives from the Hebrew word *pardes,* which means 'garden or citrus grove'.) They have been given but one commandment: they must never eat the fruit from the Tree of the Knowledge of Good and Evil. Satan, disguising himself as a serpent, tempts Eve by encouraging her vanity: 'Knowledge forbidden? / Suspicious, reasonless. Why should their Lord / Envy them that? Can it be sin to know? / Can it be death?'

Eve is persuaded to eat the fruit: 'Greedily she engorg'd without restraint / And knew not eating death'. Adam is overwhelmed when he learns what she has done:

> How can I live without thee? How forgo
> Thy sweet converse, and love so dearly joined
> To live again in these wild woods forlorn?
> Should God create another Eve, and I
> Another rib afford,* yet loss of thee
> Would never from my heart; no, no, I feel
> The link of nature draw me: flesh of flesh,
> Bone of my bone thou art, and from thy state
> Mine never shall be parted, bliss or woe.

Thus Adam too commits the same sin, and tastes the fruit. At this point it is worth noting that, in the opinion of many critics, 'Milton portrays Adam as a heroic figure, but also as a greater sinner than Eve, as he is aware that what he is doing is wrong'.

Having both consumed the fruit, Adam and Eve are overcome with desire for one another. After they have sated their lust, their fall from grace, they are overcome with guilt and shame. They are then cast out from the paradise of the Garden of Eden, but they remain God's creation: 'For so / I formed them free and free they must remain'.

The Archangel Michael (the chief angel of Heaven) assures Adam that even in their fallen state they may now experience 'a paradise within thee, happier far'. On the other hand, their relationship with God will never again be real as it was in the Garden of Eden. Instead they will experience a more distant God, who remains omnipotent but invisible to them. The Archangel Michael reveals to Adam that they will be able to redeem their original sin through the King Messiah (Jesus Christ).

At the same time, we see Satan in Hell, triumphant amongst his

---

* In Genesis, the first book of the Old Testament Bible, God creates the first woman, Eve, out of a rib he has taken from Adam.

fallen angels. He relates to them how his scheme has succeeded, but as he finishes his tale the fallen angels are transformed into grotesque writhing serpents. Then he too suffers the same fate, becoming deprived of his limbs and unable to speak any longer.

On the surface, *Paradise Lost* is essentially a religious text, following the early events described in the Bible. Milton's stated aim was to 'justify the ways of God to man'. As such, it is a work of considerable theological depth and subtlety, often rendered more palatable to modern sensibilities by its psychological insight. Yet such is Milton's compelling portrait of Lucifer that it is difficult not to see God's adversary as a superhuman rebel. 'Better to reign in Hell than to serve in Heaven,' he proclaims. Indeed, just over a century later, the less religiously inclined of the English Romantic poets – in particular Shelley and Byron – would see Lucifer as an exemplary figure: a visionary rebel against tyranny.

At the same time, it is not difficult to discern political echoes in this tale of rampant evil and humanity's fall from grace. During the years before Milton began his work and was still pondering its content, Thomas Hobbes was in exile writing his *Leviathan*, which would appear in 1651, seven years before Milton began writing his great epic. At one point in *Paradise Lost*, Milton even compares Lucifer to Leviathan, 'that sea-beast / Leviathan, which God, of all His works / Created hugest that swim the ocean stream'. However, Aubrey, writing of Milton, claimed: 'His widowe assures me that Mr T. Hobbes was not one of his acquaintance, that her husband did not like him at all, but he would acknowledge him to be a man of great parts, and a learned man. Their Interests and Tenets did run counter to each other.'

This last claim is something of an understatement. Though Aubrey's further assertion on Milton's behalf undoubtedly falls into the category of overstatement: 'Whatever he wrote against Monarchie was out of no animosity to the King's person, or owt of any faction or interest, but out of a pure Zeale to the Liberty of Mankind, which he thought would be greater under a free state than under a Monarchiall government.'

This may be questionable, but it does illustrate the paradox of Milton's views. He was undeniably a Republican, yet this belief is in direct conflict with any libertarian aspect of republicanism. As he wrote in one of his sonnets: 'License they mean when they cry, Liberty!' Here he equates liberty with licentiousness. The revolution required to establish a republic may be led by the cry 'Liberty!' – yet ironically it is frequently followed by a puritan authoritarianism or insistence upon orthodoxy. This was as much the case in the English Commonwealth as it would be in the subsequent French and Russian revolutions.

Milton would live on in London – blind and difficult, but dutifully tended by his daughters as he dictated his epic – while the collapse of the Puritan Commonwealth in 1660 would be followed by the Restoration period of compensatory licence. Despite Milton's disgrace, upon the publication of *Paradise Lost* in 1667 it would quickly be recognized as a transcendent work of English literature. Its shorter sequel, *Paradise Regained*, would appear in 1671. More in keeping with the tenor of the age would be his prose work *Of True Religion*, which argued for freedom of religion – for all except Catholics, who were condemned as heretics, their teachings an abomination. By the time Milton died in 1674, at the age of sixty-five, he had lived, unseeing, through yet more events which would transform England forever.

Restoration England is remembered as a time of celebration, with the theatres reopening and the return of Christmas festivities to dispel the Puritan gloom. (This was not without its vengeful side: Cromwell, who had died two years before the end of the Commonwealth, was exhumed, his cadaver publicly hanged in chains at Tyburn, his head then exhibited on a pole outside the Houses of Parliament, where it remained for fifteen years.) The new young Charles II was a popular monarch, and his contravention of Puritan ethics was widely welcomed. He would be observed walking in St James's Park with his favourite mistress, Nell Gwyn – formerly an orange-seller on the streets of London, she came to Charles II's notice when he visited the theatre. She was a talented comic actress: the diarist Samuel Pepys refers to her as 'pretty, witty Nell'. She is said to have persuaded Charles II to found the Royal Hospital Chelsea, which to this day remains the home of the Chelsea Pensioners, retired British army soldiers in bright red coats (also said to have been Nell's idea).

However, Charles II also had a more serious side. In 1660, the very year he was restored to the throne, he founded the Royal Society of London for Improving Natural Knowledge (now known simply as the Royal Society). To put this into context, this was six years prior to the founding of the Académie des Sciences in Paris (where Huygens had become a leading light). But it was also a direct beneficiary of the so-called invisible college – which evolved amongst a group of natural philosophers (scientists) in order to facilitate the exchange of ideas during the Commonwealth. Ironically, Puritan intellectuals had a positive attitude towards science and 'evidentialism' (the verification of truth by experimental evidence). In the words of the leading Puritan theologian Stephen Charnock: 'there was more clarity in the book of Scripture than in the book of nature, but because the Author of both has joined both together, we should not put it asunder'.

However, even here it is possible to detect an element of ambivalence towards science. And this was very much the case amongst rank-and-file Puritans, who distrusted such pursuits, viewing them as heresies similar to alchemy and hermeticism.

The Royal Society adopted as its motto *Nullius in verba* (Nothing in words), i.e. belief in experiment rather than the appeal to an ancient authority such as Aristotle. As already mentioned, the first Secretary of the Royal Society was the German-born diplomat and scientist Henry Oldenburg, whose circle of friends extended from the chemist Robert Boyle to John Milton, and saw it as his duty to keep in contact with scientists throughout Europe. The Royal Society held regular meetings in London at Gresham College, where the polymathic scientist Robert Hooke was appointed curator of experiments.

Robert Hooke was born in 1635, the youngest of five children. His father was a Royalist Church of England vicar on the Isle of Wight. Hooke showed early signs of a precocious mechanical talent. He is known to have dismantled a brass clock and constructed an identical one made of wooden parts that worked 'well enough'. He also became proficient in drawing, a talent he would develop to describe his scientific experiments.

Hooke's father died when he was thirteen, leaving him £40 – whereupon he set out for the capital to seek his fortune. In London, he went to Westminster School, and thence to Oxford, where he became a friend of Christopher Wren. By now Hooke had long since spent his inheritance, and his lack of cash meant that he had to find employment. For some years he worked as an assistant to Robert Boyle, the father of modern chemistry. Boyle was a renowned experimentalist, but Hooke was more than up to the task of acting as his assistant. Indeed, it is generally recognized that Hooke supplied the mathematical calculations for Boyle's law, which describes how the pressure of a gas decreases as the volume increases.*

Hooke's impecuniosity made him a difficult, quarrelsome character, often in dispute with his fellow scientists. His first biographer, Richard Waller, writing two years after Hooke's death, claimed that he was 'in person but despicable... melancholy, distrustful and jealous'. Although there is undoubtedly an element of truth in this assessment, it is far from being the whole story. He may have been professionally sensitive and suspicious of others, but his friendships with the likes of Wren and Boyle speak volumes. And there is no denying the originality of his thought, with the science historian Allan Chapman even going so far as to describe him as 'England's Leonardo'.

Today Hooke remains best known for Hooke's law, which was the first to describe and mathematicize the elasticity of a spring. He initially disguised this discovery as an anagram: 'ceiiinosssttuv'. This enabled him to claim priority before he published the full extent of his findings, including the solution to the anagram: *Ut tensio, sic vis* (As the extension, so the force).† Basically, Hooke's law states that when we

---

* Yet it was Boyle who drew the vital conclusion from this law. If gases behaved in this manner, it indicated that they consisted of particles suspended in a void. Compression simply forced the particles closer together. This was to prove an important step on the way to understanding that elements consist of atoms.

† Some claim this as evidence of Hooke's paranoia, but as with Huygens's 'aaaaaaac-ccccdeeeeeghiiiiiiilllmmnnnnnnnnnnoooooppqrrsttttttuuuuu' this was a common method for establishing priority. It had been so at least since Galileo's time.

extend a spring, the force pulling it back towards its original position is proportional to the distance it has been pulled. (This applies to any elastic material.)

The practical application of Hooke's law resulted in him developing a machine for cutting teeth in miniature cogwheels, as well as a hairspring for the first 'portable timepiece' (watch). Characteristically, this latter resulted in a bitter priority dispute with Huygens, who (wrongly) claimed that he had used an identical device in his pendulum clock.

Hooke developed a reflecting telescope, which he used to discover that Mars and Jupiter rotated as they orbited the sun, in a similar fashion to the earth. He was also the first to discover a double-star system when he observed the binary star Gamma Arietis. However, his attempt to measure the distance of this double-star system from the earth proved faulty – hampered by the inadequacy of his equipment. Even so, his astronomical observations led him to formulate a theory of gravity, which he described to the Royal Society in 1666:

> I will explain a system of the world very different from any yet received. It is founded on the following positions. 1. That all the heavenly bodies have not only a gravitation of their parts to their own proper centre, but that they also mutually attract each other within their spheres of action. 2. That all bodies having a simple motion, will continue to move in a straight line, unless continually deflected from it by some extraneous force, causing them to describe a circle, an ellipse, or some other curve. 3. That this attraction is so much the greater as the bodies are nearer. As to the proportion in which those forces diminish by an increase of distance, I own I have not discovered it.

This accounted for how and why the planets orbited the earth. Hooke went on to explain that this gravitation was a universal law, applying to 'all celestial bodies'. And over the years he would fill in the gap in his discovery, working out 'the proportion of this attraction'. He claimed that it obeyed a 'rule of the decrease of Gravity, being reciprocally as the squares of the distances from the Center'.*

Hooke's most celebrated discovery would come when he reversed the notion of the telescope and created a number of microscopes. These consisted of two – or sometimes three – convex and concave lenses enclosed in a tube. The distance between the lenses could be lengthened in order to focus upon the object, which was illuminated by a light.

What Hooke saw through this instrument, which was capable of 50 times magnification, astonished him. Before his eyes a new world emerged. He described what he saw when he placed a sliver of cork beneath his lens:

> I could exceedingly plainly perceive it to be all perforated and porous, much like a Honey-comb, but that the pores of it were not regular... these pores, or cells... were indeed the first microscopical pores I ever saw, and perhaps, that were ever seen, for I had not met with any Writer or Person, that had made any mention of them before this...

This was the first use of the word 'cell' in a biological context.

Hooke's artistic talents enabled him to make precise drawings of the creatures and substances that inhabited this previously unseen world. He drew a louse, a fly's monstrous eye, a fully magnified flea... wherever he looked he saw something as it had never been seen before. And a scientific mind such as Hooke's was soon drawing conclusions from what he saw.

Hooke's microscopic investigations of fossils such as petrified ammonites (marine molluscs) led him to conclude that species could become extinct, and that others might have come into being later. This contradicted current theology and went some way towards a theory of

---

* Hooke began developing his notion of gravity in 1666, unaware that Newton had conceived of an almost identical idea, which he would only publish in his *Principia Mathematica* in 1687. This would result in a furious priority dispute, whose details will be discussed in a later chapter on Newton.

evolution. His examination of fossilized wood convinced him that the world was much older than the 6,000 years allotted by the Bible.[*]

Hooke would collect his drawings in the book *Micrographia*, which was published by the Royal Society in 1665. This became an overnight sensation, arguably the first scientific bestseller, with all English society wondering at the new universe discovered by Hooke. Pepys described it as 'the most ingenious book that ever I read in my life'.

This was no mean praise coming from Pepys, who was an elected member of the Royal Society. In common with the polymathic expertise of many of its early members, Pepys not only kept himself abreast of the latest scientific developments, but was also a member of parliament and held high office as chief secretary of the navy. Here his reforms modernized the increasingly archaic practices of England's navy, thus enabling it to become a fighting force capable of resisting the powerful Dutch navy, and laying the foundation for 'the most powerful maritime force in the world'. All this, to say nothing of him being arguably the finest diarist in English history.

Other early members of the Royal Society included Hooke's former employer Robert Boyle, whose methodical recording of his chemical experiments introduced a new rationality into science as a whole. Boyle's template with regards to his experiments included a clear statement of the intention, the proportions of the chemical ingredients used, the ordered processes to which they were subjected and the equipment involved, as well as the result, and the conclusions to be drawn from it. Such clear methodology broke with the previous secrecy of chemists (especially alchemists) in their experimental work. Any scientist now had the equivalent of a recipe for how to conduct an experiment, and how to write it up afterwards – thus enabling others to check its veracity. By this means, the chemist could build upon a certain foundation of experimental expertise to create further experiments and findings (which could

---

[*] The Irish Anglican archbishop James Ussher had recently used a combination of biblical reference and historical dates to calculate that the world was created around six o'clock in the evening on 22 October 4004 BC.

be confirmed). In many ways, Boyle was doing for chemistry what Euclid had done for mathematics some two millennia previously. Euclid had placed mathematical truths arrived at by intuition, or inductive reason, on a firm foundation: their truth could be proved. For Boyle, the truths of science arrived at by deductive reason had their means of verification – experimental proof.

Boyle's experimental method brought about the rational separation of true chemistry from the esoteric and essentially irrational secretive methods and aims of alchemy.* As such, Boyle rightly deserves his place as the founder of modern chemistry – and much beyond. Physics, biology, astronomy and other sciences would all adopt this method, which is now familiar to any student who conducts experiments in a lab.

Boyle was also responsible for clarifying the notion of a chemical element: this he defined as any substance that could not be reduced to simpler substances. Take a basic example: water was long thought to be an element; however, it is now known that when an electric current is passed through water, it separates into hydrogen and oxygen. These cannot be reduced to simpler substances, and are thus elements. Boyle's notion of an element was cannily prescient, though he was not able to produce any experimental evidence to confirm his conjecture – such as splitting water, which would only be achieved by a later generation of chemists.

Unfortunately, old habits die hard – at the same time as Boyle was conceiving of this pioneering notion of the elements, he was also continuing with his covert pursuit of alchemy, attempting to transmute elements much as the alchemists of old had sought to transmute base elements into gold. Illogically, he still mistakenly believed that it was possible to change one element into another. Despite denials of Boyle's belief in alchemy by those keen to protect his status as 'the father of

---

* Ironically, the new chemistry, purged of the irrational elements of alchemy, would still rely heavily upon many of the techniques developed by alchemists. These included such basics as filtration and purification, chemical processes involving oxidation and reduction, as well as equipment such as crucibles, distillation jars and all manner of glass tubes and vessels.

chemistry', evidence for this can be found in his writings, as well as the leading role he played in the repeal of the 150-year-old statute 'against multiplying gold and silver'.

For many years Boyle suffered from frail health, and it is now known that his sister Katherine assisted him in his experiments after Hooke left his laboratory. Indeed, it is more than possible that she played a role every bit as important as that of Hooke in many of Boyle's findings.

Other early luminaries of the Royal Society included a wide range of talents, from the maverick political economist Sir William Petty to Edmund Halley of Halley's Comet, as well as Hooke's old Oxford friend Christopher Wren, who became professor of astronomy at Gresham College.

It is no accident that so many of these early members of the Royal Society counted astronomy amongst their many pursuits. During the Age of Reason, European science would expand as never before. This was to a great extent enabled by advances in the technology of lens-grinding, which resulted in the invention of the telescope and the microscope. The former opened up the exploration of the universe; the latter revealed a hitherto unsuspected microverse. This expansion of European vision was matched by the spread of European discovery across the globe – which was in turn inextricably linked with trade, and emergent colonial empires on distant continents.

The great enthusiasm for astronomy amongst early members of the Royal Society is nowhere plainer than in John Flamsteed, the first Astronomer Royal, who was born in 1646 and would discover the planet Uranus (though he mistook it for a star) and go on to prepare a catalogue which mapped the position of 3,000 stars. Flamsteed's precocious interest in astronomy was such that at the age of twelve he had observed, and well understood, the astronomical movements responsible for a partial eclipse of the sun. Six years later, he would certainly have followed the passage of the bright comet which passed across the sky above London at the end of 1664. This event caught the imagination of all who saw it, from the people of London to members of the Royal Society. Pepys recorded how one afternoon he attended Gresham College, 'where Mr Hooke read a second very curious lecture about the late Comett; among other things proving very probably that this is the very same Comett that appeared before in the year 1618, and that in such a time probably it will appear again, which is a very new opinion'.

In 1682, the future Astronomer Royal Edmund Halley observed what is now known as Halley's Comet. He was the first of the era to understand that this comet had an orbit, which could be calculated. His observations and calculations led him to predict (correctly, as it transpired) that this comet would reappear in 1758 – when it would posthumously be named in his honour. It is evident from Pepys's diary entry that Hooke had undertaken similar calculations regarding the comet of 1664. Members of the Royal Society such as Pepys, Halley and Hooke recognized that comets were in fact astronomical phenomena, with their passage amenable to scientific reason. However, this was certainly not the case amongst the population at large. Here comets remained superstitiously regarded as evil omens, presaging great disasters.

And with regard to the 1664 comet, the irrational superstition appeared justified. The following year, England was stricken by the first of a succession of catastrophic events. Firstly, 1665 saw the arrival in England of the Great Plague, a similar bubonic affliction to the Black Death which had swept Europe over three centuries previously. The new outbreak spread from parish to parish, town to town, city to city across the land, borne by rats carrying infected fleas. The disease proved particularly virulent as it spread through the winding medieval streets and tiny lanes of the City of London, with the core of its teeming population of 80,000 crammed between the old Roman city walls and the north bank of the River Thames.* Raw sewage flowed down the cobbles of many

---

* By now London had begun to spread beyond these confines – south across London Bridge into Southwark, east beyond Spitalfields and Shoreditch, and west across the open ground that lay between the City of London and Westminster, which contained the royal palace of Whitehall, Westminster Abbey and the Houses of Parliament. In all, this conurbation had a population of around 400,000, making it second only to Paris and Constantinople in Europe. Though, compared with the elegant architecture of central Paris and other major European cities,

thoroughfares, its pungent odour mingling with the choking black coal smoke that wafted from the chimneys of the crowded cheek-by-jowl tenements, whose windows overhung the passageways below. In such unsanitary conditions, the plague soon began to take hold.

On 7 June 1665 Pepys recorded in his diary: 'This day, much against my Will, I did in Drury Lane see two or three houses marked with a red cross upon the doors, and "Lord have mercy upon us" writ there; which was a sad sight to me, being the first of that kind that to my remembrance I ever saw.' The red cross was the ordinance, enforced by the city authorities, to identify infected homes, whose inhabitants were confined to isolation. Later in the day, muffled men dragging carts would pass down the street calling, 'Bring out your dead!' The wrapped cadavers would then be manhandled on to the carts and carried off to the local churchyard.

By 30 January 1666, Pepys was recording how, when he passed St Olave's, his local church, he was shocked and frightened 'to see so many graves lie [piled] so high upon the churchyard... where so many have been buried of the plague'. The following day he recorded that 'many about the city that live near the churchyards [are] solicitous to have the churchyards covered with lime'. But by now the ravages of the plague were such that there was a shortage of all commodities, which meant that it was no longer possible to cover the corpses in this manner. The result was an 'offensive and unwholesome stench' emanating all around.

By now, most of the cadavers carried off by handcarts, or shipped away by lighters (rowing barges), ended up being emptied into common graves. Soon more than two dozen large pits were dug, mostly outside the City walls. There were 68,594 officially recorded deaths, though it is now believed that some 100,000 cadavers were disposed of in such fashion.

Throughout the long hot summer of 1666 there was a drought, leaving the old wooden houses of the City tinder-dry. Just after midnight on Sunday, 2 September 1666, a fire broke out in a bakery on Pudding Lane. The family living upstairs managed to escape through an upper

---

London remained a 'wooden, northern and inartificial [i.e. unplanned] congestion of houses'.

window and across the rooftops, leaving behind a maidservant who was overcome by fright and burned to death in the flames. The neighbours vainly attempted to douse the fire, until the parish constables arrived and ordered the nearby houses to be demolished to create a fire-break. The householders vigorously protested, and when the Lord Mayor of London Sir Thomas Bludworth arrived on the scene he countermanded this order, remarking dismissively of the fire that 'a woman could piss it out'.

Pepys records how the following morning he climbed to the battlements of the Tower of London to view the fire. By now a high easterly wind had stoked the flames into a conflagration which had destroyed some 300 houses and spread as far as the riverfront and the houses at the City end of London Bridge. He took a boat up the Thames, where he saw 'a lamentable fire':

> Everybody endeavouring to remove their goods, and flinging into the river or bringing them into lighters that lay off. Poor people staying in their houses as long as till the very fire touched them, and then running into boats or clambering from one pair of stairs by the water-side to another. And among other things, the poor pigeons I perceived were loath to leave their houses, but hovered about the windows and balconies till they were some of them burned, their wings, and fell down.

Within four days, the City of London inside the ancient walls and west beyond the River Fleet had been gutted. The centuries-old St Paul's Cathedral, with its high nave and tower, which had for so long dominated the London skyline, was 'now a sad ruine'.

The fire would reach within a stone's throw of Gresham College. The entire heart of the City was left smouldering amongst the ashes. Even the Royal Exchange, which had by now become London's answer to the Amsterdam Stock Exchange, was burned to the ground. The centuries-old Guildhall, the City's town hall, was still standing, but its interior was gutted. How could London possibly recover?

At the time, England was in the midst of another naval war against the Dutch. In June 1667, the Dutch fleet conducted the notorious Raid on the Medway, setting fire to many of the ships in England's most strategic harbour, and even towing away the *Royal Charles*, pride of the English navy. This has been described as 'the most humiliating defeat suffered by British arms'.

First the Great Plague, then the Great Fire of London, then the Raid on the Medway... this should have been the end of England's rise. Yet if anything these events only served to galvanize the country to even-greater ambition. And Fellows of the Royal Society, as well as Gresham College, would prove central to the new London, which rose from the ashes of the old city. Hooke, who was in lonely residence at Gresham College, was soon joined by refugees from the Guildhall, led by Lord Mayor Bludworth. And others also sought accommodation.

> Gresham College now became the hub of London's business activities too. For the next five years Hooke lived cheek by jowl with the merchants and financiers from the Royal Exchange, whose displaced activities were also relocated to Gresham College... with over a hundred makeshift stalls erected around the buildings, the College was turned into a combination of Town Hall and market place.

Despite all that had taken place, it was business as usual. More significantly, Hooke was hired as a surveyor for the City of London, assessing in detail the ravages of the Great Fire. As such, he became chief assistant to Christopher Wren, who had been commissioned to oversee no less a task than the rebuilding of the capital. This latter task would take years – during which Wren, assisted by his young protégé Nicholas Hawksmoor, would rebuild in his own style more than fifty churches whose spires, towers and domes would remain a feature of the London skyline until the twentieth century and beyond. But the crowning glory of Wren's achievements would be the building of a new domed and towered St Paul's Cathedral, which remains to this day one of London's leading landmarks. This would not be completed until 1711, when the final stone was placed on the lantern by Wren's son in the 'topping out' ceremony. A contemporary poet described the new St Paul's: 'Without, within, below, above, the eye / Is filled with unrestrained delight.'

The new London that rose from the ashes of the Great Fire was soon more than a rival for Amsterdam, its importance rivalling even Paris.

CHAPTER 11

A QUIET CITY IN SOUTH HOLLAND

D ELFT HAD ONCE BEEN the capital of the Dutch Republic, during the 1500s when William of Orange ruled the newly independent province of Holland. These were turbulent times, as the Dutch fought for their freedom from Spanish Habsburg rule. When Philip II of Spain offered a reward of 25,000 crowns to anyone who would assassinate the Prince of Orange (also known as William the Silent), this was taken up by a French Catholic named Balthasar Gérard. On 10 July 1584, Gérard leapt from his hiding place in the hall of Delft's Prinsenhof brandishing a pair of long-barrelled pistols, and shot the prince. According to legend, as William of Orange lay dying he uttered the words: '*Mon Dieu, ayez pitié de moi et de mon pauvre peuple*' ('My God, have pity on me and my poor people').* Even though it remains unlikely that William the Silent actually said these words, they would become a rallying call during the struggle for independence.

---

* French was the language of the court, and this is also indicative of William's descent from the House of Orange and its origin in southern France.

Amidst the confusion, Gérard managed to escape from the Prinsenhof, with William's attendants in hot pursuit. Gérard intended to make it to the city walls and dive into the moat. (He had a pig's bladder tied to his waist to keep him afloat.) On the other side, a saddled horse stood ready to carry him away. But Gérard was caught by his pursuers when he slipped on some rubbish in a lane leading up to the walls.

Gérard was put on trial, and then sentenced to a death of remarkable brutality even in those times. For days he was subjected to numerous ingenious and excruciating tortures (at one point he was hung on a pole and whipped, with heavy weights suspended from his big toes). On the day of his execution his right hand was burned off with a red-hot iron, before he was quartered and disembowelled while still alive, and then beheaded. According to historian Lisa Jardine, Gérard was the first recorded assassin of a ruler using a firearm. The bullet marks in the wall of the Prinsenhof can be seen to this day.

After this, history moved on from Delft. The royal court assembled elsewhere, leaving the city and its surrounding waterways to provincial calm. The quiet streets, canals and everyday life of this world would be captured in the timeless oil paintings of Jan Vermeer, who was born in Delft in October 1632.

During his lifetime, Vermeer would achieve little recognition beyond his home city. He would paint fewer than three dozen paintings, and seems never to have ventured further from Delft than Gouda or The Hague, both within a dozen or so miles. Until recently, little was known of his life – indeed, even today Vermeer remains something of an enigma. In Holland during his lifetime, there was a popular saying: '*Zoo den man was, was zyn werk*' (So the man, so the work). Most of what we can glean of Vermeer must therefore be found in his work.

Vermeer's deceptively clear and straightforward *View of Delft* depicts the city from across the expanse of the outer canal. Beyond the smooth, slightly dappled stretch of water we see the city walls, with the Schiedam Gate and its clock linked by a stone bridge across a small canal leading to the twin towers of the Rotterdam Gate. Close inspection reveals a number of working barges, their dark shapes pricked out with pointillist white dots of paint. On the sandy shore in the foreground stand several unremarkable figures going about their business. And this is the point: despite the overall stillness and muted shadowy shades of the buildings beneath the partially clouded sky, this is a working city, as it would have been in 1661. Much as its inhabitants saw it, and wished to see it.

It is difficult to comprehend the mayhem of William the Silent's assassination taking place here. Indeed, it is even more difficult to comprehend that just seven years previously, this city had been rocked by the Delft Thunderclap, when a cellar in a storehouse containing thirty tons of gunpowder exploded, wreaking havoc on this city of just 15,000 souls.* But what was all that gunpowder doing there? This seemingly peaceful city existed in the midst of an age of war (the Thirty Years' War, the War of Independence, the wars against the English). The Delft Thunderclap, and the ensuing fire, destroyed entire neighbourhoods of wooden houses, killing more than a hundred citizens and injuring ten times that many. By the time of Vermeer's painting, these houses had been replaced by red-brick buildings. Are those the red rooftops glimpsed away in the sunlight at the centre of the painting? The calm of Vermeer's painting would appear to be all but illusory; the history of its details reveals a very different picture.

Nowhere is this more apparent than in Vermeer's other surviving cityscape, *The Little Street* of 1658. This small matter-of-fact painting depicts two unremarkable red-brick houses, whose age certainly predated the Thunderclap. The houses have windows made up of small lead-framed squares of glass, and some of these windows are shuttered. The worn red brick and pale shutters are precisely rendered. Such a weathered effect was achieved by painstakingly delicate overpainting, using a mixture of dusty sand and expensive muted pigments (red ochre and madder lake, as well as grit for the red bricks). A woman bowed over her sewing sits in the doorway of the right-hand house. At the end of its side passageway another woman is bent over a washtub. Against the wall beside her leans a mop or a broom, with a trickle of soapy water beside the drain leading into

---

* At the time, the central city of Amsterdam had a population of 60,000.

the cobbled street. Between the women, beneath the shuttered windows of the house, we can see the backs of two kneeling children, who appear to be intent upon some game they are playing on the squared flagstones in front of the house.

In the words of modern art critic Maurizia Tazartes, this entire scene is 'typical of Vermeer's subtle poetry and extraordinary sensitivity... [making for a] silent, absorbed picture'. Only on closer inspection do we become aware, beyond the masterfully precise rendering, of the overall shabbiness of the buildings beneath the partly clouded northern sky – as well as the resignation in the posture of the two women. Indeed, an overall air of melancholy pervades the scene. The main building with the woman in the front doorway has been identified as the local workhouse, the last sanctuary for the poor and destitute of Delft. Vermeer's painting was made in 1658, when he probably knew that this house was due for demolition – ironically to make way for the headquarters of the local painters' guild, of which he was a member. As in so much of Vermeer's work, here is art fulfilling its most profound mission – as an object of contemplative insight, where we come to our own conclusions.

However, Vermeer's penchant was for interior scenes. He obsessively returned to variations of the same window-lit corner of the same room (probably in his house), often featuring a young female figure. In one of these pictures we see a sturdy maid pouring milk from a jar into an earthenware bowl, which is on a table beside a basket and loaves of bread. How does this apparently simple scene achieve its almost monumental power? This is perhaps the one instance where Vermeer conforms with Ernst Gombrich's reductionist view that 'his paintings are really still lives with human beings'. The same certainly cannot be said of Vermeer's painting of a seated young woman playing a lute beneath a large map of Europe, her fresh face gazing towards the light coming from the window. Are her eager eyes staring out beyond the glass of the window, or is this the absorbed expression of concentration on playing the music? This is a human question, not applicable to a still life. And the answer lies in our imagination.

Then there is the painting of another young woman adorned with a yellow satin jerkin lined with ermine; she is holding out the pearl necklace she is wearing as she gazes into a mirror hanging on the wall by the same window. As Tazartes puts it: 'He has captured the young woman's fascinated delight perfectly.' This painting is another intriguing object of contemplation with no easy answers. It is what it is, and at the same time it is the suggestion of an entire life laid out before you. As so often, Vermeer evokes the imagination of the viewer. The painting itself is a mirror, and what we see in it reflects our view of the world he has depicted.

Then we come to the painting many critics regard as his finest work: *Woman in Blue Reading a Letter*. This features another young woman standing by the window, using its light to enable her to read the letter she is holding. Behind her is a large map, this time featuring the provinces of Holland and West Friesland. She is heavily pregnant, her body bulging beneath the blue jacket she is wearing. What are the contents of the letter? It is impossible to tell from the young woman's intent expressionless face. Words of love from the absent father-to-be? News of his death in the wars? This peaceful domestic scene is focused on the unknown drama contained in the letter.

The historian Kenneth Clark, in his *Civilisation*, compares Vermeer to Descartes, 'first of all, in his detached, evasive character'. Like Descartes, Vermeer 'wanted to cut away all preconceptions and get back to the facts of direct experience, unaffected by custom and convention'. In support of this view, Clark tells us an anecdote about an eminent collector, who travelled some way to visit Vermeer, only to be told that the artist had no pictures he could show him, 'which was just untrue because when he died his house contained unsold pictures of all periods'. Vermeer was not interested in such visitors; all he wanted was 'tranquillity, in order to enjoy fine discrimination and discover the truth through a delicate balance'.

This is only partly true. One of the few facts we know for certain about Vermeer's life is that at twenty he married Catharina Bolnes. She was two years older than him and came from a wealthy Catholic family. (Vermeer converted to Catholicism in order to marry her.) The couple were to have fifteen children, four of whom died in infancy. Although Vermeer and his bride moved into the spacious house of his mother-in-law, using two rooms as his studio, the constant presence of so many children must have made for a particularly noisy and eventful domestic milieu. Similarly, the presence of his mother-in-law and his lack of apparent worldly success cannot have helped.

In the same year as Vermeer married, his father died, passing on to him his art dealership, as well as numerous debts from his other commercial interests. Vermeer welcomed the prospect of entering the art trade. He loved collecting and studying paintings. However, he seems to have been unable, or unwilling, to sell the paintings he acquired. His business activities were a constant drain on his finances; he took out several loans, and ran up lasting debts. The 'detached, evasive' character to which Clark alludes may well have only been achieved in his paintings.

Vermeer remained meticulous in his art. He chose to use the most expensive pigments, and took so long seeking perfection in his paintings that only thirty-five of these have come down to us. The calm reason of the paintings was created against a background of unreason: of domestic pandemonium, commercial incompetence, political uncertainty and war. They were appreciated by few in his lifetime, but the few who did appreciate them recognized them for what they were: consummate works of art. Evidence of this can be seen in the fact that Vermeer would be visited by Cosimo III de' Medici, the future Grand Duke of Tuscany, during his tour of northern Europe.

Then, in 1672, came the *Rampjaar* (Year of Disaster). The country was in the midst of a third war with England, the French army of Louis XIV invaded from the south, and German forces launched an attack from the east. A local saying from that year famously described the Dutch people as '*redeloos, radeloos, reddeloos*' (irrational, distraught, beyond salvation). The economy collapsed, and with it the art market. Any hope Vermeer might have had of selling his collection of his own and other works of art vanished overnight.

Vermeer died suddenly in 1675 at the age of forty-three, leaving his wife with eleven children and a mountain of debt. In the petition she wrote to her creditors, she described how:

During the ruinous war with France he not only was unable to sell any of his art, but also, to his great detriment, was left sitting with the paintings of other masters that he was dealing in. As a result and owing to the great burden of his children having no means of his own, he lapsed into such decay and decadence, which he had so taken to heart that, as if he had fallen into a frenzy, in a day and a half he went from being healthy to being dead.

Following Vermeer's nervous breakdown and ensuing death, Catharina would be forced to sell off two of his last paintings to pay off their large debt to the baker. The difficult task of acting as Vermeer's executor was taken on by his friend Antonie van Leeuwenhoek (pronounced 'Lay-van-hook'), the other extraordinary inhabitant of this quiet city in South Holland.

Antonie van Leeuwenhoek's surname translates as 'Lion's Corner', probably after the district in Delft where his family originated, which takes its name from a carved lion on a corner house. Van Leeuwenhoek was born just a week or so after Vermeer, in October 1632. His father was a basket-maker who died when young Anton was just five years old. His mother, who came from a prosperous brewing family, then remarried – to a painter. The fact that the family had links with the local artistic circle probably accounts for how Van Leeuwenhoek came to be a friend of Vermeer.

At the age of sixteen, Van Leeuwenhoek left school and travelled to Amsterdam, where he became an apprentice bookkeeper at a linen-draper's shop on Warmoesstraat, the street on which the original stock exchange had been founded in 1611.* It was in this shop that Leeuwenhoek first came into contact with the glass buttons used by drapers to magnify the surface of cloth so as to determine its quality.

---

* This draper's shop happened to be owned by a successful Scottish businessman named William Davidson, who is now known to have been a spy for the English during the Third Dutch War. He would later become instrumental in the education of the child who grew up to become William III of Orange. In 1689, William would be invited to accept the throne of England, Scotland and Ireland, whereupon he and his wife would ascend as joint monarchs William and Mary.

In his early twenties Van Leeuwenhoek returned to Delft and established his own drapery business. Around the same time, he married a local woman named Barbara de Mey. In time they would have five children, only one of whom survived infancy – a daughter named Maria. The drapery business provided him with a comfortable income, but it was his hobby that became his overriding passion. Like many in the Dutch Republic, Van Leeuwenhoek became fascinated by the new craze for lens-grinding. Magnifying lenses may have been used by scientists such as Galileo, Huygens and Hooke to scour the heavens, but in the Dutch Republic these also served a more everyday purpose. Middle-aged folk – from scholars to citizens who wished to read the latest news sheets – found that instead of having lines of print read out to them they could simply don spectacles, whose lenses enabled them to decipher print into comparative old age.*

Besides producing glasses, a number of lens-grinders sought to produce lenses of ever-greater magnification. Here Van Leeuwenhoek discovered that he had a unique advantage. He also took to using globules of glass, such as those employed by drapers to examine their cloth.

He soon discovered how to make these for himself. By holding a glass rod over a flame, and then stretching this, he was able to produce a filigree of glass, which could then be broken and its fragments polished into tiny glass buttons. He also made lenses by chipping off the small glass nodule that forms on the bottom of a blown glass bulb. Van Leeuwenhoek became so practised at this that he could produce tiny glass buttons almost as small as a pin's head. When polished these became miniscule biconvex

---

* The effect of these new spectacles would transform society during the Age of Reason in a way that is often overlooked. Now that people could read, and see clearly, well beyond middle age, this meant that learning became extended. At the same time it also spread: knowledge became democratized. The result was a wide increase in understanding, articulation and even self-realization, which extended the range of the educated classes. Aided by the spread of cheaper printing presses, this led to the widespread appearance of dictionaries, instruction manuals and popular (often plagiarized) versions of scholarly works, as well as a growing market for pamphlets containing all manner of news, political ideas, scurrilous gossip and the like. This was the birth of a new information age.

lenses capable of considerably higher magnification than anyone had yet achieved by constructing microscopes with two or three larger polished lenses, such as those used by Hooke in his *Micrographia.*[*]

The only drawback with Van Leeuwenhoek's method was that these ever-smaller globules of glass became increasingly difficult to manipulate and actually use as a magnifying lens. They also had a very short focus. Van Leeuwenhoek managed to solve this problem by clamping the tiny glass globule between two metal plates with tiny holes drilled in them. The plates could then be raised or lowered in order to focus the lens gripped between the two tiny holes. By this means, he was able to focus his miniscule glass button-lenses on all manner of objects.

What Van Leeuwenhoek saw intrigued him: he appeared to have discovered a new world filled with all manner of wonders and tiny beings – 'animalcules', he called them, as his lenses burrowed ever deeper into the unknown. By now, he was approaching middle age. His wife had died and he remarried. His commercial and civic standing in Delft led to him being given the post of janitor of the city hall, a purely honorary sinecure.

However, there is evidence that this honour may also have been granted to Van Leeuwenhoek in recognition of his scientific pursuits, knowledge of which must already have spread amongst some of the cognoscenti of the city. Evidence that his discoveries were not entirely ignored in his home city can be seen from two works by his friend Vermeer. Amongst the unsold paintings found in Vermeer's possession on his death were two portraits – one called *The Geographer*, the other *The Astronomer*. Both of these depict their subjects at work with the objects of their profession. The geographer appears lost in thought as he leans over a map, a measuring compass in his right hand. The astronomer is similarly absorbed in concentration as he leans forward, his right hand moving the surface of a celestial globe on his desk. The surface of the globe depicts the patterns of the stars in the night sky. Both portraits are evidently of

---

[*] It is important to stress that at this early stage Van Leeuwenhoek was unaware of Hooke's work. Initially he not only used a different type of microscope, but his results were of a different order.

the same man, and were painted around 1668. These two portraits are now thought to be of Van Leeuwenhoek, who would have been in his mid-thirties around this time. Vermeer seems to have understood that his friend was every bit as much of an explorer of an unknown world as any geographer or astronomer.

Unbeknownst to Van Leeuwenhoek, the experiments he was undertaking exceeded far beyond anything before achieved. Even Hooke and his microscope could only perceive a magnified version of the world we could glimpse with our own eyes. Van Leeuwenhoek's lenses enabled him to gain access to an entire universe far beyond previous human conception. Nothing scientists had previously seen had led them to suspect the existence of this utterly new realm of 'animalcules'. For the first time, an entire zoology of new creatures was made accessible to human investigation.

Van Leeuwenhoek continued with his hobby, though his miraculous findings remained unknown – except locally, to his friends and acquaintances amongst the citizens of Delft. Certainly no one outside this small provincial city seemed either aware, or interested, in what he was discovering. And so things might have continued, had Van Leeuwenhoek not encountered the celebrated Dutch physiologist Regnier de Graaf, who had come to live in Delft. De Graaf had invented a syringe to inject dye into human organs so that their structure and function could be studied, and it was he who coined the term 'ovary'. More pertinently, De Graaf was also a member of the Royal Society of London.

One day Van Leeuwenhoek happened to invite De Graaf to his house so that he could see for himself the world he had discovered with his tiny lenses. As De Graaf screwed up his eye and peered through Van Leeuwenhoek's bead of glass he immediately understood the scientific importance of what he was seeing. On returning home, De Graaf immediately wrote to Oldenburg, the secretary of the Royal Society, about Van Leeuwenhoek's astonishing findings and his amazing instruments.

De Graaf's intervention on Van Leeuwenhoek's behalf proved most timely – within a few months De Graaf had died of malaria. Sometime later, a letter for Van Leeuwenhoek arrived from the Royal Society.

Unfortunately this letter was written in Latin, still the international language of scholars, and was thus incomprehensible to Van Leeuwenhoek, who had never completed his education. Fortunately, De Graaf had been so impressed with Van Leeuwenhoek's discoveries that he had mentioned them to Constantijn Huygens, the polymath father of the distinguished scientist Christiaan Huygens. It was Huygens senior who ensured that Van Leeuwenhoek understood the contents of the letter from Oldenburg, which invited him to submit examples of his work to the Royal Society. Van Leeuwenhoek was so overjoyed with this prestigious recognition that he was soon bombarding the Royal Society with letters and drawings of what he had viewed through his novel microscope.

The Royal Society was initially somewhat suspicious of Van Leeuwenhoek's voluminous communications. For a start he was Dutch, and England was at the time in the midst of the Anglo-Dutch wars. Secondly, although Van Leeuwenhoek wrote to them in Dutch, the Royal Society soon managed to work out from his drawings that he was using a single-lensed microscope, which he claimed had a magnification of 200 times. Hooke's sophisticated two- and three-lensed microscopes were barely capable of achieving much more than a quarter of this magnification.

If what Van Leeuwenhoek claimed he saw was true, then there did indeed exist an entirely new microscopic realm filled with all manner of 'animalcules'. These inhabited everything from drops of water to spermatozoa. Indeed, his investigation of the flea went far further than Hooke's famous example: he observed that fleas themselves appeared to harbour their own tiny parasites. It was this last finding that would later inspire the Irish cleric and satirist Jonathan Swift to write: 'Great fleas have little fleas upon their backs to bite 'em. / And little fleas have lesser fleas, and so *ad infinitum*.'*

This newly discovered world seemed without end. As the American

---

* Some have speculated that Hooke's *Micrographia*, as well as work by Van Leeuwenhoek, may well have inspired Swift's *Gulliver's Travels*, in which the hero voyages to Lilliput where he is a giant, and later to Brobdingnag where he is a midget in a giant world.

historian of science and futurist Isaac Asimov would observe: 'Leeuwenhoek was the first to discover the one-celled animals called protozoa and in 1677 opened up a whole world of living organisms as alive as the elephant and the whale yet compressing all that life into a space too small to see without mechanical help.'

In 1677 Hooke decided to create a microscope using Van Leeuwenhoek's methods and specifications. At the same time, Van Leeuwenhoek despatched some two dozen examples of his own. All this confirmed that his method was indeed superior. His work was vindicated, and in 1680 he was unanimously voted a Fellow of the Royal Society.

But this did not distract him from his work. Three years later he would make what many regard as his most pioneering discovery. At the very limit of which his tiny glass-beads were capable of reaching, he managed to discern living organisms we now know to be bacteria. It would be well over a century before scientists were able to confirm the existence of this form of life.

Van Leeuwenhoek continued working in Delft until he was ninety years old, assisted in his task by the only surviving member of his family, his daughter Maria. It was she who would welcome the many dignitaries who now beat their way to the door of the obscure microscopist of Delft, whose observations had changed our understanding of the world. Amongst others, he received visits from William and Mary, the King and Queen of England, as well as Frederick I of Prussia and Peter the Great of Russia.

Ironically, although Van Leeuwenhoek's microscopes and his findings went far beyond those of Hooke, it was the Englishman's methodology that would prevail. In Van Leeuwenhoek's skilled hands, the single-lensed microscope reached its limit. As the art of lens-grinding improved, and the techniques of microscopy were better understood, it was the mounted two- and three-lensed microscopes that managed to see further into the world which Hooke and Van Leeuwenhoek had been the first to explore.

During the Age of Reason both Holland and England would produce single-minded scientists of the order of Van Leeuwenhoek, as well as many consummate polymaths such as the early members of the Royal Society and the Huygenses (father and son). So it comes as something of a surprise that the authorities of both Holland and England should during this period be taken in by the activities of a highly talented charlatan named Johann Becher, whose 'expertise' (genuine and otherwise) ranged from economics to chemistry, and much in between.

Johann Becher was born on the Rhine upstream from the Dutch border, in the Protestant German city of Speyer, in 1635. When he was just thirteen his father died, in the very year that saw the end of the Thirty Years' War. Despite his youth, Becher took to the road, tramping the highways and byways of a ravaged Europe. He is known to have reached as far north as Sweden, and also to have travelled to Italy. Becher was gifted with a keen intellect, and during the course of these wanderings he gathered a wide range of knowledge, though this was untrammelled by the discipline of academic learning.

The ruined German lands consisted of a myriad of quasi-independent states, each trying to re-establish its civic and commercial life. As a result, the rulers of these states were much in need of expert advisers. At the age of just twenty-six, Becher managed to talk himself into just such a post at the court of the Elector of Mainz, one of the more powerful states in the Rhineland. He quickly converted to Catholicism so that he could marry the daughter of a powerful imperial councillor, who granted him a degree in medicine as a wedding present. Building on this slender foundation, Becher soon managed to have himself appointed professor of medicine at the University of Mainz, and personal physician to the elector himself.

Not long after drawing his considerable annual salary for these posts, Becher absented himself from Mainz and made his way south to the more powerful state of Bavaria, where his novel suggestions for commerce soon came to the notice of the elector, Ferdinand Maria, who appointed him *Hofmedicus und Mathematicus* (court physician and mathematician). Becher advised the elector that in order to thrive, Bavaria needed to restrict its reliance upon trade with France, particularly with regard to the import of luxury items such as silk. He proposed the establishment of a home-grown silk industry in Bavaria, but this was bitterly resented by the powerful merchants who had made their fortunes in the French silk trade.

Becher decided that his talents were not sufficiently appreciated in Bavaria, and removed himself to Vienna, which was now becoming established as one of the major centres of Europe. Becher presented his credentials to the Emperor Leopold I of Austria, boasting of his expertise in previously running no less than two states. Once again, Becher suggested that the remedy to Austria's economic ills lay in the establishing of an indigenous silk industry. This quickly ruined the nascent silk industry he had set up in nearby Bavaria, but then ran into difficulties of its own.

During Becher's stay in Vienna he would prove a fount of knowledge, not all of which was spurious. He is said to have arrived in the capital of the Austrian empire 'brimming over with plans and projects'. One of these was a suggestion for a canal linking the upper waters of the Danube to the Rhine river basin, in order to facilitate trade with landlocked Austria and the opportunities presented by Holland's thriving inland and overseas commerce. (This was a project centuries ahead of its time.) It was during these years that Becher also made major contributions in various fields. His economic ideas are still recognized as playing a leading role in the development of mercantilism, now regarded as the formative school of political economy prior to economics becoming a recognized field of study.*

Becher's form of mercantilism stressed that a nation's prosperity lay in exporting goods, and limiting as far as possible the import of goods it could produce itself. Profits from trade should be stored in the form of gold, which must on no account be tapped, except in case of extreme necessity. It was this gold reserve that was the measure of a nation's wealth.

Becher also pioneered the notion of cameralism: the science of public administration. This fostered the belief that a strong centralized authority

---

* The Scotsman Adam Smith's *The Wealth of Nations*, published in 1776, is generally recognized as the founding work of economics.

should be established to administer political and commercial activity for the benefit of the state. Such political and economic ideas were much needed in a Europe laid low by the Thirty Years' War.

Quite apart from these beneficial practical notions, Becher also made major contributions in more intellectual spheres. It was he who transformed chemistry by proposing the Phlogiston theory, which would remain central to science for at least another century. This explained combustion (burning) by proposing that in this process materials released a fire-like substance called phlogiston into the atmosphere. Proof of this process was supported by experimental evidence. When a burning substance was placed in an enclosed space, its fire soon went out. Why? Because the air became saturated with phlogiston, and could absorb no more of it.

However, experimentalists soon discovered that when a substance burned it in fact *gained* weight, rather than losing it by releasing phlogiston. But the proponents of Phlogiston theory were quick to counter this argument, by suggesting that phlogiston must have *negative* weight. This argument only seems unreasonable in hindsight. Even the great Robert Boyle believed in phlogiston; indeed it was he who proposed the 'negative weight' theory.

Unfortunately, Becher also shared another enthusiasm with Boyle – namely, a persistent belief in alchemy. However, where Boyle kept quiet about his activities in this sphere, Becher was all for loudly promoting it as a panacea. To back up his mercantilist ideas he suggested that the Viennese authorities should add to their nation's gold reserves by transmuting the sands along the banks of the Danube into gold, using alchemical means.

Becher may appear now to have been a charlatan, but there is little doubt that he was quite sincere in his belief in alchemy. But how could such an original thinker – in economics, political administration, chemistry and so forth – also believe in such an unscientific idea as alchemy? Despite Becher's habit of switching from Protestantism to Catholicism, and back again, when it suited him, he remained a firm believer in Christianity. For him the world had been created by God the chemist, who maintained his creation by a continuous process of alteration and transformation. (This idea can be seen as the basis of his economic thought, and his political ideas, as well as his chemistry.) Indeed, Becher's article of faith is one of the most inspiring in the cause of science:

> The chemists are a strange class of mortals, impelled by an almost maniacal impulse to seek their pleasures amongst smoke and vapour, soot and flames, poisons and poverty, yet amongst all these evils I seem to live so sweetly that I would rather die than change places with the King of Persia.

Armed with his indestructible belief in alchemy, Becher arrived in Holland sometime in the mid-1670s. Here he returned to his old hobby horse of silk manufacture, attempting to set up a manufactory in Haarlem. However, when he learned that Holland was beginning to suffer from an increasing shortage of gold reserves, he could not resist this opportunity. Presenting himself before the States General, he once again outlined an ambitious scheme for transmuting the vast tracts of sandy beaches along the Dutch coast into gold, by alchemical means. The hard-headed businessmen who filled the assembly were unconvinced. So Becher proceeded to overcome their lack of faith with a spectacular demonstration. He set up an experiment involving sand and a small amount of silver, which miraculously succeeded in producing gold. The Dutch assembly then enthusiastically backed Becher's scheme.

However, Becher now explained that in order to operate on the vast scale he had suggested, he would of course require a considerable amount of silver to start off with. A few days before Becher's enormous project was due to begin, he disappeared and caught the ferry to England.

It is difficult to delineate the aspects of reason and unreason in Becher's exceptional personality. Alongside the con man, there certainly existed an element of genius – to say nothing of an excess of self-conviction. Becher believed in himself, and (like Boyle) believed in alchemy; even if he had not quite cracked its ultimate transmutational riddle – yet. On the other hand, he was certainly not above providing an element of 'encouragement' to his belief. He evidently saw this as being on a par with talking himself into posts and tasks for which he was not officially qualified, but nonetheless fulfilled with some satisfaction – and not always just to himself.

Becher turned up in London in 1678, where he completed the final volumes of his *Physica Subterranea*. Ostensibly about mining (hence its title), this was to be Becher's masterwork, and was brimming with all manner of original ideas. It attracted the attention of Prince Rupert, a member of the royal family and also a Fellow of the Royal Society, who commissioned him to undertake an inspection of mines in Scotland and Cornwall. Towards the end of this undertaking – for which Becher was untypically qualified – he decided to extend his commission by a few months and settle down to complete a number of unfinished works. (According to the preface of his *Laboratorium Portabile*, this was completed in Falmouth, a major port and seaside resort in Cornwall.)

However, a leopard cannot change its spots – on his return to London, Becher wrote a thesis describing a clock that worked by perpetual motion, which he submitted to the Royal Society. To his chagrin this was rejected, as was his application to become a Fellow, despite the fact that he had cited Boyle in many of his works. (Or possibly *because* he had cited Boyle, on alchemical matters.) Becher would die a year or so later, at the age of forty-seven. By this time he was penniless, but still ruing his rejection by the Royal Society – even going so far as to reconvert once more to Protestantism in the hope of furthering his cause. Posthumously, Becher would be acknowledged for his genuine contributions, with no less than the great twentieth-century Austrian-born Harvard economist Joseph Schumpeter going so far as to claim that 'his vigor and originality were universally recognized even by men like Leibniz'.

CHAPTER 12

EXPLORATION

Antonie van Leeuwenhoek and Robert Hooke may have discovered the wonders of the microworld, and the likes of Christopher Wren and John Flamsteed had expanded our understanding of the universe, but there still remained our earthly globe in between these extremes. The Age of Reason would see an expansion of European knowledge of the globe, which built upon the spectacular territorial discoveries of the earlier Renaissance era – by the likes of Columbus (the New World), Dias (the sea route around Africa to the Indian Ocean), and Magellan (the circumnavigation of the globe).

As already described, by the early 1600s the English and the Dutch had begun making inroads on the Portuguese monopoly of trade all over East Asia. This was largely the doing of the English East India Company in India, and the Dutch VOC in South-East Asia, where it had established its headquarters at Batavia (now Jakarta) on the island of Java, in modern Indonesia.

Willem Janszoon was already an experienced trader when he set sail from Holland in 1603 as captain of the *Duyfken* (Little Dove), one of a flotilla of a dozen ships under the command of the VOC's Admiral

Steven van der Haghen. When the flotilla disembarked from Batavia for the return voyage, van der Haghen ordered Janszoon to undertake an exploratory voyage to seek out further opportunities for trade, especially in 'the great land of New Guinea and other East and Southlands'.

Janszoon duly set sail on the *Duyfken* for the south coast of New Guinea, arriving at what is now known as the Torres Strait.* This 100-mile stretch of water separates New Guinea from Cape York at the northern tip of Queensland. Janszoon made landfall some hundred miles south-west of Cape York, thus becoming the first European to see and set foot on the subcontinent of Australia. The exact spot where he landed is the mouth of Pennefather River, near modern-day Weipa. Janszoon then sailed south, mapping the coastline. Remnants of this voyage can be found in the names of several geographical features – such as the spit of land twenty miles south of the Pennefather known as Duyfken Point, and Cape Keerweer some hundred miles further south, where Janszoon turned the *Duyfken* round and headed back north (*keerweer* is Dutch for 'turnaround').

The coastline had proved inhospitable and swampy, and the few indigenous people the Dutch encountered were hostile. During various expeditions ashore, Janszoon lost ten of his crewmen. As Janszoon had not sailed all the way through the Torres Strait, he was convinced that he was mapping the southern coast of New Guinea, and decided to name this region Nieu Zeelandt, after the Dutch province of Zeeland.

Janszoon's geographical error would be repeated in the 1622 world map produced by the Dutch cartographer Hessel Gerritsz, though he decided against calling the territory Nieu Zeelandt. Gerritsz's map would contain one of the earliest modern references to Australia Incognita (Unknown Southern Land), though this too was an error. A few years earlier, the Spanish explorer Pedro Fernandes de Queirós had made landfall on the Pacific island of Vanuatu; wildly misjudging its size, he

---

* Named after the Spanish explorer Luís Vaz de Torres, who in fact reached this stretch of water several months later. In the description of Janszoon's voyage I have continued to use the modern names of locations.

had named it 'Australia del Espiritu Santo' (Southern Land of the Sacred Spirit).

In fact, the name 'Australia' had on occasion been used by mapmakers since the classical era for the purely hypothetical southern continent which was presumed to balance out the landmasses of the northern hemisphere. Following the first circumnavigation by Magellan's expedition in 1522, the notion of an unknown great southern continent had been revived – in particular in the 1569 world map by Mercator. The above concoctions of genuine exploration, informed guesswork and pure speculation give an indication of the difficulties faced by the earliest explorers of the southern hemisphere. In an attempt to sort fact from fiction, and avoid conflicting piecemeal assemblages from various sources, it was the Dutch who first came up with a solution.

The Dutch Golden Age extended into the field of cartography. The finest cartographer of the era was undoubtedly Hessel Gerritsz, who was appointed the first exclusive cartographer of the VOC. All captains returning from VOC-sponsored voyages were ordered to report any geographical findings to Gerritsz. This centralization of knowledge was soon reaping rewards for the Dutch merchants in the East India trade. In a reciprocal move, captains setting out on VOC-sponsored voyages were granted the use of Gerritsz's latest maps to chart their route.

Not surprisingly, a clearer picture of East Asia, the East Indies and Australia gradually began to emerge from the collated knowledge of Dutch sailors. However, not all the knowledge received by Gerritsz was positive, or even useful. The tragic wreck of the *Batavia* in 1629 was a case in point.

Dutch ships sailing west around the Cape of Good Hope had discovered how to sail south and take advantage of the Roaring Forties, the strong westerly winds that prevail between latitudes 40° and 50° South. This became known as the Brouwer Route, named after the Dutch captain who first made use of it. An English East India Company ship following a VOC trading ship soon discovered this Dutch trick, which was so useful that it all but halved the sailing time from Europe to the Spice Islands. However, what ensuing East India Company ships failed to understand was that it was necessary to keep a precise watch on the ship's longitude and turn sharp north before running into the west coast of Australia. Dutch ships were not above falling into this trap either.

In October 1628, the VOC's new flagship the *Batavia* set sail on her maiden voyage, leading a flotilla of VOC ships to Batavia, the capital city of the Dutch East Indies. On board the *Batavia* was the commander of the flotilla, the senior merchant Francisco Peisaert, with Ariaen Jacobsz as captain. Peisaert and Jacobsz were old enemies. On an earlier trip to India, Jacobsz had got drunk and insulted Peisaert in front of his fellow merchants, whereupon Jacobsz had received a public dressing-down, humiliating him in front of his crew.

Crammed aboard the *Batavia*, which was just 149 feet long and 34 feet wide, were 300 or so passengers, amongst whom was a bankrupt thirty-year-old apothecary named Jeronimus Cornelisz, who was a member of a notorious heretical sect. He had managed to evade his debtors and escape prosecution for heretical beliefs by signing up with the VOC. Locked in the cargo hold were twelve wooden chests containing 250,000 silver guilders – money for the purchase of spices and other cargo for the ship's return.

According to evidence later given by Peisaert, Captain Jacobsz and the heretic Cornelisz had secretly planned to stage a mutiny, seize the ship's treasure, and start a new life on a remote spice island. Once the *Batavia* rounded the Cape of Good Hope, Jacobsz managed to steer the ship off course so that it became separated from the rest of the flotilla.

On the night of 4 June 1629, the lookout in the crow's nest reported seeing white water ahead breaking over a reef. Jacobsz dismissed this as reflected moonlight, and as a result the *Batavia* crashed into the coral reef of one of a string of islands now known as the Houtman Abrolhos, some fifty miles off the coast of western Australia.

As the ship broke up, 300 of the ship's company managed to make their way ashore, though thirty or so others died. It soon became clear that there was no fresh water on the island, and only seals and seagulls for sustenance. Peisaert decided to set off with Jacobsz and the ship's officers in one of the *Batavia*'s thirty-foot longboats in search of fresh water.

As the heretic Cornelisz was a signed-up member of the VOC, it was decided that he should be left in charge of the remaining crew, soldiers and passengers – despite his lack of either military or naval experience.

The merchant Peisaert's longboat reached the mainland, but was still unable to discover any source of fresh water. So he made the bold decision to set sail for Batavia in his longboat, in order to seek help at the VOC headquarters. Meanwhile Cornelisz despatched the other longboat full of soldiers, under the command of Wiebbe Hayes, to look for water on the nearby islands. Two of the soldiers had secretly been told by Cornelisz to abandon Hayes and the other soldiers, and sail back without them. This they duly did, leaving Hayes and his fellow soldiers to die. When the two soldiers arrived back, Cornelisz persuaded them and some other soldiers to massacre the remaining survivors. In the end, 110 men, women and children were killed, while several younger women's lives were spared so they could be kept as sex slaves.

By now, Cornelisz and his men had managed to salvage some of the treasure chests from the wreck of the *Batavia*, as well as some weapons and supplies. He and his cronies plotted to overcome the crew of any ship sent to rescue them. They would then go ahead with Cornelisz's plan to sail to one of the more hospitable of the distant Spice Islands, where they would set up their own private kingdom.

However, unbeknownst to Cornelisz, Hayes and his soldiers had discovered fresh water and sufficient sources of wildlife to survive. The soldiers then learned of the massacre that Cornelisz had organized, from a survivor who had managed to escape using wood from the wreck of the *Batavia* as a primitive raft. There now followed a series of skirmishes, raids and battles between Hayes and his soldiers on their island, and Cornelisz and his men on theirs. During one of these, the soldiers managed to capture Cornelisz and held him prisoner.

Meanwhile Peisaert and his men in the first longboat had sailed and rowed and steered their craft for more than 130 days, until they finally reached the south coast of Java. Here they were picked up by a Dutch trading ship which carried them to the capital Batavia, where Piesaert reported the shipwreck of the VOC flagship. The governor of Batavia then gave Peisaert and his men the use of the small merchant yacht *Saardam*, which ironically had been one of the original flotilla that had set out under the command of the *Batavia*. Together with a number of soldiers, Peisaert and his men set sail to find the wreck of the *Batavia*, with the aim of rescuing any survivors.

The *Saardam* finally sighted what was left of the *Batavia*, but Piesaert was surprised to see what appeared to be a pitched battle taking place. This was the abandoned soldiers led by Hayes attacking what was left of Cornelisz's ruthless band of cronies.

Upon catching sight of the *Saardam*, both sides immediately broke off fighting and set sail towards the rescue ship – each intent upon telling their side of the story first. Hayes and his soldiers managed to reach the *Saardam* well ahead of Cornelisz's men. In breathless haste, Hayes recounted to Peisaert what had happened. Piesaert believed him, and after a brief skirmish the remnants of Cornelisz's gang were taken prisoner.

As there was not sufficient room aboard the small trading yacht *Saardam* for its crew and all the survivors of the *Batavia*, Peisaert decided to hold an ad hoc trial on the mainland. Cornelisz, his replacement leader, and the senior members of his gang were found guilty. Peisaert ordered that their hands be cut off, and they should then be hanged. On account of their youth, the cabin boy and a young sailor were spared the death sentence, and instead were left marooned on the Australian mainland. According to one source: 'This made them the first Europeans to have permanently lived on the Australian continent.*

The remaining members of Cornelisz's group were marched aboard the *Saardam* and confined below decks. Peisaert was able to recover ten

---

* Whether this 'permanence' lasted for more than a few days remained an open question. Not until over three centuries later was evidence discovered that they might have survived. In the twentieth century, a local Aboriginal community was found to suffer from occasional outbreaks of a rare disease previously unknown in Australia. This disease was found to have been prevalent in Holland during the early 1600s. Though there is no certainty that this came from the cabin boy or the young sailor from the *Batavia*, as other Dutch ships are known to have been wrecked on this coast, possibly leaving other Dutch survivors who were absorbed into this particular Aboriginal community.

of the twelve chests of treasure, and these too were stowed aboard; the *Saardam* then set sail back to Batavia. Of the original ship's company of 341, just 122 are thought to have survived.

On arrival in Batavia, an official commission was set up. This ordered that five more of Cornelisz's men be hanged, and the others subjected to floggings and various brutal punishments. Peisaert reported his suspicions that Captain Jacobsz had originally plotted a mutiny with Cornelisz. Despite being subjected to torture, Jacobsz confessed to nothing. He is thought to have died in jail in Batavia the following year.

The commission decided that Hayes was the hero of the day, and he was immediately promoted to sergeant, with his men all being made corporals. Peisaert himself was subjected to a long and vigorous interrogation. Despite all his efforts – reaching Batavia in his longboat, sailing back to rescue the survivors, capturing Cornelisz and his men, as well as rescuing almost all the treasure – the commission concluded that he was in fact the man responsible for the entire episode. Peisaert was severely reprimanded for failing to show leadership, as well as a lack of proper authority – as a result he was stripped of all he owned. He would die the following year, a broken man.

This story, reminiscent of several tragic adventures during this period of exploration, is characteristic of its age. As such, it is all but impossible to disentangle the strands of reason and unreason which constitute its threadbare surviving narrative.

Further exploration of Australasia would be undertaken by VOC captain Abel Tasman, the finest of all the Dutch explorers. Tasman was born in a village in the northern Dutch province of Groningen around 1603, and appears to have signed on as a VOC sailor while still in his youth. By his early thirties he had become a senior naval officer, serving on a number of VOC-sponsored expeditions east of Java. In this way, he had visited Luzon (the main island of the Philippines), made landfall on Japan, and visited the Dutch fortress-station of Zeelandia on the island of Formosa (in modern Taiwan).

When Tasman was thirty-nine years old, the VOC governor-general in Batavia, Anthony van Diemen, commissioned him to undertake an expedition consisting of two small ships. His orders were to sail into unknown regions of the Southern Pacific Ocean in search of a southern landmass rich in gold, which had begun appearing on European maps as a result of a misprint in an edition of Marco Polo's *Travels*.

Tasman's first expedition left Batavia on 14 August 1642, heading some 3,000 miles east to the VOC supply station on Mauritius.* Here his two small ships, the *Heemskerck* and the *Zeehaen,* rested for a month, while the ships were repaired and took on sufficient victuals for a long voyage. Tasman then sailed directly south, reaching around 50° South, almost certainly further than any previous explorer. From here he took advantage of the Roaring Forties, heading east. However, such was the rough sea, bitter cold, snow and hail, that he was forced to sail on a slightly more north-eastern course.

On 24 November 1642 Tasman made landfall on what he named Van Diemen's Land, after his VOC sponsor (now known as Tasmania). Tasman sailed around the southern tip of Tasmania, but after some days his attempt to sail north was hampered by the high winds of the Roaring Forties as they passed through the Bass Strait. He thus did not realize that Tasmania was not connected to mainland Australia. As the sea was too rough to make landfall, he instructed the strongest swimmer aboard (the ship's carpenter) to swim through the breakers and plant a flag on the land, thus claiming it for Holland. Despite his error, Tasman had established the important fact that Australia was not joined to any great south island, which many still presumed occupied the southern polar regions.

---

* As an aid to their sailors, the VOC had established a string of supply stations along their 12,000-mile main route from Holland to Batavia. In the Atlantic, just south of the equator, they established a supply station at Ascension Island, which they did not occupy, but to which they introduced a herd of goats for passing VOC captains to replenish their meat supplies. Further south in the Atlantic they occupied Saint Helena, which soon had fruit and vegetables, but this fell into abeyance with the establishment of a more permanent colony at Capetown in 1652. Flotillas which had become separated after rounding the Cape of Good Hope on the return route to Holland were ordered to rendezvous at Saint Helena. All of these spots had originally been discovered by the Portuguese, and would later be taken by the East India Company with the advent of British naval supremacy.

Tasman then continued due east, carried forward by the Roaring Forties, with nothing but his compass to guide him through the rough seas of the vast empty ocean. On 13 December he caught sight of land ahead, becoming the first European to set eyes on New Zealand. This was the north-west coast of South Island.

Tasman sailed north, to North Island. Here he made contact with indigenous tribesmen, but they proved hostile, and four of his men were clubbed to death. Tasman's journal entry at this point is particularly evocative:

In the evening about one hour after sunset we saw many lights on land and four vessels near the shore, two of which betook themselves towards us... with the hiding of the sun (which sank behind the high land) they had been still about half a mile from the shore... [The] people in the two canoes began to call out to us in gruff, hollow voices. We could not in the least understand any of it; however, when they called out again several times we called back to them as a token answer. But they did not come nearer than a stone's shot. They also blew many times on an instrument, which produced a sound like the moors' trumpets. We had of our sailors (who could play somewhat on the trumpet) play some tunes to them in answer.

As Tasman and his men turned to sail away from the bay, he observed a large group of double-hulled canoes (*waka*) filled with angry armed warriors speeding across the water towards them. After a brief skirmish, he managed to sail away. What Tasman had not realized was that the local people were trying to protect one of the rare fertile valleys they relied upon for food, and had already spent years defending this spot against marauding tribes.

From New Zealand, Tasman sailed north as far as the Solomon Islands, which had been 'discovered and claimed' by the Spanish in 1568, but had since been abandoned, leaving the native population in peace. Tasman then headed west past northern New Guinea and back to Batavia, arriving on 15 June 1643.

Such was the success of this voyage that Tasman was commissioned by Anthony van Diemen to undertake a second voyage. This would map the north coast of Australia, starting from the Cape York coast mapped by Janszoon and continuing over 2,000 miles around the Gulf of Carpentaria, as far as the north-west tip of Australia, before returning via southern New Guinea to Batavia.

The VOC authorities in Batavia were more than a little disappointed by Tasman's second great voyage of discovery. He had discovered no new territory with which the VOC could trade, and neither had he discovered any new important shipping route to anywhere! In future, they decided, they would commission a more 'persistent explorer'. However, in the event no such explorer could be found, and the VOC abandoned any further expeditions into the Southern Pacific Ocean.

With hindsight, it is possible to see that Tasman had left what resembled a tantalizing preliminary artist's sketch of the southern world. These ghostly lines on the blank page of the Southern Pacific Ocean would not be used for well over a century, when the Englishman Captain James Cook took up the challenge that Tasman's incomplete explorations had posed.

Meanwhile, on the other side of the globe, the outline of the New World was mostly complete on European maps. There may have been an unaccountable bulge on the west coast of South America, and the absence of much reliable evidence for the northern coastline of North America, but otherwise the outline is quite recognizable to modern eyes. However, much like the Australia partly mapped by Tasman, and the African continent mapped by the Portuguese, little was known of the North American continent beyond the immediate hinterland occupied by the first European settlers: the Spanish in Florida, the English in what became New England, and the Dutch VOC that occupied southern Manhattan island (New Amsterdam). The English contested with the French for the Canadian east coast and hinterland, making the first real inroads into the interior of the subcontinent by way of the St Lawrence

River. French explorers reached the first of the Great Lakes in the early decades of the seventeenth century, directed by indigenous people who spoke of a 'Fresh-Water Sea'. Members of the Huron nation led them to the Mer Douce (Sweet Sea), now known as Lake Huron.

These early French explorers were financed by the French government or various commercial enterprises, such as the Company of One Hundred Associates – loosely modelled on the VOC and the English East India Company. The Hundred Associates was mainly interested in the fur trade, with trappers hunting for beaver, otters, lynx, mink and other pelts. Along with these were despatched various Jesuit and Franciscan missionaries whose aim was to 'civilize' the native peoples by converting them to Christianity. But such was the nature of their mission that these priests venturing into unknown territory were often explorers themselves. It was the Franciscan friar Joseph Le Caron who first set eyes on Lake Huron in 1615: 'His garb was the customary rude garment of coarse, gray cloth, girt at the waist with a knotted cord, and surmounted by a peaked hood. He was shod with wooden sandals an inch or more in thickness.'

It was a Jesuit priest and a young French fur-trader who together in 1673 would make the first great inroads into the vast heart of the North American continent, a territory hitherto unknown to Europeans. Father Jacques Marquette had been born in Laon in northern France in 1637. He came from an old French family with distinguished military and administrative ancestors. At the age of seventeen he chose to join the Jesuits, one of the most prestigious and certainly the most intellectual of the Roman Catholic orders. Marquette's combination of learning, enterprise and self-sufficiency led his superiors to send him at the age of twenty-nine on a mission to New France (Canada). Within two years of arriving at the settlement of Quebec, Marquette had mastered no less than seven languages of the Iroquois, the confederacy who occupied the entire St Lawrence Valley and territory south of the Great Lakes.

Marquette was then sent by his superiors to spread the word amongst indigenous peoples of the newly opened-up Great Lakes region. Here he helped found a mission at Sault Sainte Marie (in modern-day Michigan). While setting up another mission station on Lake Superior (in modern-day Wisconsin), he had dealings with the Illinois, who told him of a large river, far to the south, which many different tribes used as a trading route. This they called the Great River – or *Misi-zibi*.

Marquette passed news of this to his superiors in Quebec, and asked for permission to go in search of the Great River. This was granted, and he teamed up with another Frenchman, Louis Jolliet, as well as five *voyageurs* of mixed Native and French ancestry.

Louis Jolliet was eight years younger than Marquette, but had a deep knowledge of the territory. He had been born in a small settlement near Quebec in 1645. Jolliet's father died when he was six, and his mother married a prosperous merchant who owned a tract of land on the Île d'Orléans, the large island in the St Lawrence River downstream from what is now Quebec City. In his youth Jolliet worked here, becoming familiar with the local indigenous peoples and learning several of their languages. However, he also had a yearning for a full education, with the possibility that he might enter the priesthood. Entering the Jesuit seminary at Quebec he studied philosophy and also became an accomplished musician (harpsichord and organ). However, at the age of twenty-two he decided against entering the priesthood. He still felt the call of the wild, which he had first experienced on the Île d'Orléans. He left the seminary and travelled west into the hinterland, becoming a fur trapper. Six years later he would meet and become friends with Marquette, who invited him to join his expedition to find the Great River.

On 17 May 1673, Marquette and Jolliet, and their five hardy *voyageurs*, set out in two canoes from St Ignace on the straits leading from Lake Huron into the top of Lake Michigan. From here they paddled and sailed their way some 300 miles across Lake Superior, and down the western inlet to the location of modern-day Green Bay. Following the instructions they had been given by the Illinois, they then voyaged south down the Fox River to the spot now known as Portage, Wisconsin. Here they did indeed portage – that is, carry their canoes loaded with equipment and supplies – across two miles of marshy wooded territory. Here they reached the Wisconsin River, part of the upper reaches of the Mississippi

River System. They paddled downstream, eventually reaching the wide waters of the Mississippi itself on 17 June, at a spot near modern Prairie du Chien (Dog's Meadow).*

Marquette, Jolliet and the five *voyageurs* now began canoeing down the widening waterway of what was unmistakably the Great River. They travelled south for over 600 miles, occasionally encountering the canoes of friendly indigenous people who traded up and down the Mississippi. They noticed that many of them were carrying in their loaded canoes goods of European origin.

The first European to discover the mouth of the Mississippi River had been the Spanish explorer Hernando de Soto more than 100 years previously, in 1541, but little attempt had been made to explore upstream beyond the treacherous waters of the delta. When the Marquette-Jolliet expedition reached the mouth of the Arkansas River, they decided to turn back. They had no wish to encounter hostile Spanish settlers, who were evidently trading with the Native Americans at the mouth of the Great River, which they assumed was just a short distance downstream. In fact, they were some 435 miles from the Mississippi Delta.

On their return journey, Jolliet and Marquette learned from friendly indigenous traders that there was a much shorter route to the Great Lakes. On their advice, they turned off the Mississippi and began paddling up the Illinois River, then up its tributary to a spot where they could portage to the Chicago River, which flowed into Lake Michigan at the location of modern-day Chicago. It was August by the time they made it back to Green Bay. Here Marquette left the expedition to join a new missionary station nearby. Jolliet continued across the Great Lakes, eventually making his way back to Quebec – where he gave a detailed description of their expedition, which had opened up the interior of the North American subcontinent.

---

* Late in the following century, a German immigrant named Johann Jakob Astor (later John Jacob Astor) would establish a fur warehouse here. The monopoly trade he set up in Prairie du Chien helped make him the first American multimillionaire, and possibly the richest man in American history, and laid the foundations for the Astor family fortune.

The French authorities in Quebec would later appoint Jolliet as Royal Hydrographer, and as such he would take further expeditions north to Labrador. After setting out on a further expedition in 1700, he disappeared without trace.

Four years after Marquette's return from the Mississippi expedition, he would travel down Lake Michigan to the mouth of the Chicago River. Such was the regard of the local people for Marquette that he was given a grand feast featuring sagamité – a delicacy consisting of a variety of well-cooked and matured ingredients, including maize, animal brains, smoked fish and grease. But a year later, Marquette would die at the age of thirty-eight, his body weakened by dysentery.

We have seen how the import of American food, such as tomatoes and haricot beans, transformed French cuisine. And it is little exaggeration to say that the arrival of the potato would revolutionize diet across the entire European continent. Ironically, this was amongst the last of the American imports to arrive, as it was not discovered by the Spanish until they moved into the high Andes.* By the end of the sixteenth century, potatoes were being cultivated as a crop in the Canary Islands, though they were not popular in mainland Spain where the potato was regarded as fodder only fit for the native peoples of the New World.

As early as 1570, Basque fishermen began using potatoes as ship's stores for their longer voyages. When they put ashore in western Ireland to dry their cod, they introduced the potato to Ireland. The arrival in England of the potato is usually credited to Sir Francis Drake, when he brought this new vegetable to the Elizabethan court in 1580 after his circumnavigation.

Despite the Spanish contempt for the potato as a food, it was regarded as being useful for medical purposes in Seville. When Philip II of Spain heard that his ambassador to the Netherlands had fallen ill, he sent him some potatoes. They were soon being cultivated across Europe, from the

---

* The sweet potato was first imported to Europe by Columbus. The name for this vegetable in the Americas was *batatas*, and this is the origin of our word 'potato', which is now more widely used to refer to tuber potatoes, despite the fact that these and sweet potatoes are unrelated species.

Netherlands to northern Italy. Regardless of rumours that the potato was 'the devil's apple' because it grew underground, in northern Europe potatoes became a dietary replacement for root vegetables such as swedes, turnips and beetroot. The underground cultivation of potatoes meant that they were also less exposed to looting.

The fact that potatoes produced three times as many calories per acre as grain had a transformative effect on diets throughout much of western Europe, leading to a diminution of sicknesses caused by malnutrition. This was particularly the case during the cold winters. The Little Ice Age may have been passing its peak, but long severe winters remained the norm. In 1658, the Swedish army was able to attack Denmark by marching across the ice between Danish islands.

European trade routes were now established across the globe. The English and the Dutch sailed around the Cape of Good Hope to the Far East. Though vulnerable to English privateers and pirates, Spanish treasure fleets continued to sail regularly across the Atlantic from South and Central America back to Spain. To this was added a Spanish treasure route sailing west across the Pacific from South America to Asia, where Spain had occupied the Philippines.* The Spanish had seen the Philippines as a stepping stone to the Spice Islands, but these were too strongly guarded by the VOC. Instead, they established a route taking silver and gold from South America to China in exchange for porcelain, silk and other luxury goods, which were then transported back across the Pacific to Acapulco. From here, they were transported overland across Mexico on mule trains to Veracruz, for shipment over the Atlantic on the regular treasure fleets.

These, and other lesser trade routes (such as the French fur trade in Canada), consistently enriched Europe during this period. However, even these lucrative commercial links were becoming eclipsed by the notorious transatlantic slave trade. As already indicated, this would come into its own during the Age of Reason, a dark underside to one of western humanity's most transformative eras.

---

* Named after Philip II of Spain. In a spectacular example of administrative overreach, the Philippines were governed by the Viceroy of New Spain in Mexico.

At the start of the 1600s, the main route was the Portuguese transport of slaves from Angola and the Congo to Brazil. During the later 1600s, the Dutch would become the leading slave traders. With the rise in English naval power came a rise in English participation in this trade. The English, and later the French, established large forts (referred to as 'factories') for keeping enslaved people along the coast of West Africa between the Senegal and the Niger rivers. It is recorded that by the end of the seventeenth century one out of every four ships which left Liverpool harbour was a slave trader.

In 1600, sub-Saharan Africa accounted for almost a fifth of the world's population. From then on, this proportion would decrease as Europe's population increased – both in numbers and prosperity. Thus the evolution of the slave trade is reflected in the evolution of Europe itself.

CHAPTER 13

A COURTLY INTERLUDE

Despite the wars during this period, it is widely accepted that in the 250 years between 1500 and 1750 the population of Europe almost doubled, from around 65 million to as much as 128 million. This rapid expansion was accompanied by a general increase in prosperity, driven by factors ranging from the cultivation of the potato to scientific innovations, from mercantile entrepreneurship to profits from the slave trade. All this encouraged a social transformation that had begun in the early years of the Renaissance in Italy and was reflected in the growth of new cultural ideas such as humanism and the emergence of scientific thought.

Although Protestantism rejected outright the flamboyant rituals of the Church, even many within the Catholic fold had begun to recognize such performances as empty, or at least lacking in behavioural conviction. Yet without such ritualistic guidelines, how was one to behave? Those secure in their social roles continued to go through the motions. Others, such as the burgeoning merchant class and newly risen courtiers in the expanding courts, found themselves wondering how to acquire manners appropriate to their social standing. The classic answer to this need would be found in the short work *Il Cortegiano* (The Book of the Courtier). This was written by Baldassare Castiglione, a courtier in the service of the Duke of Urbino, and was first published in Venice in 1527.

The main text of *Il Cortegiano* features fictional conversations between the Duke of Urbino, the papal diplomat Count Ludovico Canossa, the Venetian poet Pietro Bembo, and various courtiers. Echoing the dialogues of Plato, the central figures and the courtiers discuss the particular qualities and behaviours that should be adopted by courtiers of different ranks. In Plato, however, a more profound discussion of the 'good life' leads on to a philosophical debate concerning an ideal society, and how citizens should adapt themselves under such utopian conditions. An indication of less prescriptive Renaissance mores can be seen in Castiglione's conscious avoidance of such matters. This may appear to trivialize Castiglione's work, but it is arguably more socially mature for avoiding any dissection of power. Four years after the first printed edition of *Il Cortegiano*, Machiavelli's *The Prince* would appear with its ruthless instructions on how to achieve – and maintain – power. *The Prince* is a work of political amorality, intended for rulers, whereas *Il Cortegiano* is a work of social morality, intended for young men who wish to achieve cultured behaviour. As such, *Il Cortegiano* is undoubtedly the more civilized of the two and is an advance in keeping with the Age of Reason.

According to Castiglione, a courtier should be well educated in the classics and the fine arts, as well as being possessed of athletic ability. However, in this discussion of the seemingly more trivial aspects of life at court, debate on more important topics begins to emerge – such as women, nobility, humour and love.

The courtier should create a good impression, taking great care over his appearance and attire. Most importantly, he should learn how to speak in a 'sonorous, clear, sweet and well sounding' voice. At all costs he should maintain a manly composure, avoiding an effeminate or uncouth demeanour, his manner 'tempered by a calm face and with a play of the eyes that shall give an effect of grace'. The notion of grace (*grazia*) takes on a central role in Castiglione's work – which is, in essence, an instruction manual. According to Castiglione, *grazia* can only be obtained by *sprezzatura*, which he defines as 'a certain nonchalance, so as to conceal all art and make whatever one does or says appear to be without effort and almost without any thought about it'.

Castiglione's guide to the attainment of manners fulfilled an unrealized need, and anyone with social aspirations could not afford to be without a copy. The popularity of *Il Cortegiano* quickly spread north across the Alps and throughout Europe, where it was widely plagiarized, translated, transmogrified, imitated and so forth – as was the fate of all books, patents and other novelties that achieved success during this era.

Galileo provides an instructive example here. Several of his original inventions were pirated, despite his taking precautions, and this deprived him of a considerable source of income. However, he finally got his own back. In 1608, the Dutch-German lens-grinder Hans Lipperhey invented what became known as the telescope (from the Greek *tēleskópos*, meaning 'far-seeing'). Word of this new wonder quickly spread across Europe, reaching Galileo in Venice the following year – long before any actual example of the invention. Such was Galileo's scientific acuity that he instantly grasped the principles by which it worked and retired to his laboratory to begin experimenting. He had such an understanding of physics that after a little tinkering with lenses he soon produced his own telescope from scratch. This proved to be almost three times as powerful as Lipperhey's original. Galileo cannily decided against selling his telescope, instead granting its free use to the Venetian authorities, demonstrating to them how they could use it from a high tower to spot any invading fleet long before it was visible to the naked eye. For this the grateful authorities rewarded him with a pension for life.

The achievements of the Age of Reason were undeniably pan-European, and evidently instilled a sense of pride in those who lived through this age. There nonetheless remained an irrational element to this self-regard. Not all countries were equal. And this was much more than just a matter of political or military power. Throughout Europe there always remained a sneaking admiration and feeling of inferiority towards many things Italian – especially music, literature, the arts in general, and even fashion. The Italians had that intangible quality which manifests itself as taste; and Castiglione's *Il Cortegiano* appeared to be the ultimate guide to how to achieve Italian fashionable behaviour and taste.

The Age of Reason saw the beginning of the notion of progress in Europe, and this was certainly reflected in many aspects of society. The population boomed, and in societies with a more democratic, liberal tendency, such as England and Holland, this meant an increase in the middle classes – the bourgeoisie. The very name derives from 'burger', has connotations of 'citizen', and indicates the predominantly urban nature of this class and its cultivation of so-called civilized behaviour (another word that has connotations of *civitas*, or 'city'). In France, and such autocratic city-states as Naples and Milan, the new aspirant behaviour would often be characterized as 'courteous', i.e. belonging to the court. In such author-itarian societies, the emphasis on manners might be associated with the privileged classes, but Castiglione realized the manners of the court could permeate beyond its 'genteel' limits.

And once again we find connotations that spread far beyond genteel behaviour – giving rise to the notion of the 'gentleman' or *le gentilhomme* (in French), with similar words appearing in other European languages. Indeed, Castiglione's definition of courtly behaviour, and its consequent influences, would remain for more than five centuries. His description of *sprezzatura* – with its nonchalance, lack of evident or earnest effort, the concept of the naturally gifted amateur – is integral to the notion of 'gentlemanly behaviour' to this day.

Le gentilhomme was already evident in French society – Molière's drama *Le Bourgeois Gentilhomme* being the supreme example – as were those who aspired beyond their class to attain such a status. Though largely modern and satirical in intent, this work still adhered to a tradi-tional format, the drama being interspersed with musical interludes and ballet.

Although the printing presses of Venice had begun producing music sheets as early as 1501, it took some time before the musical revolution that had taken place in Italy during the Renaissance began to spread across Europe. Ballet, opera, castrato singers, chamber music ensembles and the like were all popular in Italy long before their influence took hold abroad. The main transformation in Italian Renaissance music was to spread beyond church music and into secular entertainments. Here opera (in part invented by Galileo's musician father) played a leading role – as did the timbre of music as a whole. The logical strictures of counterpoint, so widespread in medieval church music, now began to expand to include more mellifluous elements of harmony and chords.

Such developments soon became evident in the French court, which had a long history of drawing on Italian artists, designers and so forth. The new wave of Italian musicians brought with them new instruments as well as new music – the sackbut (a form of slide-trumpet or trombone), various types of lute and viola, the piccolo (small flute), and the newly invented violin.

An example of the speed at which these instruments were evolving can be seen in the case of the violin. The modern violin was invented in Italy around 1550 – probably in the northern towns of Cremona and Brescia. Indeed, Cremona was the home town of Antonio Stradivari (Latinized to Stradivarius), who was born there in 1644. Such was his skill as a violin maker that by the end of the century he was crafting violins which to this day are recognized as the finest of their kind. Many experts have sought to discover the secret of how Stradivarius produced such marvels of musicality – but they remain at a loss. Some put it down to his use of particular varnishes, or the borax he incorporated to protect the wooden body of the violin from woodworm; others suggest that the fine wood he used is no longer obtainable owing to the evolution and pollution of Italian forests.

As with many such unique accomplishments, few are willing to accept them for what they are – a manifestation of superior skills allied to an expert knowledge in the handling of materials. This lack of acceptance in many ways stems from the Age of Reason. Scientists examining Stradivariuses have subjected them to minute examination, hunting for deft hints of technique, ingredients or method, using the most modern precision equipment – to no avail. Any rational answer to the secret of Stradivarius's methods continues to elude them. Here, in essence, is the irrationality that lies at the heart of all artistic creation – and which will continue to elude rational investigation for as long as artificial intelligence fails to replicate the full range of human nature.

If such can be said of a consummate violin maker, how much more is this the case with a composer of genius. Despite the despoliation of the local forests, there must have been something in the air (or the gene pool) of Cremona – for this was also the birthplace of Claudio Monteverdi, the greatest composer of the age. It was he, more than any other, who would create the bridge between the rational disciplines of Renaissance music and the glorious flourishes of the early baroque era. Ironically, it was to be the very boldness of the advances he introduced which would lead to the neglect of his compositions during the centuries following his death. Not until the early twentieth century would the full richness, originality and cadence of his music be once again recognized for what it was (and this, despite the fact that over the intervening years so much of his output had been lost).

Claudio Monteverdi was born in 1567 in the small city of Cremona, which was part of the Duchy of Milan. Significantly, it was close to the borders of the rich and powerful Venetian Republic, as well as the smaller Duchy of Mantua, both of which would play a formative role in his long life.

Monteverdi's father was an apothecary, but he seems to have introduced his son to the city's rich musical life from an early age. Young Claudio is not known to have entered into any formal education. On the other hand, he is known to have received a thoroughgoing musical education from the *maestro di capella* (master of the cathedral choir) Marc'Antonio Ingegneri, a talented but otherwise somewhat mysterious figure whose work is mostly lost. Ingegneri's lasting memorial is the comprehensive yet progressive musical schooling he imparted to the young Monteverdi, inspiring the boy's imagination in many hitherto-inconceivable ways.

Monteverdi's first known work is a collection of motets (Renaissance polyphonic vocal compositions), produced at the age of just fifteen. He continued to publish works, mainly madrigals (secular vocal works unusually involving several unaccompanied voices, typical of the Renaissance period) dedicated to a succession of rich and influential aristocratic music-lovers, in the hope of attracting a patron – an indispensable part of an Italian musician's life at the time.

Finally, in 1591, at the age of twenty-four, Monteverdi secured an appointment as a musician at the court of Duke Vincenzo of Mantua, who was eager to establish his provincial city as a leading centre of Italian musical life. Monteverdi would remain at Mantua for twenty-two years, marrying the court singer Claudia de Cattaneis in 1599, and two years later being appointed *maestro di capella*. Yet it was during these years that the influential critic Giovanni Artusi launched a vicious attack on Monteverdi's music (without actually naming him) in a treatise named *On the Imperfections of Modern Music*.

In 1606, Monteverdi was commissioned by Duke Vincenzo's heir, the young Francesco, to compose an opera. The result was *L'Orfeo*, claimed to be Monteverdi's finest early work (apart from a single aria, the score of this work is now lost). Despite his evident and burgeoning talent, this was a low period in his life. He was overworked, underpaid, subjected to the constant jealous calumnies endemic at such small courts – and to top it all his wife died in 1608. Overcome by nervous exhaustion, he retired home to Cremona, but was persuaded to return to Mantua the following year. Four years later, as the victim of further court intrigue and professional jealousies he fled back to Cremona, an embittered and all but penniless forty-six-year-old. To add insult to injury, highway robbers would relieve him of his last fifty ducats on his way home.

But Monteverdi's luck soon changed. In 1613 he was appointed musical director at the church of San Marco in Venice. Here he was given the freedom to hire new musicians and singers, and it was during the course of this work that Monteverdi did so much to formalize the various sections of what has come down to us as the modern orchestra. He also found time to compose new works. Free from the claustrophobic small-city politics of Mantua, his work blossomed, expanding and delineating the new baroque form.

In later life, Monteverdi would take holy orders, but still continued to compose secular music. The year 1637 saw the opening in Venice of San

Cassiano, the world's first public opera house. This encouraged the ageing composer to produce one more burst of major works: operas, madrigals, ballets... Yet once again his superlative skills roused bitter jealousies. Typical of such attacks was the 1637 denouncement: 'The Director of Music comes from a brood of cut-throat bastards, a thieving, fucking, he-goat... and I shit on him and whoever protects him...' Despite such coarse insults, Monteverdi produced his final, and one of his finest, operas, *The Coronation of Poppea*, in 1643, the year of his death. In the introduction to this work, Monteverdi at last received his due, being named as the leading musician of his time: 'he will be sighed for in later ages, for his compositions will surely outlive the ravages of time'. Ironically, it would take almost 250 years for the fulfilment of this prophetic assessment.

Despite Monteverdi's personally neglected legacy, the introduction of Italian music to the French court was already widespread by the time of Louis XIII, the son of Marie de' Medici. And it was during this era that we see the many elements of Italian music and the expectations of the French court fuse, to achieve their early baroque apotheosis during the Age of Reason.

It was said that during the reign of Louis XIII, whose Parisian residence was then the Louvre Palace, not a day passed without a musical performance of some kind at court. Louis XIII himself composed songs, and from 1618 onwards maintained La Grande Bande, an ensemble consisting of twenty-four violin players who performed at royal concerts, grand balls and other official occasions.*

In 1644, the young Louis XIV's chief minister Cardinal Mazarin introduced Italian opera to the French court. Mazarin had been born and spent his formative years in Italy, with the result that he was something of a connoisseur of opera. He knew what he was doing, and chose the finest Italian exponents of this art to present to a French audience. Ironically,

---

* This was, as its name suggests, a band rather than an orchestra. Collections of musicians playing different instruments together were not unknown, even in the Renaissance, but these were more correctly described as an 'ensemble', or in a larger group a 'consort'. The origins of the orchestra as we know it evolved in Italy under the auspices of Monteverdi.

this proved to be a resounding failure – the musical taste and appreciation of French audiences was in fact far more sophisticated than their Italian counterparts during this period. French audiences were in the habit of remaining hushed during performances, the ladies fanning themselves and their partners breaking into polite applause at the end of musical interludes. Such restraint was observed only amongst the small audiences at court performances in Italy. Concerts attended by the wider public were far more raucous affairs. Artists who were disliked or inept were liable to be booed, or subjected to cat calls and abuse. Musical interludes were regarded as opportunities for conversation amongst the audience, often to the point where the music itself was inaudible. So why did Mazarin's introduction of Italian opera to French audiences start off as a fiasco? The French audiences may have been respectful of certain courtly conventions with regards to the performances they attended, but they also expected the performances themselves to be respectful of the current dramatic conventions in France. They were quite used to having their drama inter-spersed with short balletic routines, or interludes of song – what they could not tolerate was the entire performance being given over to singing and ballet, with no hint of any intervening drama. French taste also inclined to reasonable exposition by the actors and singers, in controlled vocal fashion – whereas Italian opera involved full-throated displays of what appeared to be almost demented vocal expression, complete with matching violent action. Such uninhibited behaviour was regarded by the French as little better than an uncouth expression of irrational emotion. But, as ever, fashions changed.

Another of Cardinal Mazarin's introductions to French musical life was rather more successful. He invited the Italian singer Atto Melani to Paris. This caused a considerable stir, for not only was Melani a vocal prodigy but he was also a castrato, a new type of singer that was well-established in Italy but remained something of a novelty north of the Alps. These singers provided an indispensable service. Women were not permitted to sing in cathedral choirs of the Roman Catholic Church, which were staffed by young boys whose voices had not yet broken. By the mid-sixteenth century, the practice of castrating young boys so that they retained their youthful high-pitched voices was becoming more commonplace. Furthermore it was soon discovered that castrati, as they became known, were capable of developing superb vocal skills not otherwise attainable by boys, nor even the finest women singers. Because castrati lacked testosterone, their bones did not harden as they grew older and their limbs grew longer. Thus most castrati were tall, with well-developed rib cages, giving them an exceptional vocal capacity, range and strength.

Atto Melani was born in 1626 in the Tuscan town of Pistoia, some twenty miles north-west of Florence. His family were noted for their fine voices and musical abilities; consequently, three of his brothers and two of his cousins were also castrated during their prepubescent years. (Two of his less vocally gifted brothers became composers.) It soon became clear that young Atto's voice was exceptional. The range and tone of his voice were only matched by his almost superhuman ability to hold on to higher notes. (Castrati were usually capable of singing as sopranos, mezzo-sopranos or contraltos.)

Melani's exceptional talents soon came to the notice of Mattias de' Medici, the third son of the ruling Grand Duke Cosimo II of Tuscany. With the help of this Medici patronage, Melani was soon receiving invitations to sing as far afield as southern Germany and Austria. However, in 1645 Cardinal Mazarin used his influence to tempt Melani to Paris, where he first performed at the age of nineteen.

Despite his young age and the fact that he had been castrated, by the time he arrived in Paris he seems to have already lived a rich and varied life. Mattias de' Medici was almost certainly homosexual, and the attraction for his young protégé is thought to have extended beyond his vocal abilities. Similarly, as Melani's American biographer Roger Freitas claims, 'circumstantial evidence is convincing' that by the time Melani reached Paris he had already had an affair with Duke Carlo II of Mantua, during the course of which 'both men had sex with the same (unidentified) page at the court of Innsbruck'. (In many cases, and Melani's certainly seems to have been one of them, castrati were capable of sexual activity but lacked the capacity for reproduction.)

Melani's arrival in Paris was a great success, and he now established himself as the leading singer in Europe's major city. However,
his ambitions were not to cease with mere artistic fame. It is likely that
Mattias de' Medici had permitted Melani to travel to France in the hope
that he might garner intelligence regarding the future attitude of France
towards the Duchy of Tuscany. Louis XIII had died in 1643, and the
underage Louis XIV had ascended to the throne under the guidance of a
circle of powerful advisers, including Jean-Baptiste Colbert and Cardinal
Mazarin. It seems that Mazarin quickly discerned Mattias de' Medici's
covert motive with regard to Melani; yet he evidently understood the
appropriateness of assigning this task to a young man of such evident
talent, charm and amorality.

Cardinal Mazarin took Melani in hand and made sure that he was
given a rigorous grounding in the art of espionage. On completion of this
expert training, Mazarin began 'loaning out' his new young maestro to the
courts of Europe. His instructions to his protégé were no simple matter:
on arrival at his destination Melani should ensure that his performances
charmed the leading figures in local society. Where possible, he should
accept hospitality in the palaces of power, rather than residing with local
French representatives. In this way he could gain as much intelligence
as possible, while at the same time paying attention to court gossip, thus
discovering who was in favour and who was liable to fall from grace. He
was also encouraged to copy down the gist of any documents that came
to his notice. The intelligence that Melani gathered was sent back to Paris
in the form of coded letters, which were to be despatched by means of
reliable sources.

An indication of the importance of Melani's espionage activities can
be seen in the mission he was given in 1657, when he was sent on a singing
engagement to Bavaria. Mazarin gave Melani explicit instructions that he
was to gain the favour of the ruler, Prince-Elector Ferdinand, who was
known to be a friend of France. Melani was to do his best to persuade
Ferdinand to stand for election as the new Holy Roman Emperor.
Unfortunately for France, Ferdinand demurred; had Melani's mission
been a success, the union of France and the Holy Roman Empire would

certainly have changed the course of European history. No other nation, or alliance, could have withstood the union of the two major powers in Europe, and Louis XIV, the Sun King, would in effect have become ruler of the continent.

Meanwhile Melani continued with his musical career. Amongst his greatest successes was playing the lead in Lully's *Ballet de l'Impatience* in 1660. However, this proved to be his last operatic triumph. The following year, Melani's sponsor and protector Cardinal Mazarin died. Melani's enemies concocted a charge of treason against him – alleging he had made copies of the letters of Louis XIV – and he was forced to flee back to Italy. Here he settled in Rome, where both his success as a singer and his more nefarious activities were soon earning him a considerable fortune.

An indication of the levels at which Melani's espionage activities were now being conducted can be seen from the role he played in Rome during 1667, when Pope Alexander VII died. Melani managed to attend the top-secret conclave of cardinals that was to elect the new pope. Here he was acting as assistant to Cardinal Giulio Rospigliosi, who was elected Pope Clement IX, with the aid of the French faction amongst the College of Cardinals.

When Louis XIV heard of this, he was so pleased with Melani that he forgave him, invited him back to France, and made him an *abbé* (abbot) with the handsome annual stipend of 3,000 gold livres. Despite his religious elevation, Melani decided to resume his professional singing career, though he was now well into middle age. In 1668 he gave his last concert, and then ostensibly devoted himself to the religious duties incumbent upon his post. In fact, he did nothing of the sort. Melani became one of Louis XIV's secret advisers on diplomatic matters, and continued with his espionage activities. Beside the friendships he had made at courts throughout Europe, he now had considerable influence amongst the College of Cardinals.

Atto Melani finally died in Paris in 1714, at the age of eighty-seven. According to modern historian Aurora von Goeth: 'Among his bequest were several estates and palazzi, bank accounts and a large library, as well as his collected correspondence with European sovereigns and people of

great importance. Apart from the index, the 108 volumes of the correspondence are lost without trace.' Such is the fate of the machinations
which take place behind the façade of diplomacy. Atto Melani knew too
much, and took his secrets to the grave, leaving them beyond the reach
of history.

Several of Melani's greatest successes were in operas written by
Jean-Baptiste Lully, who also played a major role in the careers of the
dramatists Molière and Racine. Lully's accolade as the 'prince of French
musicians' was well deserved. Not only was he a superb instrumentalist
and a nimble dancer in his own ballets, he arguably brought French
baroque music to its first peak.

Here too we see another instance of the widespread exaggerated regard
for Italian taste. The French composer we know as Jean-Baptiste Lully
was in fact born Giovanni Battista Lulli in Florence in 1632. His father
was a lowly miller, though in later life, during his fame in France, Lully
would describe himself as '*écuyer... fils de Laurent de Lully, gentilhomme
Florentin*' (Esquire, son of Laurent de Lully, gentleman of Florence).

Perhaps it was little Giovanni Battista's evident intelligence, or
his equally evident wish to draw attention to himself... either way, he
attracted the interest of a local Franciscan friar who took it upon himself
to educate the miller's son. The young Lully's self-appointed tutor must
have been a man of considerable polymathic talents, for by the time his
pupil was a teenager he had learned how to read and write (both books
and musical scores), as well as becoming more than proficient at playing
the guitar and the violin. But this prodigious learning rested lightly on
Lully's shoulders, as he also developed a lively wit, daring attitude and
boisterous character. During the Mardi Gras celebrations in 1646, Lully
took it upon himself to dress up as a harlequin and entertained passing
revellers in the streets by clowning as he played the guitar.

It was this that brought him to the attention of the visiting French
aristocrat Roger de Lorraine, whose young niece Mademoiselle de
Montpensier had made it known that she wished for a lively and intel-
ligent young Italian with whom she could converse to improve her
mastery of this fashionable language. Lully evidently fitted the bill, and

the fourteen-year-old street performer was transported to Paris, where he entered the household of the nineteen-year-old woman who would in time become known as 'one of the greatest heiresses in history'. Born in the Louvre Palace and related to Louis XIII, she would inherit no less than five dukedoms whose landed estates covered large tracts of Burgundy, Auvergne and several other French provinces. Over the years she would receive proposals from aristocrats across Europe, as well as three kings (including Charles II of England), but instead chose to fall in love with one of her courtiers.

However, Mademoiselle de Montpensier is now also remembered for fostering the musical skills of the young Italian who entered her entourage as a mere *garçon de chambre* (chamber boy). Her voluminous household also included several dozen musicians, amongst whom were three of France's most able court composers. Initially, they referred to Lully somewhat snootily as '*le grand baladin*' (the great street-entertainer), but they were quickly won over by his prodigious talents and also by the fact that he already knew how to compose musical scores. Flourishing under such tuition, and using his clowning to gain their affection, Lully quickly became a court favourite.

Then, disaster struck. Mademoiselle de Montpensier became involved in a plot against Louis XIV and was banished to one of her distant country estates. Boldly, Lully decided to stay behind in Paris, where he soon caught the attention of the king, who was so enchanted by his music and his witty character that he appointed Lully 'Superintendent of the Royal Music'. It was in this role that he came into contact with, and began working with, the likes of Racine and Molière. Though Lully believed in enjoying himself, and made sure that his saucy humour endeared him to the king, he also worked prodigiously. In between singing and ballet dancing, composing music for church and court, he managed to complete operas at the rate of almost one a year, frequently ensuring that there were roles in which Melani could show off his own great talents.

Then, in 1683, Louis XIV shocked the French court by unexpectedly marrying his mistress Madame de Maintenon, who was renowned for her baleful influence over his majesty and her deep religious devotion. It took some time, but eventually, as Lully's biographer Jérôme de La Gorce observes, 'The king's enthusiasm for opera dissipated; he was revolted by Lully's dissolute life and homosexual encounters'. In 1686, at the age of fifty-four, Lully fell from grace.

But this was not to be his only fall. While conducting at a church service, he collapsed after accidentally striking his foot with his long heavy conducting staff while he was emphatically beating time for the musicians. His wound developed gangrene, which soon spread; but he refused to have his leg amputated as he was determined to retain his prowess at dancing, of which he remained inordinately proud. The gangrene then spread throughout his body, finally affecting his brain, causing him an agonizing death. The great French chronicler Titon du Tillet would justly call him 'the inventor of that beautiful and grand French music, such as our operas and the grand pieces for voices and instruments that were only imperfectly known before him'.

The English were not renowned as a musical nation, yet it was during their emergence in so many other fields, from science to literature, that they produced their finest composer yet. Namely, Henry Purcell, whose masterwork, his opera *Dido and Aeneas*, is regularly performed to this day. To the modern ear, more attuned to the unrestrained emotion of the classical era, the taut and measured tones of Purcell may appear as the epitome of rationality; yet closer listening reveals the profound subtleties of harmony and emotion amidst his baroque flourishes.*

Henry Purcell was born in 1659 in the district of Westminster, which would later become a notorious slum known as the Devil's Acre. This was just a couple of hundred yards west of the soaring towers of the medieval Westminster Abbey, the traditional site of the coronation of England's

---

* During the late 1960s, one such discerning listener was Pete Townshend, lead singer of the anarchic English rock band The Who. He would absorb Purcell's harmonic influence in several of his hits, especially 'Pinball Wizard', whose very name can be read as an apt metaphorical take on the rhythmic spontaneity found in several of Purcell's works.

monarchs. Purcell's family were not poor, but they lived in this district owing to the family's musical connections to the Abbey. When Purcell's father died, Henry was just five years old and was taken in by the nearby family of his uncle, who had sung at the coronation of Charles II in 1649 and later became a member of the Chapel Royal (the king's personal choir). During his early childhood, young Henry received a musical education and showed early talent. By the time he was eleven he had composed an ode for Charles II's fortieth birthday, on 29 May 1670. (There is some evidence that by this stage Purcell had already been composing music for two years.) After this he was given a musical scholarship to the prestigious Westminster School, eking out his finances by becoming a copyist at the nearby Abbey. This painstaking chore proved an instructive discipline, and his talent was further developed by the Abbey's organist, Dr John Blow.

Purcell's big break came in 1679, when Blow resigned so that Purcell could succeed to his post.* Purcell was lucky in that his career coincided with the Restoration period, which enabled him to collaborate with a number of talented literary figures when writing his operas. His first collaboration was with the Irish poet and lyricist Nahum Tate, who would go on to become poet laureate but is today largely forgotten, except for providing the lyrics to Purcell's *Dido and Aeneas*. This takes its theme from Virgil's *Aeneid* and recounts the tragic love of Dido, Queen of Carthage, and the Trojan hero Aeneas. When Aeneas dutifully obeys the god Jupiter and departs Carthage for Rome, Dido is overcome with grief. She orders her funeral pyre to be built on the battlements so that Aeneas can see the flames rising as he sails away. Dido's lament, 'When I am laid in earth' – which she sings before she stabs herself and falls into the flames – remains one of the most technically accomplished and moving arias in opera to this day.

---

* There is some suggestion that Blow's action might not have been quite so philanthropic as it appears, however, and he may have been dismissed from his post for creative accounting when it came to the Abbey's finances. Either way, he would go on to lucrative posts at St Paul's Cathedral and the king's residence at Hampton Court, where he built himself a nearby house to add to the other eight he owned in Westminster.

Indeed, many see *Dido and Aeneas* as the first English opera. However, Blow would dispute this, claiming that his *Venus and Adonis* predates Purcell's claim. In fact, of the two only Purcell's work is sung throughout in true Italian operatic fashion. Although Blow's work does not resort to the spoken word, it does make use of Italian recitative, which is declamative rather than choral and was highly popular in France at the time.

Here we can see that English composers were in thrall to Italian music, as well as making use of French influences. The passage from Renaissance polyphony to full-blown baroque music may have taken longer to reach England, but its composers were quick to adapt to the transformative elements of the new style, at the same time giving them a character of their own. This was particularly the case with Purcell, whose French and Italian influences would develop a uniquely English flavour.

Purcell was also fortunate in having a number of exceptional contemporary singers who were willing to work with him. The most notable amongst these was the Reverend John Gostling, a basso profundo whose exceptionally powerful voice was matched by his great vocal range, which extended over more than two octaves. The best-known of Purcell's work for Gostling was 'They That Go Down to the Sea in Ships', written to commemorate the escape from drowning by shipwreck of Charles II (and also Gostling, who was amongst his entourage).

Purcell also benefitted from the range of English literature that had continued to flourish since the Elizabethan era. Amongst his successes were a semi-opera, *The Fairy-Queen*, based on William Shakespeare's *A Midsummer Night's Dream*, and several collaborations with William Congreve, a classic dramatist of the Restoration era whose witty satirical works parodied the social pretensions of the time.

By contrast, Purcell also produced music for the poet John Dryden's tragedy *Tyrannick Love*. This is often remembered for the fact that one of the main supporting roles was played by Nell Gwyn, then at the height of her fame as Charles II's favourite mistress before she fell from favour and came close to penury. (Charles II, on his deathbed, is reported as saying to his successor James II: 'Let not poor Nelly starve', a wish that was fulfilled.)

These remained difficult times politically, an exemplar of which is well supplied by the life of the poet Dryden, who was obliged to take a number of 'pragmatic' decisions in order to maintain his career. As a young man he was educated at the most Puritan college in Cambridge (Trinity), after which he found employment with Oliver Cromwell's secretary. He even went so far as to write a eulogy on the death of Cromwell in 1659. However, he evidently sensed that change was in the air, for his so-called eulogy has been characterized as 'cautious and prudent in its emotional display'. Ten years later, upon the succession of Charles II, Dryden wrote a fawning panegyric celebrating the Restoration, as well as a succession of works in favour of the Church of England. When the Catholic James II ascended the throne in 1685, Dryden composed an allegory in heroic couplets celebrating his own conversion to Catholicism.

Despite such weather-vane willingness to follow the prevailing wind of the time, Dryden also displayed a remarkable ability for getting into trouble on his own account. In 1679, he published 'An Essay in Satire'. This not only mocked Charles II and his succession of mistresses, but also lampooned a number of his more influential courtiers, including the rakish poet the Earl of Rochester. Whereupon Rochester hired a gang of thugs to beat up Dryden in a Covent Garden alley as he was on his way home one night.

By the time Dryden died in 1700 at the age of sixty-eight, he had become established in the English poetic succession, following on from the likes of William Shakespeare and John Milton, and was accorded the honour of being buried in Westminster Abbey.

Purcell was also forced to navigate the treacherous political waters of seventeenth-century England. Charles II was notorious for his philandering, and produced at least a dozen known illegitimate children with more than half a dozen mistresses (i.e. those women who retained his favour for more than a brief interlude). However, he proved unable to provide a surviving legitimate heir by his Portuguese queen Catherine of Braganza. Consequently, when he died at the age of fifty-four in 1685, he was succeeded by his Catholic brother James II. Within three years James II had proved so unpopular that he fled the country when parliament invited the Protestant Dutch prince William of Orange and his wife Mary to take over the throne as 'constitutional monarchs'.*

When Queen Mary died in 1694, Purcell composed a popular and moving anthem for her funeral. This would prove to be of such enduring appeal that it would frequently be used at ensuing royal funerals, including that of Queen Victoria in 1901. The heartfelt element of this work is hardly surprising: Purcell was no stranger to grief. He had married his wife Frances as early as 1682, when he was twenty-three years old; she would give birth to six children, four of whom would die in infancy.

Purcell himself would die unexpectedly in 1695, at the age of just thirty-six, when he was at the height of his powers. The circumstances of his death remain something of a mystery. It is generally agreed that he died at his home in Marsham Street, a quarter of a mile or so south of Westminster Abbey. Some sources claim that he died of tuberculosis; others adhere to the unlikely claim that he died of 'chocolate poisoning'. However, these appear to be a cover to protect his reputation. A more persistent and credible story maintains that he caught a chill when his wife locked him out of the house after he returned late on a cold November night from carousing with his friends.

Like his friend Dryden, Purcell would be accorded the signal honour of being buried in Westminster Abbey. Whereas Dryden was buried in Poets' Corner, the slab above Purcell's grave can be seen in the north choir aisle of the Abbey.

Purcell's music has retained its popularity and high reputation over the centuries. Apart from his influence on Pete Townshend, his music for Queen Anne's funeral was adapted by Wendy Carlos to great dramatic effect in Stanley Kubrick's 1971 film *A Clockwork Orange*. Purcell's work

---

* Theoretically, England had been ruled by a constitutional monarchy since at least 1215, when King John was forced to sign the Magna Carta, which granted certain constitutional rights. These had gradually been eroded by the time Charles I ascended the throne, guided by his belief in the divine right of kings. William and Mary were 'invited' by parliament to become heads of state, and their ruling powers were severely curtailed by the Bill of Rights they were made to sign in 1689.

has also appeared as background music in films ranging from *Kramer vs. Kramer* to the 2005 version of Jane Austen's *Pride and Prejudice*. 'Dido's Lament' is tellingly used as a leitmotif to the collapse of Nazi Germany in the 2004 film *Downfall*, set in Hitler's bunker during the final days of the Second World War. Such recurring and varied influences speak of the range and lasting effect of England's finest baroque composer.

So far the courts and courtiers we have described have been a largely male affair. Powerful female monarchs, such as the Medici queens of France and Elizabeth I of England, may have flourished at the heart of European power, but their influence to a large extent belongs in the earlier Renaissance age. However, there was to be another exceptional female monarch, who ruled at what was then the very outer edge of Europe. This was Queen Christina of Sweden, the wilful ruler who 'invited' Descartes to Stockholm to teach her philosophy.

Christina was born in 1626, and succeeded to the throne in 1632, but only took full power when she reached the age of eighteen. She has been dubbed 'one of the wittiest and most learned women of her age', and she is known to have mastered no less than seven languages, including Arabic and Hebrew. Despite this she did not let her intellectual pursuits interfere with her determination to rule her country as she saw fit. (She began learning this role early, attending meetings of the ruling council when she was just fourteen.) Indeed it was only through her astute political manoeuvres that Sweden did not collapse into class conflict and civil war following the end of the Thirty Years' War – in which her father, King Gustavus Adolphus, had died while leading the Protestant Swedish-German forces to victory over the Holy Roman Imperial forces at the decisive Battle of Lützen.

Christina's intellectual ambition was to turn Stockholm into the 'Athens of the North', and it was to this end, as much as for her own philosophical education, that she browbeat Descartes into travelling to her court. She also made arrangements for the transportation of Descartes's precious 2,000-book library, knowing that he would not try to escape and leave this behind.

Christina also persuaded many other European scholars, artists and scientists to join her in Stockholm. After the Swedish army took Prague in 1648, she ordered that the library and other treasures collected by the Holy Roman Emperor Rudolf II be transported to Sweden. She was also keen to encourage music and the performing arts; Christina was herself a talented amateur actress. (She even irritated Descartes by obliging him to write a drama for performance at court.) She also imported a French ballet troupe whose master was required to give her lessons in deportment.

Christina was inspired by the example of Queen Elizabeth of England, and wished to emulate her as a 'virgin queen', though unfortunately her nation required her to produce an heir. Like Elizabeth, she understood the importance of having a strong navy, and in 1650 she instructed the Dutch-Swedish banker Louis De Geer to found the Swedish Africa Company, modelled on the Dutch and English East India companies. (De Geer would later turn this company into a major profiteer of the slave trade.)

Despite devoting considerable time and energy to her royal duties, she continued with her educational pursuits, conducting intense dialogues on all manner of subjects with her imported intellectuals in her private chambers. Inevitably, malicious rumours of sexual misconduct began to spread. Meanwhile, in her journal she expressed 'an insurmountable distaste for marriage [and] for all things that females talked about and did'.

For almost two decades, Christina continued with her intellectual pursuits, ruled her country, and resisted all attempts to find her a husband. Throughout this time she remained in the habit of working for ten hours a day. Not surprisingly, in 1651 she had a nervous breakdown.

By now, Christina had long been in intimate conversation with Antonio Macedo, the secretary to the Portuguese ambassador. These conversations were initially limited to scientific matters, such as the works of Copernicus, Galileo and Kepler. But Macedo was a Jesuit priest, and when he steered the conversation to more philosophical subjects, she soon became fascinated with concepts such as free will and determinism, as well as the immortality of the soul.

Christina's succession of intense, intimate conversations with men led the royal historian Arnold Johan Messenius to brand her a 'Jezebel'. This was too much, and she ordered him to be executed. Messenius had been a popular figure, and his execution stirred considerable dissent. By now the queen's wilfulness and extravagance had begun to jar with many at court and throughout the land. And when Christina let it be known that she agreed with so many of Macedo's arguments that she had decided to convert to Catholicism, this proved the last straw.

In 1654, Queen Christina abdicated, and then fled the country in men's clothing, making her way through Europe to Rome. But she was never one to renounce her royal ways, and by the time she eventually arrived in Rome she had accumulated a retinue of 255 assorted courtiers and 247 horses.

Initially, Pope Alexander VII was so overjoyed by the fact that Her Majesty had converted to Catholicism that he allowed Christina and her court to occupy a wing of the Vatican. However, her opinions and general manner soon led to a falling-out and a change of address, with Alexander VII declaring her to be 'a queen without a realm, a Christian without faith, and a woman without shame'.

Over the coming three decades, Christina would continue to have similarly fluctuating relations with no less than five successive popes. She also made occasional sorties to the capitals of Europe. At the court of Louis XIV, she caused a considerable stir with her unfashionable attire and decidedly masculine forthrightness. Despite this, she won over Cardinal Mazarin, who granted her permission to stay permanently at his residence at Rome.

Upon learning that her successor to the throne, Charles X Gustav, had died, Christina turned up in Sweden expecting to be crowned his successor. When informed of the impossibility of this happening because she was a Catholic, she reluctantly staged a second public renunciation of the throne. She then embarked upon a series of travels through Germany and France, though the possibility of a visit to England was firmly turned down by the Commonwealth authorities.

Back in Rome, her insistence upon close relationships with the popes continued with varying success. She so won the affections of Clement IX that when he lay dying she was one of the few permitted to visit his bedside. Relations with his successor Clement X proved less cordial when she insisted that he prohibit the popular local custom of chasing Jews through the streets during Carnival, and issued a 'royal proclamation' taking them under her protection.

Christina finally died in 1689 at the age of sixty-two. Despite gossip-mongers spreading tales of male and female love affairs, she almost certainly died a virgin. Her modern biographer Veronica Buckley suggests that she was probably intersex or non-binary. Pope Innocent XI arranged for her to be buried in St Peter's.

Christina can be seen as a pioneering spirit of the new age, or a classic case of wilful unreasonableness. Either way, there is no denying that she played a leading role in bringing her comparatively backward kingdom at the edge of Europe firmly into the fold of the Age of Reason.

Beyond Europe, the era of empire-building continued apace. With the advent of the slave trade, exploitation and brute power, there was little evidence that all this was taking place in an Age of Reason. However, there were the occasional exceptions. And like Queen Christina, women were few and far between in this rare category.

Juana Inés de la Cruz is an all but unique example of a polymathic talent who advanced the cause of the Age of Reason in a location far beyond its normally accepted European territory. Besides contributing to the literature of the Spanish Golden Age (without ever visiting Spain), she also wrote philosophy, studied mathematics – and in particular wrote poetry and composed music. These last two endeavours were vital to her creative development. To paraphrase the modern writer Sarah Finley: the visual is related with patriarchal themes, while the sonorous offers an alternative. And nowhere was the 'patriarchal' so dominant as in the Spanish life of this and other periods – especially in the colonies of New Spain.

Juana Inés de la Cruz was born in 1648 in New Spain, on a hacienda near what is now known as Mexico City. She was the illegitimate daughter of Don Pedro de Asuaje, a Spanish naval officer, and Doña Isabel de

Santillana, daughter of the wealthy Spanish family who owned the large estate. Her father soon absented himself, and Juana grew up with her mother and her extended family. Possibly owing to Juana's illegitimacy, and thus lowered expectations for a socially advantageous marriage, she was allowed the free run of the family mansion and the surrounding countryside. There she discovered her grandfather's wide-ranging library, which is said to have contained some 4,000 books. As girls were not permitted to read, she took to removing books and studying them in secret in the next-door chapel. By this and other subterfuges she taught herself Latin. (As Spanish is a Romance, i.e. Roman, language, derived from the Latin spoken in Iberia during the Roman Empire, this feat is not quite so unlikely as it may sound to English-speakers. Spanish evolved from one direct source, whereas English evolved mainly from a mixture of Anglo-Saxon, the Latin spoken in England during Roman times, and 'Romance' Norman French.)

Juana's wanderings through the fields of the estate, and curiosity about its workings and account books, soon taught her the rudiments of mathematics. These wanderings also brought her into contact with the native workers and their native-speaking overseers. In this way she learned to speak and write the local Aztec language Nahuatl (pronounced Nāw'tl). By her teenage years she was already reading and writing philosophy, as well as mastering the complexities of mathematics and Aristotelian logic.

But such freedom could not last, especially for a young girl developing into maturity. So in order 'to have no fixed occupation which might curtail my freedom to study' she chose to enter a monastery of Hieronymite nuns, a closed yet comparatively relaxed order where her social status ensured that she could continue to study. Around this time, her grandfather left her his library, and it seems that she was able to have it donated to the monastery, enabling her to continue her studies in her cell. Here she became known as Sor (Sister) Juana.

Word of Sor Juana's extraordinary gifts soon spread, and she was visited at the monastery by Don Carlos de Sigüenza, seen by many as the first great intellectual *criollo* (the name given to Spanish born in the

New World). Such was Don Carlos's breadth of intellectual talents and
expertise that he would become known as the 'Mexican da Vinci'. He
and Sor Juana would converse together in the monastery's *locutorio* – a
room set aside for nuns to meet outsiders, with whom they communicated through a metal grille. Don Carlos was just three years older
than Sor Juana, and had received a formal education. Yet despite the
lacunae in Sor Juana's autodidact knowledge, they were soon conversing
as equals.

Sor Juana now began writing a series of dramas and poems. One of her
poems was entitled *Hombres Necios* (Foolish Men) and presents a rational
argument against the irrationality of men seeing themselves as superior
beings to women. Her poems are both autobiographical and spiritual,
describing the soul's philosophical search for knowledge: 'I don't study to
learn more, but to ignore less'. This suggests a knowledge of Plato's idealistic philosophy – there is an ideal world beyond the ephemeral world we
humans inhabit. This world of ideas is pre-existent, waiting to be discovered by all who seek to apprehend it. In which case, she implies, such
knowledge is just as available to women as it is to men.

It was around this time that seemingly exaggerated stories of Sor
Juana's exceptional intellect came to the attention of the Marquis of
Mancera, the Viceroy of New Spain. In order to test the veracity of
these claims, he invited her to court, where she was subjected to close
questioning by a gathering of philosophers, theologians, poets and other
intellectuals. The answers she gave more than satisfied the viceroy and
his wife, Leonora, concerning her talents. The vicereine Leonora was
descended from a distinguished Italian family, and had grown up as a
menina (a young lady-in-waiting, or girl page) at the Spanish court in
Madrid. A woman of some learning herself, it has been suggested that
Leonora may have arranged for Sor Juana to receive further expert tuition;
more certain is the fact that she became Sor Juana's protector.

This last fact would prove vital to Sor Juana, and indeed her very
existence as an intellectual free spirit. Her questioning of male superiority had ensured her enemies in high places, especially in the Church. A
senior New Spain cleric, the Bishop of Acapulco, now chose to publish

(under a pseudonym) one of Sor Juana's texts, suggesting that her defence of women challenged the authority and hierarchy of the Church.*

Sor Juana's cloistered existence enabled her to foster her creativity, yet at the same time it repressed her ability to live a 'normal' life commensurate with her intellectual freedom. Despite this, her poems and her music were far from limited to experiences of spirituality or arguments undermining the patriarchy. In both arts she found an outlet for her entire being, especially her feelings of sensuality and secular love. The modern Colombian writer Jaime Manrique declares that 'her love poems are expressions of a complex and ambivalent modern psyche, and because they are so passionate and ferocious... when we read them we feel consumed by the naked intensity she achieves'. Despite such 'naked intensity', Sor Juana was capable of wry reflection: 'The very distressing effects of love, but no matter how great, they do not equal the qualities of the one who causes them'.

Owing to the location and content of Sor Juana's vast output, much of her work has been lost – only known by reference to it in other sources. Music played a central part in her poetry, and her practical knowledge of the subject is evident in her surviving writings – especially concerning the tuning of various instruments and her ambitious attempt to create a new simplified form of musical notation.

Sor Juana would continue her cloistered life for some twenty-seven years, until she died in 1695 at the age of forty-six – almost certainly as a result of treating plague victims within her monastery. Don Carlos, the Mexican Leonardo, would deliver the eulogy at her funeral.

After her death, her life and works would soon be forgotten. Not until the twentieth-century Nobel Prize-winning Mexican poet Octavio Paz would they receive their due as the most important body of poetic work produced in the Americas until the arrival of nineteenth-century figures such as Emily Dickinson and Walt Whitman.

---

* For this, and many other ideas in her work, Sor Juana is now regarded as a proto-feminist, i.e. a feminist before the idea had been conceptualized.

CHAPTER 14

SPINOZA AND LOCKE

THE AGE OF REASON would reach its apogee in the philosophy of
Baruch Spinoza, the most rational of all the great thinkers of this
age. Indeed, it is all but impossible to overstress the centrality of reason
in his thought. In the words of his biographer Margaret Gullan-Whur:
'Logical inference was his yardstick for drawing conclusions in all areas
of human concern, including emotion. He believed – an ancient assumption – that the ordering of the universe was causally logical. Reasons and
causes being thus identical, the paradigm of *adequate* knowledge was
mathematics.'

The rational power of Descartes's doubt, which led him to doubt
everything until he arrived at one ultimate truth ('I think therefore I am')
was nothing compared to the all-pervading rigour of Spinoza's philosophy.
In the words of Bertrand Russell, Spinoza's major work – his *Ethics* – 'is
set forth in the style of Euclid, with definitions, axioms, and theorems;
everything after the axioms is supposed to be rigorously demonstrated
by deductive argument. This makes him difficult reading.' Russell's final
remark here may not be a logical deduction, but it is undeniably true. This
is a pity, as Spinoza's philosophy is highly appealing – as well as being

open to wildly differing interpretations which would surely have annoyed its rational author.

Some have seen Spinoza's philosophy as atheism; others have regarded it as diametrically the opposite, i.e. pantheism, the belief that the world is God and God is the world. Such a belief harks back to the beginnings of human thought, and yet at the same time continues to flourish over the centuries – as can be seen from the following assertion by Albert Einstein: 'I believe in Spinoza's God who reveals Himself in the orderly harmony of what exists, not in a God who concerns Himself with fates and actions of human beings.'

Spinoza was born in 1632 in Jodenbuurt, the Jewish district in Amsterdam – where Rembrandt found inspiration in the faces and wisdom of the local scholars. Spinoza was of Sephardic Jewish ancestry, his family having fled persecution by the Inquisition in Portugal, and finding refuge in the more liberal atmosphere of the Netherlands. His father, Miguel, was a merchant, with a 'warehouse on the Prinsengracht filled with sugar, Brazil wood, candied ginger and dried fruit'. His mother, Ana Débora, was from a comparatively rich merchant family, but died when Baruch was six years old. An English traveller who visited Amsterdam during this period noted that the local Jewish population was mostly from Portugal, and consisted of many 'Ritch Merchants... living in liberty, wealth and ease.'

Young Baruch was brought up and educated in a traditional Sephardic Jewish school of the period.* This was comparatively strict in its teachings and observation of Jewish customs. However, young Baruch would not go on to any advanced education in the Pentateuch (the first five books of the Old Testament of the Bible, upon which the Jewish faith is based). Instead, his father made him abandon his education and join the family business when he was seventeen.

Spinoza's father would die four years later, leaving the business heavily in debt. Baruch petitioned the Amsterdam authorities to be classified as

---

* A teacher at this school was Rabbi Menasseh ben Israel, one of the authorities who was consulted by Cromwell on how to set up a religious state.

an 'orphan', which meant that his inheritance from his mother could not be used to pay off his father's debts. His intention was to use this money so that he could devote himself to the study of modern philosophy, especially Descartes and the natural philosophy of optics (especially with regard to light passing through lenses). His older sister Rebekah claimed that this inheritance was rightly hers, and took him to court. She lost the case, but Spinoza then seems to have given her the money, claiming that he only wished to prove a point.

From this emerges a young man of determined philosophical interests, and an equal determination to prove himself right. By this period Spinoza was also beginning to learn the practical side of optics: understanding how to grind lenses. This was a thriving enterprise in an age which saw the increasingly widespread use of spectacles – though for the time being Spinoza regarded this as merely experimental work alongside his study of optics.

More importantly, Spinoza spent long hours studying contemporary philosophy, and forming ideas of his own. He came to the conclusion that there was no evidence, either in the Bible or modern philosophy, for the belief that God had a body, that the soul was immortal, or that angels existed. Such ideas were central to the teachings of the Pentateuch. Regardless of this, Spinoza took to hanging around outside his local synagogue discussing his ideas with other young Jews. Such was the rational power of his arguments that he began to convince a number of his youthful audience. According to Spinoza, the authors of the Pentateuch were scientific simpletons, and not much better as theologians.

The synagogue elders naturally took umbrage at this behaviour and went to some lengths to silence him. First Spinoza was threatened, and then told that if he went somewhere else and kept his ideas to himself, they were willing to pay him an annual stipend of 1,000 florins. (At the time, a student could live on 2,000 florins a year.) Despite being all but penniless, Spinoza chose to refuse this generous offer. He was nothing if not headstrong, especially with regard to getting his own way.

Just as troubling to the religious authorities was the fact that Spinoza had begun reading Aristotle – the basis of Christian medieval thought.

However, he appears to have come to this by reading commentaries on Aristotle by the great Jewish scholars Maimonides and Hasdai Crescas, both of whom had been renowned Sephardic scholars some two and a half centuries previously. Their writings were still read by Portuguese Jews, but were controversial nonetheless. Crescas's readings of Aristotle had led him to the conclusion that matter was eternal and that the Creation was no more than the imposition of order upon the primeval chaos of the cosmos. Spinoza's absorption of these ideas would colour his entire outlook.

The Jewish religious authorities in Amsterdam were understandably worried by Spinoza's behaviour. The immigrant Jewish population was tolerated, as was their religion – but such toleration had its limits. Heretical ideas such as those peddled by Spinoza were definitely not welcomed in Protestant Holland. By persisting in trying to spread his ideas, Spinoza was putting the entire Jewish community at risk.

One night, as Spinoza left the synagogue, a man stepped up beside him. In the nick of time, Spinoza noticed the raised dagger in his hand and instinctively raised his cloak to protect himself. The dagger slashed through Spinoza's cloak, but left him unharmed. It remains unclear whether Spinoza's assailant had been hired to kill him, or was an Orthodox Jewish zealot. Either way, the Jewish authorities became determined to cut themselves off from Spinoza and all he stood for.

In July 1656, Spinoza was ceremonially excommunicated from the Jewish community. As Russell described it: 'He was cursed with all the curses in Deuteronomy and with the curse that Elisha pronounced on the children who, in consequence, were torn to pieces by the she-bears.' This meant that he was completely ostracized from all contact with Jews: no one was allowed to communicate with him, let him into their house, or have any dealings with him whatsoever.

Spinoza now took refuge with a certain Franciscus van den Enden, a former Jesuit priest who had become a freethinker and a man of polymathic learning. He had run an art shop in central Amsterdam, where he published and sold prints by the likes of Rubens and Van Dyck. This shop had become a gathering place for dissenting intellectuals. Even so, van den Enden was careful to maintain a veneer of religious respectability;

he was 'Catholic with Catholics and Protestant with Protestants'. In fact, he was an atheist and a democrat, and is thought to have acted as a spy for Johan de Witt, the leading statesman during the First Stadtholderless Period, after the House of Orange was deposed.

When the bookshop went bankrupt, Van den Enden opened a school on the outskirts of Amsterdam. Spinoza was taken on as a resident teacher, and in the evenings he learned Latin from Van den Enden, who was sympathetic with the more daring views of Descartes – which Descartes himself had abjured when he learned of Galileo being summoned to trial in Rome. In particular, Spinoza learned of Descartes's comprehensively mechanistic view of the workings of the universe. It was now that he was introduced to the ideas of Giordano Bruno, who had proposed that the universe was infinite, just as God was infinite, suggesting that God and the universe were one and the same. These ideas would play a formative role in Spinoza's mature philosophy. In a characteristic act of defiance, he changed his first name from Baruch (Portuguese Jewish) to Benedictus (Latin), thus indicating his wish to be regarded as a non-Jewish scholar.

Van den Enden's sixteen-year-old daughter, Clara Maria, was also on the staff at the school, where she taught classics and music. The twenty-three-year-old Spinoza is said to have fallen in love with her, but his advances were rejected, and she eventually married one of her adult pupils. Though those who seek to regard Spinoza as living a saintly life – his thoughts absorbed in philosophy, his regard for himself and the world as one of a pantheistic union with God – utterly reject the idea of Spinoza falling in love.

However, it is difficult to regard Spinoza as the sexually dormant unworldly figure his hagiographers would have us accept. As much as any other philosopher prior to the modern age, he displayed a penetrating psychological awareness of secular love and sexual jealousy. In his *Ethics*, he proposed: 'The stronger the emotion which we imagine the person we love to feel for us, the more we are filled with self-pride'. He also claimed: 'If anyone thinks that there is between his beloved and another person the same or a more intimate feeling of love than there was between them when he alone loved her, he will feel hatred for the one he loved and be gripped with envy for his rival.' He described this 'envy' (jealousy) as 'the swings of feeling arising from the simultaneous experience of love and hatred, together with bitter envy for a third person'.

This sounds very much like the self-knowledge of someone who has undergone just such a situation. In another work, he described how he was 'like a sick man with a fatal disease, who is faced with death if he does not find a cure'. His cure for this disease was 'love for the eternal and infinite which alone feeds the mind pleasure and frees it from all pain'.

Van den Enden would eventually disappear, and his school close down. (It is now known that he crossed secretly into France, where his democratic ideas led to him becoming involved in a failed plot to assassinate Louis XIV. The conspirators were apprehended, and van den Enden was hanged outside the Bastille.) Spinoza retired to the country-side outside Leiden, where he devoted his life to his philosophy, earning his living as a lens-grinder. However, he would never forget the active democratic ideals instilled in him by Van den Enden. He may have lived a frugal life of the mind, in tune with his modest needs (according to a lifelong friend who rented him a room at one point, he subsisted on a diet of gruel and raisins), but such apparent withdrawal from the world did not prevent him from airing his controversial opinions on the matters of the day. This he did in his private correspondence with the likes of Henry Oldenburg of the Royal Society, and various close friends who recog-nized his exceptional philosophic mind. When he moved to a suburb of The Hague, these friends began meeting at his house to discuss politics – amongst them such distinguished figures as Christiaan Huygens and the leading republican Johan de Witt.

Over the coming two decades until his early death, Spinoza devoted himself to setting down his ideas on philosophy, politics and theology. His initial ideas on these subjects would appear in the only substantial work he published during his lifetime: *Tractatus Theologico-Politicus*. On the surface, this work was in no way subversive. His philosophy appeared highly abstract; his politics seemed to follow those of Hobbes, in that he invoked the authority of the state; and his theology was compatible with the liberal climate which prevailed in the Dutch Republic at the time.

Spinoza had already gained notoriety amongst the Jewish community, and possibly as a result of this his *Tractatus* soon began to attract adverse critical attention, despite its seemingly inoffensive nature. He now became a controversial figure throughout Holland and beyond. And why was this the case? On closer examination, it was seen that his philosophy clashed with that of Descartes, his politics were deemed subversive, and his theology was regarded as atheistic. Despite this, Spinoza was offered the prestigious chair of philosophy at the University of Heidelberg, the oldest in Germany, but turned it down as he wished to pursue a life of thought 'in accordance with his own mind'.

Spinoza's notoriety ensured that *Ethics* would not be published in his lifetime. This was his major work, upon which his reputation rests, and it would ensure him both posthumous execration and saintly admiration. Even his unwitting attempts to render this work unreadable, by casting it in the form of geometric proofs, would not save it from the furore that ensued.

From the outset, *Ethics* is an uncompromising expression of his extremely rational and abstract view of the world. As such, it may be compared with Euclid's *Elements*, which dates from around 300 BC. The *Elements* begins with a series of self-evident definitions, upon which Euclid builds the foundations of his mathematics, deducing proofs of geometry and number theory. The rigour of Euclid's thought becomes evident from his opening definitions: 'A point is that which has position but no dimensions'; 'A line is a length without breadth'; 'The intersection of lines and their extremities are points'...

A similar rigour is evident at the outset of Spinoza's *Ethics*, whose definitions begin:

> A thing which is its own cause (*causa sui*) I understand as
> something whose essence involves existence and whose nature
> cannot be conceived except as existing.
> A thing is finite (*in suo genere finito*) when it can be limited by
> another thing of the same nature. For example a body is said to
> be finite because we can always conceive of another, larger body.

Similarly, a thought is limited by another thought. However, body cannot be limited by thought, nor thought by body.

Spinoza continues by including two definitions which are all-important for his system: God and Eternity.

> By God (*Deus*) I understand an absolute infinite being – that is, a substance consisting of infinite attributes, each of which expresses eternal and infinite essence...
>
> By Eternity (*aeternitas*) I understand existence itself, conceived as following necessarily from the definition of the thing which is eternal. *Explanation*: For existence so conceived is an eternal truth, inasmuch as it is the essence of the eternal thing...

However, the rigour of Spinoza's argument immediately seems less compelling than that of Euclid. Why should this be? Because despite its rational deduction, it contains metaphysical concepts which are alien to modern thought, such as 'essence', 'eternal truth' and 'eternal thing'. Despite this, Spinoza's thought contains many ideas that are persuasive, appealing and wide in scope. (Einstein was to believe in Spinoza's world because of its all-encompassing reach, divine beauty and rigid causality.)

Spinoza's universe was pantheistic – he referred to it as *Deus sive Natura* (God or Nature). This is the only substance that there is, or can be; and as such it contains an infinite number of attributes. As mere mortals we are only capable of apprehending two of these attributes – namely, extension and thought. Our entire world appears to consist of these two attributes, which may be compared to two dimensions; while we remain unaware of the infinite dimensions beyond. Spinoza's universe harks back to medieval thought (where God permeated every aspect of life), yet at the same time it uncannily echoes ultra-modern concepts such as string theory (where in addition to the four dimensions of space-time we perceive, there are in fact six, or more, extra dimensions beyond our apprehension).

Spinoza's view of the world manages to overcome the mind-body problem that Descartes was unable to resolve. Namely, how does the mind (which operates by abstract reason) manage to interact with the body (whose corporeal reality operates by mechanical means)? For Spinoza, 'mind and body are one and the same individual which is conceived now under the attribute of thought, and now under the attribute of extension'. Mind and body are simply different aspects of the same thing – *Deus sive Natura* perceived through just two of His infinite attributes.

Our apprehension may be limited to just two of God's infinitely numerous attributes, but these nonetheless conform to the rigid logic inherent in the entity of God or Nature. Where mind is concerned, one idea follows another with the same rigid logical order as the deterministic cause and effect which operates between things in the attribute of substance. Logic, determinism, order... the chain of cause and effect is necessary, inevitable and irreversible.

Where Galileo saw mathematics as the language in which God had written the universe, Spinoza went one further: God or Nature is the embodiment of logic. God did not write the universe; He *is* the universe. And how do we know that this divine being exists? Because we are part of it. And our finite beings (limited to the attributes of mind and substance) proceed necessarily from His infinite attributes.

Spinoza was aware of the element of circularity in this argument, and in order to eliminate any such flaw in his divine conception of things he produced a philosophical proof of God's existence. Despite the disparities between the philosophies of Spinoza and Descartes, Spinoza's proof of God's existence is much the same as one of the two proofs that Descartes found necessary to ensure God's existence. Namely, the ontological argument, which states that as God is possessed of all possible perfections, he must of necessity be possessed of the attribute of existence (or he would be lacking in perfection). This originally medieval argument is recognizably more suited to Spinoza's philosophy than Descartes's with its emphasis on doubt. Indeed, this proof seems in many ways an inevitable consequence of Spinoza's thought. Consider how Spinoza characterizes the notion of substance:

So if someone says that he has a clear and distinct – that is to say, true – idea of substance and that he nevertheless doubts if such a substance exists, this would be just the same as if he said that he has a true idea but nevertheless suspects it may be false.

From this it follows: 'Since existence appertains to the nature of substance, its definition must of necessity involve existence, and therefore from its mere definition its existence can be concluded.'

To the modern ear, this may sound like so much medieval sophistry. Yet there remains that undeniably modern aspect to the God or Nature universe. Contemporary scientists use uncannily similar arguments to account for several central notions, including the Big Bang and the elusive theory of everything (or unified field theory). Stephen Hawking was not above asking: 'Is the unified theory so compelling that it brings about its own existence?'

Spinoza may have spent his days pondering such metaphysical realms, in between working at his lens-grinding to support his meagre existence, but he did not live an entirely otherworldly existence. He always kept abreast of political developments, especially those involving his friend Johan de Witt – whose life would take a drastic turn during these years. Holland may have provided a refuge for freethinkers such as Descartes and Spinoza, but it should not be regarded as some utopian haven of liberal thought. Far from it. There may have been an element of democracy under the stadtholder rule of the House of Orange, but debate within this framework was robustly contested. And the newly independent Free States remained under constant threat from their former imperial masters – the Spanish – as well as neighbouring France, England and the German states.

During the First Stadtholderless Period, when the House of Orange was displaced, Johan de Witt became the leading republican statesman. Then in 1672 came the calamitous *Rampjaar*, with England, France and the German states all at war with Holland. The invasion by the troops of Louis XIV caused consternation throughout the land,* as the Dutch

---

* This was when Vermeer went bankrupt in Delft.

flooded the polders and French troops ran amok. Wild rumours circulated and the populace turned against De Witt and his brother. They were set upon by the mob, who literally tore their bodies to pieces: 'With unprecedented butchery, pieces of flesh were hacked off and sold as souvenirs, or roasted and eaten.' News soon reached Spinoza, who was renting a room nearby. Such was his outrage at what had happened that:

[he was] prompted, on the day of the massacre of the De Witts, to go out in the night and put up somewhere near the place a paper [placard] saying ULTIMI BARBORUM [lowest of barbarians]. Abuse in Latin would not have been understood by the rabble, but, chillingly, the crowd had not consisted entirely of 'canaille'. Spinoza's... presence would have been recognized, and his weak frame would not have got him home alive. But his host had shut the house to prevent him going out... for he would have been exposed to the risk of being torn to pieces.

Spinoza would live out his days in and around The Hague, dying prematurely at the age of forty-four in 1677, his death hastened by phthisis, which was almost certainly caused by the glass dust from his lens-grinding lodging in his lungs.

Bertrand Russell would describe Spinoza as 'the noblest and most lovable of the great philosophers. Intellectually, some others have surpassed him, but ethically he is supreme. As a natural consequence, he was considered, during his lifetime and for a century after his death, a man of appalling wickedness.'

Somewhat surprisingly, Spinoza's twentieth-century biographer Gullan-Whur appears to incline more towards the latter view. She rubbishes the saintly picture which has accrued around Spinoza's name, suggests he was homosexual, and characterizes him as 'an intellectually supercilious man, whose arrogance seldom tallied with his criterion for rational self-esteem, and whose testiness was ingrained'.

While Spinoza was extending philosophy into the extremities of reason, the Englishman John Locke proposed an entirely antithetical philosophy. This can only be regarded as belonging to the realms of unreason insofar as it is not based upon rational premises. Apart from this lacuna, Locke's philosophy was expounded in a most reasonable fashion, and was in accord with the Scientific Revolution which thrived during the Age of Reason. Locke's new philosophy was known as empiricism: the theory that all our knowledge is based upon experience, as perceived through our five senses.

Like his older contemporary Thomas Hobbes, Locke would live through one of the most turbulent periods in English history. Consequently, he – and his philosophy – would be forced to navigate their way through the full panoply of unreason that unfolded during his lifetime. This would include the troubled reign of Charles I into which he was born, the consequent English Civil War, the Puritan Commonwealth, the libertarian era of the Restoration, and the brief Catholic rule of James II. This would be followed by the Glorious Revolution, which saw the ascension of William of Orange and his wife Mary to the throne.

This last may have been the crowning achievement that brought peace and constitutional monarchy to the land, but it was also a crowning achievement of unreason. While the Dutch ruler William of Orange had been busily preparing his fleet to invade England and launch into a fourth Anglo-Dutch War in as many decades, the English took the unusual step of inviting the leader of the enemy forces, and his wife, to take over as rulers of their country. Thus William and Mary ascended to the throne in a Glorious Revolution which involved no revolution at all. And at the same time, Britain embarked upon the delicate constitutional experiment which continues in the present day. This balancing act ensures that the monarch has supreme power in theory, yet remains all but powerless in practice.

John Locke was born in 1632 in a remote village in Somerset. His father was a country lawyer who supported the Puritan cause, and on the outbreak of the Civil War in 1642 he joined the Parliamentarian army. Around this time the family moved to a village on the outskirts of Bristol, which was beginning to thrive from trade with the New World, especially the notorious triangular trade in slaves. At the age of fifteen, Locke was sent to London to study at Westminster School (where the poet Dryden was a contemporary pupil).

At this time Westminster School was a microcosm of the divided world around it. A majority of the pupils came from a Parliamentarian background, while the headmaster, Dr Busby, was as enthusiastic for the Royalist cause as he was for flogging his pupils. On the day that Charles I was beheaded in nearby Whitehall, Dr Busby locked his pupils within the school so that they could not witness this historic event. Locke was a gentle soul of frail constitution who did not flourish amidst such a robust atmosphere.

At the age of twenty, Locke went to study at Christ Church, Oxford. England's oldest university was still very much living in the past where its educational curriculum was concerned. Aristotelian Scholasticism was very much the order of the day in all subjects – from science to theology. Indeed, according to the statutes of the university, a scholar was liable to be fined one shilling if he contradicted the word of Aristotle, and a further shilling for every time he repeated this misdemeanour.

During the 1650s Oxford was very much under Puritan control, and many of the traditional student pursuits had been curtailed. The taverns only served 'small beer',* the bordellos were closed down, and even the celebration of Christmas was banned. Despite this repressive atmosphere, Locke managed to obtain works by Descartes, which inspired him to begin thinking about philosophy independent of Aristotelian orthodoxy. This led him to become interested in science, in particular medicine.

After reading William Harvey's *De Motu*, which first described the circulation of the blood, Locke began to reject the accepted medical teachings of Galen. Along with his circle of university friends he began undertaking a series of daring scientific experiments. Amongst these

---

* Containing less than 2 per cent alcohol, it was widely drunk throughout the population, even by children. The minimal alcoholic content acted as a sterilizing agent, eliminating the many bacteria that contaminated the water supply.

friends was Richard Lower, who is known to have undertaken one of the first successful blood transfusions during this period.

After graduating, Locke became a lecturer in Ancient Greek. However, he spent most of his time conducting experiments with his circle of like-minded friends, including the chemist Robert Boyle and the physicist Robert Hooke. He also discussed Descartes, as well as pursuing philosophical ideas of his own. Despite this, Locke would never become a fully fledged Cartesian. He admired Descartes's use of doubt, which encouraged him to see beyond the obfuscating clouds of Aristotelian orthodoxy, but he was inclined to reject Descartes's belief in the primacy of reason. This simply did not chime with the method he found himself employing in his scientific pursuits. Medicine was not based upon reason; it was based upon the findings of experiments. These alone had enabled him to see beyond the mistakes in the time-honoured teachings of Galen. Facts, rather than doubt, led to the ultimate reality of experience.

Despite entertaining such unorthodox thoughts, Locke was not inclined to incite controversy. Temperamentally averse to such confrontation, he kept his ideas to himself, only discussing them with his close-knit circle of friends. He was by nature cautious and secretive, and only recorded his more revolutionary ideas in coded notebooks. By now, he was beginning to piece together his original ideas to form a coherent philosophy.

It was around this time that Locke started to read Hobbes's political masterpiece *Leviathan*. Initially he was inclined to concur with Hobbes's authoritarian belief that any form of government, no matter how repressive, was better than none. This seemed self-evident to anyone who had grown up amidst the turmoil of the Civil War. On the other hand, his natural inclination to question authority soon led him towards a more nuanced picture – one more in accord with his own experience.

Locke now embarked upon the two subjects which would dominate his thought – namely, epistemology (how we obtain true knowledge) and modern political theory (how liberty can thrive under government rule). And in 1666, he met the man who was to change his life and enable him to terminate his academic career. This allowed Locke to emerge from the world of ideas into the reality of politics and clashing beliefs. His ideas would now undergo the purgatory of practical application, from which would emerge his empirical philosophy and the pragmatic idealism of his political theory.

The man who took Locke under his wing was Lord Ashley: a man of diminutive stature but nonetheless forceful character; an aristocrat possessed of many talents and burning ambition. Ashley had originally supported the Royalists in the Civil War, but had switched sides when he suspected that Charles I was planning to sell out to the Catholics. During the Commonwealth he was appointed by Cromwell to the ruling Council of State, but soon chafed under Cromwell's restrictive ideas. Despite this, Ashley was one of the party appointed by parliament to approach Charles II with the offer of restoration to the throne. By the time Locke entered his service, Ashley was one of the most powerful figures in the country. However, beneath his robust manner was a man of afflicted health. He intended for Locke to take on the role of his personal physician. And during his first years in Ashley's service, Locke duly delivered his wife of a child, and prescribed a bold intervention to cure Ashley of a suppurating abscess of the liver.

In 1672 Ashley was appointed a peer of the realm, taking on the name Lord Shaftesbury; he was then appointed Lord Chancellor, the senior political post in the land. Whereupon he appointed Locke Secretary of the Board of Trade and Plantations. This involved him in the administration of the American colonies, in particular the Province of Carolina.* Locke survived Shaftesbury's downfall in 1675, but eight years later was forced to flee for sanctuary to Holland after being (wrongly) suspected of involvement in a plot against Charles II. Here Locke is thought to have met Spinoza, and certainly studied the latter's *Ethics* in some detail. Although Locke's burgeoning philosophical ideas were diametrically opposed to Spinoza's rational approach, he found himself in accord with Spinoza's political ideas. These inclined Locke's thinking towards the liberty of the individual and religious tolerance, as well as the separation of church and state.

---

* Named just nine years previously after Charles II (*Carolus* in Latin).

During Locke's period in exile he would complete the bulk of his major works – his *Two Treatises of Government* (on politics) and his *Essay Concerning Human Understanding* (on philosophy).

The first of Locke's *Treatises on Government* contains a penetrating critique of absolute monarchy and the divine right of kings – two long-standing notions that had recently been defended by the English political thinker Robert Filmer, a staunch opponent of the Parliamentary cause who had been imprisoned in Leeds Castle during the Commonwealth. Filmer's *Patriarcha, or The Natural Power of Kings* sidestepped Hobbes's philosophical argument for the necessity of government, and instead appealed to the authority of 'Old Testament history from Genesis onwards'. To modern eyes, this may appear a weaker argument than that of Hobbes, but it indubitably carried more force at the time. And with good reason. Filmer traced the divine power of kings back to the 'kingly power' originally bestowed upon Adam by God, which thus descended to his heirs.

As Filmer argued, 'the desire of liberty was the first cause of the fall of Adam'. Hence our inclination to liberty was in fact an impiety, contrary to God's will. There was no question of any social contract, as proposed by Hobbes. Nor was there any consideration of the public good. God's will was uppermost. But this derived its force from our most powerful instinct: namely, the authority of a father over his family and children.

In modern parlance, there is a compelling sociological and psychological argument here which would appear to trump philosophical or ethical considerations. It also had the weight of history behind it. Thus Locke's argument against Filmer may be regarded as an attempt to establish a modern legitimacy – one which flies in the face of all that had gone before it. As such, it may be regarded as political theory on a par with Cartesian doubt – where all previous certainties are subjected to scepticism. However, Locke does not arrive at any political bedrock similar to Descartes's 'I think therefore I am'. Instead he attacks the very core of the belief in the divine right of kings: how can we possibly tell if any political ruler is a direct descendant of Adam? Without the certainty of any such identity, the ruler's power does not have God's authority, and cannot be absolute. In which case, resistance to such rule is justifiable if his commands are not deserving of obedience.

In Locke's second treatise, he extended this argument using his own reading of historical development. This reading denies both the biblical view (of Adam's communication with God), and Hobbes's picture of life as 'nasty, brutish and short'. In Locke's view humanity originally lived in a state of nature, in families and loose groups which were free from external authority. Under such conditions each person had a duty to God not to 'harm another in his life... liberty, or... goods'. The echoes here of the United States Constitution are no accident. Locke's arguments for 'people [to] agree to unite, and to enter into society to make one people, one body politic, under one proper government' are precisely those used in the following century by the American colonists to justify their break with British rule.

In this last aspect, Locke's political philosophy was undeniably ahead of its time. However, his epistemological philosophy, as set down in his masterwork *Essay Concerning Human Understanding*, is very much in accord with contemporary European thought – following the Scientific Revolution instigated in the previous century by Galileo. This method of thought had not been properly accounted for in the rational philosophies of Descartes and Spinoza. Descartes had suggested that when confronting a problem it should first be fully analysed and reduced to its simple component parts. Only then could any argument proceed by 'clear and distinct' rational steps towards a conclusion. Spinoza's philosophy was even further removed from current scientific practice – despite the fact that it employed the language in which, according to Galileo, God had written the universe.

Locke's bedrock was prior to rational thought: it was the very stuff of sensation itself. His empirical experience preceded the possibility of rational thought, which could only be applied to our sensations after we had experienced them. As he explained: 'My purpose [is] to enquire into the original, certainty, and extent of human knowledge; together with the grounds and degrees of belief, opinion, and assent'.

Here Locke makes it evident that he is taking into account Descartes's 'malicious demon' who is capable of deceiving our senses. And like Descartes he is determined to avoid any preconceptions or false beliefs which may cloud the mind. To this end, he posits that when we are born, our mind is a *tabula rasa* ('white paper, void of all characters'). All our consequent ideas – our perceptions – are derived from experience. These experiential ideas, these perceptions apprehended by our senses, imprint themselves upon the white paper of the mind. Only then do we use our reason to work out connections between our experiences. What we make of this raw data is human knowledge: 'Empiricism about ideas is combined with rationalism about knowledge... without reason, all we have is belief, not knowledge.'

And Locke makes another important distinction, between the qualities of our perceptions. The primary qualities are those which reside in the objects of our experience – that is, 'solidity, extension, figure, motion or rest, and number'. The secondary qualities are all the other aspects of our perception, such as colours, sounds, smells and so forth. The primary qualities are actually in the bodies which we perceive, whereas the secondary qualities are only in the perceiver. It is with our eyes that we see colours, with our ears that we hear sounds, with our nose that we smell odours, etc.

Only the secondary qualities of our experience are those which can be deceived by Descartes's malicious demon; these alone are subject to mirages and diseases such as jaundice that distort our vision. Or so Locke would have us believe. In fact, the primary qualities are just as prone to deception. A mirage misleads our experience of solidity and motion just as much as it deludes our eyes. But as Bertrand Russell pointed out, 'even his errors were useful in practice'. The distinction between primary and secondary qualities 'dominated practical physics until the rise of quantum theory in our own day... The theory that the physical world consists only of matter in motion was the basis of the accepted theories of sound, heat, light, and electricity.' In other words, Locke may have been wrong, but his distinction was useful. And as Russell comments, 'This is typical of Locke's doctrines.'

Locke would return from his exile in Holland in triumph. He was aboard the ship that transported William of Orange's wife Mary to England for the Glorious Revolution of 1688. Two years later, his two masterworks – *Two Treatises on Government* and *Essay Concerning Human Understanding* – would be published in London, where they met with the acclaim that was their due. And Locke's achievements were recognized across the board; he was befriended by such disparate figures as Newton and Dryden, who both held his intellectual opinions in high regard. By now his frail constitution meant he was beginning to succumb to illness. Despite this, he would live beyond the turn of the century, finally dying in 1704 at the age of seventy-two.

CHAPTER 15

THE SURVIVAL AND SPREAD
OF THE CONTINENT
OF REASON

WHILE FRANCE, ENGLAND, HOLLAND and the German states squabbled in northern Europe, the entire continent of the Age of Reason faced an existential threat in the east. For years the Ottoman Empire had occupied the Balkans and virtually the entire littoral of the Black Sea. By 1660, the Ottoman army had occupied Transylvania, Moldova and part of Hungary, moving ever closer to Vienna, capital of the Habsburg Holy Roman Empire under Leopold I. In a desperate attempt to prop up his position, Leopold I formed an alliance with Venice and Pope Innocent XI. He then signed the Treaty of Warsaw with John III Sobieski, King of Poland, promising support for Poland if the Ottoman Empire marched into eastern Poland and attacked Warsaw, with Poland pledging support for the Holy Roman Empire in the event of any attack on Vienna.

It soon became evident that, to the Ottomans, Vienna held the key to eastern Europe. The city straddled the Danube, which led to the Black Sea, with its Austrian hinterland protecting the trade route between southern

Germany and the eastern Mediterranean. In early 1683, the 150,000-strong Ottoman army of Sultan Mehmed IV, under the command of the grand vizier Kara Mustafa Pasha, prepared to advance across the Balkans. Mehmed IV now despatched a menacing letter to Leopold I, making clear his intentions:

> I will make myself your master, pursue you from East to West, to trample upon all that is pleasant and accessible to your eyes. I resolve to ruin you and your people and to leave your empire a commemoration to my dreadful sword. I will establish my religion and pursue your crucified God whose wrath I do not fear. I will put your sainted priests to the plough [and] I will rape your women. Forsake your God, your religion, or I will order that you be consumed by fire.

In the words of one modern historian, Kim Seabrook: 'the long struggle between the Habsburg and Ottoman Empires for the mastery of Central Europe… was always more than a conflict over territory or between dynasties. It was a battle of ideas, of culture and most of all of faith – it was a clash of civilisations.'

In Belgrade, Mehmed IV left his army to return to his capital, Istanbul, making it plain to Mustafa Pasha that nothing short of victory would be acceptable. The forty-eight-year-old grand vizier was a seasoned warrior. In 1676 he had fought a war against Poland, overrunning the eastern province of Podolia. A man of arrogance and a fanatical hate for Christians, Mustafa Pasha was described by the Venetian diplomatic representative in Istanbul as 'wholly venal, cruel and unfair'.

Mustafa Pasha and the Ottoman army reached the gates of Vienna on 14 July 1683, and immediately began besieging the city. By now Leopold I had fled to southern Germany, leaving the city to be defended by his imperial commander Ernst Rüdiger von Starhemberg and 20,000 soldiers, aided by 10,000 citizen volunteers, along with some 140 functioning artillery pieces. By this stage Mustafa Pasha's army had been reinforced by a further 20,000 men, including the elite janissary corps and Tatar cavalry.

The defences of Vienna had been considerably reinforced since the previous siege of the city in 1529. Now the massive walls of the city rose fifty feet above the surrounding sixty-foot-wide ditch. Starhemberg ordered that all houses and dwellings outside the city walls be razed to the ground, giving the soldiers atop the ramparts a clear range of fire.

Meanwhile, Mustafa Pasha ordered his besieging army to begin digging deep trenches, from which mining tunnels were dug beneath the city walls. When complete, these would be filled with barrels of black gunpowder, to be detonated beneath the foundations, thus causing breaches through which the attacking Turks could pour into the city.

As the Turks painstakingly dug their tunnels, taking weeks to reach under the defensive ditch, hunger began to spread through the besieged citizens and soldiers. However, Mustafa Pasha refrained from pressing home his advantage by firing cannonballs over the walls into the city. Some sources have speculated that the Turkish general wished to leave the treasures of the city intact, so that they would be preserved for him and his army to plunder.

By August, Starhemberg's troops and the citizens of Vienna were becoming desperate. All the cats and dogs throughout the city had already been eaten, and those inside the city walls were now reduced to eating rats and drinking contaminated water. Hunger and widespread fatigue began to set in – to such an extent that Starhemberg gave orders that any soldier found asleep at his post was to be shot.

In early September, after more than fifty days of siege, news reached Vienna that the imperial forces led by Charles V, Duke of Lorraine, were approaching the city from the north. Meanwhile Sobieski was marching his Polish troops towards Vienna with the intention of linking up with the imperial forces. With the addition of troops from the German states, this would make a combined army of some 80,000 men, a formidable force – though still far less than the vast Ottoman army of 150,000.

When Charles V reached the approaches to Vienna, he noticed that the Ottoman forces had not occupied the Kahlenberg hill that overlooked the city. He realized that from these heights he would be able to attack the rear of the Ottoman forces, and also gain a strategic vantage point from which to direct his troops. But it soon became clear that Sobieski and his Polish troops had strayed into the Vienna woods to the north-west of the city, and were making heavy weather of finding their way through the undergrowth.

By this stage, the tunnelling Ottomans had detonated their gunpowder mines and blown several large holes in the city walls. On seeing what was happening, Starhemberg ordered his men to dig their own tunnels, fill them with gunpowder, and detonate them to hold back the Turks. Meanwhile his forces fought a rear-guard action retreating into the inner city. At points along the walls, men listened for the digging of further tunnels. In the words of an eyewitness:

> We had a simple but brilliant idea, we put dried peas on a drum, if the peas moved then somewhere below us the Turkish sappers were at work. A new explosion was coming. Starhemberg had a rocket sent up into the night sky, our last desperate cry for help to the army of our Allies.

Charles V noted the signal, and grasped the seriousness of the situation. At daybreak, he ordered his men to attack the rear of the Ottoman lines – without waiting for Sobieski's Polish troops. The Ottomans soon realized what was happening, and Mustafa Pasha ordered his troops to break off the siege and launch themselves against the imperial forces. Not all of his men obeyed this order, for many remained intent upon breaking into the city and plundering its treasures. Despite this, an overwhelming force of Ottoman soldiers stormed up the slopes of the Kahlenberg, brandishing their banners and blaring their horns as they charged towards the imperial troops. The imperial forces resisted bravely, as best they could, but by the end of the day it was evident that they would soon be defeated. Then, as dusk was falling, Sobieski and his Polish forces emerged from the woods on to the Kahlenberg.

What followed has been called 'the greatest cavalry charge in history'. Eighteen thousand horsemen, armed with twenty-foot lances, swords, and hammers launched themselves on to the Ottoman lines. According to a Turkish chronicler: 'It was like a tide of black pitch rushing downhill, burning and crushing everything in their path.' What followed was a rout. In the aftermath of the battle, Sobieski wrote – incoherent with joy – to his wife of his victory:

> When the Champions of Islam saw the enemy advancing to attack they all lost the desire to fight, utterly devastated by the terrible defeat which had occurred with the Supreme Will of Allah, Kara Mustafa took the Holy Flag of Islam and turned to flee. Fighting and shedding bloody tears everyone tried to escape with life and limb from the Infidel swine.

He went on to describe the plunder his troops had seized from the fleeing Ottomans:

> Our treasures are unheard of, tents, chattels, sheep, cattle, and no small number of camels. It is a victory as no one has ever seen before, the enemy completely ruined, everything is lost for them, they run for their lives. General Starhemberg has hugged and kissed me, and called me his saviour.

The Battle of Vienna, as it came to be known, was the greatest defeat inflicted on the Ottoman army since its inception in 1299. As soon as news reached Istanbul of what had happened, Sultan Mehmed IV was so enraged that he ordered the execution of his grand vizier. When Mustafa Pasha finally made it to Belgrade on 25 December, riding on a donkey, he was executed in the customary manner: strangled with a silk cord pulled tight by janissaries.

The Battle of Vienna signalled the end of any further expansion by the Ottoman Empire into the lands of eastern Europe. Cultural legends attached to this historic victory include the baking of a celebratory crescent-shaped pastry (mimicking the crescent of the Ottoman flag), which became known as the croissant. According to another legend, the citizens of Vienna came across so many sacks of coffee beans, abandoned by the fleeing Turks, that they opened the first coffee house in the city.

During the following decade, another power on the fringes of Europe would seek to enter the continent – not to destroy it, but to learn from it. This would be a mission led by Peter the Great, Tsar of Russia, which took place during the final three years of the seventeenth century.

Peter the Great was born in Moscow in 1672. Just ten years later he would succeed to the throne, under the guardianship of his half-sister Sophia. Peter would preside at meetings of the ruling council, but Sophia would advise him on what to say, communicating with him through a hole in the back of his throne. His education was conducted by private tutors. One of these was the Scotsman Patrick Gordon, who became a general in the Russian army. Another was Paul Menesius (the Latinized form of Menzies) – also a Scot – who encouraged Peter to play boisterous games in the palace gardens with live ammunition.

These early years saw a number of unsuccessful palace coups, during the course of which Peter personally witnessed the murder of several of his relatives. On two occasions he was forced to flee fifty miles north-east in the dead of night to take refuge in the fortified monastery of Troitse-Sergiyeva Lavra, the spiritual home of the Russian Orthodox Church. When Peter reached the age of seventeen, he was obliged to enter an arranged marriage with an older, round-faced Russian woman named Eudoxia Lopukhina, whom he grew to detest. (He would later despatch her to a nunnery, leaving him free to marry someone else.)

Peter did not gain full power until he was twenty-two, by which time he had grown up into something of a physical oddity. He had sprouted to the exceptional height of six foot eight inches (at least a foot higher than most of his contemporaries), though other aspects of his development had not kept pace. Consequently he had small feet and hands, and his narrow shoulders were topped by a small head. As if this was not enough, he also had unsettling facial tics. (Expert medical diagnosis, with the benefit of historical hindsight, has ascribed these tics to ailments ranging from epilepsy to childhood psychological trauma, or simply acute embarrassment at his own conspicuous physical presence.)

Despite such setbacks, Peter proved a masterful tsar from the outset. The early years of his reign saw sweeping reforms in a wide range of social and political matters. Both the army and the navy were radically restructured. The latter reform was long overdue, as Russia's navy was for the most part a purely internal force. Its only seaport was Archangel, in the distant frozen north on the White Sea, which was icebound for several months each winter. The Baltic was under Swedish control, and the Black Sea was controlled by the Ottoman Empire. But Peter's Scottish tutors had fed his dreams with tales of British sea power, and Peter was determined that Russia should one day have a navy whose power belied its geographic disadvantages.

In 1695, Peter impulsively launched a campaign against the Ottomans by the Sea of Azov, which links the River Don to the Black Sea. The Russian forces proved no match for the Ottomans and their allies the Tatars of Crimea. So Peter returned to Moscow and launched a shipbuilding programme. The following year he sailed thirty ships down the River Don and into the Sea of Azov, where the Ottomans were defeated. Peter established Russia's first modern naval base at Taganrog on the Sea of Azov, thus gaining access to the Black Sea.

Other reforms were cosmetic, but indicative – including the banning of beards from his court. (Both Gordon and Menesius were conspicuously clean-shaven, whereas the ruling boyars prided themselves on the luxurious bushiness and inordinate length of their facial adornment.) When the boyars proved recalcitrant, Peter brought in astute measures to reinforce his decree – swingeing taxes. If a boyar wished to demonstrate his privileged position by wearing a beard, he would have to pay for it.

At the same time, European dress was introduced, and long heavy Russian coats were banned. Peter was doing his best to try to make his court *look* European. And this was the point. Appearance was intended to transform behaviour. His aim was nothing less than to change old Russia into a modern European nation. But this could not be done overnight, when even he himself had little notion of what it meant to be a contemporary European in the Age of Reason.

In order to remedy these defects, Peter decided to embark upon a tour of Europe. In 1697, he left Russia accompanied by an entourage of some 250 'experts' on a 'Grand Embassy' to western Europe. Peter was determined that he should not receive any special treatment during this tour: he wanted to see things as they really were, not some glorified version mocked up to impress the Tsar of Russia. In pursuance of this plan he chose to travel incognito (adopting the pseudonym 'Sergeant Pyotr Mikhaylov'). From now on he would just be another member of the Russian delegation. Though this proved difficult, owing to his towering stature – as well as his visible outrage when a fellow member of the delegation presumed to address him as an equal.

The Grand Embassy did not get off to a good start when Austria initially refused Peter's request for a visit. Political alliances in western Europe had undergone a drastic change in recent years. Following the Battle of Vienna, Austria wished to maintain peace with the Ottoman Empire, so that it could pursue its wars in western Europe. France also demurred at playing host to the Grand Delegation, as it too wished to remain on good terms with the Ottoman Empire – for similar reasons. Consequently, Peter was forced to reduce his previous ambitions for a grand tour, and instead he travelled to Holland. Despite Holland's democratic politics being the diametric opposite of Peter's autocratic rule, he was nonetheless impressed by what he learned during the course of his visit to what was in many ways Europe's most advanced nation.

The incognito sergeant was housed in the suitably modest wooden dwelling of a local master blacksmith in Zaandam. (The widow with whom he lived was paid to seek alternative accommodation.) In Amsterdam, Peter was received as a guest by Jacob de Wilde, the head of the admiralty. Here Peter was able to admire his host's extensive collection of coins and Dutch art, and the daughter of the house made an engraving of the historic meeting between her father and his incognito guest. (Upon leaving, the sergeant made his host an offer he couldn't refuse, and his precious collections of art and coins were then shipped to Russia.) Peter was also given an opportunity to try his hand at carpentry while visiting the VOC shipyard, the largest in the world at the time. He was so enthused by this chance to become a craftsman that he stayed on for four months, hewing and sawing alongside the workmen and helping the local shipbuilders construct a two-mast frigate, which was then named after him. (Later, Peter would have many of the carpenters, shipwrights and seamen involved in the building of the good ship *Peter* shipped to Russia.) At the end of his stay in Amsterdam, Peter arranged for Dutch engineers with experience of building fortresses and canal locks to be invited to Russia to pass on their skills to local craftsmen. He also visited the distinguished scientist Frederik Ruysch, who instructed him in the latest advances in dentistry as well as how to catch butterflies; later he would meet Jan van der Heyden, the inventor of the fire hose.

From Holland, the Grand Embassy travelled to England, where the visiting sergeant was presented to William of Orange. In London, Peter was able to see how the city was being rebuilt after the Fire of London, and he visited the half-completed St Paul's Cathedral. Although Sir Christopher Wren vetoed the idea of having his stonemasons shipped en masse to Russia, a seed was planted in Peter's mind: it was possible to build a complete stone city from scratch.

From England, the Grand Embassy journeyed through Germany to Prague, and then on to Vienna, where Peter was at last able to meet the Holy Roman Emperor Leopold I. However, news reached the tsar from Moscow that there had been a revolt by the crack army units known as the Streltsy, who were attempting a coup in favour of his half-sister Sophia.

The tour was immediately abandoned, and Peter hastened back to Moscow. Forgetting for the moment all the enlightened ideas he had learned in Europe, he savagely put down the revolt – with the defeated Streltsy subjected to a series of gruesome tortures. Some victims were roasted alive, while others had their flesh torn apart by red-hot pincers or were clubbed to a pulp. Over a thousand died, with the remainder whipped and branded before they were marched off to Siberian exile. Having dispensed justice, Peter once again returned to his strategic aims, implementing a programme of reforms which sought to bring the Age of Reason to his backward nation.

In 1699, Peter instigated a highly symbolic change. He decreed that instead of the Russian New Year beginning on 1 September, it would now begin on 1 January, thus conforming with European practice. In a further move, which angered the Orthodox Church, he adopted the Julian calendar (established by Julius Caesar in 46 BC). This counted the years from the birth of Christ – unlike the old Russian calendar, which counted the years from the purported creation of the world. Henceforth the year 7207 would be transformed into the year 1700.

Peter then signed a peace treaty with the Ottoman Empire, which cemented Russian gains in the Sea of Azov. This meant that Peter was free to turn his attention to the Baltic. As before, he launched into an impulsive declaration of war, with disastrous effect. This time the enemy was Sweden, which proved far too powerful, both on land and at sea. Peter's campaign culminated in the Battle of Narva, where the Swedish army under Charles XII put to flight a Russian army four times its size.

Such was the extent of Charles XII's victory that he now ignored Russia and turned his attention to attacking Poland. This gave Peter the respite he needed, and he at once embarked upon his most ambitious project of all. It was intended to establish Russia once and forever as a European nation: a power to be reckoned with throughout the continent. This scheme involved the building of a vast new capital city on the swampy marshland at the headwaters of the Baltic.

It is difficult to overestimate Peter the Great's role in the foundation of St Petersburg. Peter himself selected the site of the new city, and in 1703 he attended the laying of the foundation stone. This would be the location of the Peter and Paul Fortress – its double name ominous of its ambiguous future role. Strategically, this fortress guarded the entrance to the Neva and Russia's route to Europe; politically, it would become the dungeon which housed dissidents championing liberal European ideas. (Amongst the first to occupy a cell here was Peter's rebellious son Alexei. Over the years other notable inmates would include a roll call of the usual suspects, including the writers Dostoevsky and Gorky, the anarchist Bakunin, and political unfortunates such as Trotsky, and Lenin's brother Alexander.)

To build his city, Peter ordered the conscription of some 40,000 serfs, who were set to work draining the delta marshes under the supervision of Dutch canal engineers. However, such was the number of serfs who absconded or died that 40,000 soon became the *annual* number of conscripts, which had to be supplied by their previous owners, all suitably equipped with tools and clothing. Meanwhile, the construction of stone buildings was forbidden throughout Russia, so that all stonemasons could report for work on the grand project. Peter himself supervised the overall building, having taken up residence in a modest wooden cabin, which he shared with his Polish peasant mistress Catherine, who cooked his meals and would in time become his second wife.

Over the coming years Peter made a number of visits abroad, especially to Paris. This enabled him to model the wide boulevards of St Petersburg, such as Nevsky Prospect, on those of central Paris; meanwhile palaces and official buildings, such as the old Admiralty Building, were loosely based on Versailles, though the naval yards behind this building are said to have been modelled on the VOC yards in Amsterdam.

The island of Kronstadt was chosen as the new Baltic naval base. The fortification of the island and the construction of a new fleet was entrusted to the Scotsman Thomas Gordon (no relation to Peter's tutor). Under Gordon, Scottish merchants took up residence on Kronstadt and began trading with Scotland and other European countries.

St Petersburg was intended to be Russia's 'window to Europe', and Peter soon transferred his capital from 'old, wooden' Moscow to the purpose-built classical ministry buildings of his new city. But despite Peter's preference for his modern, rationally laid-out city, Russia would retain many of its traditional ways – as epitomized by Moscow, which remained the centre of the Russian Orthodox Church. This was a country which still stood apart from Europe, its history never joining the mainstream of European development. Russia was a nation that had experienced no Renaissance, no Reformation, and no separation of powers (the tsar was God's representative on earth, and thus above any secular law). Even Russia's Cyrillic script was alien to most European eyes.

Peter's attempt to open up his country to the continent of reason would remain at best a partial success. Russia's geography encouraged isolation and self-sufficiency. Its empire was a land empire, extending to the east into Asia. Northern Europe's empires, on the other hand, extended westward across an ocean to the Americas, or overseas to Asia, introducing a cosmopolitan aspect that was almost entirely missing from Russia's traditional history.

CHAPTER 16

NEW REALITIES

Fortunately, mathematics did not disappear down the philo-sophical blind alley into which Spinoza had attempted to lead it. As we have already seen, mathematics as we know it was conceived by the Ancient Greeks – more particularly by the philosopher Thales of Miletus, around 600 BC. Babylonian, Chinese, Indian and Ancient Egyptian mathematics all predate Thales – introducing such vital concepts as minus quantities, trigonometry and geometry. But these earlier forms of mathematics lacked one basic concept: namely, the notion of proof. When this was introduced by the Ancient Greeks, it brought a hitherto-unknown degree of rigour into mathematics.

This is perhaps best illustrated by Euclid, when faced with the question of how many prime numbers there are.* Euclid provided a simple and beautiful proof that there are an infinite number of primes. (This was the beauty which had so enraptured Bertrand Russell when

---

* A prime number is one which is only divisible by one and itself. For instance: 2, 3, 5, 7, 11... But not 4, which is divisible by 2; or 6, which is divisible by both 2 and 3. Or 8, 9, and 10, all of which are divisible by prime numbers.

he was introduced to Euclid at the age of eleven.)*

Ancient Greek mathematics was largely rediscovered during the Italian Renaissance (a rebirth of classical learning). However, by the Age of Reason the necessity for proof had become somewhat restrictive: it had begun to limit the sheer creativity of the mathematical mind.

Breaking free of the requirement for generalized proof enabled mathematicians to venture into entirely new areas. Here they could use ad hoc methods and algorithms (processes, or set of rules, used to solve a problem), which enabled them to discover how something worked without necessarily proving it to be true. This was particularly the case in mathematical physics – especially astronomy – but, most intriguingly of all, it also allowed mathematicians to venture into a new field that appeared to be as philosophical as it was mathematical. Paradoxically, this field would become a key concept in practical mathematics and indeed all forms of predictive calculation – in subjects ranging from the movement of stars to gambling. It would become known as probability, and it enabled mathematics to take its first tentative steps into the hitherto unknown (incalculable) realm of the future.

Probability theory as we know it today can be traced to a particular incident which took place in Paris in 1654. The gambler and self-styled nobleman Chevalier de Méré† approached the mathematician Blaise Pascal and challenged him to solve an ancient gambling problem known

---

* The proof is roughly as follows: Suppose we multiply all known primes together, and then add one. Now, if the resulting sum is prime, this is a prime that was not in our original list. Hence we have a further prime. This process can be repeated ad infinitum; thus there are an infinite number of primes. If, on the other hand, the sum number arrived at by multiplying all primes, and then adding one, is not a prime, it must be divisible by some prime. But it cannot be divided by any of the multiplied primes, since any division will leave the remainder of the added one. Hence the prime that it can be divided by cannot be amongst all the primes previously multiplied. This process too can be applied ad infinitum. Both cases always end up with a further prime. Therefore there is an unending, infinite number of primes.

† He was in fact a commoner from Poitou named Antoine Gombaud, who adopted the title *chevalier* (knight) in order to gain access to the fashionable salons of Paris, where he earned a living gambling with mathematically illiterate aristocrats.

as the problem of the points. In one version of this, two players agree to play dice for a stake, which will be won by the first to win seven games. However, the contest is interrupted and has to be abandoned when one player has won three games and the other has won one game – how should the initial stake be divided? What was the probability of any outcome?

Pascal became intrigued by the problem of points, and wrote to his fellow mathematician Pierre de Fermat in Toulouse on the matter. The exchange of letters that followed between Pascal and Fermat is seen as laying the foundations of modern probability theory.

Fermat's suggested solution was to list all possible paths to the required number of wins, count how many paths led to each player, and divide the pot accordingly. This method certainly worked, but it became increasingly complicated as the number needed to win got higher.

Pascal's solution made use of an ancient arrangement of numbers that is now known as Pascal's triangle. In this, the numbers in each row are formed by adding the two numbers immediately above it. This combination of numbers contains a surprising amount of solutions to particular problems. For instance, it reveals a number of probabilities.

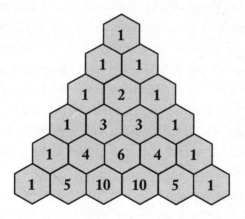

Pascal's Triangle, showing the first six descending rows.

If you toss a coin once, it can land either head or tails (1). If you toss a coin twice, there are four possible combinations: HH, HT, TH, TT. Taking HT and TH as variations on the same outcome, we get 1, 2, 1.

Toss the coin three times, and the combinations can be read off from the third row of the triangle: 1, 3, 3, 1...

Pascal's triangle has many other intriguing properties. For instance, the upper-left diagonal row contains all 1s. The next diagonal row down lists the counting numbers 1, 2, 3... The following diagonal down lists the triangular numbers (these can be represented by a pattern of dots in the form of an equilateral triangle): 1, 3, 6, 10... And the next diagonal row down lists the tetrahedral numbers: the three-dimensional version of the triangular numbers, in the form of a regular triangular pyramid.

Another property of Pascal's triangle is that if we add up the horizontal lines of the triangle we get 1, 2, 4, 8... These are the powers of two: $2^0, 2^1, 2^2, 2^3$...

These are but a few of the many remarkable properties of Pascal's triangle.

Blaise Pascal was born in 1623 at Clermont-Ferrand in the mountainous Massif Central region of central France. His father was a gifted mathematician who earned his living as a tax collector, and his mother died when he was just three years old. Pascal proved to be a paradoxical child. Physically, he was so sickly that he was not expected to live. On the other hand, it soon became evident that he had the mind of a child prodigy – especially with regard to mathematics and theology. When he was just sixteen, Pascal wrote an original paper on conic sections (the curves obtained by slicing through a cone at various angles). This paper was shown to Father Mersenne, who was so impressed that he passed it on to Descartes for comment. In the event, Descartes refused to accept Pascal's paper, on the grounds that such ideas 'would scarcely occur to a 16-year-old child'.

By 1642, when Pascal was nineteen, his father was working as a tax inspector in the port of Rouen, in northern France. Despite his mathematical ability, Pascal's father found the seemingly endless calculations involved in tax collecting almost overwhelmingly onerous. In order to assist his father, Pascal constructed an ingenious mechanical calculating machine. Later known as a Pascaline, this machine was capable of adding and subtracting. Such was its originality that in 1649 it came to the notice of Louis XIV, who granted it a royal privilege (the equivalent of a patent). Pascal would go on to construct no less than fifty of these Pascalines, which may be seen as an early form of a cash register – and as such, an analogue forerunner of the modern computer.

Over the coming years Pascal would apply himself to various mathematical and physical problems. In physics, he extended Torricelli's work on the barometer. Pascal reasoned that the mercury in Torricelli's barometer was affected by the pressure of the earth's atmosphere, which Pascal proposed would grow less dense the higher the altitude. In order to test this conjecture, he suggested an experiment: the barometer should be taken up a mountain, and the height of the mercury column recorded at each stage of the ascent.

By now Pascal's health was increasingly frail, so he passed the experiment on to his brother-in-law, who took the barometer on a climb up the Puy-de-Dôme (the mountain close to where Pascal had been born). Pascal's theory was duly tested, confirming that the earth's atmosphere grew less dense the higher one climbed. He concluded that, above the earth's atmosphere, space would be a vacuum. This view proved controversial on several counts. According to the prevailing Aristotelian teaching, 'Nature abhors a vacuum.' It also denied Descartes's modern scientific view that all space was filled with matter.*

Pascal had always been a troubled soul, and in 1654 he had an intense religious experience. This led him to become an adherent of the Jansenists

---

* During the ensuing centuries, Pascal's view would prevail. Not until the advent of quantum theory would Descartes's theory be confirmed – though not in any way that Descartes could possibly have foreseen. This is a classic illustration of how scientific understanding can evolve as our knowledge of the world grows more extensive. Science is merely a series of hypotheses which agree with experimental findings. The experiments do not *prove* the findings with the rigour of a mathematical proof. As experiments become more precise or extensive, so they frequently undermine previous findings. However, later findings frequently refine the previous experimental evidence, rather than simply contradicting it. As previously noted, this is why the calculations of Newtonian physics were sufficient to send a rocket to the moon, despite the fact that Newtonian physics had been superseded by Einstein's more complex relativity.

of Port-Royal, the intense Catholic religious sect in which Racine had been involved. As a result, Pascal gave up mathematics and his scientific investigations, devoting himself to religious writings. These would eventually be published as his *Pensées*, widely viewed as containing some of the finest religious writing of the era. The work makes clear that, despite his frail health and bouts of extreme suffering, Pascal had not abandoned his mathematical view of the world – in particular his understanding of probability theory.

For example, Pascal's most compelling argument in favour of religious belief comes in the form of what is now known as Pascal's wager, which is straight probability theory. As such, it is very much a product of the Age of Reason. According to this argument, any rational person should believe in the existence of God, and commit to a life of faith. If it turns out that God does not exist, the rational person has only denied themselves trivial pleasures and luxuries. If, on the other hand, God does exist, they will receive the ultimate gain of entry into Heaven, and avoid the ultimate loss of an eternity spent in Hell. (The counterargument to this points out that Pascal does not actually prove the existence of God, merely the probable benefits of belief in such an entity. Or indeed any divine entity in any religion.)

Another of Pascal's arguments would appear even more convincing, and much more relevant to the modern age. In his *Pensées* he claims: 'The heart has its reasons which reason knows nothing of.' This is, if anything, one of the most compelling arguments against the supremacy of reason. Not until Freud's notion of the unconscious mind would a reasonable argument be found to account for Pascal's claim.

The Age of Reason was one of growing human self-awareness. The supreme example of this can be seen in the quasi-philosophical introspection of Montaigne. In the intellectual sphere, Locke's empiricism marks a deepening of our self-understanding. But this trend was not limited to the purely personal, individual sphere. Harvey's discovery of the circulation of the blood, and Van Leeuwenhoek's discovery of an entirely new microworld, remain outstanding as purely physical advances in our inner knowledge. The Age of Reason also saw the beginnings of a wider introspection in the social sense, with thinkers pondering the workings of society itself – the very way in which they lived. As nations throughout the continent continued with their troubled evolution through civil and religious strife, thinkers sought to analyse precisely what society was, and to what it should aspire. Here Hobbes sketched a somewhat pessimistic paradigm, with Locke proposing a liberal approach more in tune with modern attitudes. At the same time, both William Petty and Johann Becher both attempted, after their own fashion, to lay down a framework for the ever-advancing commercial activities that epitomized the progressive element of the age.

So much for theory; a seminal advance now came in the practical understanding of what precisely was taking place in society. This came with the unexpected birth of an entirely new branch of scientific enquiry – namely, statistics. The father of modern statistics is widely acknowledged to be John Graunt, who was born in London in 1620. According to John Aubrey, who counted him as 'my honoured and worthy friend', Graunt 'was bred-up (as the fashion then was) in the Puritan way'. He went into the family haberdashery business, where he showed that he had 'an excellent working head'. The business thrived to such an extent that by the age of twenty-one he was running his own shop, specializing in buttons and lace collars. At the same time he was also appointed a freeman of the Drapers' Company, the guild to which the haberdashers belonged.

As if this were not enough, Graunt also 'rose early each morning to study before Shop-time'. The field which he chose to study was not only original but quite outside the scope of his work. In this, Graunt's life bears a curious resemblance to that of his contemporary, Dutch pioneer Antonie van Leeuwenhoek. But where Van Leeuwenhoek pioneered microscopy, Graunt pioneered statistics. Before starting work each morning he began copying down details from the City of London bills of mortality (i.e. death registers). It has been suggested that his original motive for doing this was professional – that he was researching the extent, age and composition of his living clientele – though this seems unlikely. Either way, Graunt's interests soon extended far beyond such limits.

The collection of bills of mortality was a comparatively recent phenomenon. As the population of England became increasingly urbanized, it was found necessary to collect details of these citizens for the purposes of tax and military service. The first regular bills of mortality for the City of London were collected in 1603, the year of Queen Elizabeth I's death, when there was an outbreak of plague. Weekly lists were made of the number of people who had died, with the figures categorized according to various causes of death. Paradoxically, listing these causes of death serves to bring the city vividly to life. Take, for instance, a typical week's list:

Aged: 13
Drown'd: 8 (…four at St Katherine's Tower)
Evil: 3
Feaver: 60
French Pox: 6
Griping in the guts: 134
Impostume [abcess]: 6
Stopping in the stomach: 9
Teeth: 38
Wind: 3
Worms: 2

Other weeks include such causes as 'Murthered and shot', 'Found dead in streets', 'kild by several accidents', 'Stone & strangury'.

Graunt would publish his *Natural and Political Observations on the London Bills of Mortality* in 1662, when he was forty-two. It contained his analysis of the Bills of Mortality using 'shop arithmetic', which is far more inventive than it sounds. The bills of mortality also included the numbers of all children christened. Graunt took these christening figures, along with the mortality figures, to calculate the rate of mortality of infants before the age of six. First he chose the categories of death that he knew only included babies or very young children – such as 'Stilborn',

'Overlaid and starved at Nurse', 'Infants' – and added these together. Then he used his own observations and intuition, and calculated accordingly. For instance, he reckoned that half the deaths from smallpox and measles occurred in children under the age of six; similarly, for one third of any plague deaths. From this he 'inferred' that 36 per cent of the overall deaths in London were of children under six. And making use of the number of baptisms he was then able to calculate the rate of infant mortality. Armed with such figures he went on to calculate 'that of 100 persons born, 36 die before age 6 and 7 survive to 70'.

Graunt may have used only shop arithmetic, but not for nothing does he emerge as the first statistician. He was also able to estimate the size of an army which could be raised in London 'based on the assumption that there are 107 males for each 100 females' (Graunt was the first to note this discrepancy).

More tellingly, Graunt was also well aware of the inaccuracies present in the figures he was dealing with. Few other than Descartes have begun with such healthy scepticism regarding their basic data. For example, Graunt observed that the figures for 'French pox' (syphilis) were invariably too low. This was because families wished to be spared the disgrace, so that 'onely hated persons, and such, whose very Noses were eaten off, were reported'. On the other hand, those who were recorded as dying of the more respectable 'old age' were inevitably exaggerated.

On publication, Graunt's *Observations* attracted the attention it deserved. Within a month it had been read by Charles II himself, who recommended that Graunt should be made a Fellow of the Royal Society. There was a little quibbling about letting a mere shopkeeper enter such exalted ranks, but the king would hear nothing of such objections: 'If they find any more such Tradesmen, they should be sure to admit them all, without any more ado'.

Alas, Graunt's fall from grace was equally swift. When the Great Fire of London broke out in 1666, he was accused of having 'some hand' in this. At the time he was an officer of a water company, but there is no certain evidence of any negligence on his behalf, nor of his encouraging the fire, despite the widespread incompetence of the firefighters.

The fact is, Graunt had converted to Catholicism – at the very moment when public opinion was turning against 'Papists'. Furthermore, Graunt's haberdashery premises were burned to the ground in the fire, leaving him facing bankruptcy. He would die in 1674, aged fifty-three, 'descended into poverty'. Not even his work would be spared – his 'friend', the unscrupulous William Petty, would put it about that he had sponsored Graunt's work, providing the original ideas which lifted his activities from mere fact-collecting to original statistical analysis.

Graunt's work inspired another member of the Royal Society, namely the polymath Sir Edmund Halley, who besides being Astronomer Royal was also an accomplished mathematician, geographer, meteorologist and physicist. Halley obtained the bills of mortality for the German town of Breslau (now Wrocław in Poland) between 1687 and 1691.* Unlike the London bills used by Graunt, these included the ages of those who had died. Following in Graunt's footsteps, Halley began analysing these figures, and in doing so laid the foundations of actuarial science – which deals with such entities as annuities, life insurance and pensions. An indication of the state of the field prior to Halley's input can be seen from the fact that one could purchase a life annuity from the government for a fixed sum, regardless of how old one was. This meant that, for the same price, a twenty-year-old and a seventy-year-old could purchase an annuity that guaranteed them an annual payment for life.

The mathematical side of political economy was now beginning to emerge. But the subject still remained without any insight into the mechanics of economic behaviour. This would be supplied by an original character whose notoriety would come to match that of William Petty, no less.

Bernard Mandeville was born in 1670 in Rotterdam, where his father was a prosperous physician of Huguenot origins. Young Bernard followed his father into the medical profession, obtaining a degree at the University

---

* According to the modern Canadian philosopher Ian Hacking, a noted historian of probability, these were supplied by the German philosopher Leibniz, who was also a member of the Royal Society.

of Leiden when he was twenty. The details of Mandeville's consequent life are sketchy at best. However, it appears he moved to England sometime after 1690, having become involved in the tax riots which took place in Rotterdam during that year. Mandeville's stated reason for going to England was to learn the language, but he was almost certainly a fugitive from justice. After starting out as a physician in his adopted country, he seems to have branched out and become a public relations officer for a gin distillery.*

Despite this switch of profession, Mandeville would achieve such success in London that he soon counted amongst his friends the likes of Lord Macclesfield, the Chief Justice, and the writer Joseph Addison, who founded the *Spectator* magazine.

Mandeville is variously described as a physician, philosopher, poet, political economist and satirist. He certainly earned his living as a physician at some stage, but the notorious book which he published in 1705 indubitably indicates his talents in the other four fields. This work is generally known by its more informative later title: *The Fable of the Bees: or, Private Vices, Publick Benefits* – with later more elaborate (and more notorious) editions appearing over the ensuing decade or so. In this work, Mandeville compares society to a hive of bees, whose individual behaviour all contributes to the collective good. However, the society collapses when the bees abandon their self-interested pursuit of honey, and instead begin behaving virtuously in an abstemious fashion. Mandeville argues that in any functioning society, it is vice and greed which lead to collective economic prosperity. When a population adopts Christian values of self-restraint this leads to economic ruin. As Mandeville put it: 'What we call Evil in this World, Moral as well as Natural, is the grand Principle that makes us social Creatures, the solid Basis, the Life and Support of all Trades and Employments without Exception... we must look for the true Origin of all Arts and Sciences.'

---

* Gin had recently been invented in Holland, and enthusiasm for this cheap spirit quickly spread to England. There it would be served in the notorious gin palaces, where clients could get 'drunk for a penny, dead drunk for tuppence'. This would later inspire the squalor of Hogarth's *Gin Lane*.

Despite this apparent advocacy of public licence, Mandeville's nihilistic view is not the whole story – it has to be placed in the context of his age. His view of virtue was decidedly narrow – very much a legacy of Puritanism. Likewise his view of personal vice. Not all the colourful or forbidding characters who ended up swinging from a rope at Tyburn were social benefactors in disguise.

Mandeville's view of the mechanics of the market was profound, despite its lack of systematic reasoning. In his view there was no need for interference in these mechanics, either by government legislation or individual altruism. The market was best left to its own devices. He also understood the division of labour (a term which he coined), as well as how labour evolves according to market forces:

> As things are managed with us, it would be preposterous to have as many Brewers as there are Bakers, or as many Woolen-drapers as there are Shoe-makers. The Proportions as to Numbers in every Trade finds itself, and is never better than when nobody meddles or interferes with it.

This is the first reasoned advocacy of what came to be known as economic laissez-faire. Mandeville also well understood the brutality of such a free market: 'To make Society Happy… it is requisite that great numbers should be Ignorant as well as Poor.'

Mandeville's uncomfortable insights, together with Graunt's statistics and the embryo of probability theory, would in time provide the ingredients for modern-day economics. It was in the Age of Reason that these ideas and a picture of economic society began to coalesce. Past facts, combined with social insights and probability, would give birth to the predictive economics without which no contemporary, fully functional government would be able to fulfil its remit.

Such thinking sought to establish political economy on a generalized scientific basis. However, there is no denying that this line of thought also included a very particular competitive element, which was as cut-throat as any who competed in the marketplace it described. Thus theoretical reason coexisted with a vital element of unreason. Financial operators were increasingly prepared to gamble their all on a project, in the hope of making a market killing… If this failed, one could always resort to flight to another jurisdiction – as exemplified by the antics of the notorious Johann Becher. Not for nothing did the phrase 'Here today, gone tomorrow' take on its modern meaning during this era.*

A prime example of cut-throat market competition can be seen in the title of a work produced by the English mercantilist Andrew Yarranton, the full version of which was published in 1681: *England's Improvement by Sea and Land to Out-do the Dutch without Fighting, to Pay Debts without Moneys, to Set to Work all the Poor of England.* Yarranton's answer to these problems was credit, which he saw as a universal panacea. This was but a small advance on the ideas first produced by the eccentric early mercantilist Johann Becher.

In many ways, mercantilism simply reflected the practice of successful merchants (hence its name). It stressed the importance of foreign trade, yet with the proviso that exports should always be greater than imports, thus ensuring a positive balance of trade. Wherever possible, imports should be obtained from distant countries, so as not to enrich neighbouring countries – and thus rival merchants. Exports helped maintain local employment, whereas imports led to unemployment.

Another great mercantilist virtue was saving, as this encouraged the growth of capital. Indeed, a nation's wealth was to be judged by the amount of gold and silver it had accrued in its vaults. Urbanism had brought about an increase in the money economy – as opposed to the barter economy, which often prevailed in rural areas. Money became wealth. Money and gold were equated – and were in fact still largely the same thing. A gold or silver coin worth one pound or one guilder was expected to contain gold or silver worth one pound or one guilder. Though over the years this equivalence would become increasingly eroded. Through

---

* The actual origin of this phrase is in a 1549 work by the extreme Protestant preacher John Calvin, who used it to illustrate the brevity of human existence. Calvin would doubtless have been horrified at its evolution to a racier application in the world of finance.

the activities of governments, or criminals, the precious-metal content of coinage could be debased. Likewise, the practice of 'clipping' coins was becoming widespread – the edges of coins were clipped off, so that these clippings could be melted down to produce further coins. Here was a prime example contradicting the time-honoured adage '*Ex nihilo nihil fit*' (Nothing out of nothing comes).

And the world of finance was now beginning to indulge an even more powerful method of achieving a conjuring trick of unreason. As we saw in the Tulipmania episode of 1637, more and more people were becoming involved in speculative markets.* During Tulipmania, speculators without sufficient capital had frequently been encouraged to lay down a deposit (a fraction of the purchase price) to secure the future purchase of an expensive tulip. But this was just the beginning of the credit market boom. And those involved in this market began to understand that credit was capable of doubling or trebling – or more – the purchasing power at one's disposal. By borrowing on spec, one could make (or lose) a multiple of the assets one actually possessed. And the collateral for one's next borrowing could be the capital obtained from the previous borrowing; such 'leverage' was theoretically limitless.

All this was very much counter to mercantilist thought. But it is necessary to bear in mind that as economic self-understanding in general and mercantilist thinking in particular progressed, it did so against an undercurrent of increasing business on credit. Reason and unreason: one step forwards, one step backwards – the true value of money remained the same, yet at the same time its purchasing power could be expanded exponentially.

It was in France that mercantilist thought came into its own. And its first noted practitioner was neither a theorist nor a merchant. As

---

* This had by now become particularly evident with the purchase of shares in the English East India Company and the Dutch VOC. Similarly widespread investments were made in the triangular slave trade and government bonds. This was the beginning of the middle class, or bourgeoisie, whose growth of influence was reflected in fields as disparate as the art market and parliamentarian politics, as well as the spread of heady aspirational ideas such as 'liberty' and 'egalitarianism'. Liberal democracy as we know it is a legacy of this growing class.

already mentioned, Jean-Baptiste Colbert was chief adviser to Louis
XIV. He would hold this post for more than twenty years, in the process
becoming the most powerful man in France apart from the Sun King
himself. During this period Colbert would evolve an economic and political doctrine known as Colbertism, which is now generally recognized as
a form of mercantilism. Colbert's rise to such an exalted post had been no
easy matter, and his exercise of power would likewise be no simple affair.
Indeed, such was his driving ambition that it is no exaggeration to say
that he worked himself to death.

Jean-Baptiste Colbert came from Reims in north-eastern
France, where his father and his grandfather had been merchants and
financiers. According to family legend they were of Scottish descent.
Little is known of Colbert's early years, but after leaving school
he worked for a banker in Paris. By the age of twenty he was a civil
servant in the War Office, eventually rising to become secretary to the
minister. During these years he married, and would in time have three
children. At the age of twenty-seven he and his wife were left 40,000
crowns – probably an inheritance from a relative. As was the custom of
the day, Colbert used this money to purchase a post as a councillor of
state (equivalent to a junior minister), which allowed him to hone his
managerial talents. Such were these talents that Colbert attracted the
attention of the chief minister Cardinal Mazarin, who had accumulated
such a vast fortune during his period in office that he needed someone
with financial expertise to manage it.

Colbert soon began advising Mazarin on ministerial matters, and even
took over his role when he was out of the country on diplomatic missions.
In this way, Colbert met and became a trusted friend of Louis XIV,
who was now in his early twenties. During this period, Colbert wrote a
mémoire to Mazarin on tax reform, revealing that of all the taxes gathered
in France only around half of these ever reached the royal coffers. The rest
was being embezzled, and one of the chief culprits was none other than
Nicolas Fouquet, Louis XIV's trusted minister of finance.

When Mazarin died in 1661, the forty-one-year-old Colbert stood in
line to succeed him. His chief rival for the post was Fouquet. Armed with

incontrovertible evidence of Fouquet's embezzlement, Colbert managed
to engineer his downfall. Fouquet was duly tried and sentenced to exile,
but Louis XIV countermanded this sentence and ensured that he was sent
to a French prison for life (where the authorities could keep an eye on
him and his activities). Whereupon Colbert was appointed chief minister.
He then further ingratiated himself with Louis XIV by revealing to him
the extent, and location, of Mazarin's secret wealth.

One by one Colbert gradually inveigled his way into taking control
of the various high offices of state: Superintendent of Buildings in 1664,
Controller-General of Finances in 1665, Secretary of State of the Navy
in 1669... with the ministries in charge of commerce, the colonies, and
supervising the building of Versailles soon to follow. Only the war department somehow eluded his grasp.

There is no hard and fast rule that those who bring benefit to their
nation – either intellectual and/or financial – should be characters of
outstanding moral stature. Indeed, anyone who qualified in this aspect
was unlikely to have risen to the top of the greasy pole of French politics
during such an age of intrigue and corruption. To get anything done,
one first had to ensure that one was in a position to do so. And Colbert
certainly managed this.

Colbert saw that England's emergence as an international commercial power posed a direct threat to France. The means by which England
had achieved this was by pursuing a policy of free trade and exploitation of its colonies, all under the protection of its powerful navy. Colbert
quickly realized that free trade only succeeded when a nation had developed a successful industrial base at home – which France had not, largely
owing to its rural economy and inefficient tax system. In order to combat
English, and to a lesser extent Dutch, free trade, Colbert developed a rival
plan. France would introduce tariffs protecting its own industries, which
could then be built up by domestic trade.*

---

* Despite the western world's present article of faith in free trade, it has become
clear that this is far from being a universal panacea. Some of the greatest economic
'leaps forward' in modern history have been accompanied by protective tariffs, along
with state investment in infrastructure and locally protected industries. To give but

At the same time, Colbert launched a three-pronged attack on the commercial malaise that was hampering the nation's economy, while still reassuring Louis XIV that France remained the major political power in Europe. (Note Colbert's mercantilist distinction between waning economic power, and actual political power in terms of bullion savings and land.) First the tax regime needed to undergo a sweeping reform. Upper class 'exemptions' were brought in line, and consumer taxes on luxury items were introduced to ensure that privileged expenditure by those who had evaded tax nonetheless contributed to the national exchequer. And in an effort to revive the national economy, Colbert financed a number of state-run industrial monopolies.

Typical of these was his encouragement of the silk industry. France already had a silk industry centred on Tours, but it was Colbert's championing of Becher's old panacea which at a stroke revived the silk-manufacturing fortunes of Lyon, the major city of southern-central France – encouraging subsidiary industries such as spinning and dyeing. France had now also become more integrated – largely owing to the policies pursued by Cardinal Richelieu and his successor Mazarin. Colbert was able to build on this by encouraging interprovincial trade. Emblematic of this was his commissioning of what is now known as the Canal du Midi – which links the Atlantic Ocean to the Mediterranean, eliminating a stormy journey around the Iberian peninsula of almost 1,500 miles.

---

three examples: First, Hamilton's protection of the newly independent United States, shielding its nascent industries from external competition and allowing it to develop the foundations of what would later become the world's leading economy. Second, Bismarck's strictly regulated protection of Prussia-led Germany, which set it on course to becoming the leading European commercial powerhouse. And most recently, China's authoritarian and protectionist policy, which in the past decades has seen it achieve the greatest 'leap forward' in all human history, lifting many hundreds of millions out of abject poverty. The west's assumption that a free market and autocratic rule are incompatible and economically unsuccessful has been shown to be no more than a modern folk belief – the paper tiger of freedom and democratic liberalism. Sadly, these may have proved sufficient for the centuries of modern progress which grew out of the Age of Reason, but it has now been revealed that they are not a necessary condition for progress.

Further encouragement to national industries came from the banning of the import of Venetian glass, and the founding of French glass-making manufactories, enabling local craftsmen to supply the mirrors for the Hall of Mirrors at Versailles. Amazingly, Colbert was able to build an efficient and improving economy, complete with a burgeoning local commercial sector, all while his reforms were under constant threat from Louis XIV's insatiable appetite for costly foreign wars.

As if this was not enough, Colbert also went out of his way to encourage French artistic and intellectual life – establishing the Académie des Sciences in 1666, as well as entrusting Huygens with the task of building a planetarium. In pursuit of his artistic policy, Colbert also invited to France the renowned Italian artist Gian Lorenzo Bernini, who would design the eastern façade of the Louvre as well as create a superb sculpture of Louis XIV. However, Colbert and Bernini proved temperamentally incompatible, and Colbert's diplomatic efforts to smooth over the difficulties soon matched his stressful attempts to rein in Louis XIV's expensive wars. (It is no accident that Colbert's one major failing was his inability to gain control of the Ministry of War.)

Colbert continued his obsessive work and micromanagement of all the many projects he instigated. Aware of how he himself had manipulated his way to power, he trusted no one. Such overwork, driven by paranoia, soon began to take its toll. He would rise at first light, and seldom made it to bed before midnight. This regimen induced ulcers, and he was soon only able to ingest bread dipped in chicken broth. Constantly in pain, he still refused to delegate or cut down in any way on his punishing schedule.

Colbert's encouragement of trade with the French overseas colonies, which now stretched from the Indian Ocean to the Caribbean, inevitably involved him in the slave trade. Here, characteristically, he drew up a table of specifications, the so-called *Code Noir* (Legislation for Black Slaves). This defined the conditions of slavery throughout the French colonial empire. Amongst its many and detailed strictures, it decreed that all slaves must be converted to Catholicism, as well as listing the specific punishments to be meted out for misdemeanours. Captured runaway slaves were to be branded and have their ears cut off. Other articles of the code determined the fate of children born of enslaved people. Those born of married slaves were automatically slaves. However, those born of a slave mother and a free father were not slaves. Likewise, freed slaves inherited the same civil rights as any French colonial citizen. In summary, the *Code Noir* was a document which epitomized the Age of Reason's unreasonable underside. It comes as little surprise that it has been labelled 'the most monstrous judicial text produced in modern times' and would stigmatize Colbert's name for centuries to come.

An often-overlooked aspect of the *Code Noir* was that it also referred to Jews, who were ordered to be expelled from all French overseas territories. (Jewish traders from Dutch and Portuguese colonies had begun settling in the ports of several French colonies.) This expulsion prompted a negative attitude towards Jews in France, especially those in the recently acquired territories of Alsace and Lorraine, who were driven across the Rhine into German territories.

The ensuing emergence of the likes of the Rothschild family in Germany, and the pan-European connections established by such banking organizations, would expose the fatal flaws in the mercantilist project and its belief in the accumulation of gold in national vaults. For better or worse, the future of commercial enterprise now lay not in national savings but in the skilful manipulation of credit on national and international markets. A nation would no longer be measured so much by its accumulated wealth, as by the power which investment and leverage of such wealth was able to generate.

A brief, simplified illustration of this financial Indian rope trick can be seen in the fact that the two most sophisticated economies in Europe – the Dutch and the English – both now operated with a national debt. As early as 1632, the Dutch national debt had reached 50 million guilders, and would continue to grow through the ensuing decades – soon matching the English national debt, which by 1671 stood at £1.3 million. This meant that in mercantilist terms the English and the Dutch had minus quantities of savings stowed away in their national vaults, and rather than *receiving* interest on their savings they were in fact *paying* interest on their debts. However, both nations managed to continue existing in this anti-mercantilist fashion through the issue of government bonds, which sought to reduce these debts. Such bonds involved the purchase by many investors of small portions of the government debt for a limited period of years. During these years the government paid an annual interest on the loan, before repaying it at the end of the agreed period. This at least had the effect of containing the national debt, if not always reducing it. And it provided the government with a useful extra form of income to cover the imbalance in its national budget.

By contrast, when autocratic nations such as France and Spain found themselves in financial difficulty, their monarchs often simply resorted to bankruptcy. (In the seventeenth century alone Spain defaulted on its payments to creditors in 1607, 1627, 1647, 1652 and 1662; while France went bust three times in less than a century.) Thus, ironically, it was the mercantilist nations who believed in the power of accumulated wealth which suffered. Meanwhile, the English and the Dutch, who resorted to financial legerdemain, survived to lead markets forward into the new era – of ever more sophisticated (and risky) manipulation.*

---

* Tulipmania had just been a rehearsal for what was to come: in 1720 the London financial market would blow up with the South Sea Bubble, while in the same year a scheme to convert the French currency to paper money would wipe out the Paris Stock Exchange.

CHAPTER 17

LOGIC PERSONIFIED

T HE THIRD KEY PHILOSOPHER of the Age of Reason, Gottfried
Leibniz, draws together many of the themes which emerged
during this period, as well as pointing the way forward beyond his
time. He would benefit from meeting, or having dealings with, several
of the leading figures of the period, including no less than Huygens,
Oldenburg, Boyle, Spinoza, Pascal and Newton. Yet out of these
encounters, he seldom emerges with credit. Nonetheless, he remains a
polymath the likes of which has rarely appeared in history. As a philosopher he produced no less than two philosophies (one optimistically
logical, the other austerely logical). As a mathematician he invented
calculus (independent of Newton), as well as championing binary
arithmetic and extending the fields of infinite series and combinato-
rial analysis. In the pursuit of statesmanship, he attempted to unite
the Protestant and Catholic churches (no less), as well as drawing up
a detailed plan for the French invasion of Egypt. He also invented a
superior calculating machine. As a diplomat he travelled far and wide
in Europe and appears to have exasperated the majority of those whom
he encountered. He also founded (and became the first president of)

the Berlin Academy of Sciences, founded a similar academy in Russia, dabbled in espionage and alchemy… and so the list goes on. Here was an ornament of the Age of Reason, if ever there was one. By contrast, his flaws were personal rather than emblematic of the age or his talents. His misfortunes were likewise.

Gottfried Leibniz was the son of a Lutheran professor of moral philosophy. His father died in 1652 when he was just six, and the precocious Gottfried appears to have been largely self-educated from the books in his father's extensive library. Here, much like any other imaginative child, he began dreaming up all manner of fantastical ideas. The difference being that Leibniz sketched out and set down blueprints for his flights of fancy. Thus he produced embryonic plans for futuristic projects ranging from a submarine to a form of motorized stagecoach, from a horizontal windmill to a machine for measuring good and evil. (These were no mere passing fads: Leibniz would often return to these inventions in later life.)

At the age of fourteen, Leibniz entered the University of Leipzig to study law. His study soon broadened to include all possible interpretations of this concept. Thus, he studied the laws of physics, the laws of philosophy, the laws of mathematics, as well as the entire political concept and history of law. In so doing, he came across the writings of Galileo, Descartes and Hobbes, whose work was by this time revolutionizing scientific, political and philosophical thought. Characteristically, Leibniz soon conceived of an idea for harmonizing all this radical thought with the Aristotelian Scholasticism it was in the process of replacing. In his spare time, he even became an avid student of alchemy (with the aim of reconciling it to chemistry) and set out a theoretical basis for a computer (some three centuries before Alan Turing's seminal work on this subject).

There is one discernible theme which runs through these myriad topics – namely, the attempt to bring disparate, or even opposing, aspects into a state of harmony. And this would remain one of the guiding principles of Leibniz's supremely broad intellectual life. The reconciling of the irreconcilable would prove his most quixotic ambition.

Five years after entering the University of Leipzig, Leibniz applied for a doctorate, an appointment for which his exceptional work had shown he was more than qualified. He was confident that he would be accepted for an academic post, following in his father's footsteps. To his astonishment, he was rejected. The American philosopher Matthew Stewart suggests that the reasons for this lay in Leibniz's curiously contradictory character:

> On the one hand, Leibniz evidently possessed an easy and winning charm, as is abundantly confirmed in his fluid rise to power and the fact that he eventually sustained fruitful relations with literally hundreds of individuals across the continent... On the other hand, he had a peculiar talent for making enemies – a talent of which he seems to have remained largely oblivious.

Having been rebuffed by the University of Leipzig, Leibniz set off 200 miles south to the University of Altdorf near Nuremberg, where he made sure that his reputation had preceded him. Here he was immediately awarded a doctorate and a post as professor on the teaching staff. The latter he turned down, explaining that he had 'very different things in view'.

And indeed he did. Leibniz now inveigled his way into the Nuremberg Society of Alchemists. This proved no mean feat, as he had invariably found himself 'baffled by their bizarre symbols and opaque texts'. So much so that in order to gain entry into the society, 'he composed a parody of their efforts, making incomprehensible claims by means of unintelligible symbols'. The president of the society was so impressed by this opaque text that he immediately offered Leibniz the post of secretary, which he accepted. Only later would it become clear why Leibniz embarked upon this abstruse charade. One of the leading members of the society was Baron Johann Christian von Boineberg, first minister of the reigning Elector of Mainz. In no time, Leibniz entered the service of the elector.

During this period, Mainz (along with other states in western Germany) was constantly under threat from Louis XIV and his expansionist wars. Leibniz proposed an ingenious scheme to divert such a threat. This would involve him travelling to Paris to present to Louis XIV a diversionary plan for France to invade Egypt.* The Elector of Mainz duly despatched Leibniz to Paris in 1672.

In Leibniz's view, Paris was 'the most knowledgeable and powerful city in the universe'. Here, as a foreign emissary, he would have the opportunity to meet the finest minds in Europe. However, the unknown and intellectually bumptious young emissary of a small German state quickly discovered that entering French high society was not quite so simple as gaining access to an alchemists' society in Nuremberg. Even such figures as might have been impressed by the youthful German prodigy were no longer available. Descartes, Mersenne and Pascal were all dead; while Hobbes had long since returned to England. And when Leibniz finally managed to gain an audience with Colbert, the first minister appeared little interested in Leibniz's ingenious and detailed tactical instructions on how to invade Egypt – making it plain that they were unlikely to reach, let alone be of interest to, His Majesty Louis XIV.

However, Leibniz's luck changed when he finally managed to meet Christiaan Huygens, who was so impressed by the fecund originality of his new young friend's mind that he arranged introductions to several of the leading lights of Colbert's new Académie des Sciences. The most notable of these was Nicolas Malebranche, widely regarded as Descartes's most talented successor.

In order to persuade Huygens to remain in Paris, Colbert had generously arranged for him to take up residence in a spacious apartment

---

* This is far from being as outlandish as it might sound. Just over a century later, Napoleon would lead a French invasion of Egypt (though he remained unaware that Leibniz had drawn up plans for an identical project). In his dream of supreme strategy and megalomania, Napoleon saw Egypt as the logical centre from which to rule the world, being the juncture of Africa and Asia, with Europe nearby. (America was considered too insignificant to matter in this scheme.)

overlooking the gardens of the Royal Library. By this time, Huygens was ailing and reduced to his bed – but he was only too pleased to receive regular visits from Leibniz, fascinated by the young man's seemingly inexhaustible font of inventive ideas. Yet when they began discussing mathematics, it soon became clear that Leibniz was severely hampered by the backward state of German mathematics. Huygens immediately suggested a course of study which would enable him to overcome his mathematical shortcomings. It also seems likely that the forty-three-year-old Dutchman tutored the twenty-six-year-old German, guiding his researches in new directions. Despite this, there is no doubting the astonishing originality of Leibniz's work in this period – during which he, on his own, made a number of sensational advances in mathematical technique. Most notable amongst these was differential and integral calculus. Calculus was undoubtedly a major scientific advance of the Age of Reason – arguably its greatest theoretical discovery (or invention).*

Prior to the introduction of calculus, mathematics could loosely be characterized as the calculation of rigid and precise, or even approximate, quantities, including the calculation of velocity (the speed of a body in a particular direction). Calculus revolutionized mathematics by introducing into this field a fundamental refinement of the concept of motion, in the form of rates of change. Descartes introduced the notion of Cartesian coordinates, showing how the solutions to an algebraic formula could be mapped as a line on a graph – Leibniz took this idea, and dramatically transformed it with differential and integral calculus. Put simply, differential calculus shows how the rate of change can be

---

* Philosophers and mathematicians continue to dispute whether mathematics is an invention of the human mind, or is pre-existent in some Platonic idealistic realm and thus simply discovered. Highly convincing arguments can be made for both these approaches. Galileo's suggestion that the world is written in the language of mathematics would seem to suggest that mathematics is already out there, waiting for us to discover it. Ingenious mathematical 'inventions' such as calculus – which creates, and even appears to conceptualize, motion in human mental terms – would seem to suggest otherwise.

calculated at a particular point on a curve. This is done by calculating the gradient of the tangent to the line at that particular point.

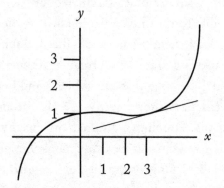

The two-dimensional plane measured by the x-axis and the y-axis. The curving line is the graph plotting the solutions to an algebraic equation. The oblique line is the tangent to the line when x = 3 and y = 1. The gradient of the line shows the rate of change at this precise point.

Thus, for instance, where a curve represents the changing speed of an object (such as a car), the actual speed of that object at any particular point can be calculated (i.e. the exact reading of the car's speedometer).

Leibniz also developed the notion of integral calculus, the inverse of differential calculus. By means of integration, the area under a graph can be calculated between two precise points.

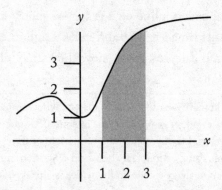

Integration enables the calculation of the (shaded) area beneath the curve between x = 1 and x = 3.

This can be used for a wide variety of purposes. By means of integration it is possible to calculate the precise amount of liquid which flows through a tube between two points in time, when the water flows in varying amounts. It can also calculate the precise area of an irregularly bounded plot of land.

An indication of the difficulties involved in calculus can be seen in the process of differentiation, which involves the identification of a point on a curve. (Integration requires identifying the exact locations of two points on a curve which is in continuous motion, but each of these must be treated as having a stationary position.) The identification of the exact point on a continuous curve is done by the use of ever-decreasing minute values known as infinitesimals, which move closer and closer to zero but never actually reach this limit (the point itself). The infinitesimals can thus be said to reach the infinity-th term in their sequence. This is infinitely small, but can be treated as zero – a conjuring trick that enables the precise calculation of a continuously changing value. (This may be seen as the very essence of attempting to impose rationality upon the irrational.) Leibniz continued developing his ideas on calculus during the years 1672–3 – but, crucially, he neglected to publish them until 1684.

In between fruitlessly pestering Colbert about his plans to invade Egypt and inventing calculus and a host of other original mathematical ideas, Leibniz also found time to draw up a detailed blueprint for a remarkable new calculating machine. Unlike Pascal's Pascaline, Leibniz's machine would be able to multiply and divide as well as add and subtract. Huygens passed on this news to his friend Oldenburg at the Royal Society, and in 1673 it was arranged that Leibniz should visit London. Here he gave a bravura description of his machine to the assembled worthies of the Royal Society, but was forced to concede that the prototype he had built was not yet fully functional. (As was evident when he attempted a demonstration.) Despite this, Oldenburg ensured that Leibniz was elected a Fellow of the Royal Society, extracting a promise that in return he would send them a working version of his calculator within a year. As a gesture of goodwill, Oldenburg even allowed Leibniz to peruse some of Newton's unpublished papers.

Leibniz now obtained a post as privy counsellor to Duke John Frederick of Brunswick at his court in Hanover. However, on his way Leibniz took the opportunity to visit van Leeuwenhoek and Spinoza. The latter had just finished his masterwork, *Ethics*, and Leibniz held intense discussions of its contents with Spinoza over several days. (Owing to Spinoza's widespread notoriety as an atheist, Leibniz would later go to great lengths to deny that this meeting had taken place. He would especially deny all knowledge of *Ethics*, many of whose ideas bear a suspicious resemblance to some of those he incorporated into his own philosophy.)

Despite Leibniz's evident disappointment with living in provincial Hanover, which had a population of just 10,000 citizens, he was soon doing his energetic best to please his new employer. He rearranged the ducal library – at the same time ordering a number of recently published volumes he himself wished to consult. And after touring the dukedom he drew up plans for an extensive canal network for the benefit of the local industries. When he travelled to the Harz mountains, he revolutionized the duke's mining operations by constructing horizontal windmills intended to drive the machinery and drain floodwater from the deep shafts.

Leibniz's employer soon tired of this cornucopia of expensive projects and insisted that he devote himself to the principal task for which he was employed: namely, to write a history of the Hanover family, tracing its ancestors back to Charlemagne. This was more than a mere vanity project, as the Hanoverians wished to advance their dynastic ambitions – chief of which was their claim to succeed to the throne of Britain.

Leibniz avidly seized his opportunity, and began making a series of extensive travels around Europe, ostensibly visiting archives which might provide documentary evidence of the Hanoverian dynasty. Over the next few years, he travelled through Germany, Italy and Austria. It was during this period that he embarked upon diplomatic efforts to unite the Catholic and Protestant faiths, and also gathered intelligence that would nowadays be regarded as espionage. He made many inspired practical suggestions to all those who graciously accommodated him. But most importantly of all, he found time to conduct regular correspondence with a number of intellectual princesses and aristocratic ladies (mostly related to his employer). It is in these letters that he began setting down his philosophical ideas, which would eventually cohere into the system outlined in his main published work, *Monadology*.

Leibniz's philosophical system is both rational and metaphysical, giving it a deceptive simplicity and considerable beauty. He held that the world consists of an infinite number of entities, called monads, which are the ultimate constituents of all things. If something occupies space, it must have extension, which means that it occupies a certain volume, no matter how small, and is thus divisible and complex. But these ultimate simple monads themselves cannot have extension and cannot be material. Thus the world consists of an infinite number of metaphysical points.

Not a few theoretical physicists have remarked on the similarity between Leibniz's monads and the modern notion of string theory, where the universe consists of infinitely minute strings that vibrate through multiple dimensions (though we are only aware of the four dimensions which constitute the space-time continuum). Like Leibniz's monads, these invisible strings are all but devoid of mass or extension, yet they alone give rise to all the particles, entities and energy out of which emerges the world we perceive. Critics of string theory question how this miraculous process takes place – a process which remains beyond the reach of experimental evidence. Leibniz, on the other hand, was able to provide a remarkable, and subtle, explanation of how his monads – an infinite number of metaphysical points – come to make up the world we perceive. Because these points (monads) can have no physical interaction, they are not subject to the laws of cause and effect. There is no causality between them, despite what appears to us to happen in the material world. The apparent interaction of the monads that make up the world is the result of a 'pre-established harmony' that exists between them, and has existed since they were first created by God.*

---

* Others have detected a resemblance here to Leibniz's description of the workings of his infinitesimal calculus. This also deals with an infinity of minute quantities that both do (and do not) exist. Yet despite this apparent irrationality, there is no denying that his infinitesimal calculus produces rational results.

From the moment each monad is created, the changes in state it undergoes are caused only by its own preceding state. They are each subject to their own chain of causality, which remains in alignment with the other monads because of the pre-established harmony that operates according to the *horologium dei* (God's clock).

This explanation prompts us to take a detour. Despite Leibniz's metaphysical ingenuity in suggesting that the world works according to an independent yet coordinated harmony, it presents us with a particularly practical novelty. This theory is one of the first comprehensive modern philosophical attempts to explain the world in terms of a complex apparatus. The Age of Reason would see a number of increasingly revolutionary technological advances – beginning with the telescope and the microscope, which introduced humanity to the wonders of the universe and the microverse. It is no coincidence that the latest technological innovation during Leibniz's lifetime was the intricate mechanical harmony of Huygens's pendulum clock – which aligned human measurement (the hours of our day) with the continuous passing of time in the real world. Leibniz's ultra-rationalistic horological harmony simply synchronizes with the age in which it was conceived. The ingenuity of its pre-established harmony is no more than the vision of a realistically possible (rather than ideal) machine that continues to function despite its necessary imperfections.*

In keeping with Leibniz's superior mathematical abilities, he was also the finest logician of his time. It thus comes as no surprise that the optimistic public philosophy he developed in his letters to his aristocratic lady friends, and that he finally set down in his *Monadology*, should have a strong logical underpinning. It is based on two fundamental principles: contradiction and sufficient reason. God may have created the world, but

---

* It is interesting to trace how in each successive age, the explanation of the universe – how it is composed and how it works – seems to echo the most advanced creation during that age. Thus in Leibniz's time the world was explained as working like a clock. Later, during the Industrial Revolution, our explanation of the world was that it was, and functioned precisely like, a huge mechanical system or complex machine. Similarly, the most modern explanations of the universe liken it to a giant computer (or sometimes a holograph).

even his infinite powers are subject to logic. The world God created had of necessity to be a possible world. And to be possible it had to conform to the principle forbidding contradiction. A self-contradictory world is not logically possible.

Likewise, for the world to be created in the first place, there had to be a sufficient reason for it to be created. This reason was of course God. Because God is good, he naturally created the best world of which he was capable. But according to the principle of contradiction, this had to be a possible world. This means that God created 'the best of all possible worlds'. A perfect world is evidently impossible, and whatever defects the world possesses are inevitable owing to the possibility of its existence.

Leibniz's strongest critics – Bertrand Russell and Voltaire – ridiculed his concept of the best of all possible worlds. How could such evils as famine, natural disasters, war and disease exist in such a world? But while Leibniz's optimistic public philosophy can be said to put a gloss on such tragedies and afflictions, the private philosophy he developed in his notebooks is more fragmentary, more logical and less comprehensive than his *Monadology*.

Yet its logical foundations are remarkably similar. In fact, many modern commentators now deny the claim by Russell that Leibniz had two different philosophies. The *Monadology* can be seen as merely an optimistic take on the fundamental logical facts that grounded Leibniz's metaphysical rational view of the world of monads. Instead of stressing that this is the best of all possible worlds, we could insist that a logically restrained God is obliged to create no other world than one with disease, famine, war and the like. It is simply not possible for there to be any other kind of world. This interpretation certainly chimes with a modern view of the human condition. If instead of Leibniz's logical constraints on God's creation we introduce the Darwinian 'survival of the fittest', then the optimistic/pessimistic divide in Leibniz's philosophy becomes superfluous. The creation of the world – either by God, or evolution – naturally entails certain logical constraints, such as sufficient reason and the absence of contradiction. Such logic renders perfection impossible. This is the world as it is – no more, no less.

Leibniz ended up as a lonely figure, occupying his room at the empty ducal residence in Hanover. Despite being widely regarded as the finest mind in Europe, he was increasingly neglected by his new employer, George of Hanover, whose main interests were visiting his hunting lodges and roistering with his friends. Indeed, Duke George was somewhat discombobulated when Peter the Great of Russia paid a visit to Hanover in 1711 and made it plain that he had no wish to participate in any bloodsports. The sole reason for his visit, he informed the duke, was to spend a few days in conversation with Leibniz in order to learn of his latest scientific discoveries, and pick his brains concerning any advances which might help him to run his vast territory. This astonished Duke George, who had not for one moment considered taking the advice of the curious resident intellectual he had inherited from his father.

In 1714, Duke George was invited to Britain to ascend to the throne. (No other suitable Protestant relatives were available.) The newly created George I was adamant that Leibniz should remain behind in Hanover. Apart from offending Oldenburg by neglecting to send the Royal Society the promised model of his calculating machine, Leibniz had also become embroiled in a dispute with Newton over who had invented calculus – a dispute of such magnitude that it split scientific opinion throughout Europe. As Newton was now president of the Royal Society, George I was given to understand that bringing Leibniz to London would be viewed as an insult to the nation's greatest scientist, who had been knighted and was regarded as a national treasure.

Back in Hanover, Leibniz continued with his desultory researches into the history of the House of Hanover. In between times he continued with his studies, covering page after page with his new ideas. For instance, after reading the latest information reaching Europe about Chinese culture, he began studying the principle of yin and yang. This led him to come up with the idea for a new binary arithmetic. This could be used to convert logical statements into mathematics, thus enabling moral conflicts to be solved by calculation, with one side 'proved' to be correct. This ingenious approach to human behaviour failed to convince, however, and to his disappointment the presiding judges in law courts were not replaced by mathematicians conducting binary calculations. In fact, the invention of binary arithmetic proved three centuries ahead of its time, and would only come into its own with the invention of the computer.

Leibniz also continued to make considerable advances in fields ranging from theology to symbolic logic, and from mining engineering to the chemical isolation of phosphorus. Indeed, such was the sheer volume and originality of his writings that they have not yet been fully catalogued to this day. It is little surprise that many have come to regard Leibniz as the Leonardo of his era.

Until the very last years of his life Leibniz was capable of concentrating on his work with such intensity that on occasion he would work for twenty-four hours at a stretch, oblivious to the trays of food brought to him by his faithful servant Eckhart. In 1716, at the age of seventy, Leibniz finally died. Although George I was at the time on a visit to Hanover, Leibniz's funeral was attended only by Eckhart.

CHAPTER 18

ON THE SHOULDERS
OF GIANTS

WHERE LEIBNIZ DESCRIBED A world constrained by logic, Isaac Newton described an entire universe constrained by just one fundamental scientific force – namely, gravity. For Newton, this force governed the behaviour of everything from the smallest particles to the largest planets, and even the stars. In a materialist age such as our own, this physical interpretation has a far greater appeal than any theoretical logical description, such as that of Leibniz. And the overwhelming advantage of Newton's idea, even in these early years of the scientific era, was that it could be tested and used to develop explanations of all manner of further material phenomena. In this aspect, Newton's understanding of the workings of gravity can be seen as the crowning achievement of the Age of Reason. When asked how he had succeeded in this supreme achievement, he explained, in a bout of uncharacteristic diffidence: 'If I have seen further it is by standing on the shoulders of Giants.'

Isaac Newton was born on Christmas Day 1642 in the hamlet of Woolsthorpe, just outside Grantham in the East Midlands of England.

By a freak of fate, his great scientific predecessor Galileo had died earlier
in the same year. Newton's father was an illiterate smallholder who died
before Isaac was born, and was said to have been 'a wild, extravagant
and weak man'. When Newton was two years old, his mother married
a sixty-one-year-old vicar named Barnabas Smith, and went to live
with him in a nearby village. Young Isaac was consequently brought
up in Woolsthorpe by his grandmother. The loss of his mother is said
to have been a traumatic event for the infant Isaac, making him prone
to outbursts of intemperate rage throughout his life. During his childhood, he would climb to the top of a nearby hill, from which he could
silently contemplate the village where his mother now lived. Although
just a few miles distant, his mother was in fact a world away, and is said
not to have visited him. Meanwhile, it was explained to him that his
father was 'in heaven'. This is said to have inspired Newton's lifelong
interest in the workings of heavenly bodies.

Other facts from this period present a slightly different picture. In
his later years, Newton would confess to 'threatening my [step] father
and [my] mother... to burn them and the house over them'. It is known
that young Newton constructed wooden shelves in his home which
contained 'two or three hundred books' from his stepfather. These were
mostly theological tomes, but they also contained a large blank notebook.
Newton would begin jotting down notes, scientific observations and
schemes in these, a habit he would continue into adulthood.*

The Civil War had broken out in the year of Newton's birth,
and would continue throughout his childhood. His modern American
biographer James Gelick well describes this: 'Motley, mercenary
armies skirmished throughout the Midlands. Pikemen and musketeers
sometimes passed through the fields near Woolsthorpe. Bands of men
plundered farms for supplies.' Morose and lonely, Newton grudgingly
fulfilled his tasks on the family smallholding – minding sheep, pulling
up turnips – and at the same time attended the village school, where he

---

* According to Richard Westfall, this notebook 'later witnessed the birth of calculus
and Newton's first steps in mechanics'.

learned to read and write, absorbed arithmetic by rote, and was inculcated with selective readings from the Bible.

In 1649, Charles I was executed and England fell under the Puritan rule of Oliver Cromwell. Three years later, Newton's mother returned home, along with her three new children. Her husband, the Reverend Barnabas Smith, had died. Isaac was packed off to school in Grantham, eight miles away. It was too far for him to return home, so he boarded with the local apothecary, sleeping in the garret. Here we gain first-hand knowledge of the gifted, troubled child he had become. On the garret wall he scratched Archimedean triangles, while in the margins of his Latin textbook he scribbled pitiful messages: 'There is no room for me... I will make an end. I cannot but weepe. I know not what to doe.' There was just one ray of light in his dark teenage years: his landlord, Mr Clarke, had built up a collection of scientific books, which he would lend to his strange solitary tenant.

When Newton was seventeen, his mother called him home to run the farm. At regular intervals, he and a farmhand would rise before dawn to drive livestock into Grantham to sell at the market. Newton would entrust the farmhand with the sale of the sheep or pigs, while he nipped around the corner to borrow some more books from Mr Clarke. One day the sheep escaped, causing widespread damage in the town and to the fences of nearby fields before they could be rounded up. Newton was brought before the courts and fined four shillings and four pence (the price of a good pair of shoes). Thus Newton's first official qualification was a criminal record – a fact which made him extremely wary of contravening the law for the rest of his life.

Luckily, this incident prompted two sympathetic mentors to realize that something had to be done about this talented young lad. Mr Stokes, the headmaster of the King's School in Grantham, contacted Newton's maternal uncle, William Ayscough, who was rector of a nearby village but also happened to be a graduate of Trinity College, Cambridge. Between them, they browbeat Newton's mother into sending him back to school in Grantham, where they could prepare him for the Cambridge entrance examination. Newton returned to board with Mr Clarke, and according to his landlord's young daughter he formed a romantic attachment with her during this period. This teenage crush appears to have been largely of her own imagining, for this is the only occasion in Newton's life when he was romantically linked to any woman.

One particular activity Newton pursued during these years was the creation of ingenious working models of various machines. He constructed a water mill, a mousetrap of his own design, and a windmill, all of which caused widespread wonder. However, most significantly of all he is known to have created out of wood a four-foot-high water clock, operated by means of intricately carved gears, levers and interlocking cogs. From the outset, it is evident that Newton was not only possessed of exceptional mental powers, but also developed considerable practical abilities. (Coincidentally, these were the very years when Huygens was inventing the pendulum clock.)

At the age of eighteen Newton passed his entrance exam and was admitted to Trinity College, Cambridge, which was acknowledged as the most academically prestigious college in the university.* However, in Newton's time it suffered from the remnant blight that afflicted so many universities away from the leading European centres of learning – such as Paris, Leiden and several Italian universities including Padua: the lecturers at Trinity still adhered strictly to the long-standing medieval curriculum of Aristotle and scholasticism. (The gatherings at Oxford attended by the likes of Boyle, Hooke and Locke were to all intents and purposes private societies.)

This was not the only blight that afflicted Cambridge undergraduates. As with so many matters English, class distinction was almost as rigid as Aristotle's philosophy. Newton was an impecunious scholar of unmistakably lesser-class origins compared to most other 'gentlemen scholars'. As such, in order to pay his way he was obliged to combine his studies with duties as a 'sizar' – who had to serve, clean, and perform other menial tasks about the college.

---

* A reputation that has continued through the centuries. During the early decades of the twentieth century, Trinity was said to have produced more Nobel Prize winners than the whole of France.

Peter Paul Rubens's interests extended far beyond his role as an artist – he was also a diplomat, adviser to royalty and businessman.

Estimated to have produced over two hundred paintings, Rembrandt van Rijn is widely considered to be the most profound artist of the Age of Reason.

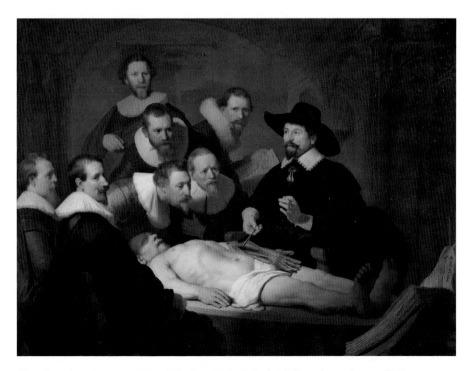

The Anatomy Lesson of Dr. Nicolaes Tulp (1632) by Rembrandt van Rijn.

Nicolas Poussin, who became First Painter to King Louis XIII, was known for severe classical restraint in his paintings, even when depicting violent scenes such as *The Abduction of the Sabine Women.*

Charles I (*above*) was intent upon establishing for England a leading role in European art and formed a lasting attachment to Flemish artist Anthony Van Dyck.

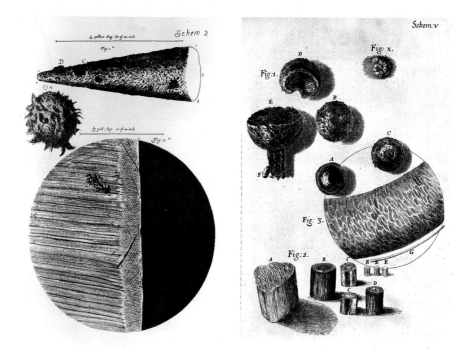

Robert Hooke's *Micrographia* was the first important work on microscopy. A needlepoint (*left*) and hair follicles (*right*) are just two of the finely detailed illustrations therein.

The search for scapegoats following the Great Plague (1665–6) and then the Great Fire of London (1666) (*above*) saw Hobbes's *Leviathan* banned for tending to 'atheism, blasphemy and profaneness'.

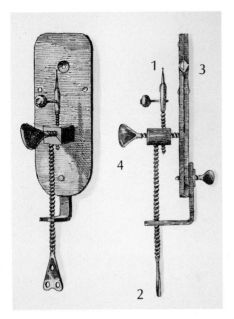

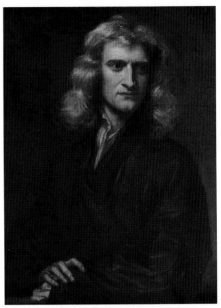

One of Antonie van Leeuwenhoek's microscopes: (1) the specimen was placed on the apparatus, (2) brought into position vertically by turning the lower screw, (3) and moved toward or way from the lens (4) by turning the shorter screw.

Isaac Newton's conceptualization of the laws of motion and universal gravitation are perhaps the most seminal discovery of the Age of Reason.

The 1999 replica of the seventeenth-century Dutch ship *Duyfken* (Little Dove) on the River Derwent in Tasmania.

Sor Juana Inés de la Cruz became one of the Spanish New World's foremost intellectuals, turning her nun's quarters into a salon.

Such was his popularity as an actor, poet and especially playwright, that French would become known as 'the language of Moliere'.

Following the death of Cardinal Mazarin in 1661, Jean-Baptiste Colbert became First Minister to Louis XIV; *Colbert presenting the Members of The Royal Academy of Sciences to Louis XIV in 1667* (c. 1670).

A Portrait of a Man in Front of a Sculpture (1666), thought to be Baruch Spinoza.

One of the great polymaths of the age, Gottfried Leibniz was a pre-eminent figure in both the history of philosophy and the history of mathematics.

Queen Christina of Sweden attempted to establish Stockholm as the 'Athens of the North'.

Claudio Monteverdi is often regarded as the greatest composer of the Age of Reason.

Mary Beale's *Portrait of a Mathematician*, thought to be of Robert Hooke, may have been deliberately discarded, lest it risk detracting from Isaac Newton's discoveries.

John Locke's empirical philosophy influenced philosophers such as Voltaire and Rousseau, as well as American revolutionaries.

Engraving of Halley's Comet of 1682 over Augsburg. Halley used his observations and Newton's law of universal gravitation to compute the periodicity of the comet, which was subsequently named for him.

The Murder of the De Witt Brothers (c. 1672) by Pieter Fris.

Scene on the West African coast with a family being separated by slave traders (1788). Many of the achievements of the Age of Reason were financially enabled by the transatlantic slave trade.

Fortunately, amongst the 3,000 volumes lining the shelves of the Trinity library were a number of works donated by more enlightened scholars. In this way, Newton was unusually fortunate in being able to absorb the works of Galileo and Descartes – both of which he immediately recognized as describing a much more accurate scientific vision than that accepted by academic orthodoxy. Most importantly, he learned from Descartes the idea that the entire universe was filled with a 'universal vortex', which caused the motion of the planets. He also discovered that Galileo – acting on his belief that the world worked according to mathematics – had used geometry to calculate the motion of the stars and the elliptical passage of the planets discovered by Kepler.

Amazingly, this important reading was all completed during his first year as an undergraduate – between attending lectures and his menial duties as a sizar. From the time of his arrival in Cambridge, Newton met few people, made few friends, and spent much of his time alone in his room. According to his definitive biographer Richard Westfall: 'He purchased a lock for his desk, a quart bottle and ink to fill it, a notebook, a pound of candles, and a chamber pot'. Little wonder that he became known as the Silent Scholar.

Such was Newton's preference for his own company, and his unwill-ingness (or inability) to conform to accepted social patterns – both at this early stage and throughout his later life – that many are convinced that he was autistic. This (of necessity unconfirmed) possibility should be borne in mind during many of the otherwise irrational incidents that character-ized his mental and social behaviour throughout the ensuing decades of his long and for the most part rational life.

During Newton's second year at Cambridge he began filling an extensive notebook he labelled *Quaestiones Quaedam Philosophicae* (Some Philosophical Questions). Indicative of his solitary, secretive nature is the fact that the opening and concluding pages of this notebook are filled with orthodox Aristotelian philosophy (possibly jotted down during lectures). Only in the middle of the notebook does he begin outlining his own original thoughts, trying to square these with what he had learned from his study of Galileo, Descartes, Kepler and Huygens.

The rigidities and blatant errors of Aristotelian science had led Newton into the habit of questioning whatever he found did not accord with his own thought. And the more he began examining the new explanations by Galileo, Descartes and Huygens, the more he began to perceive that these too had their shortcomings. They were certainly original explanations, and they indubitably worked in their own fields of application. But there was one fatal flaw which ran throughout the new world view: it remained provisional. It became increasingly evident to him that Descartes's vortexes, Kepler's ellipses and Huygens's invisible 'subtle matter' were lacking something. Even when such ideas appeared to be in accord with mathematical calculations, they did not present a complete picture.

In 1665, news reached Cambridge that the Great Plague had broken out in London and was beginning to spread through the country at an alarming rate. The university immediately closed down and its students dispersed. The twenty-three-year-old Newton tramped a hundred miles back home to Grantham, where he and his family prepared to remain in isolation in the hope of avoiding the scourge.

Fortunately, Woolsthorpe was spared, and Newton set up his room as a place where he could study and carry out experiments. Living in untroubled isolation, his mind began to clear of all distractions and trivialities. No longer was he a sizar at the beck and call of 'gentlemen scholars'. The result was Newton's *annus mirabilis*, a year during which he made a series of major scientific breakthroughs of all but unprecedented proportions.[*] These he wrote down in 'the nearly blank thousand-page commonplace book he had inherited from his stepfather and named... his Waste Book'.

Newton's first major discovery during this period was differential calculus by means of entities he called 'fluxions'. As we have seen,

---

[*] The only near-comparison is Einstein's miraculous year while he was working as a patent clerk in Berne. During 1905, he produced four papers which contained unprecedented scientific breakthroughs: the special theory of relativity, the proposal that light consisted of quanta, the proof that Brownian (random) motion of pollen on the surface of water confirmed the existence of atoms, and his deduction that matter and energy are equivalent according to the formula $E = mc^2$.

differential calculus determines the rate of change of a curve; this is done by discovering the tangent to the curve at a particular point, which gives its rate of change or velocity at this point. (The more vertical the tangent, the greater the rate of change.) However, philosophers and mathematicians would point out a flaw in this method. Velocity involves the measurement of distance covered in a particular time. This is the distance covered between two separate times (e.g. 20 mph means an object covers twenty miles in an hour). Differentiation at a precise point involves an irrational contradiction. A precise point has no extension; there is thus no distance or time by which the velocity can be measured (0 miles in 0 hours). Newton skilfully found a way around this problem by using fluxions, the very name of which indicates flowing or movement. Newton's calculus involved taking a section of a (flowing) curve, then reducing this fluent section, making it ever smaller until it *approached* its infinitely small limit. Although the decreasing fluxions never actually reached the infinitely small limit, it was possible to make a very close approximation of the rates of change either side of it.

The Irish philosopher Bishop Berkeley, no mean mathematician himself, would later correctly point out that this was a trick, a mathematical sleight of hand: 'And what are these fluxions. They are neither finite Quantities, nor Quantities infinitely small, nor yet nothing. May we not call them the Ghosts of departed Quantities?'

Logically (and mathematically), Berkeley was of course correct, but Newton's method of using ever-smaller fluxions – which by their nature were never at rest – was a stroke of genius that circumvented this incontrovertible point. On the other hand, Leibniz's infinitesimals were ever-smaller points, with increasingly precise (immobile) locations. However, although both of these explanations fall foul of Berkeley's objection, in practical terms the calculus of both Newton and Leibniz was found to work.*

---

* Not until the following century would the French mathematician Augustin-Louis Cauchy succeed in placing calculus on a firm theoretical footing. This was not the first time that a practical discovery made during the Age of Reason would take many years before it was proved to have a rational basis. To name but two other examples: Spinoza learned how to eliminate the blurring rainbow

As if this was not enough, Newton's *annus mirabilis* would also include a number of similarly revolutionary advances. One of these was his theory of colours, which he discovered by passing a beam of white light through a prism of glass. The prism refracted the light into its constituent rainbow spectrum. When he passed these rainbow colours through a further prism, they were refracted back to become white light. He thus demonstrated that white light was in fact made up of different colours. This prompted him to the ingenious claim that coloured light must travel in minute corpuscles of different sizes, which move at different speeds when passed through more dense media, such as glass.

However, by far the greatest scientific advance made by Newton during his year at Woolsthorpe was his conceptualization, and explanation, of the notion of gravity. It is all but impossible to exaggerate the import of this discovery – by far one of the most momentous in the history of science.* Newton's unravelling of and accounting for gravity literally changed the universe (at least from humanity's point of view).

His theory posed the hypothesis that every known object throughout the solar system, from the miniscule to the planetary realm, exerted a force of physical attraction between one another. The larger the object concerned, the greater its attractive force. Gravity was the force that drew the planets on their orbits around the sun, and governed the movement of the moons around their respective planets. It was also the force that drew the lightest snowflake down from the sky towards the earth. And it was gravity that made objects fall to the ground when we dropped them. On another scale, it caused the passage of the moon around the earth to attract the liquid of the oceans, causing the regular rise and fall of tides.

---

defects which marred his polished lenses; similarly, Kepler observed that Copernicus's circular orbits around the sun were in fact elliptical. Coincidentally, years later it was Newton who provided a rational explanation for both these phenomena.

* Its only serious rival would come almost two centuries later, in the form of Charles Darwin's theory of evolution. Where Newton posited for the first time how the physical nature of the entire universe worked, Darwin explained how this had evolved to include our place within its vastness and complexity.

By using his powers of deduction, observation and imagination – along with his recent understanding of fluxions – Newton succeeded in calculating a universal law of gravity, which accounted for all aspects of the gravitational effect. This would later result in a formula whose apparent complexity is in fact simply explained:

$$F = \frac{G\,(M_1 \times M_2)}{r^2}$$

The formula clearly describes how the force of gravity (F) causes two bodies (M_1 and M_2) to be attracted to one another, with the magnitude of this attractive force being proportional to the product of their two masses ($M_1 \times M_2$). This in turn is multiplied by the gravitational constant G (approximately 6.4743), which enables the formula to balance out. The upper sum on the right-hand side of the equation is divided by the square of the distance (r) between the two masses, i.e. r^2. Calculate the measurements, feed in the numbers, and the answer is plain.

For example, the force of gravity between the earth and the moon involves multiplying the mass of the earth by the mass of the moon, multiplying this by the gravitational constant, and then dividing the resultant sum by the squared distance between the earth and the moon, taken from the centre of each body. For evident reason, today this is generally known as an inverse-square law (because the force between two bodies varies in inverse proportion to the square of the distance between them).

During the course of his conception of gravity, Newton also came up with three laws of motion:

1. An object remains at rest or continues at a constant speed in a straight line, unless another force acts upon it.
2. The force of an object is equal to its mass times its acceleration.
3. When a body exerts a force upon a second body, there is an equal but opposite force (a reaction) exerted on the first body by the second.

These laws laid the scientific foundation for modern mechanics, conceptualizing its objects and their properties. Perhaps most significantly, the idea of 'force' – conceived as an invisible metaphysical agency operating over a distance – had been evolving since at least Ancient Greek times. However, it was here in these laws that Newton precisely conceptualized in purely physical terms the idea and proportions that we as a matter of course refer to as 'force'. In this instance, any remnant element of metaphysics was eliminated.

Newton's three laws were transformative. One example will suffice: Why does the moon not gravitate ever closer to the earth, attracted by our planet's greater mass? The moon is obeying Newton's first law of motion, continuing in a straight line at a constant speed. However, according to the third law, the gravitational force of the earth should draw it closer to the earth. It is the *conjunction* of these two forces interacting and balancing each other out that ensures that the moon continues on its orbit around the earth. The first law of motion impels it in a straight line, yet at the same time it is drawn by the earth's gravitational force, thus combining to form the moon's continuous orbital passage around the earth. Similarly, this combination of the law of inertia and gravity accounts for why the planets orbit the sun. (Though Newton was unable to give a full account of why the solar system remained stable, despite the fact that the gravity of the orbiting planets acting on each other must surely have involved them in a host of minor complex gravitational interactions, which would surely end up by unbalancing the entire system. To explain the continuing stability of the solar system under such circumstances Newton was forced to invoke the occasional minor intervention by God, who corrected any imbalance that might have led to the planets spinning away into outer space, or falling towards the sun.*)

---

* Today this difficulty has been reduced to what is known as the three-body problem, or how three bodies can maintain continuous movements in relation to each other according to Newton's laws of motion and the force of gravity. Though modern scientists discount Newton's answer, to date they have yet to find a fully generalized solution. In other words, we still do not really know why the solar system remains stable, or whether it is liable to collapse at any moment.

On returning to Cambridge in 1667, the ever-secretive Newton decided against publishing his sensational findings. Even so, he could not refrain from discussing them with a number of inquisitive colleagues, and even sent a sheaf of his writings to Oldenburg at the Royal Society. (These were the unpublished papers which Oldenburg showed to Leibniz on his visit to London in 1673.) It was soon clear to such scientists that Newton's discovery revolutionized everything from cosmology to the dripping of a tap. This was no more no less than the way the physical world worked.

When asked how he had conceived of such a comprehensive world-changing idea, Newton was in the habit of replying: 'By thinking on it continually.' When further pressed, he would become irritated at having to explain complicated scientific terms to the uninitiated. So he invented the story that while sitting in his garden at Woolsthorpe one summer's day, he had noticed an apple fall from a tree. This had prompted him to wonder what force was responsible for such an event, and why the apple fell directly to earth. Over the centuries this myth gained an element of credence: it remains the simplest explanation for an insight into one of the most universal ideas in scientific history.

The solitude of Newton's year at Woolsthorpe may have helped to concentrate his intellect and his creative faculties, but it soon became clear that this isolation was detrimental to other aspects of his nature. His minor eccentricities became more exaggerated – and instead of exclusively pursuing his mathematical, physical and cosmological inter-ests, he increasingly diverted his attention to more dubious pursuits. He launched into an intense and active study of alchemy, even setting up his own laboratory and kiln. He began studying prophecies and descrip-tions of the Apocalypse (the cataclysmic events which according to the Bible were said to presage the 'end of days'). At the same time he also started an exhaustive study of the Old Testament – in search of clues concerning the dimensions of Solomon's Temple in Jerusalem, which had been completed in the tenth century BC and destroyed by the Babylonians in 586 BC. In order to reinforce the accuracy of his studies he even taught himself Hebrew, so that he could glean hints concerning the precise layout of the inner temple, the dimensions of the tabernacle and the location of the Holy of Holies.*

Yet still Newton refrained from publishing his genuine scientific findings. The reasons for this seem to have been predominantly personal – in the main, his reticent nature, as well as his aversion to becoming involved in public controversies. These engrained traits in his personality – perhaps related to the trauma of being abandoned in his infancy – would gradually become more apparent during his mature years, and appear to have shaped Newton's spiritual life in a number of profound ways. He utterly rejected the notion of the Trinity, one of the central tenets of the Christian religion. This asserts that there is one God, but he exists in three forms – namely, God the Father, God the Son (Jesus Christ) and God the Holy Ghost (whose visitation caused Mary to become pregnant while still a virgin). It is not difficult to see how the young Newton was affected by uncomfortable psychological resonances between his own childhood situation and the ideas of the Holy Trinity. By the time he was a teenager, Newton had become convinced there was only one God, an unseen paternal figure, who was 'in heaven'.

Such a belief was regarded as heresy – one of the most serious contraventions of the Christian faith. England may have been a divided religious country at this time, but there was no denying the intensity of the belief of its citizens. By dismissing the central Christian tenet of the Trinity, and believing in just one unseen God who was hidden in Heaven, Newton became an apostate – to both Protestants and Catholics alike. He had become what was known as a Unitarian.

As ever, Newton kept this secret to himself. Yet the fears and contradictions it inspired in his life would never leave him. If anything, they increased as he grew older. He was gripped by a perpetual and increasing fear that one day he would be 'found out' – exposed as a heretic. (The irony that he studied, and rose to great eminence, at a Cambridge college named after the Trinity, only exacerbated his maturing paranoia.)

---

* The so-called Wailing Wall in Jerusalem, one of the holiest sites of Judaism, is in reality a remnant of the containing wall of the Second Temple of Jerusalem, built in 516 BC by King Herod and destroyed in AD 70 by the Romans.

The second psychological defect arising from his childhood trauma was that, as his life continued, he felt an ever-greater need to find a surrogate for the 'man of God' (his stepfather) whom he had grown to detest. Long after this man of God had died, Newton still hated the man who had robbed him of his mother. And just like his paranoia at being unmasked as a heretic, this particular aspect of Newton's precarious mental state would also deepen – until it became a fixation. Indeed, it is more than possible that his paranoia and his hatred were but differing aspects of the same mental affliction, one reinforcing the another.

Meanwhile Newton's life in Cambridge blossomed. In 1669 he was given the post of Lucasian Professor of Mathematics.* Three years later he was appointed to the Royal Society. By now his unwillingness to publish a paper describing his sensational results was beginning to upset the Royal Society. Hooke was despatched to Cambridge in an effort to persuade Newton to submit a paper. The reason Hooke was sent was because it was known that he had been researching similar subjects such as the orbits of the planets and various notions concerning gravity. During the course of their meetings, Newton became incensed when Hooke had the temerity

---

* Newton was only the second person to hold this post, after Isaac Barrow, who had been instrumental in encouraging Newton's exceptional talent. In 1669, Barrow selflessly resigned from the professorship on the understanding that Newton would be elected his successor. The Lucasian professorship has over the years become one of the most prestigious academic posts in Britain. Other distinguished occupants of this chair include the computer pioneer Charles Babbage, who held the post between 1828 and 1838. He seldom visited Cambridge, and rarely gave lectures, spending most of his time in London constructing his ground-breaking difference engine, an early analogue computer. Paul Dirac, who received the Nobel Prize for his ground-breaking work on quantum mechanics, was professor from 1932 to 1969. Dirac's autism was of a similar power to that of Newton, but took a different form, i.e. extreme reticence and rigid addiction to rationality. During an important lecture, a member of the audience said, 'I don't understand that second equation, Professor Dirac.' Dirac remained silent. 'Aren't you going to answer the question?' asked Dirac's colleague. 'That was not a question, that was a statement,' replied Dirac. In 1979 the cosmologist Stephen Hawking, who suffered from motor neurone disease, was appointed Lucasian professor at the age of thirty-seven, on the expectation that he would soon die. He went on to hold the post for thirty years.

to suggest that he too had conceived of a 'system of the world'. The fact that this bore a resemblance to the ideas which Newton had allowed to be circulated amongst trusted members of the Royal Society, but had not yet published, only deepened his suspicions. When Newton challenged Hooke, the latter was forced to admit that he had not yet succeeded in formulating a mathematical foundation for his idea. Whereupon Newton accused Hooke of plagiarizing his idea without even understanding it. Following this meeting, Hooke would be regarded as an enemy by Newton to the end of his days.

In 1684, the Royal Society despatched the astronomer Halley to try to persuade Newton to publish his ideas. During the course of their conversations, Halley informed Newton that he had also developed a version of the inverse-square law concerning the movements of the planets. This time, Newton appeared unaccountably impressed. He brought out some papers and began explaining how he had overcome the problems which had defeated Halley. He even went so far as to allow Halley to take away with him a manuscript copy of Newton's work, so that he could publish it as a book. This would eventually appear in London under the title *Philosophiae Naturalis Principia Mathematica* (The Mathematical Principles of Natural Philosophy), now usually known as the *Principia*.

The publication of Newton's *Principia* in 1687 was greeted with great acclaim – even though none but the most elite mathematical cognoscenti understood either its contents or their significance, except in the crudest sense (apple falls from tree). In recognition of Newton's increasing renown, he was chosen as the member of parliament for Cambridge (at the time an appointed rather than an elected post). Ever fearful of conflict, he refrained from participating in parliamentary debates. Indeed, his only known words from the floor of the house during his long period as an MP were a request for a window to be opened.

By now, Newton was spending much of his time in London. Astonishingly, he is even known to have socialized, though only on rare occasions. And later he also began attending the meetings of the Royal Society. As a result, he met, or corresponded with some of the finest minds of the period – including the likes of Locke, Boyle, Huygens, Flamsteed and even Leibniz (Hooke remained in disgrace). In order to aid him in his day-to-day business, Newton hired a handsome young Swiss mathematician called Nicolas Fatio de Duillier. Newton soon fell in love with Fatio, though such were his rigid principles that he could not admit this unthinkable fact, especially to himself. When Fatio left his post and returned home, Newton suffered a serious nervous breakdown, during the course of which he lost control of his mind. Consequently, he despatched a number of violently antagonistic letters to friends and acquaintances. In one of these he even claimed that Locke had 'endeavoured to embroil me with woemen [sic]'.*

It took Newton some time to recover from his mental turmoil, but in 1696 he was made Warden of the Royal Mint. This was intended mainly as a sinecure, to enable Newton to support himself in style. However, at this time the British currency was undergoing a serious crisis. Its coinage had been so widely debased by forgers, clippers, makers of base metal copies and the like that it was beginning to lose trust on the continental exchanges and many foreign merchants were refusing to accept it as payment. This threatened Britain's export trade, upon which its entire prosperity depended, and the Mint was working at full stretch from 4 a.m. till midnight in order to fulfil a policy of 're-coinage'. This latter was intended to reform the currency and re-establish its credibility by removing suspect and deliberately damaged coins from circulation, issuing only the genuine article. As the Warden of the Mint, Newton was merely expected to put in the occasional appearance, while his two main deputies performed the arduous task of actually implementing the re-coinage.

But Newton had never been one to shirk what he saw as his responsibilities. And such was his diligence that in 1699 he was appointed Master of the Mint, taking full charge of the re-coinage. Newton pursued his new employment with utmost vigour. Counterfeiting coins of the realm was fraudulence, and as such a matter of moral concern. From the very outset

---

* There is a widespread belief that Newton died a virgin. In 1733, Voltaire claimed, 'I have had that confirmed by the doctor and the surgeon who were with him when he died.' However, his biographer Westfall gives the merest suggestion that this may not have been the case.

of his appointment, Newton took the situation personally. Here were men of evil intent doing their best to undermine his credibility – and thus expose him to other charges of dishonesty, even the possibility that he might be revealed as a Unitarian. So Newton embarked upon an unprecedented strategy. He decided to see for himself how this debased currency was used, and how it circulated. Accompanied by two burly employees of the Royal Mint, he took to disguising himself and visiting low-life taverns. Here he would observe counterfeiters, and even innocent dupes, attempting to pass off this fake currency which threatened his exposure.

As a result of these visits, Newton's name soon became feared throughout the London underworld – a large and thriving demographic at the time (these were the streets where the original 'Mack the Knife' plied his trade). But it was one particular felon – a highly successful figure named William Chaloner – who soon became Newton's bête noire. Over the years, Chaloner had made such a fortune from his successful counterfeiting operations that he had set himself up as a gentleman – counting amongst his friends members of parliament, successful businessmen, bankers and even magistrates, all of whom were welcomed to social events at his London mansion. Chaloner had even purchased for himself membership of the prestigious 400-year-old Society of Merchant Venturers. Here was a pillar of society, a captain of industry, worthy of respect throughout the City of London and far beyond. Indeed, the shipping register for the port of Bristol even recorded how he had been the major investor in no less than thirteen triangular voyages (i.e. slave trade ventures) between 1709 and 1714. This would have made him amongst the most cash-rich plutocrats in the land.

When Chaloner learned of the charges being brought against him by Newton, he dismissed them as ludicrous, and soon saw to it that he had the protection of his friends in high places. Following another tack, he even covertly contacted Newton, offering to go into business with him, suggesting that his own knowledge of a new method for minting coins would be of inestimable value to Newton in his pursuance of widespread re-coinage. One aspect of this had almost certainly already been introduced by Newton. This involved collecting all coins of the realm, melting them down, extracting their genuine content, and then re-minting them in such a way that they could no longer be forged. One element of this process involved 'milling' the edges of the coins, i.e. adding ribbed indentures so that any clipping would immediately be detectable. Chaloner's advice sounded admirably above board. The only slight flaw in his plan was that he insisted he should be granted entry to the Royal Mint so that he could supervise the engravers' dies – the tools that stamped the royal design on to the faces of blank new coins. (His previous purloining of some such dies had been the foundation of his successful counterfeiting career.)

Newton had formed a low opinion of Chaloner from the start, but realized that pursuing a man with friends in such high places might well lead to his exposure as a heretic by his enemies – an ever-increasing section of the population, both in Newton's paranoid mind and in the reality of the criminal underworld thriving on forgeries. However, it was now that Newton's supremely confident adversary made a fatal mistake. Chaloner challenged Newton on the one topic to which he clung with his innermost being: 'He accused the New Warden [Newton] of incompetence, even alleged fraud in his management of the Mint.'

Driven by his utmost fear of being exposed as a fraud, Newton at once abandoned all pretence at equanimity. William Chaloner became an obsession, and Newton determined that he would hunt down his detractor with every means at his disposal. Chaloner was soon apprehended and flung into the notorious Newgate Prison. He was then tried and sentenced to be hanged at Tyburn. (Few witnesses dared to come forward for fear of incurring Newton's wrath.) Even while Chaloner lay in his cell awaiting his sentence, Newton made sure he was spied on at all times, for fear that he might attempt to pass on incriminating evidence.

To the end, Newton's persecution complex remained indefatigable. When he learned in 1684 that Leibniz had published a work claiming to have invented calculus, Newton once more descended into paranoia. He knew that he personally had discovered calculus as early as 1665 (even though he had omitted to publish this fact). But he was also aware that Oldenburg had shown Leibniz some of his unpublished papers during his visit to London in 1673. Newton had made use of calculus in measuring the movement of the planets and in his cosmological computations; it was obvious that here was where Leibniz must have stolen his ideas. In Newton's eyes, Leibniz's false claim was no less than a declaration of war, and Newton communicated as much to all his scientific colleagues. Meanwhile the scientists and academies of Europe were inclined to support Leibniz – who had, after all, published first.

The so-called Calculus Wars would persist for decades. When Newton took over as head of the Royal Society in 1703, he browbeat its Fellows into composing papers attacking Leibniz as a fraud. He even assembled an 'unbiased committee' to consider this question of priority. The committee members duly submitted their papers to the chairman of the committee, Newton himself, who then blatantly rewrote the findings of the committee in a final report, which he ordered to be read out before the Fellows of the Royal Society and entered into the records. Even after Leibniz's death in 1716, the mere mention of his name during meetings of the Royal Society was liable to bring an abrupt end to the subject under discussion. The chairman would then deliver an extempore diatribe in which he made plain his feelings towards the deceased.

The irony of all this was that there should have been no real issue at all between Newton and Leibniz. Few disputed that Newton had certainly discovered a method of calculus involving fluxions many years before Leibniz discovered his own method. And Leibniz's method was markedly different, relying more upon his own interpretation using infinitesimals. Leibniz did not make use of Newton's notion of fluxions – the method so central to his original invention. Newton's method was complicated and in certain ways incomplete. It worked, but this required a certain sleight of hand, and was only as rigorous as contemporary mathematics permitted. (Bishop Berkeley's 'ghosts of departed quantities' posed a very real rational difficulty.)

In truth, Leibniz's method may have been ingenious but it was no better at overcoming the difficulties faced by Newton, and in fact Leibniz would make little attempt to exploit the use of his discovery. On the other hand, Newton's use of calculus would play a part in leading him to the concept which explained how the world worked.

However, by a trick of fate, although Leibniz's discovery of calculus took place several years after Newton's original discovery, Leibniz's methods and their usage proved far more efficacious than Newton's painstakingly determined pioneering method. It was Leibniz's method that would increasingly be used by continental European mathematicians, who not only adopted the Latin names which he gave to the two processes – *differentialis* (showing differences) and *integralis* (bringing together) – but also adopted his notation, which is the one which we still use to this day.*

Newton may have been the first to discover calculus, but when his technique was adopted by consequent generations of British mathematicians, this caused a very real problem. While European mathematicians flourished, making novel discoveries and undertaking transformative researches in such matters as partial differentiation equations, British mathematics languished, hampered by patriotic adherence to an outmoded methodology. Newton's ideas may have led the British scientific world in his lifetime, but his archaisms would consequently hamper its progress – if only in the field of calculus.

---

* i.e. dy/dx for differentiation, and ∫ y dx for integration.

EPILOGUE

THE AGE OF REASON began with Descartes's ultimate mental introspection reducing all human knowledge to doubt – other than the simple fact of its own mental functioning. As this age advanced, art, science, politics, human and social self-understanding – as well as global exploration – expanded into new territory. For the most part, art cast off the restraints of classical perfection, giving way to the mannerism and expression of the human spirit – as well as the introspection and profound spirituality of the likes of Rembrandt. The Reformation and the ensuing Thirty Years' War had destroyed forever the hegemony of the Catholic Church in western Europe. In countries such as England and recently liberated Holland the development of novel financial techniques unleashed a social evolution whose direction, let alone destination, remained unclear. Merchant venturers set out on trading expeditions that led to the occupation of ports in distant continents, and these soon began spreading inland to become colonies. An increasing amount of the capital financing this expansion came from the highly lucrative triangular trade from West Africa to the Americas – i.e. slavery.

One of humanity's most heinous enterprises, it was slavery that had provided the wealth for empires since pre-Babylonian times. The Romans, the Vikings, the Chinese, the Aztecs, the Ottomans – all of these empires involved slavery. Even the Italian Renaissance, coming into being in a Europe severely depleted by the Black Death, had employed slaves. And in the Age of Reason, it was slavery that produced the capital which led to the progress of western European civilization, laying the foundations upon which its empires were built. At the same time, it also prompted a few rare spirits such as Montaigne to recognize the contagious barbarity of all who took part in it – to say nothing of the absurdity of its claims regarding racial superiority.

From its most introspective Cartesian beginnings, the Age of Reason broadened out into an undreamt-of vision of the planet itself: the discovery of Australia, the circumnavigation of the globe, the first glimpses by Van Leeuwenhoek and Hooke of the microworld that inhabits and sustains us. And ultimately, the mental penetration that would enable us to understand that, far beyond our wildest visions, the entire cosmos – further even than humanity was able to detect at that time, let alone imagine – operated according to basic rules that were now becoming known. The chaos of the cosmos obeyed its own rational laws.*

Newton died in 1727 at the age of eighty-four. His funeral was held at Westminster Abbey, an honour usually only granted to royalty up to that point. On the day of the funeral, his coffin was carried into the seven-centuries-old nave of the Abbey. This had been the final resting place of kings and queens of England since Edward the Confessor in 1066. Newton's coffin was borne aloft by the Lord Chancellor, two dukes, three earls and members of the Royal Society.

This historic event was almost certainly witnessed by the thirty-three-year-old French writer Voltaire, who was living in exile in London at the time, supposedly to avoid imprisonment in the Bastille. As a progressive thinker from an autocratic regime, Voltaire as much as any other realized the significance of what he was witnessing: 'His countrymen honoured him… and interred him as though he had been a king who had made his people happy.' Isaac Newton, a man born a commoner, whose mind had soared above all others in his age, was being honoured by the entire population of his country. Such an event would have been unthinkable in France at the time. In order to match and compete with such an event,

---

* Arguably, even the randomness and idiosyncrasies inherent in quantum theory conform to this rationality – being amenable to scientific explanation. Only recent speculation concerning dark matter, as well as what takes place within black holes, has raised the first serious questioning of such scientific universality.

France's moribund autocratic rule would have to change. Instead of paying lip service to the glories of art and military power, from now on science, reason, commerce and human endeavour were the qualities which would increasingly begin to lead the world. And in this, Voltaire understood the beginnings of the new age coming into being. One in which he himself would play a leading role – the Age of Enlightenment.

Yet still the vital question posed at the start of this work remains unanswered. Will human progress – much of which was initiated during the Age of Reason – end up destroying the very civilization which it did so much to create? A number of footnotes and passing references in the text have hinted at the situation we now face. And many contemporary figures have drawn attention to this potentially tragic predicament – the endgame of our civilization – yet they have provided little in the way of any realistic remedy. Can we save progress? Is this indeed possible given the freedoms (mental, political, physical) that the Age of Reason did so much to foster? Will the widespread foundations laid down during the Age of Reason (and Unreason) need to be demolished? Will we need to start again if we are to save our civilization, our very planet? Will our organic contained world – a self-regulating complex system which the far-sighted James Lovelock named Gaia – finally come to an end, preceded by a long and disaster-filled era of agony and impotence during which it withers and finally dies?

Gaia was the first of the Ancient Greek deities, born out of chaos. This very chaos consisted of the void, the vast formless state (home of the random and the unreasonable). Chaos was originally created out of the separation of heaven and earth. Out of this emerged the ordered, rational harmony of the cosmos, which yet retained elements of its earlier chaotic incarnation – most notably an element of freedom. Freedom to create, to think, to act, to destroy... even the ubiquitousness of the 'accidental'. And, of course, humanity's guiding freedom: morality. To say nothing of the unreasonable opposites to these largely progressive qualities.

Yet how can such legends as Gaia (arising out of our primeval imagination) possibly bear any relevance to, let alone answer, the larger question of our survival, as posed at the opening of this book? How can we save our planet, even as the last grains of sand trickle through the narrow glass neck of our nature's hourglass? How can we, and our planet, outlast the ever-accelerating progress which the Age of Reason did so much to set in motion? Can there possibly be an answer, even while our last minutes of time are quickly running out?

Paradoxically, the answer would appear to be progress itself... along with the reasonable advances and unreasonable convulsions that the idea of progress seems somewhat inevitably to trail in its wake. The universal adoption of a controlled and benign form of progressive (and adaptive) capitalism would seem to be the only answer left at our disposal. Such capitalism, which is capable of living alongside and interacting with ameliorating socialistic ideas (welfare), has undeniably played a major role in getting us into our present 'pre-apocalyptic' state. Yet it seems that the kernel of democratic liberalism that exists within it, and continues to drive it – to both its greatest improvements and its worst excesses – remains the only practicable remedy to our present ills. But even this, on its own, will never be enough to undo the harm we have inflicted upon our planet and ourselves.

Our greatest – and perhaps only – remedy would seem to lie in the inventive freedom of thought (and yes, excessive wealth) that this social process brings to certain individuals who inhabit this system. Even as I write this, known (and unknown) advances continue to be made – far too many to outline here – several of which have already attracted billions of dollars' worth of investment. Might one, or more, of these prove to be our saviour? There are three examples from our modern history which continue to encourage hope amidst the wholly justifiable unfurling turbulence of pessimism as we appear to sleepwalk our way towards Armageddon.

First: in 1903 the American brothers Orville and Wilbur Wright assembled a heavier-than-air machine-driven contraption that 'flew' 120 feet at less than seven miles per hour. Sixty-six years later, Neil Armstrong set foot on the moon. Second: in 1990 CERN (the European Organization for Nuclear Research) on the French-Swiss border faced a major problem owing to the ever-expanding complexity of academic papers being produced for their library by the many visiting international scientists. What was needed was a means to facilitate new researchers hunting for papers on their chosen subject and cross-referencing them to related or even unexpected fields of previous research. Eventually this problem was solved by the British scientist Tim Berners-Lee, who assembled a glorified computerized filing system whose workings he refrained from patenting and simply donated to the world. This quickly developed into a vast interconnected system now known as the World Wide Web.* Third: after several decades of chicanery and 'almost but not quite' experiments, on 13 December 2022, the Livermore Laboratory in California announced that it had succeeded in producing 'fusion'. This process is common in stars – and even our own star, the sun – where amidst extreme heat and pressure smaller atoms are 'fused' into larger ones, releasing energy in the process. The Livermore experiment achieved fusion by focusing laser beams that released a greater amount of energy than was required to cause the fusion. As pointed out by its detractors, in this case the excess energy produced would barely have been enough to power a kettle.

The twentieth and twenty-first centuries have seen more, and faster, advances in science than in any previous age. Should developments in fusion happen at a far greater rate than achieved by aeroplanes or the web, it might even be able to supply our planet with an almost limitless supply of clean energy. And thus in the foreseeable future provide a solution to climate change, pollution, global degradation, and many of the other ills that beset the world we inhabit.

If it succeeds, we will be forced into the ironic recognition that much of this rational progress has been a direct result of research funds intended to aid the two major events of the twentieth century: its two world wars. These two cataclysmic outbursts of unreason may have deeply damaged our civilization, but they did not destroy it. Though ironically it was during the second of these two irrational episodes that humanity did in fact for

---

* It has been variously calculated that this was the greatest ever act of individual charity in human history. Even if Berners-Lee had charged just $0.01 for each use of his web, he would by now have accumulated a personal fortune equivalent to at least that of the world's three top billionaires *combined*.

the first time develop the nuclear capability to destroy itself and its world. How long will it take to produce nuclear fusion at the necessary quantity and quality? As yet, a tiny minority are optimistic. But it is always worth remembering the words of Wilbur Wright: 'I confess that in 1901 I said to my brother Orville that man would not fly for fifty years.'

NOTES

PROLOGUE

p. 1 the Sun King: Much as the sun's rays illuminate the earth, the power and glory of Louis XIV were said to illuminate every corner of his realm.

p. 1 'threescore years…': Psalms 90:10.

p. 3 'At the age of eleven…': Bertrand Russell, *Autobiography of Bertrand Russell, Vol. 1: 1872–1914* (Allen & Unwin, 1967), p. 36.

CHAPTER I: REASON AND RATIONALE

p. 5 'years without summer': See Richard Watson, *Cogito, Ergo Sum: The Life of René Descartes* (David R. Godine, 2002), p. 95.

p. 7 'a noise like…': René Descartes, *The Philosophical Writings of Descartes*, trans. J. Cottingham, R. Stoothoff and D. Murdoch, vol. 11: *Meditations* (Cambridge University Press, 1984), pp. 3–62.

p. 8 'Since I desired to devote…' et seq.: René Descartes, *Oeuvres de Descartes*, ed. Charles Adams and Paul Tannery (Vrin, 1987), vol. II, pp. 31–2.

p. 9 'If you cut off…': Ibid., vol. XI, pp. 241–2.

p. 9 'There the soul comes…': Bertrand Russell, *The History of Western Philosophy* (Allen & Unwin, 1979), p. 545.

p. 9 'the most ignorant people…': Letter, 12 January 1646, see Descartes, *Oeuvres de Descartes*, vol. IX, p. 213.

p. 10 'Those long chains…': Descartes, *Philosophical Writings*, trans. and ed. E. Anscombe and P. T. Geach (Open University Press, 1954), pp. 21–2.

p. 10 'served with the Catholic…': See William Guthrie, *Battles of the Thirty Years' War from White Mountain to Nordlingen, 1618–1635* (Greenwood Publishing Group, 2002).

p. 11 'frenzies of despair': Cited in the 'Thirty Years' War' Wikipedia entry, section 'Social and Cultural Impact', accessed 28 December 2021.

p. 11 'The adventures of a simpleton...': See frontispiece of the first edition for the original German.

p. 13 'refused to deal...' et seq.: 'Fabio Chigi', Histouring.com, accessed 31 December 2021.

p. 13 'lodged above a wool...': Peter Wilson, *The Thirty Years' War: Europe's Tragedy* (Harvard University Press, 2009), p. 673.

p. 15 'null, void, invalid...': Kalevi Jaakko Holsti, *Peace and War: Armed Conflicts and International Order, 1648–1989* (Cambridge University Press, 1991), p. 25.

p. 16 'The Westphalian concept took...': See Henry Kissinger, *World Order* (Penguin Books, 2015), p. 27.

p. 17 'the father of...': Galileo is widely recognized as such in many sources. See, for instance, https://www.history.com/topics/inventions/galileo-galilei, accessed 13 June 2023.

p. 18 'When someone says 'I am thinking...': See *The Philosophical Writings of Descartes*, vol. 2, p. 100.

p. 18 'The word "I" is grammatically...': Russell, *The History of Western Philosophy*, p. 550.

p. 19 'Clearly, the brain...': Ralph Lewis, 'How Could Mind Emerge from Mindless Matter?' *Psychology Today*, 28 January 2019.

p. 19 'You're nothing but...': Francis Crick, *The Astonishing Hypothesis* (Simon and Schuster, 1994), cited in Mariano Artigas, *The Mind of the Universe: Understanding Science and Religion* (Templeton, 2000), p. 11.

p. 19 'to divide up each...': See Thomas K. Rehfeldt, 'Descartes and Scientific Method: Four Precepts', Rasch Publications, https://www.rasch.org/rmt/rmt72h.htm.

p. 20 'My geometry is to...': Cited in Watson, *Cogito, Ergo Sum*, p. 198.

p. 21 Copernican 'heresy': In March 1616, the Catholic Church issued a prohibition against the Copernican heliocentric view of the solar system, thus declaring it to be a heresy.

p. 21 'at least twenty addresses' et seq.: See Russell Shorto, *Descartes' Bones* (Random House, 2008), pp. 251–2.

CHAPTER 2: TWO ITALIAN ARTISTS

p. 23 'Italy was less inclined...': See Diarmaid MacCulloch, *Reformation: Europe's House Divided, 1490–1700* (Penguin Books, 2004), pp. 1–5.

p. 24 'Desertion, it seems, was a reality...': Brian Hoefling 'The Thirty Years' War in Italy', *First Things*, 10 August 2014.

p. 24 'By the age of six ...': Andrew Graham-Dixon, *Caravaggio: A Life Sacred and Profane* (W.W. Norton, 2011), extract on https://www.andrewgrahamdixon.com, consulted 20 January 2022.

p. 25 'naked and extremely needy...': See Peter Robb, *M: The Man Who Became Caravaggio* (Picador, 2001), p. 35, citing contemporary sources.

p. 29 'After a fortnight's work...': Floris Claesz van Dijck, a contemporary of Caravaggio, cited in John Gash, *Caravaggio* (Chaucer Press, 2003), p. 13.

p. 30 'Why have you...': Cited in Gilles Lambert, *Caravaggio, 1571–1610* (Taschen, 2000), p. 66.

p. 31 'A lot has been made...': Graham-Dixon, *Caravaggio*, p. 412.

p. 33 'prove' et seq.: See Mary G. Garrard, *Artemisia Gentileschi* (Princeton University Press, 1991), which includes the available transcripts of the trial.

p. 36 'A beautiful woman ...': Cesare Ripa, *Iconologia* (1593), cited in Keith Christiansen and Judith W. Mann, *Orazio and Artemisia Gentileschi* (Yale University Press, 2001), pp. 417–18.

p. 37 'the only woman...': Ward R. Bissell, *Artemisia Gentileschi and the Authority of Art: Critical Reading and Catalogue Raisonné* (Pennsylvania State University Press, 1999).

p. 37 'Artemisia Gentileschi was simply...': Camille Paglia, *Vamps & Tramps: New Essays* (Vintage Books, 1994), p. 115.

CHAPTER 3: SPREAD OF THE SCIENTIFIC REVOLUTION

p. 39 'mathematics is the language...': Galileo Galilei, *Il Saggiatore* (1623). See, for instance, *Discoveries and Opinions of Galileo*, trans. Stillman Drake (Doubleday, 1957), pp. 237–8.

p. 41 'the very exemplar...': Glasgow University Library Special Collections Department, 'Book of the Month: *De motu cordis*', June 2007, https://www.gla. ac.uk/myglasgow/library/files/special/exhibns/month/june2007.html, consulted 28 January 2021.

p. 41 'the greatest contribution...': K. F. Russell, cited ibid.

p. 41 'no wayes different from other toades...': See Geoffrey Keynes, *The Life of William Harvey* (Oxford University Press, 1966), citing Aubrey's *Brief Lives* entry 'William Harvey'. See also Matthew Wood, 'Harvey and the Witch', https://history.rcplondon.ac.uk/blog/harvey-and-witches, 13 April 2018.

p. 41 'He writes philosophy...': D'Arcy Power, *William Harvey: Masters of Medicine* (T. Fisher Unwin, 1897), p. 72.

p. 44 'he might almost...' et seq.: Huygens, *Oeuvres Complètes*, 22 vols (Martinus Nijhoff, 1888–1950), vol. 1, cited in Hugh Aldersey-Williams, *Dutch Light: Christiaan Huygens and the Making of Science in Europe* (Pan Macmillan, 2020), p. 122.

p. 46 'moated chateau...': Margaret Gullan-Whur, *Within Reason: A Life of Spinoza* (Peter Owen, 1998), p. 170.

p. 47 'a system of multiple vortices...': Aldersey-Williams, p. 296.

p. 48 'aaaa…': Cited in the 'Rings of Saturn' Wikipedia entry, giving source as Huygens's letter *De Saturni Luna* (On Saturn's Moon), consulted 10 January 2022.

p. 48 *'Annuto cingitur, tenui…'*: Christiaan Huygens, *Systema Saturnium* (1659), https://library.si.edu/digital-library/book/cristianihugeni00huyga-0, p. 47.

p. 51 'I have been…': Huygens, *Oeuvres Complètes*, vol. 2, pp. 309–10.

p. 51 'so finely adjusted…': Ibid., pp. 270–4.

p. 51 fn 'increased the accuracy…': see 'Huygens invents the Pendulum Clock', Jeremy Norman's HistoryofInformation.com, citing source as 'Pendulum clock' Wikipedia article.

p. 53 'the new Archimedes' fn: Joella Yoder, *Unrolling Time: Christiaan Huygens and the Mathematization of Nature* (Cambridge University Press, 1989), pp. 174–5.

p. 55 'any exceptional Alteration…': Huygens, *Oeuvres Complètes*, vol. 8, pp. 93–5.

p. 55 'because it was mixt…': Cited in Aldersey-Williams, p. 297.

p. 55 'virtuous old men…': Cited in ibid., p. 177.

p. 56 'heretical': Huygens, *Oeuvres Complètes*, vol. 3, p. 431.

p. 56 'to demonstrate the true paths…': Aldersey-Williams, p. 348.

p. 57 'the size of dinner…': Ibid., p. 350.

pp. 57–8 'the first attempt to…': Cited in ibid., p. 394.

p. 58 'convinced himself that…': See 'Christiaan Huygens', *Cambridge Dictionary of Scientists* (Cambridge University Press, 2002).

CHAPTER 4: THE ENGLISH CIVIL WAR AND THOMAS HOBBES

p. 62 fn 'He told me that he…': John Aubrey, *Aubrey's Brief Lives*, trans. Oliver Dick (Penguin Books, 1987), p. 211.

p. 64 *'L'État c'est moi'*: Widely attributed to Louis XIV by many sources. See, for instance, Delaure's *History of Paris* (1834) and Thomas Carlyle's *A History of the French Revolution* (1837). Some now believe these actual words to be apocryphal, but they certainly capture the spirit of his reign.

p. 64 'What is the good…' et seq.: See Plato's *Crito*, a dialogue between Crito and Socrates; *Apology*, which describes Socrates's conversations prior to his death; and *Republic*, his description of the ideal society.

p. 65 'the rule of reason' et seq.: See Aristotle, *Politics*, Book III, Chapter 11.

p. 65 'in parts abhorrent…' et seq.: See Jonathan Barnes, 'Aristotle', in *The Blackwell Encyclopedia of Political Thought* (Wiley, 1998).

p. 65 'His mother fell in labour…' et seq.: See Aubrey, p. 227.

p. 65 'my mother gave birth…': Thomas Hobbes, *Opera Latina*, in William Molesworth (ed.), *Vita Carmine Expressa*, vol. 1 (1679), p. 86.

p. 65 'Hobs stroke…': Aubrey, p. 227.

p. 66 'When he was a Boy...' et seq.: Ibid., p. 228.

p. 67 'brutishness and misery': See George Robertson, 'Thomas Hobbes', *Encyclopaedia Britannica Eleventh Edition*, vol. 13 (Cambridge University Press, 1911), p. 546.

p. 67 'to unite the separate...': Paraphrase of ibid. See 'Thomas Hobbes' Wikipedia entry, consulted 1 January 2022.

p. 68 'It does not seem a...': Cited in Kaitlyn Yanes, 'Descartes and Hobbes', Early Modern Ideas (blog), https://earlymodernideas.wordpress.com/2015/10/03/descartes-and-hobbes-investigating-the-nature-of-the-human-mind/, consulted 1 January 2022.

p. 68 fn 'it is the last feather...': See George Latimer Apperson, *Dictionary of Proverbs* (Wordsworth, 2006), p. 324.

p. 69 'who succeeded in making...' et seq.: Russell, *History of Western Philosophy*, p. 532.

p. 70 'worst of all...': See Thomas Hobbes, *Leviathan*, Chapter XIII, 'Of the Natural Condition of Mankind'.

p. 70 'and is a king...': Job: 41: 33–4.

p. 70 'Every man...': Hobbes, *Elements*.

p. 71 'Hobbes provided some...': Richard Tuck, 'Thomas Hobbes', in *The Blackwell Encyclopedia of Political Thought*, p. 212.

p. 72 'The covenant must confer...' et seq.: Russell, *History of Western Philosophy*, pp. 534–5.

p. 73 'For his last...' et seq.: Aubrey, pp. 234–5.

p. 74 'should be empowered...': *Journal of the House of Commons*, vol. 8 (His Majesty's Stationery Office, 1802), https://www.british-history.ac.uk/commons-jrnl/vol8.

p. 75 'A great leap...': Aubrey, pp. 234–5.

CHAPTER 5: THE NEW WORLD AND THE GOLDEN AGE OF SPAIN

p. 79 'in the seventeenth century...': Alan Rice, 'The Economic Basis of the Slave Trade', http://revealinghistories.org.uk/africa-the-arrival-of-europeans-and-the-transatlantic-slave-trade/articles/the-economic-basis-of-the-slave-trade.html, consulted 14 March 2022.

p. 80 'the first official...': Rodney Coates, 'Law and the Cultural Production of Race and Racialized Systems of Oppression', *American Behavioral Scientist*, vol. 47, no. 3 (2003), pp. 329–51.

p. 81 'an action so hateful': Nathaniel Philbrick, *Mayflower: A Story of Courage, Community and War* (Viking Press, 2006), pp. 253, 345.

p. 82 'women were inherently...': See Elizabeth Reis, *Damned Women: Sinners and Witches in Puritan New England* (Cornell University Press, 1997), p. 2.

p. 83 'the Salem witchcraft was…': George Lincoln Burr (ed.), *Narratives of the Witchcraft Cases, 1648–1706* (Charles Scribner's Sons, 1914), p. 195, note 1.

p. 83 'separation of powers': This phrase does not appear in the original US Constitution, but is generally accepted as a paraphrase of Thomas Jefferson's intention when drafting the First Amendment.

p. 83 'a cautionary tale about…': Paraphrasing Gretchen Adams, *The Specter of Salem: Remembering the Witch Trials in Nineteenth-Century America* (University of Chicago Press, 2008).

p. 83 'collaboration with devils': Wolfgang Behringer, *Witches and Witch-Hunts: A Global History* (Wiley, 2004), p. 19.

p. 83 For the details of Midelfort's findings, see H. C. E. Midelfort, *Witch Hunting in Southwestern Germany 1562–1684: The Social and Intellectual Foundations* (Stanford University Press, 1972).

p. 85 'extravagant, out-sized…': J. H. Elliott, *The Count-Duke of Olivares: The Statesman in an Age of Decline* (Yale University Press, 1986), p. 293.

p. 89 'lost the movement…': Ning Ma, *The Age of Silver: The Rise of the Novel, East and West* (Oxford University Press, 2016), p. 99.

p. 91 'a princess of…': Cervantes, *Don Quixote*, trans. John Ormsby (Smith, Elder and Co., 1885), Part 1, Chapter 13.

CHAPTER 6: TWO TRANSCENDENT ARTISTS

p. 96 'the Michelangelo…': See 'Giorgio Clovio' Wikipedia entry, consulted 1 June 2022, citing Vasari; also *The Catholic Encyclopedia*, which has Vasari describing him as 'the unique' and 'little Michelangelo'.

p. 96 'a rare talent…': Marina Lambraki-Plaka, *From El Greco to Cézanne* (exhibition catalogue) (National Gallery, 1992), p. 42.

p. 97 'inner light': Mary Acton, *Learning to Look at Paintings* (Oxford University Press, 1991), p. 82.

p. 97 'he was a good man…': Lambraki-Plaka, pp. 47–9.

p. 98 'foolish foreigner': Maurizia Tazartes, *El Greco* (El Mundo, 2005), p. 32.

p. 101 'city of the spirit': See, for instance, David Davies, 'The Byzantine Legacy in the Art of El Greco', in Nicos Hadjinicolaou (ed.), *El Greco of Crete* (Iraklion, 1995), pp. 425–45.

p. 102 'Velázquez's supreme…': Hugh Honour and John Fleming, *A World History of Art* (Laurence King, 1982), p. 447.

p. 103 fn 'weakened due to…': See Bernhard Kathan, 'Frühe Gebärmaschinen', https://www.hiddenmuseum.net/fruehe_gebaermaschinen.html, consulted 28 October 2016.

p. 103 'What exactly does it…' et seq.: E. H. Gombrich, *The Story of Art* (Phaidon, 1995), p. 408.

p. 104 'the theology of...' et seq.: Cited in Ronald Sutherland Gower, *Sir Thomas Lawrence* (J. Boussod, Manzi, Joyant, and Co., 1900), p. 83.

p. 104 'Velázquez is sometimes...': Laura Cumming, *The Vanishing Man: In Pursuit of Velázquez* (Chatto & Windus, 2016), p. 23.

p. 105 'perhaps the most important...': 'Francesco Pacheco', in Peter and Linda Murray, *The Penguin Dictionary of Art and Artists* (Penguin, 1997).

p. 106 'breathtaking veracity': Cumming, p. 29.

p. 106 'I would rather be...': Pacheco, cited in Michael Jacobs (ed.), *Lives of Velázquez* (Pallas Athene, 2007).

p. 107 'Puffy, adenoidal, so...': Cumming, p. 31.

p. 109 'it depicted Philip III...': See 'Diego Velázquez' Wikipedia entry, consulted 11 April 2022, citing Dawson W. Carr and Xavier Bray, *Velázquez* (exhibition catalogue) (National Gallery, 2006), p. 31.

p. 109 'hesitant, under-confident...' et seq.: Cumming, p. 33.

p. 111 'are the most remarkable...' et seq.: Ibid., p. 87.

CHAPTER 7: THE MONEY MEN AND THE MARKETS

p. 114 'All the residents of these...' et seq.: Jacob Goldstein, *Money: The True Story of a Made-Up Thing* (Hachette, 2020), p. 47.

p. 118 'Nobles, citizens, farmers...': See Charles Mackay, *Extraordinary Popular Delusions and the Madness of Crowds* (Richard Bentley, 1841), Chapter 3.

p. 119 'A member of the Exchange...': Cited in ibid., p. 49.

p. 120 fn 'irrational exuberance': This phrase first appeared in a speech delivered by Alan Greenspan, Federal Reserve chairman, on 5 December 1996; it would subsequently become the title of a book by Nobel Prize winner Robert J. Shiller (Doubleday, 2000).

p. 120 fn 'worse than the tulip mania...': Nout Wellink, quoted in Alex Hern, 'Bitcoin hype worse than "tulip mania", says Dutch central banker', *Guardian*, 4 December 2013.

p. 121 'Stockbrokers were not...': A. E. W. Mason, *The Royal Exchange: A Note on the Occasion of the Bicentenary of the Royal Exchange Assurance* (Royal Exchange, 1920), p. 11.

p. 121 'The best and most agreeable...': See 'Stockbroker' Wikipedia entry, consulted 27 April 2022, citing Joseph de la Vega, *Confusion of Confusions* (1688).

p. 121 'George, Earl of Cumberland...': 'Early European Settlements', *Imperial Gazetteer of India*, vol. 2 (1908), p. 454.

p. 124 'the most remarkable...' et seq.: Taken from the entry for Sir William Petty in *Aubrey's Brief Lives*, as well as *The Diary of John Evelyn*. Both Aubrey and Evelyn knew Petty, and were his contemporaries as early Fellows of the Royal Society.

p. 125 'She was not aware...': See Laura Gowing, *Common Bodies: Women, Touch and Power in Seventeenth-Century England* (Yale University Press, 2003); Laura Gowing, 'Anne Greene', in *Oxford Dictionary of National Biography* (Oxford University Press, 2020); and 'Anne Greene' Wikipedia entry, consulted 29 April 2022.

p. 125 'At her own request...': Paraphrasing contemporary pamphlets: Richard Watkins, *Newes from the Dead* (1651) and W. Burdet, *A Wonder of Wonders* (1651). See also 'Anne Greene' Wikipedia entry.

p. 125 'heating odoriferous Clyster...': Watkins, pp. 3–5.

p. 127 'from Mount Mangorton...': Aubrey, p. 244.

p. 127 'ruthless' et seq.: John Gibney, 'Sir Hierome Sankey (sic)', in *The Dictionary of Irish Biography* (online), consulted 2 May 2022.

p. 127 'mathematics is the language...': Galileo, *Il Saggiatore*, pp. 237–8.

p. 128 'the true father...': An increasing number of sources are coming round to this point of view. See, for instance, Satyajit Mishra, 'Sir William Petty: Inventor of Economics', Qrius (website), consulted 2 May 2022.

p. 128 'To express myself in Terms...' et seq.: See the preamble to Petty's report on his survey of Ireland, initially known as the *Down Survey* (1655–6), and published twenty years later as *Hiberniae Delineatio*. A facsimile edition was published in 1970 in Dublin. See also Petty's *Essays in Political Arithmetick and Political Survey or Anatomy of Ireland* (1672).

p. 131 'contemporaries described him...': See 'Sir William Petty' Wikipedia entry, consulted 28 June 2022.

CHAPTER 8: TWO ARTISTS OF THE DUTCH GOLDEN AGE

p. 135 'all by him': From Jan's original tombstone in St Peter's Church, Cologne. See 'Jan Rubens', in P. C. Molhuysen et al. (eds), *Nieuw Nederlandsch Biografisch Woordenboek*, 10 vols (A. W. Sijthoff, 1911–37).

p. 137 'the two serpents': Cited in Vincenzo Farinella, *Vatican Museums, Classical Art* (Monumenti, 1985), p. 18.

p. 137 'the prototypical icon...': Nigel Spivey, *Enduring Creation: Art, Pain, and Fortitude* (University of California Press, 2001), p. 25.

p. 140 'exchanged ideas with...': Gombrich, p. 420.

p. 142 'deserved to be called Apelles...': Taken from Rubens's gravestone, cited in Michael Robinson, *Rubens* (Prestel, 2020), p. 42.

p. 143 fn 'Fewer things are more...': See Percy Gardner, 'Apelles', in *Encyclopaedia Britannica Eleventh Edition*.

p. 146 'His mind was steeped...' et seq.: Kenneth Clark, *Civilisation* (John Murray, 1971), p. 203.

p. 147 'The mood is neither...': Ibid., p. 34.

p. 147 'you were silly like us': See W. H. Auden, 'In Memory of W. B. Yeats', https://poets.org/poem/memory-w-b-yeats.

p. 147 'All has gone...': John Berger, *Ways of Seeing* (Penguin, 1972), p. 112.

p. 148 'The group portrait...': Michael Kitson, *Rembrandt: Colour Library* (Phaidon, 1992), p. 66.

CHAPTER 9: THE SUN KING AND VERSAILLES

p. 154 fn *'Après moi...'*: There are several sources for this widely repeated remark. See, for instance, Michael Mould, *The Routledge Dictionary of Cultural References in Modern French* (Routledge, 2011), p. 43.

p. 154 'busy without cease...': Pierre Rosenberg and Renaud Temperini, *Poussin: Je n'ai rien négligé* (Gallimard, 1994), p. 14.

p. 155 'His work predominantly...': See https://gallery.lulja.com/artist/Nicolas_Poussin, consulted 27 May 2022.

p. 156 'Imagine how Poussin entirely...': Quote by Cézanne, 1907.

p. 160–1 Scene from *Le Bourgeois Gentilhomme* (1670) taken from Act II, Scene IV.

p. 161 'the language of Molière': See, for instance, Colin Randall, 'France looks to the law to save the language of Molière', *Daily Telegraph*, 24 October 2004.

p. 161 'in comparison to...' et seq.: Martha Bellinger, *A Short History of the Drama* (H. Holt, 1927), pp. 178–81.

p. 162 'examples of neo-classical...': D. G. Muller, 'Phedre', *Theatre Journal*, vol. 51, no. 3 (1999), pp. 327–31.

p. 164 'prince of...': Maximilien Titon du Tillet, *Le Parnasse François* (J. B. Coignard, 1732), pp. 393–401.

CHAPTER 10: ENGLAND COMES OF AGE

p. 169 'the best of...': Cited in Christopher Brown, *Anthony Van Dyck 1599–1641* (exhibition catalogue) (Royal Academy of the Arts, 1999).

p. 170 'the standard iconography...': See 'Anthony van Dyck' Wikipedia entry, which cites a wide range of informed art experts, consulted 12 July 2022.

p. 171 'the portrait of...': Lionel Cust, *The Burlington Magazine for Connoisseurs*, vol. 14, no. 72 (1909), pp. 337–41.

p. 171 'virtually a production...': Lionel Henry Cust, 'Van Dyck, Anthony', in *Oxford Dictionary of National Biography*, vol. 58 (1899).

p. 172 'His complexion exceeding...' et seq.: Aubrey, pp. 270–5.

p. 172 'a lofty and steady...': Samuel Johnson, *Lives of the Most Eminent English Poets*, vol. 1 (F. C. & J. Rivington and others, 1820).

p. 172 'the greatest English author': See Iain McCalman et al. (eds), *An Oxford Companion to the Romantic Age: British Culture, 1776–1832* (Oxford University Press, 2001), p. 605.

p. 173 'Love virtue, she alone...': John Milton, *Comus*, Scene 3, Epilogue.

p. 173 'a masque in honour...' et seq.: See *'Comus* (Milton)' Wikipedia entry, which draws on a number of authoritative sources, ranging from *Encyclopaedia Britannica* to *The New Groves Dictionary of Music*, consulted 14 July 2022.

p. 173 'Licence they mean...': Cited in Paul A. Rahe *Against Throne and Altar* (Cambridge University Press, 2008), pp. 104–38.

p. 173 'which I have always admired...' et seq.: John Milton, *Complete Prose Works*, 8 vols, gen. ed. Don M. Wolfe, vol. IV (Yale University Press, 1959), Part 1, pp. 615–17.

p. 173 'sad tidings...': Ibid., pp. 618–19.

p. 174 'acrimonious and surly...': Arthur Murphy, 'An Essay on the Life and Genius of Samuel Johnson L.L. D.', in *The Works of Samuel Johnson* (G. Dearborn, 1837).

p. 175 'And when Night...': This and all subsequent quotes are taken from John Milton, *Paradise Lost* (Penguin, 2000), which follows the revised version.

p. 176 'Milton portrays Adam...' et seq.: See *'Paradise Lost'* Wikipedia entry, consulted 14 July 2022, which draws on a wide range of authoritative and critical sources, particularly John Broadbent, *Paradise Lost: Introduction* (Cambridge University Press, 1972).

p. 177 'His widowe assures...' et seq.: Aubrey, p. 274.

p. 178 'License they mean...': John Milton, Sonnet 12: 'I did but prompt the age to quit their clogs', line 11.

p. 178 'pretty witty...': Ibid., p. 480n.

p. 179 'there was more clarity...': David Murray, 'The Puritan Passion for Philosophy and Science', *The Aquila Report*, 8 December 2017, consulted 19 July 2022.

p. 179 'well enough': See 'John Hooke' Wikipedia entry, which cites Aubrey (who knew him), as well as his earliest biographer, Richard Waller, and Hooke's own diary; consulted 9 July 2022.

p. 180 'in person but despicable...': Robert Hooke, *The Posthumous Works of Robert Hooke, M.D. S.R.S.*, ed. Richard Waller (Smith and Walford, 1705).

p. 180 'England's Leonardo': Alan Chapman, 'England's Leonardo: Robert Hooke (1635–1703), and the art of experiment in Restoration England', *Proceedings of the Royal Institution of Great Britain*, vol. 67, pp. 239–75; archived from the original on 6 March 2011.

p. 181 'I will explain…' et seq.: Cited in Dugald Stewart, *Elements of the Philosophy of the Human Mind*, vol. 2 (T. & T. Clark, 1877), Chapter 2, section 4.2, pp. 304 ff.

p. 183 'the most ingenious…': Pepys, *Diary*, entry for 21 January 1665.

p. 183 'the most powerful maritime…': See 'Anglo-Dutch Wars' Wikipedia entry, which draws on such authorities as James Rees Jones, *The Anglo-Dutch Wars of the Seventeenth Century* (Longman, 1996).

p. 185 'against multiplying…': This statute dated from the reign of Henry IV. See also 'Robert Boyle' in *Encyclopedia Britannica Eleventh Edition*.

p. 185 'where Mr Hooke read …': Wikisource free online version of *The Diary of Samuel Pepys*, entry 1 March 1665, https://en.wikisource.org/wiki/Diary_of_Samuel_Pepys, consulted 18 July 2022.

p. 186 fn 'wooden, northern…': Cited in Adrian Tinniswood, *By Permission of Heaven: The Story of the Great Fire of London* (Jonathan Cape, 2003), p. 3.

p. 187 'This day, much against my Will…' et seq.: Pepys, *Diary*, entries for 17 June 1665, 30 and 31 January 1666.

p. 188 'a woman could…': Ibid., p. 44.

p. 188 'a lamentable fire…' et seq.: Pepys, *Diary*, entry for 2 September 1666.

p. 188 'now a sad ruine': William Benham, *Old St. Paul's Cathedral* (Seeley and Co., 1902), pp. 74–5.

p. 189 'the most humiliating…': Charles Ralph Boxer, *The Anglo-Dutch Wars of the 17th Century, 1652–1674* (HM Stationery Office, 1974), p. 39.

p. 189 'Gresham College now became…': Lisa Jardine, *The Curious Life of Robert Hooke* (Harper Perennial, 2004), p. 139.

p. 189 'Without, within, below…': James Wright, *The Choire* (1693), cited in Xavier Baron (ed.), *London 1066–1914: Literary Sources and Documents* (Helm Information, 1997), pp. 117–19.

CHAPTER II: A QUIET CITY IN SOUTH HOLLAND

p. 191 *'Mon Dieu, ayez pitié…'*: For the full story of these events, see Lisa Jardine, *The Awful End of William the Silent: The First Assassination of a Head of State with a Handgun* (HarperCollins, 2005).

p. 192 *'zoo den man was…'*: See Jonathan Janson, 'Vermeer: The Man and the Painter', http://www.essentialvermeer.com/vermeer_the_man.html, consulted 26 July 2022.

p. 194 'typical of Vermeer's subtle…': Maurizia Tazartes, *Vermeer* (Prestel, 2007), p. 54.

p. 194 'his paintings are…': Gombrich, p. 453.

p. 195 'first of all…' et seq.: Clark, pp. 209–10.

p. 196 *'redeloos, radeloos…'*: See *'Rampjaar'* Wikipedia entry, citing *Stichting Platform Rampjaarherdenking*, consulted 28 July 2022.

p. 197 'During the ruinous war…': See Jonathan Janson, 'Vermeer's Life and Art (part four)', http://www.essentialvermeer.com/vermeer%27s_life_04.html, consulted 26 July 2022.

p. 201 'Great fleas have little fleas…': Variously attributed to Swift and Augustus De Morgan in his *Budget of Paradoxes* (1872).

p. 202 'Leeuwenhoek was the first…': Entry 192, ' Leeuwenhoek', in *Asimov's Biographical Encyclopedia of Science and Technology* (Pan Books, 1975).

p. 204 'brimming over with…' et seq.: Joseph Schumpeter, *History of Economic Analysis* (Routledge, 1954), p. 283.

p. 206 'The chemists are a strange class…': See Johann Becher, *Physica Subterranea* (1669).

p. 207 'his vigor and…': Ibid., note 10.

CHAPTER 12: EXPLORATION

p. 210 'the great land…': T. D. Mutch, *The First Discovery of Australia* (Royal Australian Historical Society, 1942), pp. 17 ff.

p. 214 'This made them…': James H. Leavesley, 'The "Batavia", an apothecary, his mutiny and its vengeance', *Vesalius*, vol. 11, no. 2 (2003), pp. 22–4.

p. 217 'In the evening…': See 'Abel Tasman' Wikipedia entry, retrieved 23 September 2022.

p. 219 'Fresh-Water Sea' et seq.: J. B. Mansfield (ed.), *History of the Great Lakes*, vol. 1 (J. H. Beers and Co, 1899), Chapter 6, https://www.maritimehistoryofthegreatlakes.ca/GreatLakes/Documents/HGL/default.asp?ID=c006, consulted 29 September 2022.

p. 219 'His garb was the customary…': Ibid.

CHAPTER 13: A COURTLY INTERLUDE

p. 226 'sonorous, clear, sweet…' et seq.: Baldassare Castiglione, *The Book of the Courtier* (Dover, 2003), p. 45.

p. 232 'The Director of Music…': See Denis Stevens (ed.), *The Letters of Claudio Monteverdi* (Oxford University Press, 1995), pp. 431–2.

p. 232 'he will be sighed…': Ibid., p. 434.

p. 234 'circumstantial evidence…' et seq.: Roger Freitas, 'The Eroticism of Emasculation: Confronting the Baroque Body of the Castrato', *The Journal of Musicology*, vol. 20, no. 2 (2003), pp. 196–249.

p. 236 'Among his bequest…': See Aurora von Goeth, 'Atto Melani, the Sun King's Spying Opera Singer', https://partylike1660.com/atto-melani-the-sun-kings-spying-opera-singer/, consulted 9 September 2022.

p. 237 'prince of...': Maximilien Titon du Tillet, *Le Parnasse François* (J. B. Coignard fils, 1732), pp. 393–401.

p. 237 *'écuyer...'*: Jérôme de La Gorce, *Jean-Baptiste Lully* (Fayard, 2002), pp. 28–9, 115–19.

p. 238 'one of the greatest...': See 'Anne Marie Louise d'Orléans, Duchess of Montpensier' Wikipedia entry, consulted 12.9.2022, citing Nancy Nichols Barker, *Brother to the Sun King: Philippe, Duke of Orléans* (John Hopkins University Press, 1989).

p. 238 'The king's enthusiasm...': La Gorce, pp. 309–13, 339–40.

p. 239 'the inventor...': Titon du Tillet, pp. 393–401.

p. 241 'Let not poor Nelly...': Charles Beauclerk, *Nell Gwyn: Mistress to a King* (Atlantic Monthly Press, 2005), pp. 317, 358.

p. 242 'cautious and prudent...': See 'John Dryden' Wikipedia entry, consulted 15 September 2022.

p. 244 'one of the wittiest...': Ruth Stephan, 'Christina, Queen of Sweden', *Encyclopaedia Britannica* (online), consulted 27 September 2022.

p. 245 'an insurmountable distaste...': Queen Christina, *Maxims of a Queen*, ed. and trans. Una Burch (Bodley Head, 1907), p. 33.

p. 245 'Jezebel': See 'The Case of Arnold Johan Messenius', in Oskar Garstein, *Rome and the Counter-Reformation in Scandinavia: The Age of Gustavus Adolphus and Queen Christina of Sweden, 1622–1656* (Brill, 1992), pp. 285–95.

p. 246 'a queen without a...': Widely cited. See, for instance, Agnes Crawford, 'The Minerva of the North: Queen Christina of Sweden and Rome', talk delivered 20 June 2022, consulted 28 September 2022.

p. 247 'the visual is related': See Sarah Finley, 'Embodied Sound and Female Voice in Sor Juana Inés de la Cruz's Canon: romance 8 and El divino Narciso', *Revista de Estudios Hispánicos*, vol. 50, no. 1 (2016), pp. 191–216.

p. 248 'to have no fixed...': 'Sor Juana Inés de la Cruz', Biography.com, consulted 15 April 2016.

p. 249 'Mexican da Vinci': See 'Carlos de Sigüenza y Góngora' Wikipedia entry, consulted 19 September 2022.

p. 249 'I don't study to...': Widely cited, see for instance AZ Quotes, consulted 25 August 2023.

p. 250 'her love poems...': *Sor Juana's Love Poems*, trans. Joan Larkin and Jaime Manrique (University of Wisconsin Press, 2003), pp. 9–11.

p. 250 'The very distressing...': Preamble, Juana Inés de la Cruz, Sonnet 17.

p. 250 'the most important...': Paraphrasing Octavio Paz, *Sor Juana, Or, The Traps of Faith* (Harvard University Press, 1988).

CHAPTER 14: SPINOZA AND LOCKE

p. 251 'Logical inference was his...': Gullan-Whur, p. xiii.

p. 251 'is set forth in the style...': Russell, *History of Western Philosophy*, p. 555.

p. 252 'I believe in Spinoza's God...': Albert Einstein, letter to Rabbi Herbert Goldstein, 25 April 1929.

p. 252 'warehouse on the Prinsengracht...': Gullan-Whur, p. 2.

p. 252 'Ritch merchants...': Richard Temple (ed.), *The Travels of Peter Mundy in Europe and Asia*, vol. 3 (Hakluyt Society, 1914), p. 70.

p. 254 'He was cursed...': Russell, *History of Western Philosophy*, p. 552.

p. 255 'Catholic with Catholics...': Cited in Gullan-Whur, p. 59, giving source as *De Nazelle Mémoires du Temps de Louis XIV* (1680), p. 101.

p. 255 'The stronger the emotion...' et seq.: Spinoza, *Ethics*, Part 2.

p. 256 'like a sick...' et seq.: Spinoza, *Treatise on the Correction of Understanding* (1661).

p. 257 'in accordance with...': Cited in Ruth Lydia Shaw, 'Spinoza', in J. O. Urmson and Jonathan Ree (eds), *The Concise Encyclopedia of Western Philosophy and Philosophers* (Hutchinson, 1975), p. 273.

p. 257 'A point is that which...' et seq.: See Euclid, *Elements*, trans. John Carey, p. 2.

p. 257 'A thing which is its own...' et seq.: See many sources, most readily available on the Project Gutenberg, including Spinoza, *Ethics*, trans. R. H. M. Elwes, and *The Ethics of Spinoza* (Carol Publishing Group, 1995).

p. 259 'mind and body are one...': Spinoza, *Ethics*, part 2.

p. 260 'So if someone says...' et seq.: Ibid.

p. 260 'Is the unified theory...': Stephen Hawking, *A Brief History of Time* (Random House, 1998), p. 190.

p. 261 'With unprecedented butchery...' et seq.: See Gullan-Whur, p. 248, citing several sources including a letter by Christiaan Huygens's younger brother Lodewijk dated 4 September 1672, and a note by Leibniz, *De Careil I lxiv.*

p. 261 'the noblest and most lovable...': Russell, *History of Western Philosophy*, p. 552.

p. 261 'an intellectually supercilious...': Gullan-Whur, p. xiii.

p. 266 'Old Testament history...' et seq.: see Christopher Hill, *The English Bible and the Seventeenth-Century Revolution* (Allen Lane, 1993), p. 20.

p. 266 'kingly power' et seq.: Russell, *History of Western Philosophy*, p. 597.

p. 267 'state of nature...' et seq.: Paraphrasing an article on John Locke by the twentieth-century English philosopher Roger Woolhouse in *The Oxford Companion to Philosophy* (Oxford University Press, 1995), p. 293 – referring to, and citing, Locke's second *Treatise of Government*, sections 6 and 89.

p. 267 'My purpose [is] to enquire...' et seq.: Locke, *Essay Concerning Human Understanding*, Book II, Chapter 1, section 2.

p. 268 'Empiricism about ideas is...': Woolhouse, *Oxford Companion*, p. 494, paraphrasing Locke, Book IV, Chapter 19, section 14.

p. 268 'solidity, extension...': Locke, Book II, Chapter 8.

p. 268 'even his errors were...' et seq.: Russell, *History of Western Philosophy*, pp. 585–6.

CHAPTER 15: THE SURVIVAL AND SPREAD OF THE CONTINENT OF REASON

p. 272 'I will make myself...': Letter from Sultan Mehmed IV to Holy Roman Emperor Leopold I, dated February 1683, cited by Kim Seabrook in 'Siege of Vienna (1683): Enemy at the Gates', 8 March 2021, https://www.prisonersofeternity.com/blog/siege-of-vienna-1683-enemy-at-the-gates/.

p. 272 'the long struggle...': Ibid, Kim Seabrook.

p. 272 'wholly venal...': Orlon Merlijn, 'Amost Agreeable and Pleasant Creature? Merzifonlu Kara Mustafa Paşa in the Correspondence of Justinus Colyer (1668-1682)', *Oriente Moderno*, vol. 83, no. 3 (2003), pp. 649–69, consulted 28 August 2021.

p. 274 'We had a simple...': George Michaelowski, emissary of the imperial forces, cited 'Siege of Vienna (1683)'.

p. 274 'the greatest cavalry...': Ibid.

p. 275 'It was like...' et seq.: Cited ibid.

p. 275 'When the Champions ...' et seq.: 'Letter from King Sobieski to his Wife', University of Gdansk, Department of Cultural Studies, Faculty of Philology, consulted 4 August 2011.

p. 281 'window to Europe': Traditional saying, widely attributed in Russian textbooks to Peter the Great.

p. 281 'old, wooden': Traditional saying. See, for instance, 'Charms of Wooden Moscow', Carusel (blog), 3 May 2020.

CHAPTER 16: NEW REALITIES

p. 286 'would scarcely occur to...': Will and Ariel Durant, *The Story of Civilization VIII: The Age of Louis XIV* (Simon & Schuster, 1980), Chapter II, subsection 4.1, p. 56.

p. 286 'calculating machine': See Georges Ifrah, *The Computer and the Information Revolution*, trans. E. F. Harding (Harvill, 2000), pp. 122–3.

p. 288 'The heart has its reasons...': Blaise Pascal, *Pensées*, (L. Brunschvicg, 1909), section 4, no. 277.

p. 289 'my honoured and worthy...' et seq.: see Aubrey, pp. 200–1.

p. 290 'Aged: 13....': 22–9 July 1679, available online, consulted 22 November 2022.

p. 290 'shop arithmetic': C. C. Hyde, 'John Graunt', in *Statisticians of the Centuries*, ed. C. C. Hyde and E. Seneta (Springer, 2001).

p. 290 'Graunt took these...': See Paul Strathern, *Dr Strangelove's Game* (Penguin, 2001), pp. 27–8, which also contains other citations and details I have used.

p. 291 'based on the assumption...' et seq.: see *Statisticians of the Centuries*, p. 15.

p. 291 'If they find...': D. V. Glass, M. E. Ogborn et al., 'John Graunt and his Natural and Political Observation', *Proceedings of the Royal Society of London, Series B: Biological Sciences*, vol. 159, no. 974, pp. 2–37.

p. 292 'descended into...': Ibid.

p. 293 fn 'Drunk for a penny...': Contemporary notices advertising gin palaces – see, for instance, Ellen Castelow, 'Mother's Ruin', https://www.historic-uk.com/CultureUK/Mothers-Ruin/, consulted 23 November 2022.

p. 293 Mandeville as physician, etc.: Many of the details of Mandeville's life are taken from the 'John Mandeville' entry in *The New Palgrave Dictionary of Economics* (Palgrave, 1987).

p. 293 'What we call Evil...' et seq.: see Richard M. Ebeling, 'The Fable of the Bees tells the Story of Society'.

p. 301 'the most monstrous...': 'Louis Sala-Molins: Le Code Noir ou le calvaire de Canaan', archive.wikiwix.com, consulted 31 May 2022.

CHAPTER 17: LOGIC PERSONIFIED

p. 305 'On the one hand, Leibniz...': Matthew Stewart, *The Courtier and The Heretic: Leibniz, Spinoza, and the Fate of God in the Modern World* (Yale University Press, 2005), pp. 40–1.

p. 305 'very different things...': Russell, *History of Western Philosophy*, p. 563.

p. 305 'baffled by their bizarre...' et seq.: Stewart, p. 48.

p. 306 fn 'Napoleon saw Egypt as...': See Paul Strathern, *Napoleon in Egypt* (Jonathan Cape, 2007), in particular p. 427.

p. 306 'the most knowledgeable...': Cited in Stewart, p. 92.

p. 312 'pre-established harmony': Urmson and Ree, p. 154.

p. 313 'the best of all...': Russell, *History of Western Philosophy*, p. 563; also see Hernán D. Caro, *The Best of All Possible Worlds? Leibniz's Philosophical Optimism and Its Critics 1710–1755*, Brill's Studies in Intellectual History, vol. 322 (Brill, 2020).

CHAPTER 18: ON THE SHOULDERS OF GIANTS

p. 317 'If I have seen...': Newton, letter to Robert Hooke, dated as 5 February 1675.

p. 318 'a wild, extravagant...' et seq.: Cited in Richard Westfall, *Never at Rest: A Biography of Newton* (Cambridge University Press, 1983), p. 47. This is the exhaustive and standard biography, from which I have drawn much material.

p. 318 fn 'later witnessed the...': Ibid., p. 51.

p. 318 'Motley, mercenary armies...': James Gleick, *Isaac Newton* (Fourth Estate, 2003), p. 10.

p. 319 'There is no room for me...': Cited in ibid., p. 14.

p. 321 'universal vortex': See, for instance, Huygens's *Oeuvres Complètes*, vol. 1, pp. 552–3, cited in Aldersey-Williams, p. 296.

p. 321 'He purchased a lock...' et seq.: Westfall, p. 66.

p. 322 'subtle matter': Aldersey-Williams, p. 296.

p. 322 'the nearly blank...': Gleick, p. 34, citing Add MS 4004.

p. 323 'And what are these fluxions...': George Berkeley, *The Analyst* (J. Tonson, 1734), p. 59.

p. 325 'An object remains at rest...': These laws appear in several forms in different sources. The original, in the language of the period, can be found in Newton, *Principia Mathematica*, vol. 2 (Cambridge, 1713), pp. 332–3.

p. 327 'By thinking on it continually...': There are many sources (and varied versions) of this quote. See, for instance, Westfall, p. 105 and n. 1, who traces it to Voltaire. Others, and other versions, tend to be less sceptical.

p. 329 'the man who had robbed...': Westfall, p. 53n.

p. 329 fn 'I don't understand that second...': Ron Edge, 'Remembrances of Dirac', *Physics Today*, vol. 5, no. 5 (2010), p. 59.

p. 330 'request for a window...': There are several reputable sources for this anecdote. See, for instance, the '9 Things You May Not Know about Isaac Newton' article on History.com, by Professor Elizabeth Nix of the University of Baltimore, consulted 21 December 2022.

p. 331 'endeavoured to embroil...': Frank E. Manuel, *A Portrait of Isaac Newton* (Harvard University Press, 1968), p. 219.

p. 331 fn 'I have had that confirmed...': See, for example, Voltaire, *Letters on England* (Cassell & Co., 1894), p. 100. On this matter, Westfall remains ambivalent, see p. 596 et seq.

p. 333 'He accused the New Warden...': Thomas Levenson, *Newton and the Counterfeiter* (Faber & Faber, 2009), p. xii.

p. 334 Calculus Wars: For the full details of this preposterous conflict, see Jason Bardi, *The Calculus Wars: Newton, Leibniz, and the Greatest Mathematical Clash of All Time* (Basic Books, 2007).

EPILOGUE

p. 338 'His countrymen honoured him…': Voltaire, *Letters Concerning the English Nation*, cited in *The Portable Enlightenment Reader*, ed. Isaac Kramnick (Penguin, 1995), p. 56.

p. 342 'I confess that in 1901…': Originally recorded in the meticulous personal notebooks and diaries kept by Wilbur Wright (1900–1901), These were originally written on the reverse side of wallpaper, and can be seen at the Franklin Institute, Philadelphia. The entire text is freely available online at Project Gutenberg.

ACKNOWLEDGEMENTS

During my research, writing, rewriting and editing of *Dark Brilliance* I have received help, guidance, assistance and useful tips from a wide variety of sources. Here are the main ones, who have each played a vital role in the writing of this work. Above all I wish to thank my *agent extraordinaire*, Julian Alexander of The Soho Agency, who as usual played a major role in making this project happen, and guiding it through any difficulties. Also a special thanks to my editor at Atlantic Books, James Nightingale, who has provided many suggestions and insights which played a significant role in improving my manuscript. Painstaking and astonishingly knowledgeable work and editorial guidance was provided once again by Gemma Wain, whose informative advice and suggestions were invaluable. I have consulted sources in many record offices and libraries, and also received help and advice from a number of academic experts. Any mistakes in the text are entirely my own. Much of my research has been done at the London Library and the British Library. As ever, in the latter my particular thanks go to the kind and friendly staff of Humanities 2 Reading Room. As so often before, my partner Amanda Bush has supplied several suggestions, and pointed out my errors. I also received encouragement and hospitality from my family, especially Oona and Matthias – as well as Tristan, who provided a useful stimulus (except with the title), and Julian, whose opinions are always worth listening to. This work is dedicated to my sister Anne.

P.S.

ILLUSTRATIONS

SECTION ONE

René Descartes, French philosopher, mathematician, and writer (*GL Archive/ Alamy Stock Photo*)

Peter the Great, Tsar of Russia (1672–1725) (1698) by Godfrey Kneller (*Wikimedia Commons*)

Dispute of Queen Cristina Vasa and Rene Descartes (*World History Archive/ Alamy Stock Photo*)

Conversion on the Way to Damascus (c. 1600) by Caravaggio (*Wikimedia Commons*)

The Fortune Teller (c. 1595–8) by Caravaggio (*Wikimedia Commons*)

Judith Slaying Holofernes (Florence) (c. 1620) by Artemisia Gentileschi (*Wikimedia Commons*)

Self-Portrait as Allegory of Painting (c. 1638–9) by Artemisia Gentileschi (*Wikimedia Commons*)

Christiaan Huygens, the astronomer (1671) by Caspar Netscher (*Wikimedia Commons*)

Side view of Huygens' clock showing the pendulum mechanism 1600s (*North Wind Picture Archives/Alamy Stock Photo*)

Cromwell in the Battle of Naseby in 1645 (1851) by Charles Landseer (*Wikimedia Commons*)

Examination of a Witch (1853) by T. H. Matteson (*Wikimedia Commons*)

Portrait of the Count-Duke of Olivares (1624) by Diego Velázquez (*Wikimedia Commons*)

Las Meninas (1656) by Diego Velázquez (*Wikimedia Commons*)

Anonymous seventeenth-century watercolour of the *Semper Augustus* (*Wikimedia Commons*)

Courtyard of the Exchange in Amsterdam (1653) by Emmanuel de Witte (*Wikimedia Commons*)

The Burial of the Count of Orgaz (c. 1586–8) by El Greco (*Wikimedia Commons*)

SECTION TWO

Portrait of the Artist (1623) by Peter Paul Rubens (*Wikimedia Commons*)

Self Portrait (1669) by Rembrandt Van Rijn (*Wikimedia Commons*)

The Anatomy Lesson of Dr. Nicolaes Tulp (1632) by Rembrandt van Rijn (*Wikimedia Commons*)

The Abduction of the Sabine Women (1634–1635) by Nicolas Poussin (*Wikimedia Commons*)

Charles I in Three Positions (1635) by Anthony van Dyck (*Wikimedia Commons*)

Illustration of a needle-point under a microscope from Robert Hooke's *Micrographia* (*Wellcome Collection/Wikimedia Commons/CC-BY 4.0*)

Several sorts of hair under a microscope from Robert Hooke's *Micrographia* (*Wellcome Collection/Wikimedia Commons/CC-BY 4.0*)

The Great Fire of London (1675) by an anonymous artist (*Wikimedia Commons*)

One Antonie van Leeuwenhoek's microscopes (*The Granger Collection/Alamy Stock Photo*)

Portrait of Sir Isaac Newton (1689) by Godfrey Kneller (*Wikimedia Commons*)

Replica of the seventeenth-century Dutch ship the *Duyfken* in the parade of sail on the Derwent River in Tasmania (*Rob Walls/Alamy Stock Photo*)

Sor Juana Inés de la Cruz (1772) (*The Picture Art Collection/Alamy Stock Photo*)

Molière (c. 1658) by Pierre Mignard I (*Wikimedia Commons*)

Colbert Presenting The Members Of The Royal Academy Of Sciences To Louis XIV In 1667 (c. 1680) by Henri Testelin (*Fine Art Images/Heritage Images/Getty Images*)

A Portrait of a Man in Front of a Sculpture (1666) attb. to Barend Graat (*Wikimedia Commons*)

Portrait of Gottfried Leibniz (1646–1716), German philosopher (c. 1695) by Christoph Bernhard Francke (*Wikimedia Commons*)

Portrait of Christina of Sweden (1661) by Abraham Wuchters (*Skokloster Castle/ Wikimedia Sverige/Samuel Uhrdin/Wikimedia Commons*)

Claudio Monteverdi (c. 1630) by Bernardo Strozzi (*Wikimedia Commons*)

Portrait of a Mathematician (c. 1680) by Mary Beale (*Wikimedia Commons*)

John Locke (n.d.) by John Greenhill (*Wikimedia Commons*)

Engraving of Halley's Comet of 1682 over Augsburg (*Science History Images/ Alamy Stock Photo*)

The Murder of the De Witt Brothers (c. 1672) by Pieter Fris (*Wikimedia Commons*)

Slave Trade (Execrable Human Traffick, or The Affectionate Slaves (c. 1788) by George Morland (*National Museum of African American History and Culture/CC0*)

INDEX

Académie des Sciences, Paris, 52, 55, 179, 300, 306

Accademia dei Lincei, Italy, 17

Adams, Gretchen, 83

Addison, Joseph, 293

Adoration of the Magi (Rubens), 139, 144n

Aeneid (Virgil), 240

Aesop (Velázquez), 111n

Albert VII, Archduke of Austria, 137, 139–40

Alcázar Palace, Madrid, 108–9

alchemy, 184–5, 205–7, 327

Alexander the Great (Racine), 163

Alexander VII, Pope, 13, 236, 246

Alexei Petrovich, Russian Tsarevich, 280

Allegory of Inclination (Gentileschi), 35–6

Allegory of the Holy League (El Greco), 99

Americas, *see* New World

Amsterdam, Netherlands, 115, 145–6, 193n, 197

Amsterdam Exchange Bank (*Wisselbank*), 146

Amsterdam Stock Exchange, 115–19

Anatomy Lesson of Dr Nicolaes Tulp, The (Rembrandt), 144–5

Ancient Greeks, 283–4

Anglo-Dutch Wars, 262

First (1652–4), 122

Second (1665–7), 122, 189

Third (1672–4), 197n

Anna of Saxony, 135

Anne of Austria, 152–3

Antonio Sebastián Álvarez de Toledo y Salazar, 2nd Marquess of Mancera, 249

Antwerp, Belgium, 135, 139–41

Apelles of Kos, 143n

Archimedes, 53n

Aretino, Pietro, 137

Aristotle, x, 17, 20, 65, 123, 162, 253–4, 263, 320–22

Armstrong, Neil, 340

Art of Painting, The (Pacheco), 105

Artusi, Giovanni, 231

Ashley Cooper, Anthony, 1st Earl of Shaftesbury, x, 265

Asimov, Isaac, 202

assientos, 78–9

Astor, John Jacob, 221n
Astronomer, The (Vermeer), 199–200
astronomy, 47–50, 56–8, 181–2,
    185–6, 321, 326, 330
Aubrey, John, x, 62n, 66, 73, 124, 127,
    172, 174, 177, 289
Australia, 214
    discovery of, 210–12, 216, 218
Austria, 151, 204, 271–6, 278
Ayscough, William, 319

Babbage, Charles, 329n
Bacon, Francis (artist), 112nm 142
Bacon, Francis (philosopher), x,
    39–41, 66, 127
Ball, Philip, 57
Ballet de l'Impatience (Lully), 236
Bamberg, Germany, 11
barber-surgeons, 88n
Barnes, Jonathan, 65
barometers, 42, 287
baroque art, 134, 230
Barrow, Isaac, 329n
Batavia (now Jakarta), Indonesia,
    209–10, 212–15
Batavia (ship), 211–15
Battle of Edgehill (1642), 62
Battle of Lepanto (1571), 89, 99
Battle of Lützen (1632), 244
Battle of Narva (1700), 280
Battle of Vienna (1683), 271–5
Battle of White Mountain (1620), 10
Bavaria, 203–4
Becher, Johann, x, 203–7, 289, 295
Béjart, Armande, 160
Béjart, Madeleine, 158, 161
Bellinger, Martha, 161

Bembo, Pietro, 226
Berger, John, 31, 147
Berkeley, George, 323, 334
Berlioz, Hector, 156n
Berners-Lee, Tim, 341
Bernini, Gian Lorenzo, 171, 300
Big Bang theory, 260
bills of mortality, 290–92
Blow, John, 240–41
Bludworth, Thomas, 188–9
Boileau, Nicolas, 163
Bolnes, Catharina, 195–7
Borghese, Scipione, 33
Bosch, Hieronymus, 99
Bourgeois Gentilhomme, Le (Molière),
    160–61, 228
bourgeoisie, 228
Boy Peeling a Fruit (Caravaggio), 25
Boy with a Basket of Fruit
    (Caravaggio), 25
Boyle, Katherine, 185
Boyle, Robert, x, 180, 183–5, 205, 264
    Boyle's law, 180
Bramhall, John, 68–9
Brant, Isabelle, 139
Brahe, Tycho, x, 43
Breslau, Germany, 292
Bristol, Somerset, 262–3, 332
British Empire, 123n
Brouwer Route, 211
Bruno, Giordano, x, 23, 43, 57, 255
bubonic plague, 6, 74, 186
Buckley, Veronica, 247
Buen Retiro Palace, Madrid, 86,
    109–10
Bungler, The (Molière), 159
Buonarroti the Younger,
    Michelangelo, 35

Burial of the Count of Orgaz, The (El Greco), 99–100

Burr, George Lincoln, 83

Busby, Richard, 263

Byron, George Gordon, 6th Baron Byron, 177

calculating machines, 286–7, 309

calculus, 303, 307–9, 333–5
    Calculus Wars, 334–5
    differential calculus, 307–8, 322–3

Calvin, John, 12, 295n

Calvinists, 12

cameralism, 204–5

Canada, 218–23

Canossa, Ludovico, 226

capitalism, 113–19, 340

Caravaggio, Michelangelo Merisi da, x, 2, 24–32, 35, 105–6

Cardsharps, The (Caravaggio), 27

Carlo II, Duke of Mantua, 234

Carlos, Wendy, 243

cartography, 210–11, 218

Carver, John, 80

Castiglione, Baldassare, xi, 226–7

castrati, 233–4

Catherine of Braganza, Queen of England, 242–3

Catholics/Catholicism, 12, 21, 61–3, 225
    art and, 27, 134n
    witch trials and, 83–4

Cattaneis, Claudia de, 231

Cauchy, Augustin-Louis, 323n

Cavendish, William, 1st Earl of Devonshire, 66, 74–5

Cerasi, Tiberio, 30

CERN (European Organization for Nuclear Research), 340–41

Cervantes, Miguel de, xi, 87–93

Cervantes, Rodrigo de, 89

Cesari, Giuseppe, 25

Cézanne, Paul, 102, 156

Chaloner, William, 332–3

champagne, 166–7

Chapman, Allan, 180

Chappell, William, 172

Charles I, King of England, xi, 36–7, 61–3, 108, 131, 141, 169–71, 243n, 262, 265, 319

Charles II, King of England, 63, 68, 73, 79, 131, 174, 178–9, 240–42, 265, 291

Charles V, Duke of Lorraine, 273–4

Charles V, Holy Roman Emperor, 138n

Charles X Gustav, King of Sweden, 246

Charles XII, King of Sweden, 280

Charnock, Stephen, 179

Chatsworth House, Derbyshire, 66, 74–5

chemistry, 184–5, 205–6

Chevalier de Méré *see* Gombaud, Antoine

chiaroscuro, 26, 31, 35

Chigi, Fabio, 13

China, 223

Christ Church University, Oxford, 263

Christina, Queen of Sweden, xi, 13, 21, 244–7

chronometry, 50–52

Church of England, 80, 126n, 242

Church, Benjamin, 81

Civilisation (Clark), 195
Clark, Kenneth, 146, 195–6
Clement VIII, Pope, 25, 30
Clement IX, Pope, 236, 246
Clement X, Pope, 247
clocks, 50–52
Clockwork Orange, A (film), 243
Clovio, Giorgio, 96–8
Clusius, Carolus, 117
Colbert, Jean-Baptiste, xi, 52, 54–6,
     152, 235, 297–302, 306
collision, laws of, 46
Columbus, Christopher, 209, 222n
commedia dell'arte, 158–9
Company of One Hundred
     Associates, 219
computers, 304
     see also calculating machines
Comus (Milton), 173
Confusion of Confusions (de la Vega),
     119
Congreve, William, 241
Conversion on the Way to Damascus
     (Caravaggio), 30
Cook, James, 218
Copernicus, Nicolaus, xi, 43, 324n
     Copernican heliocentrism, 21, 23
Corey, Giles, 82–3
Cornaro, Elena, 41n
Cornelisz, Jeronimus, 212–15
Coronation of Poppea, The
     (Monteverdi), 232
Cosimo II de' Medici, Grand Duke
     of Tuscany, 35, 234
Cosimo III de' Medici, Grand Duke
     of Tuscany, 149, 196
Cosmotheoros (Huygens), 57–8

Coster, Salomon, 51n
Council of Trent (1563), 101
Counter-Reformation, 83, 99–101
courtly behaviour, 225–8
Courtois, Alexandre, 155
Cremona, Italy, 229–30
Crescas, Hasdai, 254
Crete, Greece, 95–6
Crick, Francis, 19
Cromwell, Oliver, xi, 63, 69, 73, 83,
     126–7, 174, 178, 242, 252n, 265,
     319
Cruz, Juana Inés de la (Sor Juana), xi,
     247–50
Ctesibius, 50
Cuisinier François, Le (La Varenne),
     165
Cumming, Laura, 104, 111

da Vinci, Leonardo, 25, 137, 140
Dalí, Salvador, 111
Dante Alighieri, 157
Darwin, Charles, 47n, 324n
David, Jacques-Louis, 156
David with the Head of Goliath
     (Gentileschi), 37
Davidson, William, 197n
de Geer, Louis, 245
de Graaf, Regnier, 200–201
de Mey, Barbara, 198
De Motu (Harvey), 263
de Wilde, Jacob, 278
de Witt, Johan, 255, 256, 260–61
Delft, Netherlands, 191–4, 197, 200,
     202
     Delft Thunderclap, 193

Denmark, 223

Descartes, René, xi, 6–10, 16–22, 42, 43, 45, 244–5, 251, 255, 264, 267–8, 287n, 321–2

  gravity, 47

  Hobbes and, 67–8

  laws of collision, 46

  mathematics and, 20, 307

  Mersenne and, 16–17, 20

  Pascal and, 286

  religion and, 22

  Vermeer and, 195

Dias, Bartolomeu, 209

Dido and Aeneas (Purcell), 239–41

Dirac, Paul, 329n

Dircx, Geertje, 148

Divine Comedy (Dante), 157

Doctor in Love, The (Molière), 159

Doctor in Spite of Himself, The (Molière), 160

Dom Pérignon, 167

Don Carlos de Sigüenza, 248–50

Don Juan of Austria, 99

Don Quixote (Cervantes), 90–92

Donne, John, 171

Downfall (film), 244

Drake, Francis, 222

drama, 156–61

Dryden, John, xi, 241–2, 269

Dutch East India Company, *see* Vereenigde Oostindische Compagnie (VOC)

Dutch East Indies, 212

Dutch Republic, 15, 43–6, 139, 143–4, 151, 191

Dutch West Indies Company, 122

East India Company, 2, 120–23, 169, 209, 211–12, 216n, 296n

economics, 123, 127–31, 204–5, 294–302

  free trade, 298

  market economics, 294–6

  national debt, 301

  political economy, 123–4, 127–31, 204–5

  see also finance

Egypt 306

Einstein, Albert, 252, 258, 322n

El Escorial, Madrid, 99

El Greco, xi, 95–102, 104–5, 138

Elements (Euclid), 257

Elements of Law, Natural and Politic, The (Hobbes), 67

Elisabeth of France, Queen of Spain, 85, 87, 107

Elizabeth I, Queen of England, xi, 84, 120–21, 169–70, 245

empiricism, 262

England, 39–40, 126n, 169–90, 322, 328, 331–2

  bills of mortality, 290–91

  British Empire, 123n

  Civil War (1642–51), 2, 61–4, 67–8, 172–4, 262, 265, 318

  Commonwealth, 63, 73, 83, 126–7, 174, 178–9, 262

  currency, 331–3

  East India Company, 2, 120–23, 169, 209, 211–12, 216n, 296n

  language, 157n

  monarchy, 243n

  music, 239–44

  politics, 61–2, 64

England (*cont.*)
    population of, 290
    religion, 327
    Restoration, 63–4, 73, 126n, 131,
        174, 178, 240–42, 262
    slave trade, 79–80, 224, 263
    witchcraft and, 41
*England's Improvement by Sea and
    Land to Out-do the Dutch without
    Fighting, to Pay Debts without
    Moneys, to Set to Work all the Poor
    of England* (Yarranton), 295
epistemology, 264
'Epitaph on the Admirable
    Dramaticke Poet, W.
    Shakespeare, An' (Milton), 172
Equestrian Portrait of Charles V
    (Titian), 138
*Equestrian Portrait of the Duke of
    Lerma* (Rubens), 138
*Essay Concerning Human
    Understanding* (Locke), 266–7,
    269
'Essay in Satire, An', (Dryden), 242
Ethics (Spinoza), 251, 255, 257–8,
    265, 310
Euclid, xi, 3, 184, 251, 257–8, 283–4
Europe, 1–3, 15–16, 64, 78, 227–8
    languages, 157, 228
    politics, 153
    population of, 6, 225
    science, 185
    see also Peace of Westphalia; Thirty
        Years' War
evolution, theory of, 47n, 182–3, 324n
*Extraordinary Popular Delusions and
    the Madness of Crowds* (Mackay),
    128n

*Fable of the Bees: or, Private Vices,
    Publick Benefits, The* (Mandeville),
    293
Fairy-Queen, The (Purcell), 241
Farnese, Alessandro, 96, 98
Farnese, Odoardo, Duke of Parma, 24
Fatio de Duillier, Nicolas, 331
Ferdinand II, Holy Roman Emperor,
    xi, 10
Ferdinand III, Holy Roman
    Emperor, xi, 110
Ferdinand Maria, Elector of Bavaria,
    203
Ferdinand, Prince-Elector of Bavaria,
    235
Fermat, Pierre de, xi, 46, 285
Filmer, Robert, 266
finance, 113–31, 294–302, 331–2
    banking, 301
    financial bubbles, 120n
    see also economics
Finley, Sarah, 247
Fiorillo, Tiberio, 159
Flamsteed, John, xi, 185
Florence, Italy, 35–6, 173
fluxions, 322–3, 325, 334
Fonseca, Don Juan de, 106–7
Fortune Teller, The (Caravaggio), 26–7
Fouquet, Nicolas, 297–8
France, 15, 151–67, 278, 297–302,
    338–9
    Company of One Hundred
        Associates, 219
    economy of, 296–302
    exploration, 219–23
    French cuisine, 164–7, 222
    French drama, 156, 159–61
    French language, 157n

French Revolution, 154n
music, 229, 232–3, 237–9
slave trade, 224, 300–301
Francesco Maria I della Rovere,
Duke of Urbino, 226
Franklin, Benjamin, 140n
Frederick Henry, Prince of Orange,
144
Freitas, Roger, 234
Freud, Lucien, 142
Freud, Sigmund, 3
Friedman, Milton, 130
Fronde, The (1648–53), 153
fusion, 341

Gaia, 339
Galen, xi, 263–4
Galileo Galilei, xii, 17, 21, 23, 35–6,
39–42, 47–50, 65, 136, 173, 227,
267, 318, 321–2
Gardner, Percy, 143n
Garzoni, Giovanna, 37
Gelick, James, 318
Gentileschi, Artemisia, xii, 24, 32–8,
170–71
Gentileschi, Orazio, 32–4, 170–71
Geographer, The (Vermeer), 199–200
George I, King of Great Britain and
Ireland, 314–15
Gérard, Balthasar, 191–2
Germany, 6, 10–11, 15, 83, 306
Gerritsz, Hessel, 210–11
gin palaces, 293n
Glorious Revolution (1688), 262, 269
Gödel, Kurt, 22
Goeth, Aurora von, 236
Goldstein, Jacob, 114, 118

Gombaud, Antoine (Chevalier de
Méré), 284
Gombrich, Ernst, 103, 140, 194
Good, Dorothy, 82
Good, Sarah, 82
Gordon, Patrick, 276–7
Gordon, Thomas, 281
Gostling, John, 241
Graham-Dixon, Andrew, 24, 31
Graunt, John, xii, 289–92
gravity, theory of, 47, 181–2, 317,
324–7
Great Fire of London (1666), 74,
187–8, 291
Great Lakes, 220–21
Great Plague (1665–6), 74, 186–7,
322
Greene, Anne, 125
Gresham College, London, 126, 179,
185, 188–9
Grimaldi, Francesco, 53
Grimmelshausen, Hans Jakob
Christoffel von, 11
Gullan-Whur, Margaret, 251, 261
Gulliver's Travels (Swift), 201n
Gustavus Adolphus, King of Sweden,
244
Guzmán, Gaspar de, Count-Duke of
Olivares, xii, 84–7, 107–10
Gwyn, Nell, 178–9, 241

Habsburg Empire, 44n, 85, 103n,
153, 271–2
Hacking, Ian, 292n
Hagendorf, Peter, 11
Halley, Edmund, xii, 185–6, 292, 330
Halley's Comet, 185–6

Hanover, House of, 310, 314

Harvey, William, xii, 40–42, 62n, 125, 263, 288

Hawking, Stephen, 260, 329n

Hawksmoor, Nicholas, 189

Hayes, Wiebbe, 213–15

Hayley, William, 172

Henri II, Duc de Longueville, 13

Henrietta Maria, Queen of England, 61–2

Henry II, King of France, 164

Henry IV, King of France, 84

Henry VIII, King of England, xii, 61, 169

Hobbes, Thomas, xii, 1–2, 17, 65–75, 124, 177, 264, 266–7, 289

Holbein, Hans, 135

Holland/Netherlands, 5–6, 114–19, 134, 191–207, 254, 260–61, 278–9
  Anglo-Dutch Wars, 189, 197n, 262
  Dutch Golden Age, 133–4, 211
  Dutch Republic, 15, 43–6, 191
  exploration, 209–18
  First Stadtholderless Period, 45, 255, 260
  Rampjaar (Year of Disaster), 196, 260–61
  slave trade, 224
  Tulipmania, 117–20, 148
  VOC (Vereenigde Oostindische Compagnie), 2, 114–17, 122, 144, 146, 169, 209, 211–18, 296n

Holy League, 89, 99

Holy Roman Empire, 12–5, 235–6

Hombres Necios (Juana Inés de la Cruz), 249

Hooke, Robert, xii, 179–83, 185–6, 189, 199–202, 264, 329–30

Hooke's law, 180–81

Horologium (Huygens), 51

House of Orange, 44n, 255, 260

Hubbard, Elizabeth, 82

Huguenots, 10, 12

Huygens, Christiaan, xii, 17, 44–59, 181, 256, 300, 306–7, 309, 320–22

Huygens (Jnr), Constantijn, 45–6, 54, 56–8

Huygens (Snr), Constantijn, 44–6, 54, 57, 144, 201

Huygens, Lodewijk, 54–5

Huygens, Susanna, 55

Il Cortegiano (Castiglione), 226–8

Imaginary Invalid, The (Molière), 161

India, 123

Ingegneri, Marc'Antonio, 230

Innocent X, Pope, 14, 111–12

Innocent XI, Pope, 247, 271

Inquisition
  Roman, 21, 23
  Spanish, 87, 101

Ireland, 63, 126–9, 222

Italy, 23–38, 42, 110–11, 227–9

Jacob Blessing the Sons of Joseph (Rembrandt), 146–7

Jacobsz, Ariaen, 212, 215

James I and VI, King of England and Scotland, 40, 170

James II, King of England, 79, 241–2

Jamestown colony, Virginia, 80

Jans, Helena, 21n
Jansenism, 162
Janszoon, Willem, xii, 209–10, 218
Jardine, Lisa, 192
Jáuregui, Juan de, 88
Jefferson, Thomas, 140n
Jerónima de Las Cuevas, 100
Jesuits, 219
John III Sobieski, King of Poland, 271, 274–5
John Frederick, Duke of Brunswick, 310
John Louis of Hadamar-Nassau, 13
Jolliet, Louis, xii, 220–22
Jonson, Ben, 171
Judaism/Jews, 43, 100–101, 146, 247, 252–4, 301
Judith Beheading Holofernes (Caravaggio), 28, 35
Judith Slaying Holofernes (Gentileschi), 35
Jupiter, 181

Kahlo, Frida, 38
Kepler, Johannes, xii, 43, 48, 321–2, 324n
Keynes, John Maynard, 129
Kılıç Ali Pasha mosque, Istanbul, 89
Kissinger, Henry, 16
Kitson, Michael, 147–8
Kramer vs. Kramer (film), 244

L'Orfeo (Monteverdi), 231
La Flèche college, France, 124
La Gorce, Jérôme de, 239
La Rochelle, Siege of (1627), 10

La Varenne, François Pierre, xii, 165–6
Laboratorium Portabile (Becher), 207
Lamentation of Christ (Van Dyck), 171
languages, 157n
Laocoön and His Sons (sculpture), 137
Last Judgement (Michelangelo), 97
laws of motion, 325–6
Le Caron, Joseph, 219
Le Maire, Isaac, 115–17
Leibniz, Gottfried, xii, 54, 292n, 303–15, 327, 333–5
Leonora María del Carretto, 249
Leopold I, Holy Roman Emperor, xii, 103n, 204, 271–2, 279
Leviathan (Hobbes), 1–2, 65, 67, 69–75, 177, 264
Lewis, Ralph, 19
Leyster, Judith, 37
Lievens, Jan, 144
light, theory of, 53
Ligorio, Pirro, 98
Lipperhey, Hans, 227
Little Ice Age, 5–6, 223
Little Street, The (Vermeer), 193–4
Livermore Laboratory, California, 341
Locke, John, xii, 1, 262–9, 288–9, 331
logic, 312–13
London, 74, 186–90, 279, 290–91
Longhi, Roberto, 37
Lopukhina, Eudoxia, 276
Lorraine, Roger de, 237
Louis XIII, King of France, 141–2, 153, 155, 158, 232, 235

Louis XIV, King of France, xii, 1, 52, 64, 151–4, 167, 235–6, 238–9, 256, 287, 306
  Colbert and, 297–300
  Huygens and, 55–6
  Molière and, 159–60
Louis XV, King of France, 154n
Louis XVI, King of France, 154n
Louvre Palace, Paris, 159, 232, 300
Lovelock, James, 339
Lower, Richard, 263
Lully, Jean-Baptiste, xii, 236–9, 164
Luther, Martin, 12
Lutherans, 12

Macclesfield, Lord, *see* Parker, Thomas, 1st Earl of Macclesfield
MacCulloch, Diarmaid, 23
Macedo, Antonio, 245–6
Machiavelli, Niccolò, 65, 128, 226
Mackay, Charles, 128n
Magellan, Ferdinand, 209, 211
Magini, Giovanni, 136
Magna Carta, 61–2, 64, 243
Maimonides, 254
Maintenon, Madame de (Françoise d'Aubigné), 163–4, 238–9
Mainz, Germany, 306
Malebranche, Nicolas, 306
Mancini, Marie, 153
Mandeville, Bernard, xii, 292–4
Manrique, Jaime, 250
Margaret Theresa, Spanish Infanta, 102–3
Maria Anna of Spain, 110
Mariana of Austria, Queen of Spain, 102–3

Marie-Thérèse, Queen of France, 153
Maringhi, Francesco Maria, 36
Marino, Giambattista, 155
Marquette, Jacques, xiii, 219–22
Mars, 49, 57–8, 181
Mary II, Queen of England, 197n, 243, 262, 269
mathematics, 3, 20, 42, 46, 49, 69, 283–7, 303, 307–9, 322–3, 333–5
  algebra, 20
  calculus, 303, 307–9, 322–3, 333–5
Maurice, Prince of Orange, 6–7
Maximilian, Duke of Bavaria, 7, 10
Mayflower, 80–81
Mazarin, Jules Cardinal, x, 152–5, 232–6, 246, 297–8
Medici family, 34–5
Medici, Catherine de', 164–6
Medici, Marie de', xiii, 141–2, 155, 164–5
Medici, Mattias de', 234–5
Meditations (Descartes), 67
Mehmed IV, Ottoman Sultan, 272, 275
Melandroni, Fillide, 29
Melani, Atto, xiii, 233–7
Menasseh ben Israel, 252n
Menesius, Paul, 276–7
Meninas, Las (Velázquez), 102–4, 112
mercantilism, 295–7
Mercator, Gerardus, 211
Merixio, Fermo, 24
Mersenne, Marin, xiii, 16–18, 20–21, 46, 52, 65, 67–8, 124, 286
Messenius, Arnold Johan, 245–6
Mexico, 247–50
Michelangelo, 25, 30, 96–7, 137
Micrographia (Hooke), 183, 199

microscopes, 182, 185, 198–202
microverse, 185, 312
Midelfort, H. C. E., 83
Milan, Italy, 24–5
Milton, John, xiii, 171–8
Minniti, Mario, 27
missionaries, 219–20
Mississippi River, 220–21
Mocking of Christ (Rubens), 137–8
modern political theory, 264
Molière, xiii, 156–63, 228
Monadology (Leibniz), 311–12
Money (Goldstein), 114
Montaigne, Michel de, xiii, 288, 338
Montano, Benito Arias, 98
Montchrestien, Antoine de, 123–4
Monte, Francesco del, 27
Monteverdi, Claudio, xiii, 230–32
Montpensier, Mademoiselle de,
   (Anne Marie Louise d'Orléans),
   237–8
Moriscos, 99, 109
Moscow, Russia, 279, 281
Münster, Germany, 12–14
music, 228–39
Mustafa Pasha, Kara, xiii, 272–5

Naples, Italy, 29, 110
Napoleon Bonaparte, 306n
*Natural and Political Observations
   on the London Bills of Mortality*
   (Graunt), 290
Netherlands *see* Holland/Netherlands
Neuberg an der Donau, Bavaria, 7–8
New World, 77–84, 218–24, 247–50
New York, 122
New Zealand, discovery of, 217

Newton, Isaac, xiii, 46–7, 53, 182n,
   269, 309, 317–35, 338
   gravity, 317, 324–7
   laws of motion, 325–6
   religion and, 327–9
   Royal Mint, 331–3
   theory of colours, 324
Nicene Creed, 75
Night Watch, The (Rembrandt), 148
North America, 80–83, 218–21
   exploration of, 80–81, 218–22
   Native Americans, 79–81
   Pilgrim Fathers, 80–81
   Salem witch trials, 1–2, 82–3
   slavery, 2–3, 80–2, 224
   United States Constitution, 267

Obama, Barack, 80n
Of True Religion (Milton), 178
Oldenburg, Henry, xiii, 52, 179,
   200–201, 256, 309, 314, 327, 333
Olivares, Count-Duke of, *see*
   Guzmán, Gaspar de, Count-
   Duke of Olivares
On the Imperfections of Modern Music
   (Artusi), 231
ontological argument, 22
opera, 231–3
optics, 53–4, 253
Osnabrück, Germany, 12–14
Ottoman Empire, 88–9, 271–8, 280
Oxenstierna, Johan, 13

Pacheco, Francisco, 104–7
Paderewski, Ignacy Jan, 140n
Paglia, Camille, 37

Paradise Lost (Milton), 174–8

Paradise Regained (Milton), 174, 178

Parc, Therèse du, 163

Paris, France, 55–6, 306

Parker, Thomas, 1st Earl of
    Macclesfield, 293

Pascal, Blaise, xiii, 5, 284–8
    Pascal's triangle, 285–6

Pâtissier François, Le (La Varenne),
    166

*Patriarcha, or The Natural Power of
    Kings* (Filmer), 266

Paz, Octavio, 250

Peace of Westphalia (1648), 2, 12–16

Peisaert, Francisco, 212–15

pendulum clock, 50–51, 58, 181, 312,
    320

Penitent Magdalene (Caravaggio),
    27–8

Pensées (Pascal), 288

Pepys, Samuel, xiii, 178, 183, 185–8

Perriquet, Marie, 55

Peter the Great, Tsar of Russia, xiii,
    276–82, 314

Peterzano, Simone, 25

Petit, Marianne, 55–6

Petit, Pierre, 55–6

Petty, William, xiii, 1, 124–31, 185,
    289, 292

Philip II, King of Spain, 98–9, 191,
    222, 223n

Philip III, King of Spain, 109, 138

Philip IV, King of Spain, xiii, 37,
    84–7, 102–3, 106–11, 153

Philippe I, Duke of Orléans, 159

Philippines, 223

philosophy, 3, 249, 251–2
    political philosophy, 63, 65

    see also Descartes, Hobbes,
      Leibniz, Locke, Spinoza

Phlogiston theory, 205

Physica Subterranea (Becher), 207

Picasso, Pablo, 102

Pilgrim Fathers, 80–81

Pius V, Pope, 89, 97–8

Plato, 72, 226, 249

Plymouth colony, 81

Poland, 272, 280

politics, 61–2, 64, 70–73, 153, 266

Polo, Marco, 216

Port-Royal colony, Nova Scotia, 80

Portrait of a Man (Rubens), 136

Portugal, 209, 224

potatoes, 222–3

Potosí, Bolivia, 77–8

Poussin, Nicolas, xiii, 154–6

Powell, Mary, 173–4

Prague, Czechia, 10, 43, 245

Prairie du Chien, Wisconsin, 221

Pride and Prejudice (film), 244

Prince, The (Machiavelli), 65, 128,
    226

Principia (Newton), 182n, 330

probability theory, 284–5

Prodigal Son in the Brothel, The
    (Rembrandt), 145

Protestants/Protestantism, 11–12,
    61–3, 225
    art and, 27, 134n
    witch trials and, 83–4

Punch, John, 80

Purcell, Henry, xiii, 239–44

Puritans/Puritanism, 63, 80–83, 173,
    179, 263

Quaestiones Quaedam Philosophicae (Newton), 321

quantum theory, 54n, 287n, 338n

Quebec, Canada, 219–22

Queirós, Pedro Fernandes de, 210

Racine, Jean, xiv, 156, 162–4

Raid on the Medway (1667), 189

Raphael, 155

Reconciliation of Mother and Son (Rubens), 142

Renaissance, 1, 27, 30, 39, 43, 136, 209, 225, 228–30, 337

Rembrandt van Rijn, xiv, 142, 143–9, 252

Restoration (England), 63–4, 73, 126n, 131, 174, 178, 240–42, 262

Rhind papyrus, 69

Richelieu, Cardinal, 155, 299

Ripa, Cesare, 36–7

Romanet, Catherine de, 163

Rome, Italy, 25–6, 96–8

Rospigliosi, Giulio, 236

Rothschild family, 301

Royal African Company, 79

Royal Exchange, London, 121

Royal Society of London, 52, 179, 181, 183, 185–6, 189, 200–201, 207, 309, 329–30, 334

Rubens, Jan, 135

Rubens, Maria, 135

Rubens, Peter Paul, xiv, 109–10, 112, 134– 43

Rubenshuis, Antwerp, 140–41

Rudolf II, Holy Roman Emperor, 245

Rupert, Prince of the Rhine, Duke of Cumberland, 207

Russell, Bertrand, 3, 18, 69, 251, 254, 261, 268, 283, 313

Russia, 276–82

Russian Orthodox Church, 276, 281

Ruysch, Frederik, 279

Ryle, Gilbert, 19

Saardam (ship), 214–15

St Anselm, 22

St Catherine, 35n

St Helena, 122n

St Paul's Cathedral, London, 188–90, 279

St Petersburg, Russia, 280–81

St Rosalia, 170

St Rosalia (Van Dyck), 170–71

Salem witch trials, 1–2, 82–3

Salvius, Johan Adler, 13

Samson and Delilah (Van Dyck), 171

San Cassiano opera house, Venice, 232

San Marco, Venice, 231

Sanchey, Hierome, 127

Sandoval, Francisco de, 1st Duke of Lerma, 138

Santa Croce church, Gerusalemme, 137

Saturn, 48, 56

School for Wives, The (Molière), 160

Schumpeter, Joseph, 207

Sea of Azov, 277, 280

Seabrook, Kim, 272

Self-Portrait as the Allegory of Painting (Gentileschi), 36–7

Seville, Spain, 104–6

Sforza family, 29

Sganarelle ou le Cocu Imaginaire (Molière), 160

Shakespeare, William, 30–31, 156n, 171

share trading, *see* stockbrokers

Shelley, Percy Bysshe, 177

Simplicius Simplicissimus (von Grimmelshausen), 11

Sinan, Mimar, 89

Sirius, 49, 57

Sistine Chapel, Rome, 137

Sixtus V, Pope, 84

slave trade, 2–3, 79–81, 224, 263, 300–301, 337–8
    Code Noir, 300–301

Smith, Adam, 129, 204n

Smith, Barnabas, 318–19, 329

Smith, John, 80

Smithson, Harriet, 157n

social class, 228

socialism, 4, 340

society, 289, 293–4

Society of Merchant Venturers, 332

Socrates, 64

Solomon Islands, 217

Sophia Alekseyevna of Russia, 276, 279

Soto, Hernando de, 221

South America, 77, 79, 84, 104, 223

South Sea Bubble, 301n

Spain, 15, 77–93, 98–112
    economy of, 302
    exploration, 77–9, 84–7, 222
    expulsion of Jews and Moriscos, 99, 101, 109
    Golden Age, 77–9, 84–7, 247
    Inquisition, 87, 101, 104–6
    language, 248
    religion, 98, 100–101
    slave trade, 79

Spanish Netherlands, 139, 153

spectacles, 198, 253

Spectator magazine, 293

Spinola, Ambrogio, 111

Spinoza, Ana Débora, 252–3

Spinoza, Baruch, xiv, 251–61, 265, 267, 310, 323n

Spinoza, Benedict, 47

Spinoza, Miguel, 252–3

Spinoza, Rebekah, 253

Stampioen, Jan, 44–5

Starhemberg, Ernst Rüdiger von 272–5

statistics, 289–92

Stewart, Matthew, 305

Stiattesi, Pierantonio, 34

stockbrokers, 115–19, 121–2

Stockholm, Sweden, 244–5

Stoffels, Hendrickje, 148–9

Stradivari, Antonio, 229–30

string theory, 311

Surrender of Breda (Velázquez), 110–12

Susanna and the Elders (Gentileschi), 32–3

Sweden, 15, 223, 244–7, 280
    Swedish Africa Company, 245

Swift, Jonathan, 201

Swiss Confederacy, 15

syllogisms, 17–18

Tartuffe (Molière), 160

Tasman, Abel, xiv, 215–18

Tasmania, discovery of, 216

Tassi, Agostino, 33–4
Tasso, Torquato, 136
Tate, Nahum, 240
Tazartes, Maurizia, 194–5
telescopes, 47–9, 56–7, 181–2, 185, 227
tenebrism, 26
Thales of Miletus, 283
Thebans, The (Racine), 163
theory of colours, 324
theory of everything, 260
Theotocópuli de las Cuevas, Jorge Manuel, 100–101
'They That Go Down to the Sea in Ships' (Purcell), 241
Thirty Years' War (1618–48), 2, 6–7, 10–16
Titian, 96, 170–71
Titon du Tillet, 239
Toledo, Spain, 98–102
Torquemada, Tomás de, 87
Torres, Luís Vaz de, 210n
Torricelli, Evangelista, xiv, 42, 46, 287
Townshend, Pete, 239n, 243
Tractatus Theologico-Politicus (Spinoza), 256–7
Traité de l'Économie Politique (Montchrestien), 123–4
Travels (Polo), 216
Treaty of the Pyrenees (1659), 15
Treaty of Warsaw (1683), 271
Trinity College, Cambridge, 320–22, 329
Triple Portrait of Charles I (Van Dyck), 170–71
Tuck, Richard, 71
Tulipmania, 117–20, 148, 296, 302n
Turing, Alan, 304

turkeys, 165n
Turner, J. M. W., 102
Two Treatises of Government (Locke), 266, 269
Tyrannick Love (Dryden), 241

Unitarianism, 328
United States Constitution, 267
University of Heidelberg, 257
University of Leiden, 125
University of Leipzig, 304–5
University of Mainz, 203
University of Padua, 40–41
Uranus, 185
Ussher, James, 183n

Valadon, Suzanne, 38
Valladolid, Spain, 138
van den Enden, Clara Maria, 255
van den Enden, Franciscus, 254–5
van der Haghen, Steven, 210
van der Heyden, Jan, 279
van Diemen, Anthony, 215–16, 218
van Dyck, Anthony, xiv, 141, 169–71
van Leeuwenhoek, Antonie, xiv, 47, 197–203, 288–9, 310
van Leeuwenhoek, Maria, 198, 202
van Nassau, Justinus, 111
van Rijn, Titus, 148–9
van Schooten, Frans, 45
van Swanenburg, Jacob, 143
van Uylenburgh, Saskia, 145, 148
van Veen, Otto, 135–6
Vanuatu, 210–11
Varin, Quentin, 155
Vega, Joseph de la, 119–21

Velázquez, Diego, xiv, 87, 102–12
Velázquez, Don José Nieto, 102
Venice, Italy, 88–9, 96, 113, 136,
    231–2, 271
Venier, Sebastiano, Doge of Venice,
    99
Venus and Adonis (Blow), 241
Vereenigde Oostindische Compagnie
    (VOC), 2, 114–17, 122, 144, 146,
    169, 209, 211–18, 296n
Vermeer, Johannes, xiv, 192– 7,
    199–200, 260n
Versailles, Palace of, 152, 154, 298,
    300
Victoria, Queen of Great Britain and
    Ireland, 123n, 243
Vienna, Austria, 204
    Battle of Vienna (1683), 271–6
View of Delft (Vermeer), 192–3
View of Toledo (El Greco), 101, 105
Vincenzo, Duke of Mantua, 231
Vincenzo I Gonzaga, Duke of
    Mantua, 136–8
violins, 229–30
Virgil, 240
Voltaire, 313, 331n, 338–9
von Boineberg, Johann Christian, 305
von Ehrenberg, Bishop Philipp
    Adolf, 11

Wailing Wall, Jerusalem, 328n
Waller, Richard, 180
Wallis, John, 69
War of Devolution (1667–8), 153
Waterseller of Seville, The (Velázquez),
    105–7
Wealth of Nations, The (Smith), 204n
Westfall, Richard, 318n, 321, 331n
Westminster School, London, 263
Wettstein, Johann Rudolf, 13
William I (the Silent), Prince of
    Orange, 44–5, 135, 191–3
William II, King of England, 45,
    197n, 243, 262, 269, 279
William II, Prince of Orange, 44–6
William III, Prince of Orange, *see*
    William II, King of England
witchcraft, 1–2, 11, 41, 82–4
Woman in Blue Reading a Letter
    (Vermeer), 195
World History of Art, A, 102
World Wide Web, 341
Wren, Chritsopher, xiv, 180, 185,
    189–90, 279
Wright, Orville and Wilbur, 340, 342

Yarranton, Andrew, 295
Young Sick Bacchus (Caravaggio), 25

A NOTE ABOUT
THE AUTHOR

Paul Strathern studied philosophy at Trinity College, Dublin, and has lectured in philosophy and mathematics. He is a Somerset Maugham Award-winning novelist, and is author of two series of books – *Philosophers in 90 Minutes* and *The Big Idea: Scientists Who Changed the World* – as well as several works of non-fiction, including *The Borgias*, *The Florentines* and *The Other Renaissance*.